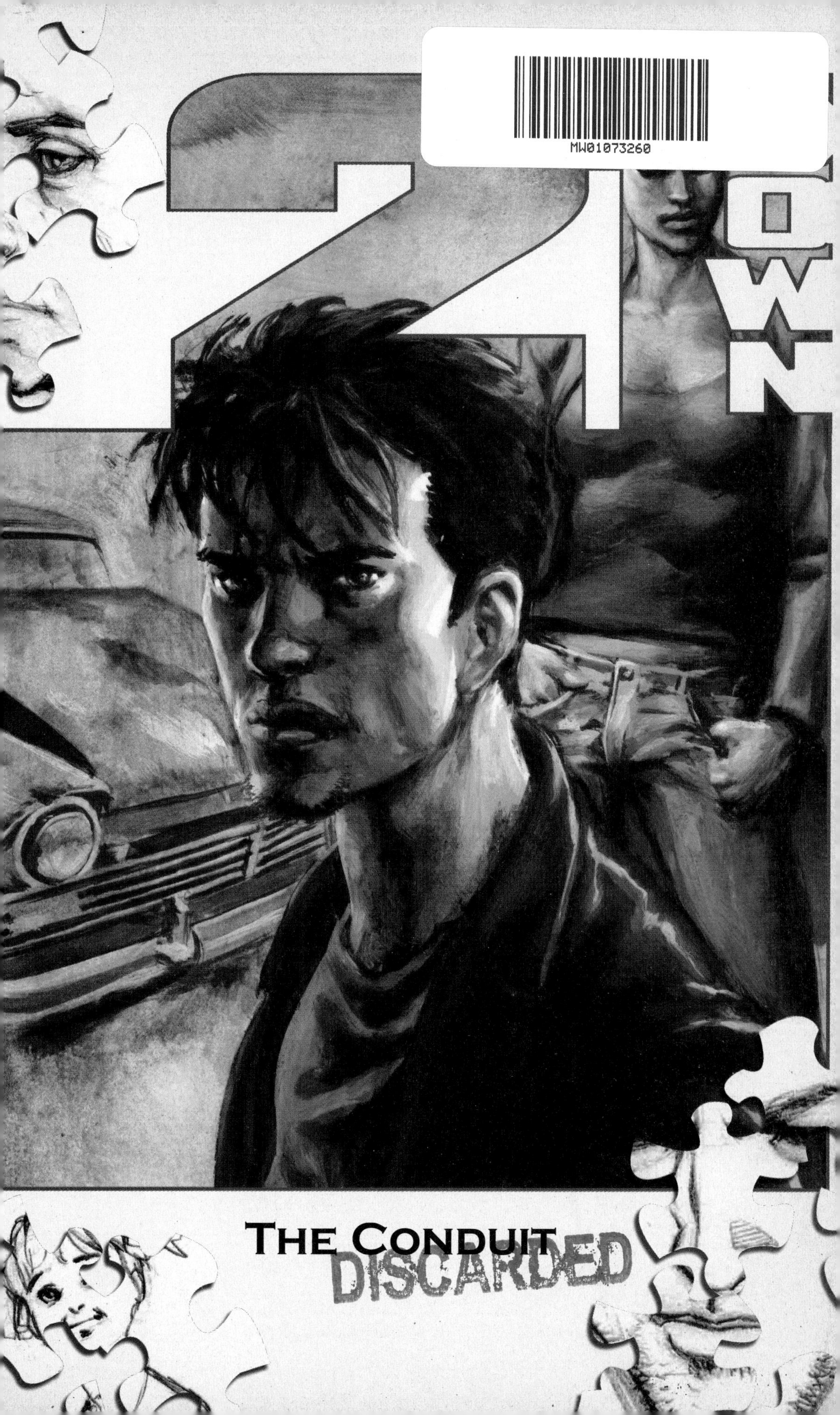

The Conduit

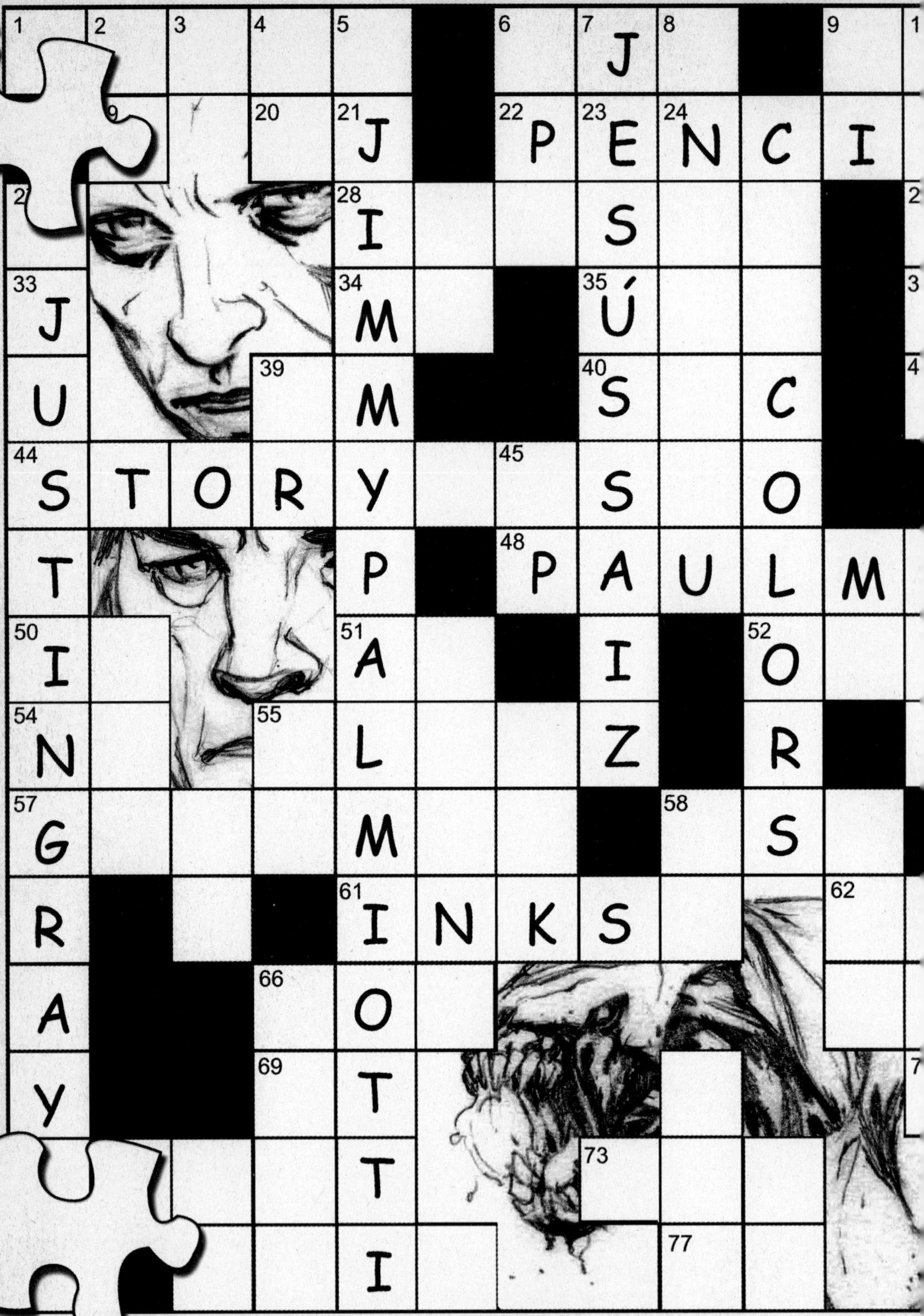
PENCI
STORY
PAULM
INKS
JIMMYPALMIOTTI
JESÚSSAIZ
JUSTINGRAY
COLORS

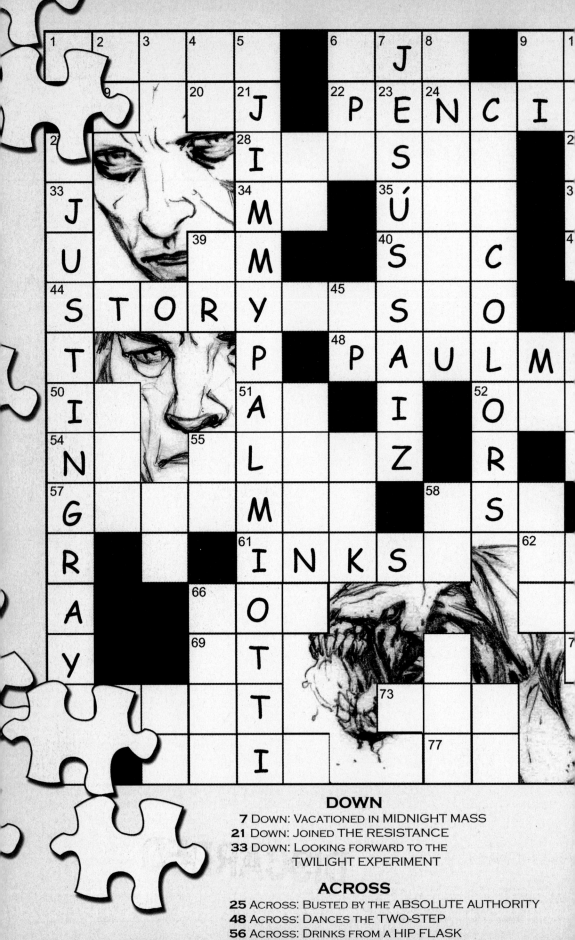

DOWN

7 Down: Vacationed in MIDNIGHT MASS
21 Down: Joined THE RESISTANCE
33 Down: Looking forward to the TWILIGHT EXPERIMENT

ACROSS

25 Across: Busted by the ABSOLUTE AUTHORITY
48 Across: Dances the TWO-STEP
56 Across: Drinks from a HIP FLASK
67 Across: He's got us COVERED

Title Page Art by: Jesús Saiz

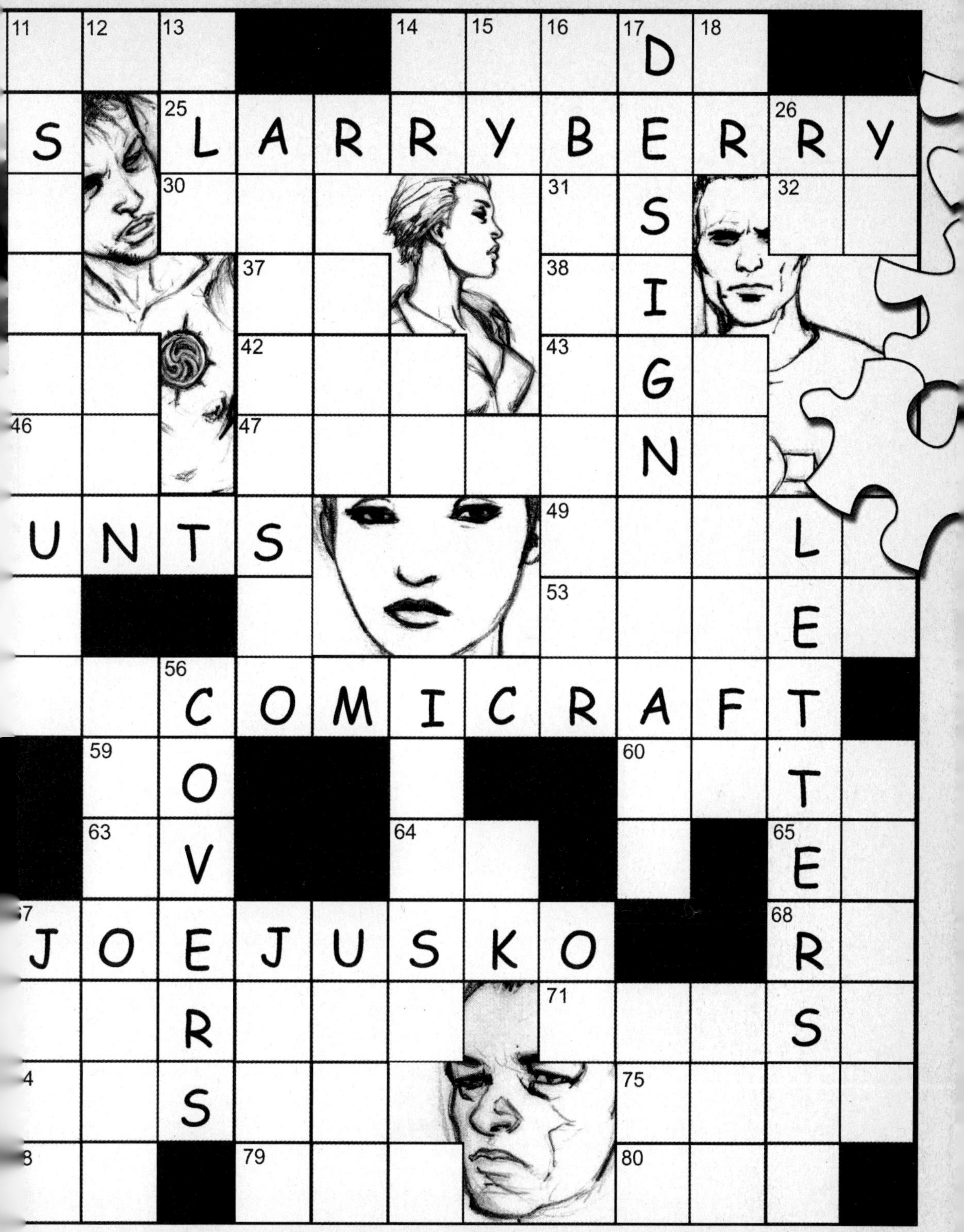
S
LARRY BERRY
DESIGN
UNTS
COMICRAFT
LETTERS
COVERS
JOE JUSKO

Jim Lee, Editorial Director ▸ John Nee, VP & General Manager ▸ Scott Dunbier, Group Editor ▸ Bob Harras, Editor—Original Series
Kristy Quinn, Editor—Collected Edition ▸ Robbin Brosterman, Senior Art Director ▸ Ed Roeder, Art Director
Paul Levitz, President & Publisher ▸ Georg Brewer, VP—Design & Retail Product Development
Richard Bruning, Senior VP—Creative Director ▸ Patrick Caldon, Senior VP—Finance & Operations
Chris Caramalis, VP—Finance ▸ Terri Cunningham, VP—Managing Editor ▸ Dan DiDio, VP—Editorial
Alison Gill, VP—Manufacturing ▸ Lillian Laserson, Senior VP & General Counsel ▸ David McKillips, VP—Advertising & Custom Publishing
Cheryl Rubin, VP—Brand Management ▸ Bob Wayne, VP—Sales & Marketing

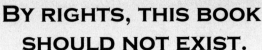

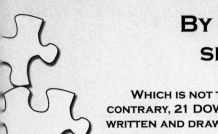

BY RIGHTS, THIS BOOK SHOULD NOT EXIST.

WHICH IS NOT TO SAY THERE'S ANYTHING WRONG WITH IT; ON THE CONTRARY, 21 DOWN IS A GREAT READ. AN INTELLIGENT STORY VERY WELL WRITTEN AND DRAWN, WITH INTERESTING CHARACTERS WHO DON'T REVEAL THEMSELVES ALL IN ONE BREATHLESS, ONE-PAGE RUSH. A BOOK THAT KEEPS YOU GUESSING. BUT THAT'S NOT REALLY ENOUGH THESE DAYS, IS IT?

COMICS—MONTHLY COMICS, AT ANY RATE—ARE NOT DOING TERRIBLY WELL AT THE MOMENT. SALES HAVE BEEN DECLINING STEADILY SINCE THE GIGANTIC ACT OF SELF-BUGGERY THAT WAS SPECULATOR-DRIVEN PUBLISHING FINALLY CAME TO AN END. PLENTY OF NEW COMICS ARE STILL BEING RELEASED, GRANTED, BUT PRECIOUS FEW OF THEM MANAGE TO SURVIVE LONGER THAN A YEAR—AND BY NEW I MEAN **NEW**, NOT SOME LONG-ESTABLISHED SUPERHERO UNDERGOING YET ANOTHER REVIVAL WITH YET ANOTHER "NEW TWIST." IT'S A HOSTILE MARKET RIGHT NOW, AND PLENTY OF GOOD STUFF GETS FLUSHED DOWN THE CRAPPER ALONG WITH THE BAD.

SO IT CAME AS QUITE A SURPRISE TO READ A BOOK THAT MAKES NO CONCESSIONS TO THE CURRENT CLIMATE WHATSOEVER.

NOW, I PERSONALLY BELIEVE THAT YOU NEED TO HIT THE READER RIGHT BETWEEN THE EYES WHEN LAUNCHING NEW MATERIAL; YOU GRAB THEIR ATTENTION FIRST AND LET THE QUIET, SUBTLE STUFF CREEP IN AROUND THE EDGES LATER. NOT THESE GUYS, THOUGH—ALL THEY CONCERN THEMSELVES WITH IS TELLING A DAMN FINE STORY. AND—WHAT I THINK I LIKE MOST ABOUT THIS PUPPY— THEY TAKE THEIR OWN SWEET TIME DOING IT, TOO.

IT WON'T BE UNTIL TOWARDS THE END OF THIS TRADE PAPERBACK COLLECTION THAT YOU'LL FULLY UNDERSTAND THE MELANCHOLY PRESTON KILLS AND THE PRICKLY RELATIONSHIP HE HAS WITH HIS BROTHER; NOT UNTIL THE VERY LAST PAGE WILL YOU EVEN BEGIN TO GET A HANDLE ON MICKEY RINALDI. THE NICE THING IS THAT YOU'RE GOING TO ENJOY GETTING THERE, WATCHING MICKEY (THE BOOK'S BEST CHARAC-TER) STRING PRESTON ALONG EVEN THOUGH HE KNOWS HE'S BEING PLAYED. 21 DOWN, YOU SEE, SPORTS SUCH AN INTRIGUING SUPPORTING CAST AND SUCH NICELY WRITTEN DIALOGUE THAT ITS STEADY PACE BECOMES AN ASSET RATHER THAN A SETBACK. YOU WON'T HAVE THE MEASURE OF THIS STORY BY THE END OF ITS FIRST OR SECOND CHAP-TER—SOMETHING FOR WHICH YOU'LL BE THOROUGHLY GRATEFUL.

SO WHAT WERE THEY THINKING, THE WRITERS OF 21 DOWN, TRYING TO MAKE A GO OF A BOOK LIKE THIS ONE WHILE OTHER COMICS WERE FALLING LIKE NINEPINS? NOT LONG AFTER THE RELEASE OF THE FIRST ISSUE I ASKED JIMMY PALMIOTTI THAT VERY QUESTION; HE WAS IN THE BASEMENT OF HIS BROOKLYN APARTMENT BUILDING AT THE TIME, WHERE I FOUND HIM RESTOCKING HIS FREEZER WITH MEAT.

"GREAT BOOK, JIMMY, BUT DO YOU REALLY EXPECT IT TO SURVIVE? NO SUPERHERO STUFF, NOT MUCH ACTION, LOTS OF TALKIE SCENES..."

"YEAH, YEAH."

"I MEAN YOU COULD MEET CHARACTERS LIKE THESE WALKING DOWN THE STREET—OR MOST OF THEM, ANYWAY..."

"YEAH, YEAH."

"YOU NEED TO HAVE SOMETHING FREAKY HAPPEN. SOMETHING THAT'LL BLOW THE READERS OUT OF THEIR SOCKS."

"YEAH, YEAH."

"THAT'S, UH...THAT'S MICKEY'S DRESS YOU'RE WEARING, ISN'T IT? FROM ISSUE FOUR?"

(CLENCHING HIS BLOOD-SLICK FISTS) "NO, IT'S HARMONY'S FROM #2. WHAT ARE YOU, BLIND?"

"I HAVE TO GO NOW, MATE."

JUSTIN GRAY WAS EVEN LESS HELP THAN JIMMY. I CALLED THE SOMETIME CHEF/FOSSIL HUNTER/BULL CASTRATOR * AT HIS HOME IN WESTCHESTER, HOPING VAINLY FOR ANSWERS...

"SO, JUSTIN, I WAS WONDERING—"

"IT WAS ALL MY IDEA."

"WHAT?"

"EVERYTHING, THE WHOLE STORY, I CAME UP WITH ALL OF IT. PALMIOTTI'S A LOSER; I'M JUST TRADING ON HIS NAME UNTIL MY GENIUS IS RECOGNIZED."

"BUT—"

"JUST PUT 'IT WAS ALL JUSTIN'S IDEA.' DO IT. DO IT OR I'LL OPEN FIRE INTO THE CROWD."

"UH..."

THUS ENDETH THE SEARCH FOR ENLIGHTENMENT...

PERHAPS, THOUGH, JIMMY AND JUSTIN HAD SIMPLY PEGGED ME AS A DIMWIT AND WERE WAITING FOR ME TO CATCH ON TO THE GLARINGLY OBVIOUS: THAT EVERYONE INVOLVED IN THE BOOK DID A BRILLIANT JOB; THAT EVEN WITH THINGS THE WAY THEY ARE NOWADAYS, THAT CAN STILL BE ENOUGH TO SWING THE DEAL; THAT 21 DOWN SURVIVES BECAUSE IT'S GREAT.

AND SURVIVE IT HAS, WITH THIS COLLECTION AND THE FORTHCOMING MATURE READERS-LABELLED RELAUNCH BEARING TESTAMENT TO ITS SUCCESS. LONG MAY IT CONTINUE, TOO; I'M KEEN TO KNOW WHERE THIS THING'S GOING, AS ARE A LOT OF OTHER PEOPLE. ANOTHER GREAT COMIC TO KEEP US ALL IN SUSPENSE—AND, I SUPPOSE, JIMMY IN DRESSES AND JUSTIN IN 30.06 AMMUNITION.

ONE LAST THOUGHT. IF, IN YEARS TO COME, YOU'RE READING THE UMPTEENTH REPRINTING OF THIS VOLUME IN SOME UTOPIAN AGE OF COMIC BOOK PUBLISHING—WITH COMICS ABOUT EVERYTHING, COMICS FOR EVERYONE, AND COSTUMED SUPERHEROES EITHER STUCK IN A TINY GHETTO-LIKE IMPRINT OR REINVENTED BEYOND ALL RECOGNITION—AND YOU'RE WONDERING ABOUT MY GLOOMY VIEW OF THE INDUSTRY, HERE'S WHAT HAPPENED: YES, THINGS WERE BAD. BUT, EVENTUALLY, THEY GOT BETTER. AND IT WAS MOSTLY THANKS TO BOOKS LIKE 21 DOWN.

- GARTH ENNIS
MAY 28TH, 2003 A.D

* ALL TRUE

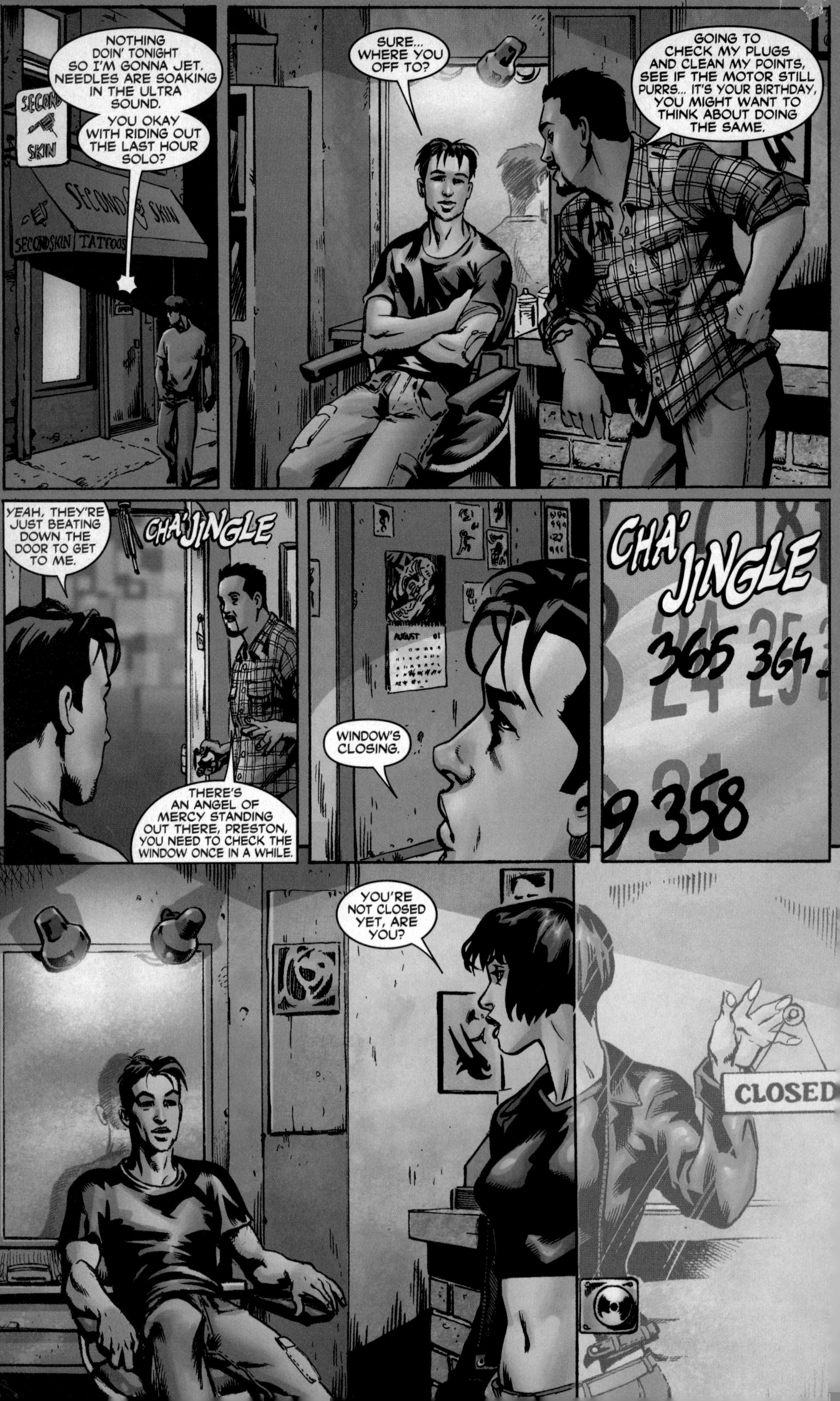
NOTHING DOIN' TONIGHT SO I'M GONNA JET. NEEDLES ARE SOAKING IN THE ULTRA SOUND.
YOU OKAY WITH RIDING OUT THE LAST HOUR SOLO?
SECOND SKIN
SECOND SKIN
SECONDSKIN TATTOOS
SURE... WHERE YOU OFF TO?
GOING TO CHECK MY PLUGS AND CLEAN MY POINTS, SEE IF THE MOTOR STILL PURRS... IT'S YOUR BIRTHDAY, YOU MIGHT WANT TO THINK ABOUT DOING THE SAME.
YEAH, THEY'RE JUST BEATING DOWN THE DOOR TO GET TO ME.
CHA'JINGLE
THERE'S AN ANGEL OF MERCY STANDING OUT THERE, PRESTON, YOU NEED TO CHECK THE WINDOW ONCE IN A WHILE.
AUGUST 01
WINDOW'S CLOSING.
CHA'JINGLE
365 364
9 358
YOU'RE NOT CLOSED YET, ARE YOU?
CLOSED

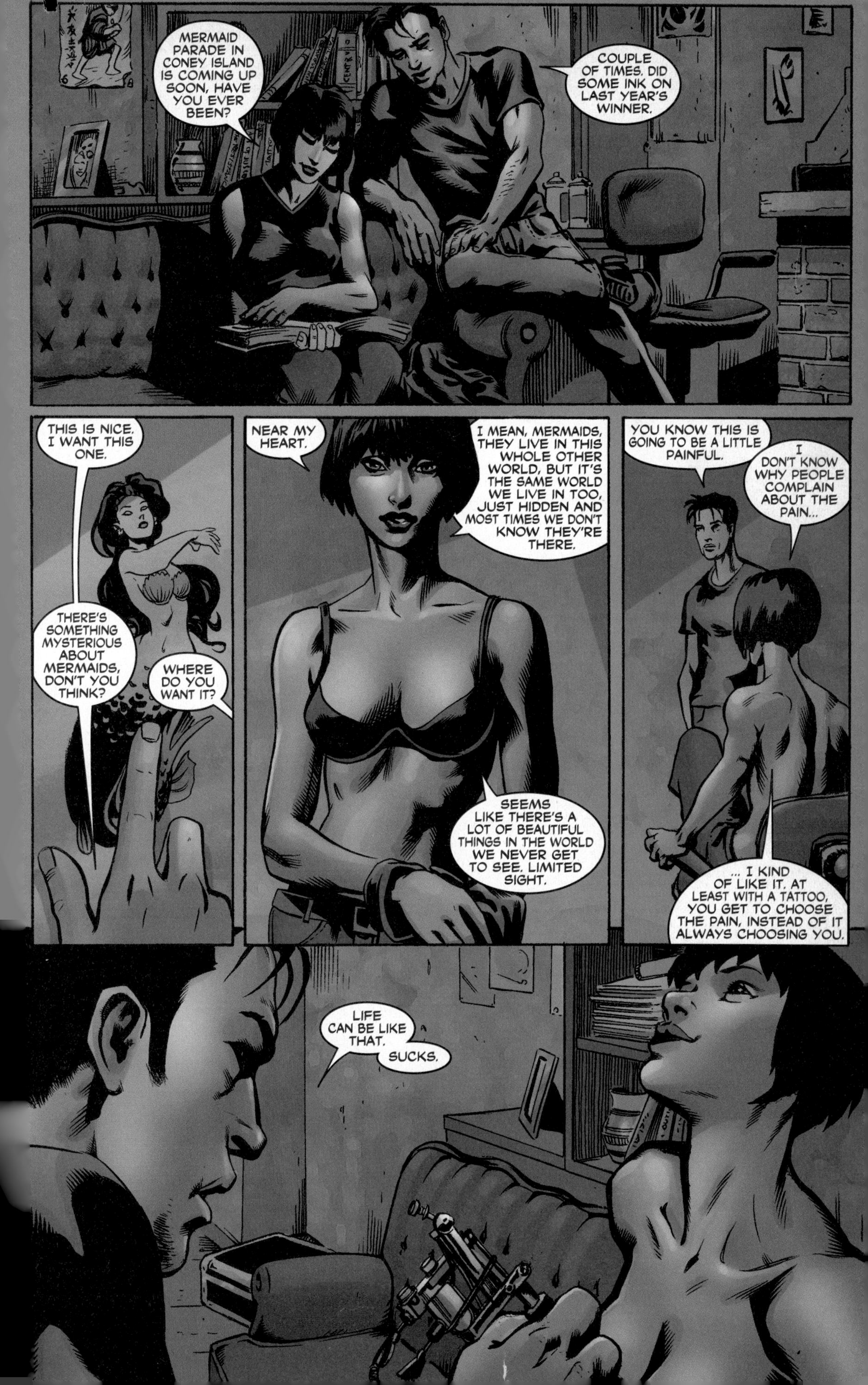
MERMAID PARADE IN CONEY ISLAND IS COMING UP SOON, HAVE YOU EVER BEEN?
COUPLE OF TIMES. DID SOME INK ON LAST YEAR'S WINNER.
THIS IS NICE. I WANT THIS ONE.
THERE'S SOMETHING MYSTERIOUS ABOUT MERMAIDS, DON'T YOU THINK?
WHERE DO YOU WANT IT?
NEAR MY HEART.
I MEAN, MERMAIDS, THEY LIVE IN THIS WHOLE OTHER WORLD, BUT IT'S THE SAME WORLD WE LIVE IN TOO, JUST HIDDEN AND MOST TIMES WE DON'T KNOW THEY'RE THERE.
SEEMS LIKE THERE'S A LOT OF BEAUTIFUL THINGS IN THE WORLD WE NEVER GET TO SEE. LIMITED SIGHT.
YOU KNOW THIS IS GOING TO BE A LITTLE PAINFUL.
I DON'T KNOW WHY PEOPLE COMPLAIN ABOUT THE PAIN...
... I KIND OF LIKE IT. AT LEAST WITH A TATTOO, YOU GET TO CHOOSE THE PAIN, INSTEAD OF IT ALWAYS CHOOSING YOU.
LIFE CAN BE LIKE THAT.
SUCKS.

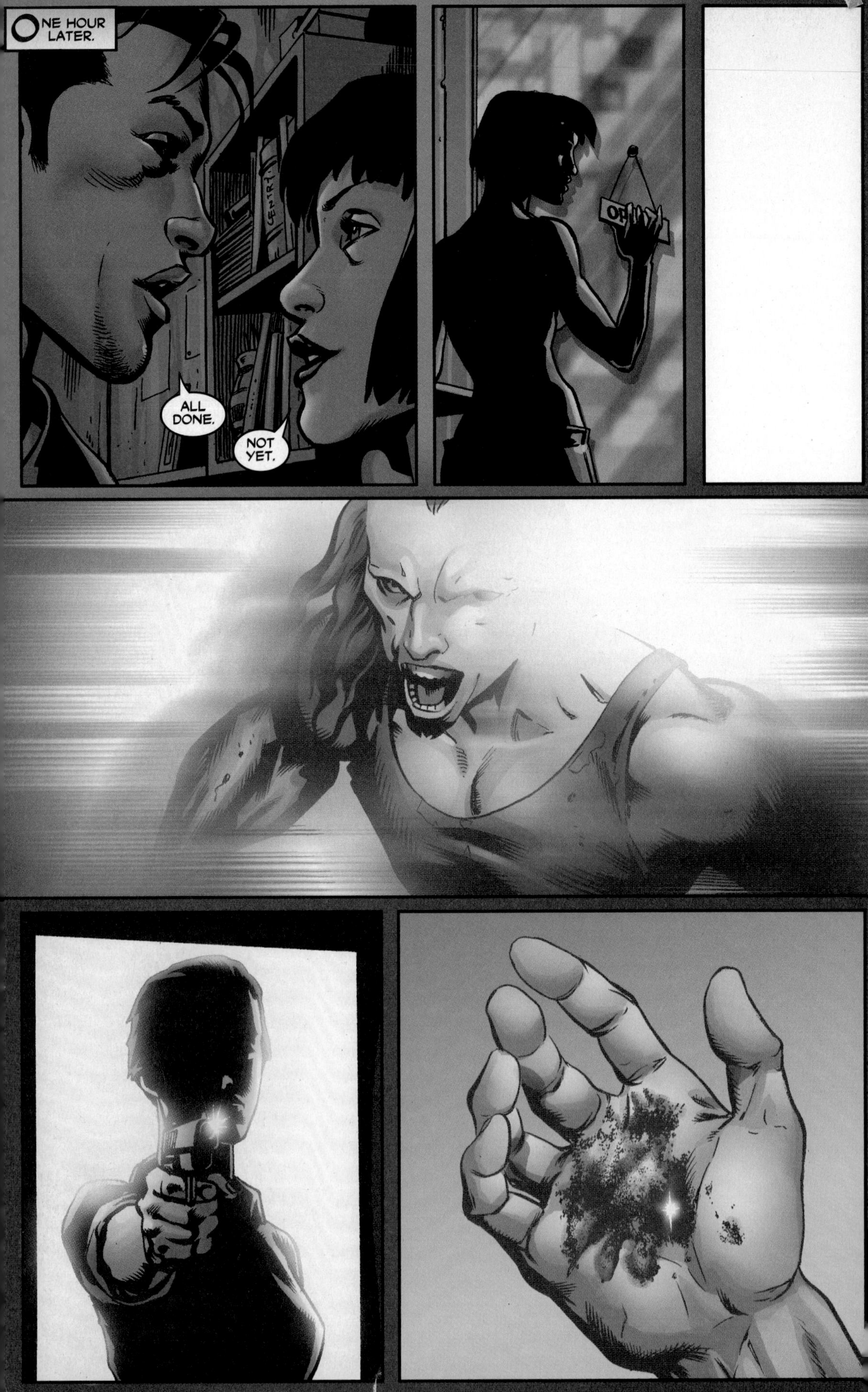
ONE HOUR LATER.
ALL DONE.
NOT YET.
OP

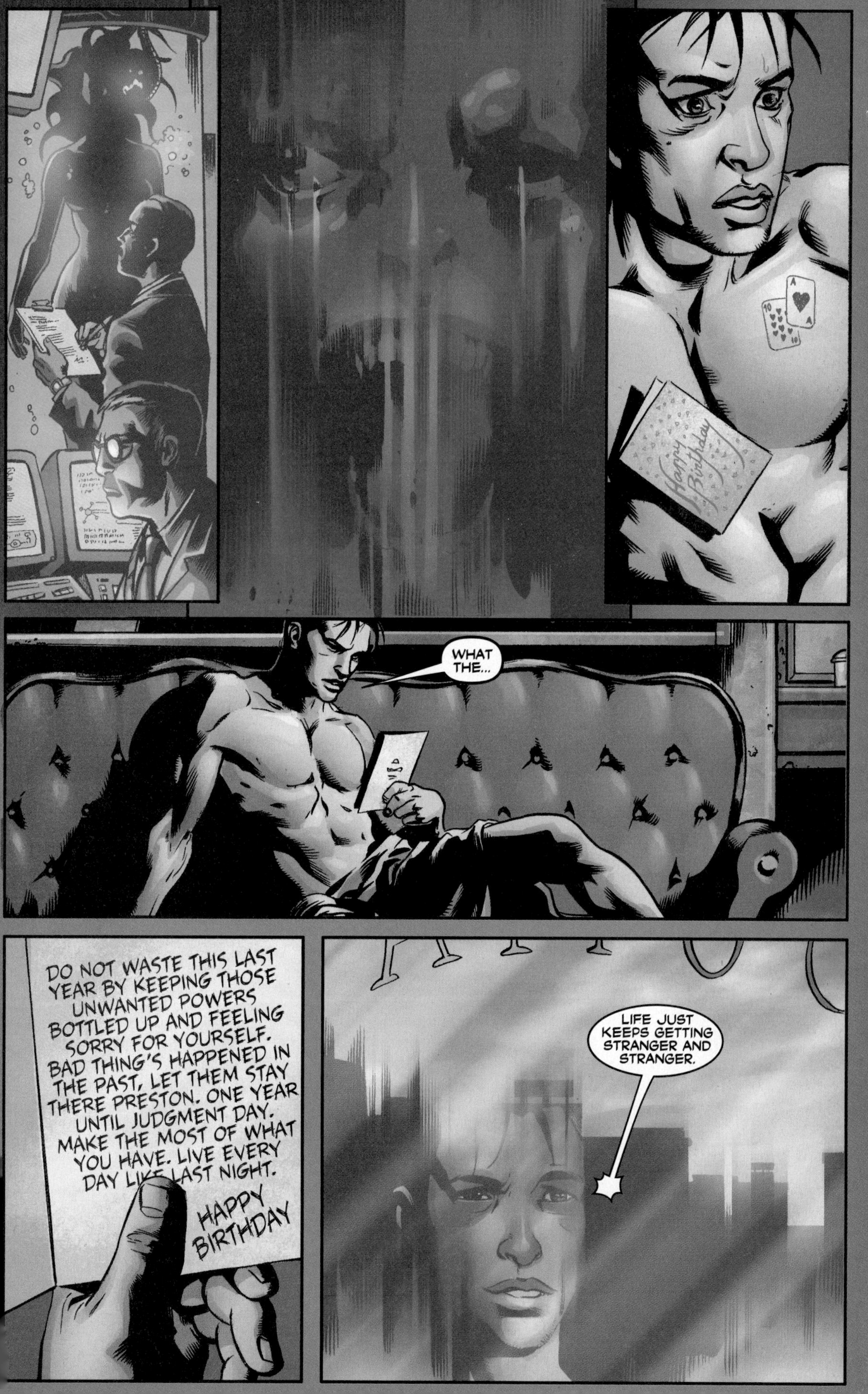

Happy Birthday
WHAT THE...
DO NOT WASTE THIS LAST YEAR BY KEEPING THOSE UNWANTED POWERS BOTTLED UP AND FEELING SORRY FOR YOURSELF. BAD THING'S HAPPENED IN THE PAST, LET THEM STAY THERE PRESTON. ONE YEAR UNTIL JUDGMENT DAY. MAKE THE MOST OF WHAT YOU HAVE. LIVE EVERY DAY LIKE LAST NIGHT.
HAPPY BIRTHDAY
LIFE JUST KEEPS GETTING STRANGER AND STRANGER.

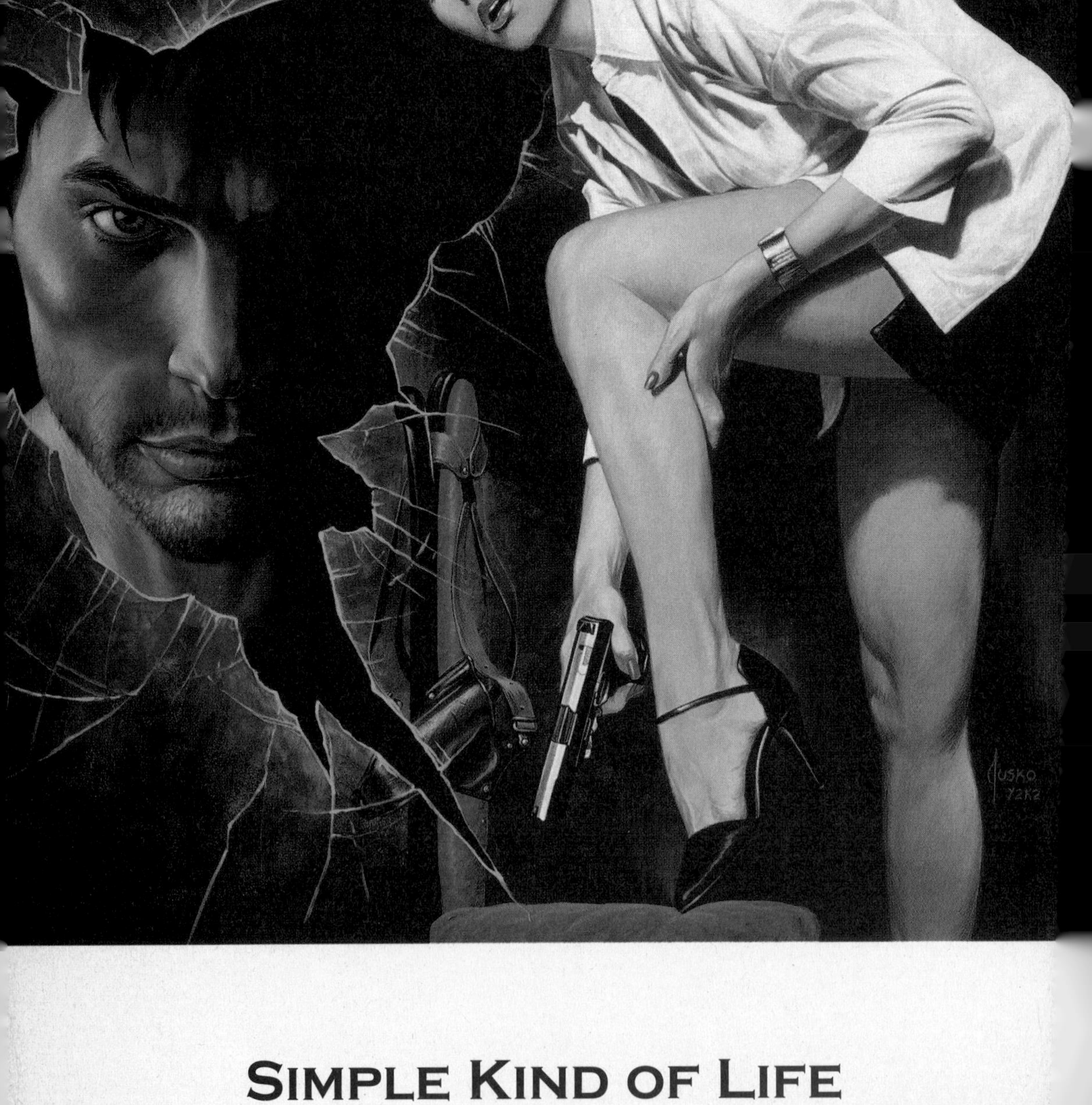

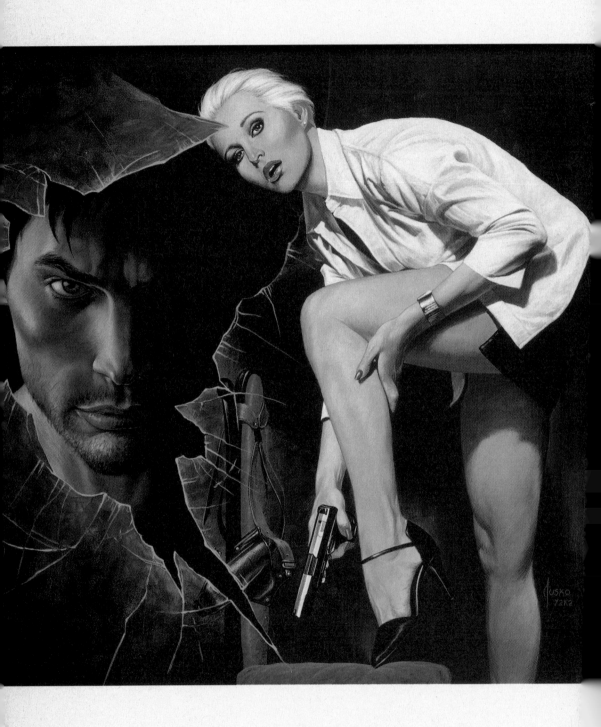

SIMPLE KIND OF LIFE

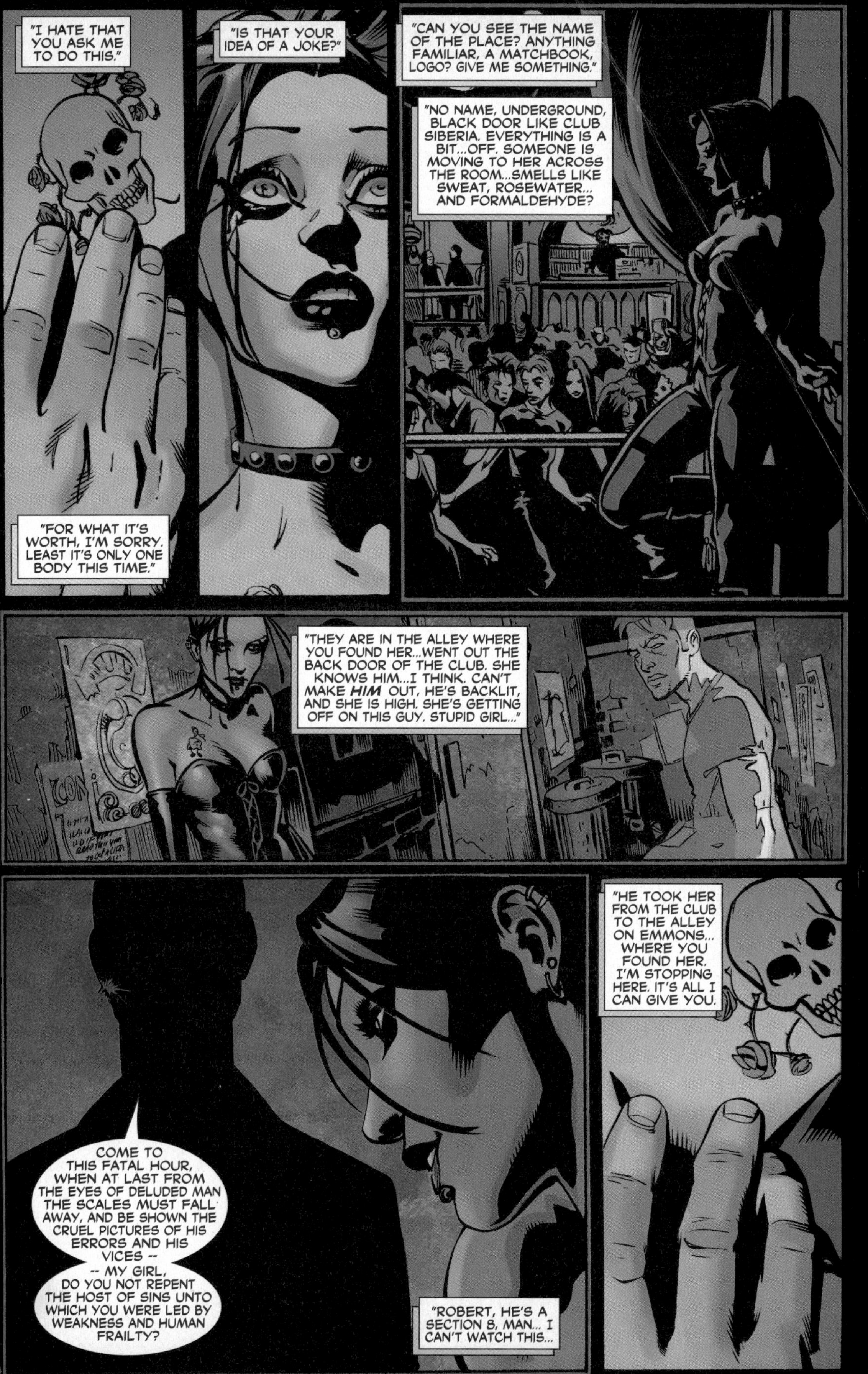
"I HATE THAT YOU ASK ME TO DO THIS."
"FOR WHAT IT'S WORTH, I'M SORRY. LEAST IT'S ONLY ONE BODY THIS TIME."
"IS THAT YOUR IDEA OF A JOKE?"
"CAN YOU SEE THE NAME OF THE PLACE? ANYTHING FAMILIAR, A MATCHBOOK, LOGO? GIVE ME SOMETHING."
"NO NAME, UNDERGROUND, BLACK DOOR LIKE CLUB SIBERIA. EVERYTHING IS A BIT...OFF. SOMEONE IS MOVING TO HER ACROSS THE ROOM...SMELLS LIKE SWEAT, ROSEWATER... AND FORMALDEHYDE?
"THEY ARE IN THE ALLEY WHERE YOU FOUND HER...WENT OUT THE BACK DOOR OF THE CLUB. SHE KNOWS HIM...I THINK. CAN'T MAKE ***HIM*** OUT, HE'S BACKLIT, AND SHE IS HIGH. SHE'S GETTING OFF ON THIS GUY. STUPID GIRL..."
COME TO THIS FATAL HOUR, WHEN AT LAST FROM THE EYES OF DELUDED MAN THE SCALES MUST FALL AWAY, AND BE SHOWN THE CRUEL PICTURES OF HIS ERRORS AND HIS VICES -- -- MY GIRL, DO YOU NOT REPENT THE HOST OF SINS UNTO WHICH YOU WERE LED BY WEAKNESS AND HUMAN FRAILTY?
"ROBERT, HE'S A SECTION 8, MAN... I CAN'T WATCH THIS...
"HE TOOK HER FROM THE CLUB TO THE ALLEY ON EMMONS... WHERE YOU FOUND HER. I'M STOPPING HERE. IT'S ALL I CAN GIVE YOU.

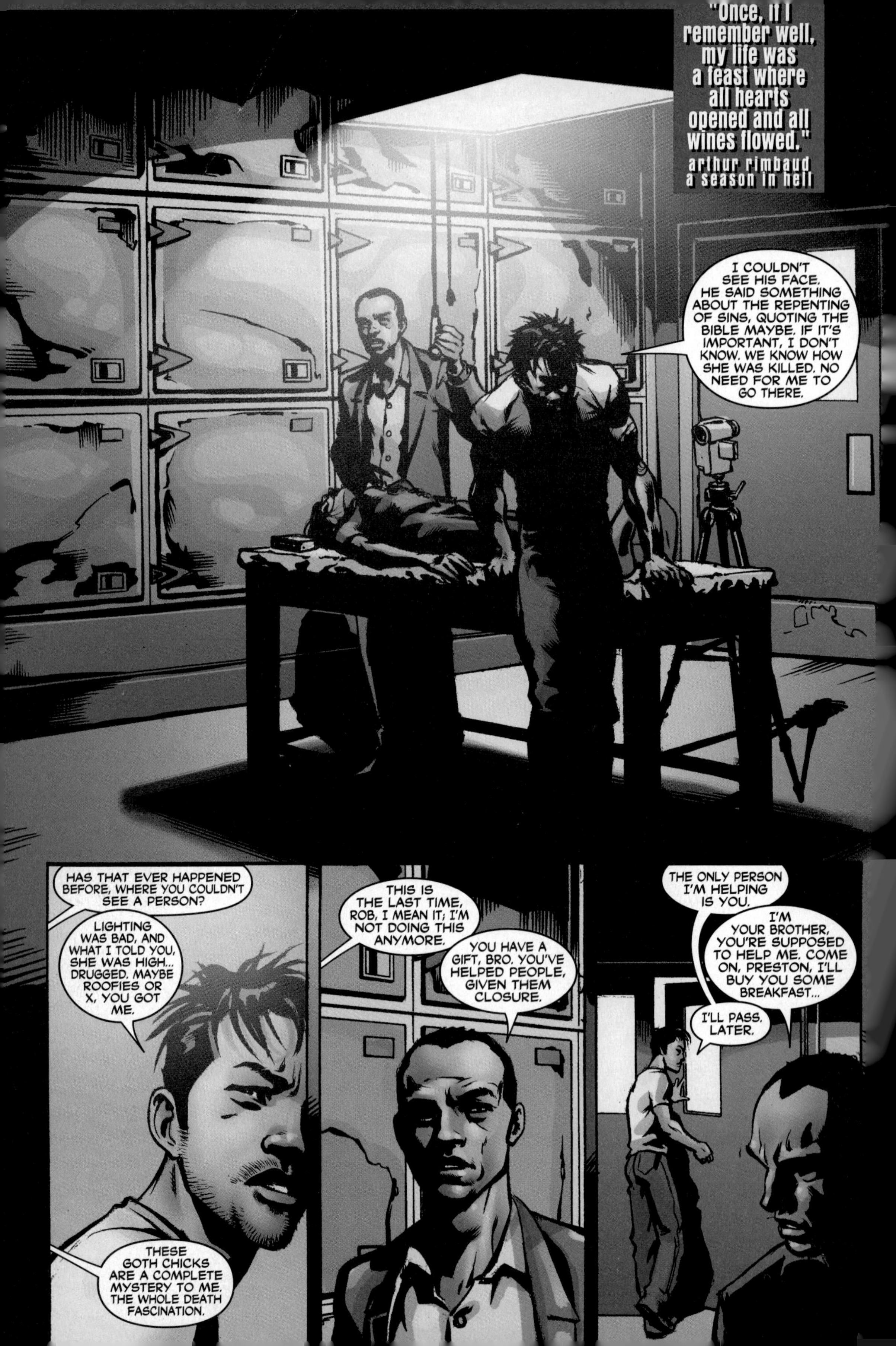
"Once, if I remember well, my life was a feast where all hearts opened and all wines flowed."
arthur rimbaud
a season in hell
I COULDN'T SEE HIS FACE. HE SAID SOMETHING ABOUT THE REPENTING OF SINS, QUOTING THE BIBLE MAYBE. IF IT'S IMPORTANT, I DON'T KNOW. WE KNOW HOW SHE WAS KILLED. NO NEED FOR ME TO GO THERE.
HAS THAT EVER HAPPENED BEFORE, WHERE YOU COULDN'T SEE A PERSON?
LIGHTING WAS BAD, AND WHAT I TOLD YOU, SHE WAS HIGH... DRUGGED. MAYBE ROOFIES OR X, YOU GOT ME.
THESE GOTH CHICKS ARE A COMPLETE MYSTERY TO ME. THE WHOLE DEATH FASCINATION.
THIS IS THE LAST TIME, ROB, I MEAN IT; I'M NOT DOING THIS ANYMORE.
YOU HAVE A GIFT, BRO. YOU'VE HELPED PEOPLE, GIVEN THEM CLOSURE.
THE ONLY PERSON I'M HELPING IS YOU.
I'M YOUR BROTHER, YOU'RE SUPPOSED TO HELP ME. COME ON, PRESTON, I'LL BUY YOU SOME BREAKFAST...
I'LL PASS. LATER.

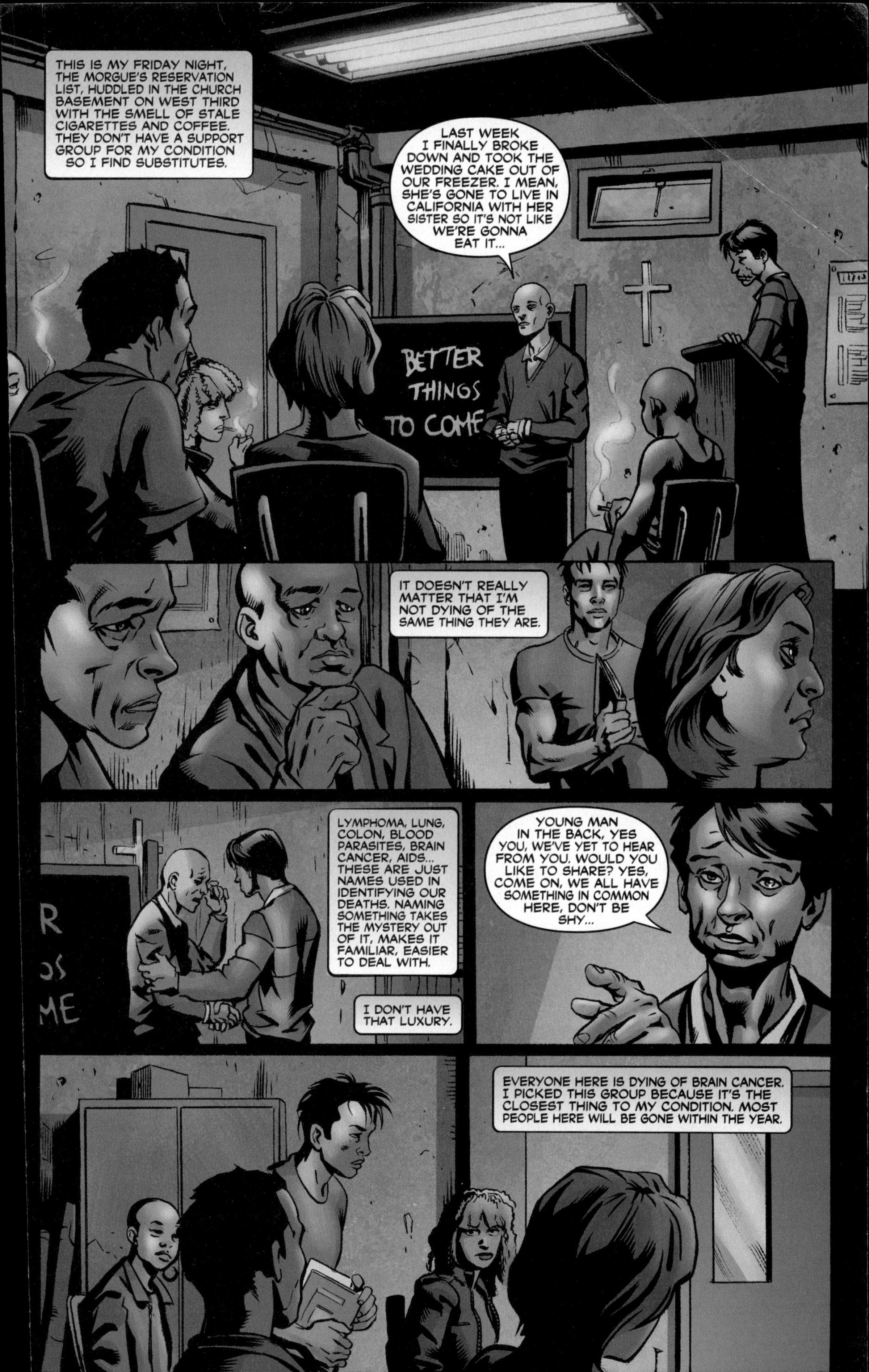
THIS IS MY FRIDAY NIGHT, THE MORGUE'S RESERVATION LIST, HUDDLED IN THE CHURCH BASEMENT ON WEST THIRD WITH THE SMELL OF STALE CIGARETTES AND COFFEE. THEY DON'T HAVE A SUPPORT GROUP FOR MY CONDITION SO I FIND SUBSTITUTES.
LAST WEEK I FINALLY BROKE DOWN AND TOOK THE WEDDING CAKE OUT OF OUR FREEZER. I MEAN, SHE'S GONE TO LIVE IN CALIFORNIA WITH HER SISTER SO IT'S NOT LIKE WE'RE GONNA EAT IT...
BETTER THINGS TO COME
IT DOESN'T REALLY MATTER THAT I'M NOT DYING OF THE SAME THING THEY ARE.
LYMPHOMA, LUNG, COLON, BLOOD PARASITES, BRAIN CANCER, AIDS... THESE ARE JUST NAMES USED IN IDENTIFYING OUR DEATHS. NAMING SOMETHING TAKES THE MYSTERY OUT OF IT, MAKES IT FAMILIAR, EASIER TO DEAL WITH.
I DON'T HAVE THAT LUXURY.
YOUNG MAN IN THE BACK, YES YOU, WE'VE YET TO HEAR FROM YOU. WOULD YOU LIKE TO SHARE? YES, COME ON, WE ALL HAVE SOMETHING IN COMMON HERE, DON'T BE SHY...
EVERYONE HERE IS DYING OF BRAIN CANCER. I PICKED THIS GROUP BECAUSE IT'S THE CLOSEST THING TO MY CONDITION. MOST PEOPLE HERE WILL BE GONE WITHIN THE YEAR.

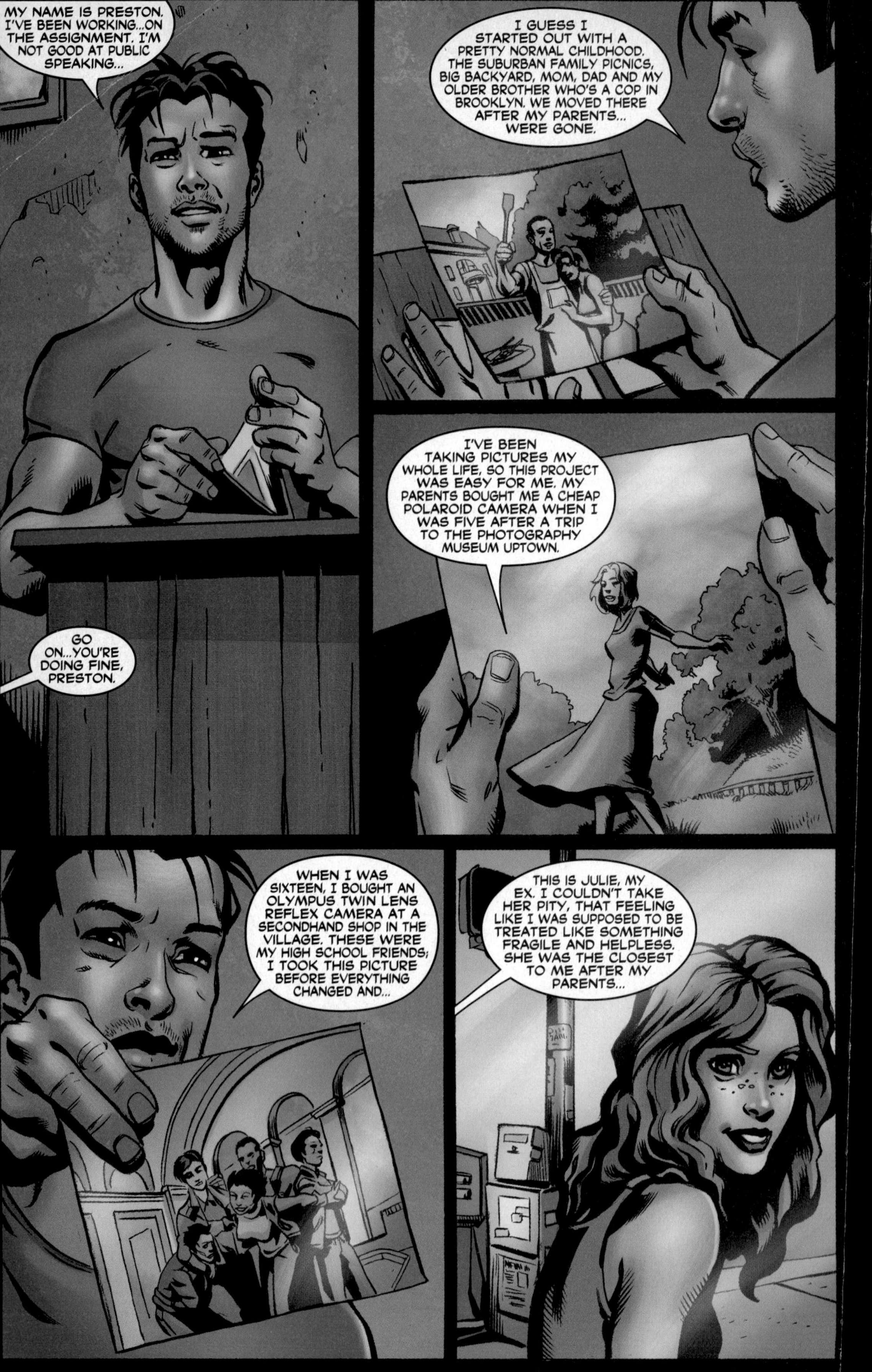
MY NAME IS PRESTON. I'VE BEEN WORKING...ON THE ASSIGNMENT. I'M NOT GOOD AT PUBLIC SPEAKING...
I GUESS I STARTED OUT WITH A PRETTY NORMAL CHILDHOOD. THE SUBURBAN FAMILY PICNICS, BIG BACKYARD, MOM, DAD AND MY OLDER BROTHER WHO'S A COP IN BROOKLYN. WE MOVED THERE AFTER MY PARENTS... WERE GONE.
I'VE BEEN TAKING PICTURES MY WHOLE LIFE, SO THIS PROJECT WAS EASY FOR ME. MY PARENTS BOUGHT ME A CHEAP POLAROID CAMERA WHEN I WAS FIVE AFTER A TRIP TO THE PHOTOGRAPHY MUSEUM UPTOWN.
GO ON...YOU'RE DOING FINE, PRESTON.
WHEN I WAS SIXTEEN, I BOUGHT AN OLYMPUS TWIN LENS REFLEX CAMERA AT A SECONDHAND SHOP IN THE VILLAGE. THESE WERE MY HIGH SCHOOL FRIENDS; I TOOK THIS PICTURE BEFORE EVERYTHING CHANGED AND...
THIS IS JULIE, MY EX. I COULDN'T TAKE HER PITY, THAT FEELING LIKE I WAS SUPPOSED TO BE TREATED LIKE SOMETHING FRAGILE AND HELPLESS. SHE WAS THE CLOSEST TO ME AFTER MY PARENTS...

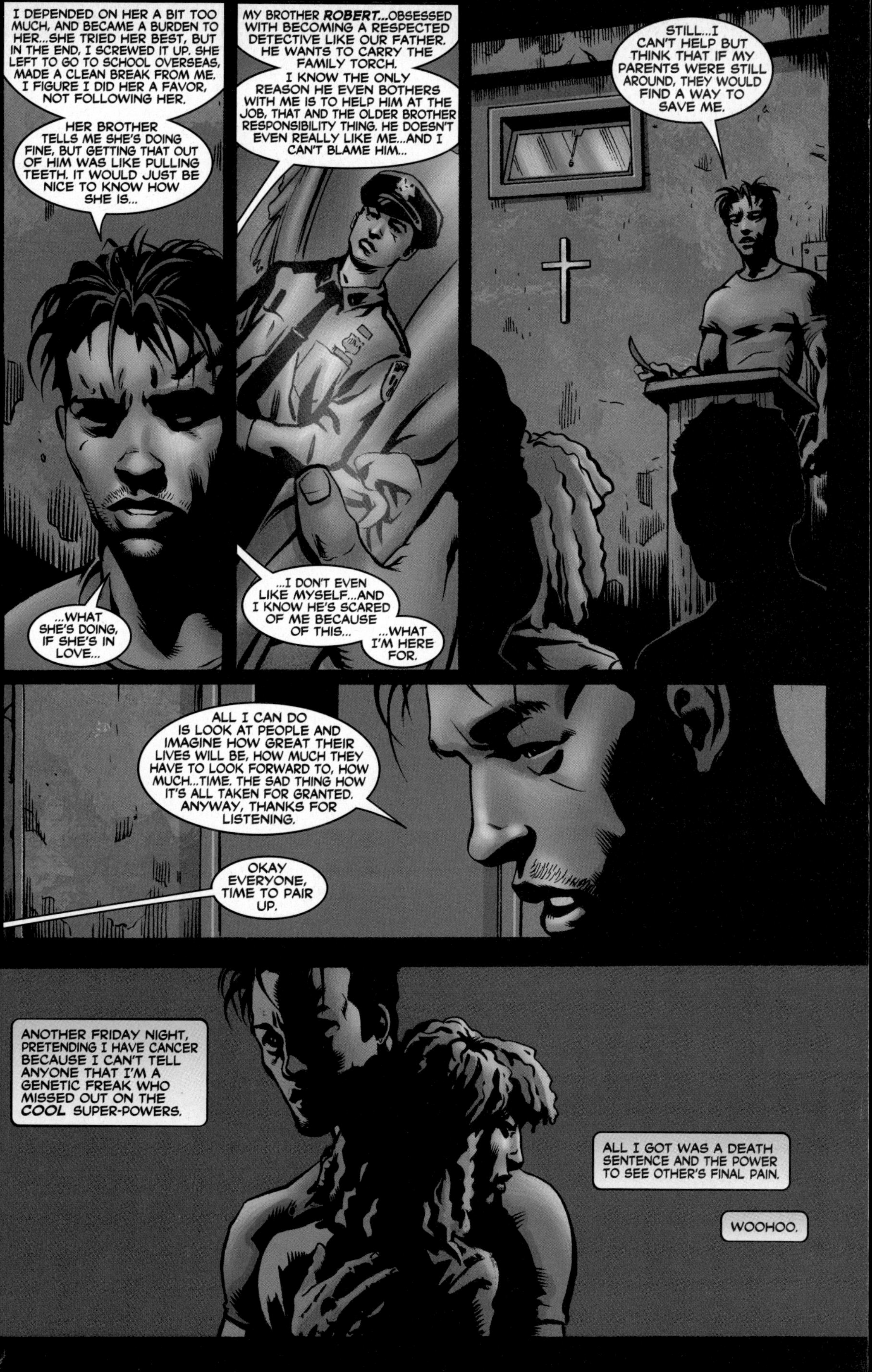
I DEPENDED ON HER A BIT TOO MUCH, AND BECAME A BURDEN TO HER...SHE TRIED HER BEST, BUT IN THE END, I SCREWED IT UP. SHE LEFT TO GO TO SCHOOL OVERSEAS, MADE A CLEAN BREAK FROM ME. I FIGURE I DID HER A FAVOR, NOT FOLLOWING HER.
HER BROTHER TELLS ME SHE'S DOING FINE, BUT GETTING THAT OUT OF HIM WAS LIKE PULLING TEETH. IT WOULD JUST BE NICE TO KNOW HOW SHE IS...
...WHAT SHE'S DOING, IF SHE'S IN LOVE...
MY BROTHER ROBERT...OBSESSED WITH BECOMING A RESPECTED DETECTIVE LIKE OUR FATHER. HE WANTS TO CARRY THE FAMILY TORCH.
I KNOW THE ONLY REASON HE EVEN BOTHERS WITH ME IS TO HELP HIM AT THE JOB, THAT AND THE OLDER BROTHER RESPONSIBILITY THING. HE DOESN'T EVEN REALLY LIKE ME...AND I CAN'T BLAME HIM...
...I DON'T EVEN LIKE MYSELF...AND I KNOW HE'S SCARED OF ME BECAUSE OF THIS...
...WHAT I'M HERE FOR.
STILL...I CAN'T HELP BUT THINK THAT IF MY PARENTS WERE STILL AROUND, THEY WOULD FIND A WAY TO SAVE ME.
ALL I CAN DO IS LOOK AT PEOPLE AND IMAGINE HOW GREAT THEIR LIVES WILL BE, HOW MUCH THEY HAVE TO LOOK FORWARD TO, HOW MUCH...TIME. THE SAD THING HOW IT'S ALL TAKEN FOR GRANTED. ANYWAY, THANKS FOR LISTENING.
OKAY EVERYONE, TIME TO PAIR UP.
ANOTHER FRIDAY NIGHT, PRETENDING I HAVE CANCER BECAUSE I CAN'T TELL ANYONE THAT I'M A GENETIC FREAK WHO MISSED OUT ON THE COOL SUPER-POWERS.
ALL I GOT WAS A DEATH SENTENCE AND THE POWER TO SEE OTHER'S FINAL PAIN.
WOOHOO.

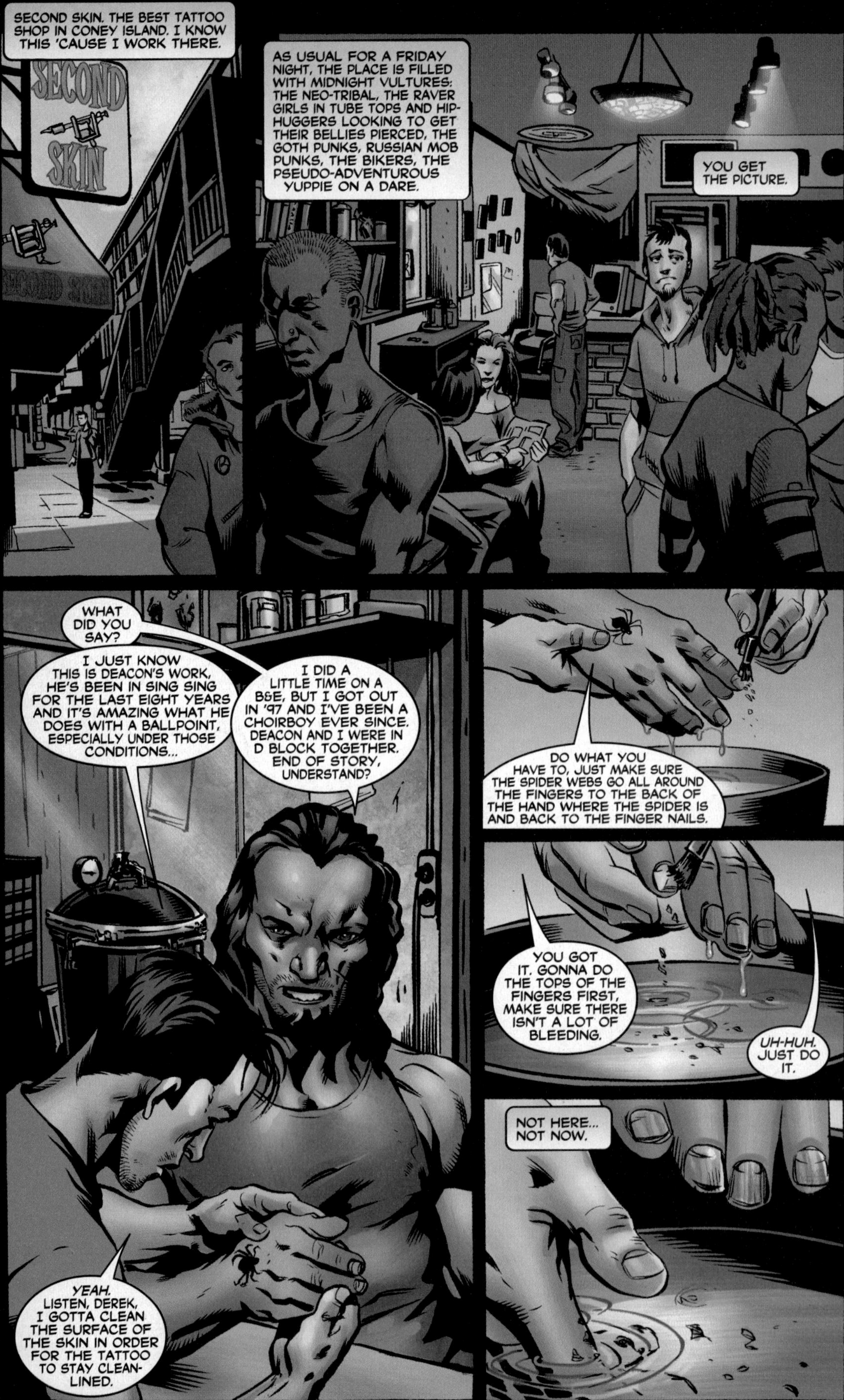
SECOND SKIN. THE BEST TATTOO SHOP IN CONEY ISLAND. I KNOW THIS 'CAUSE I WORK THERE.
SECOND SKIN
SECOND SKIN
AS USUAL FOR A FRIDAY NIGHT, THE PLACE IS FILLED WITH MIDNIGHT VULTURES: THE NEO-TRIBAL, THE RAVER GIRLS IN TUBE TOPS AND HIP-HUGGERS LOOKING TO GET THEIR BELLIES PIERCED, THE GOTH PUNKS, RUSSIAN MOB PUNKS, THE BIKERS, THE PSEUDO-ADVENTUROUS YUPPIE ON A DARE.
YOU GET THE PICTURE.
WHAT DID YOU SAY?
I JUST KNOW THIS IS DEACON'S WORK, HE'S BEEN IN SING SING FOR THE LAST EIGHT YEARS AND IT'S AMAZING WHAT HE DOES WITH A BALLPOINT, ESPECIALLY UNDER THOSE CONDITIONS...
I DID A LITTLE TIME ON A B&E, BUT I GOT OUT IN '97 AND I'VE BEEN A CHOIRBOY EVER SINCE. DEACON AND I WERE IN D BLOCK TOGETHER. END OF STORY, UNDERSTAND?
YEAH. LISTEN, DEREK, I GOTTA CLEAN THE SURFACE OF THE SKIN IN ORDER FOR THE TATTOO TO STAY CLEAN-LINED.
DO WHAT YOU HAVE TO, JUST MAKE SURE THE SPIDER WEBS GO ALL AROUND THE FINGERS TO THE BACK OF THE HAND WHERE THE SPIDER IS AND BACK TO THE FINGER NAILS.
YOU GOT IT. GONNA DO THE TOPS OF THE FINGERS FIRST, MAKE SURE THERE ISN'T A LOT OF BLEEDING.
UH-HUH. JUST DO IT.
NOT HERE... NOT NOW.

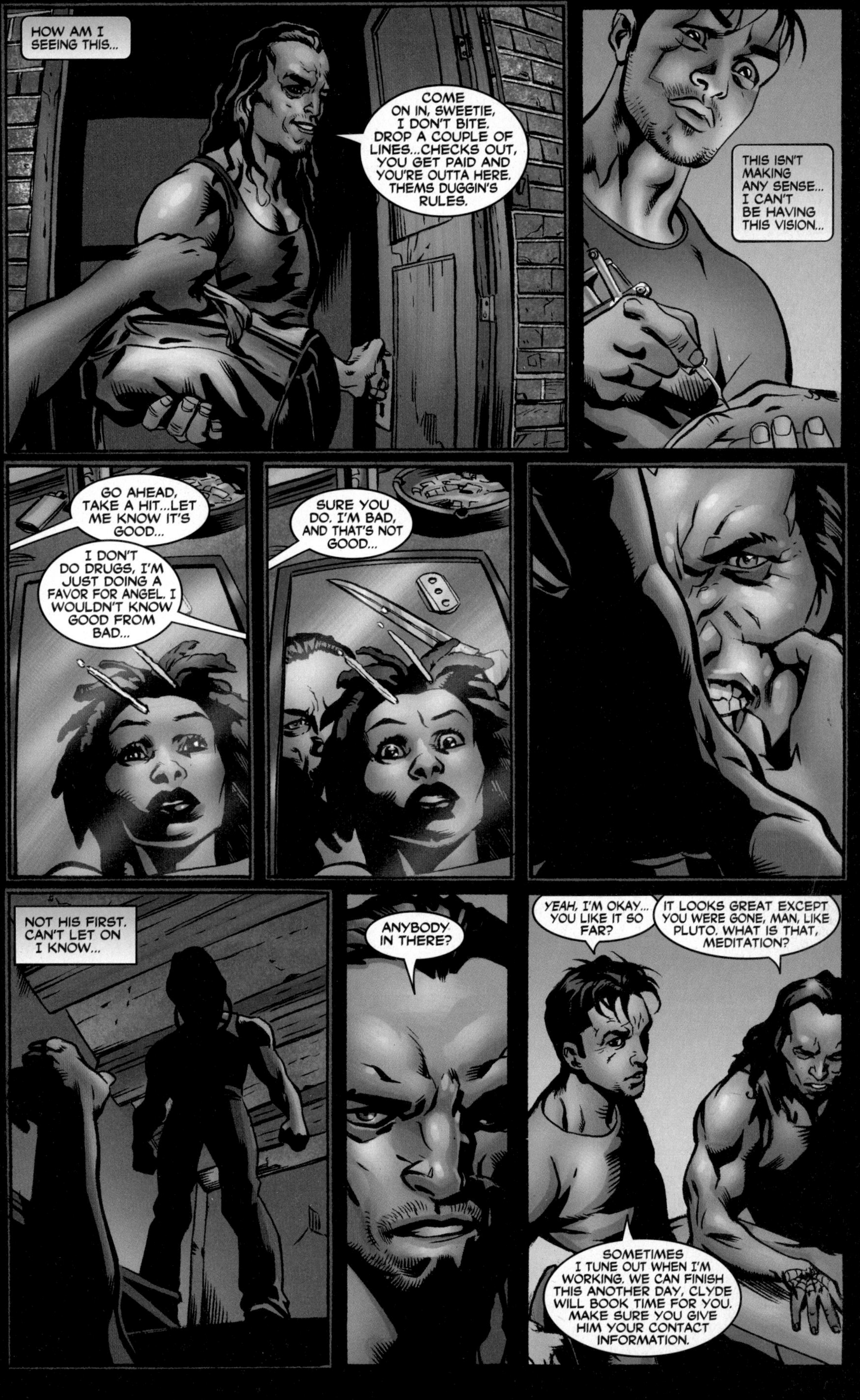
HOW AM I SEEING THIS...
COME ON IN, SWEETIE, I DON'T BITE. DROP A COUPLE OF LINES...CHECKS OUT, YOU GET PAID AND YOU'RE OUTTA HERE. THEMS DUGGIN'S RULES.
THIS ISN'T MAKING ANY SENSE... I CAN'T BE HAVING THIS VISION...
GO AHEAD, TAKE A HIT...LET ME KNOW IT'S GOOD...
I DON'T DO DRUGS, I'M JUST DOING A FAVOR FOR ANGEL. I WOULDN'T KNOW GOOD FROM BAD...
SURE YOU DO. I'M BAD, AND THAT'S NOT GOOD...
NOT HIS FIRST. CAN'T LET ON I KNOW...
ANYBODY IN THERE?
YEAH, I'M OKAY... YOU LIKE IT SO FAR?
IT LOOKS GREAT EXCEPT YOU WERE GONE, MAN, LIKE PLUTO. WHAT IS THAT, MEDITATION?
SOMETIMES I TUNE OUT WHEN I'M WORKING. WE CAN FINISH THIS ANOTHER DAY, CLYDE WILL BOOK TIME FOR YOU. MAKE SURE YOU GIVE HIM YOUR CONTACT INFORMATION.

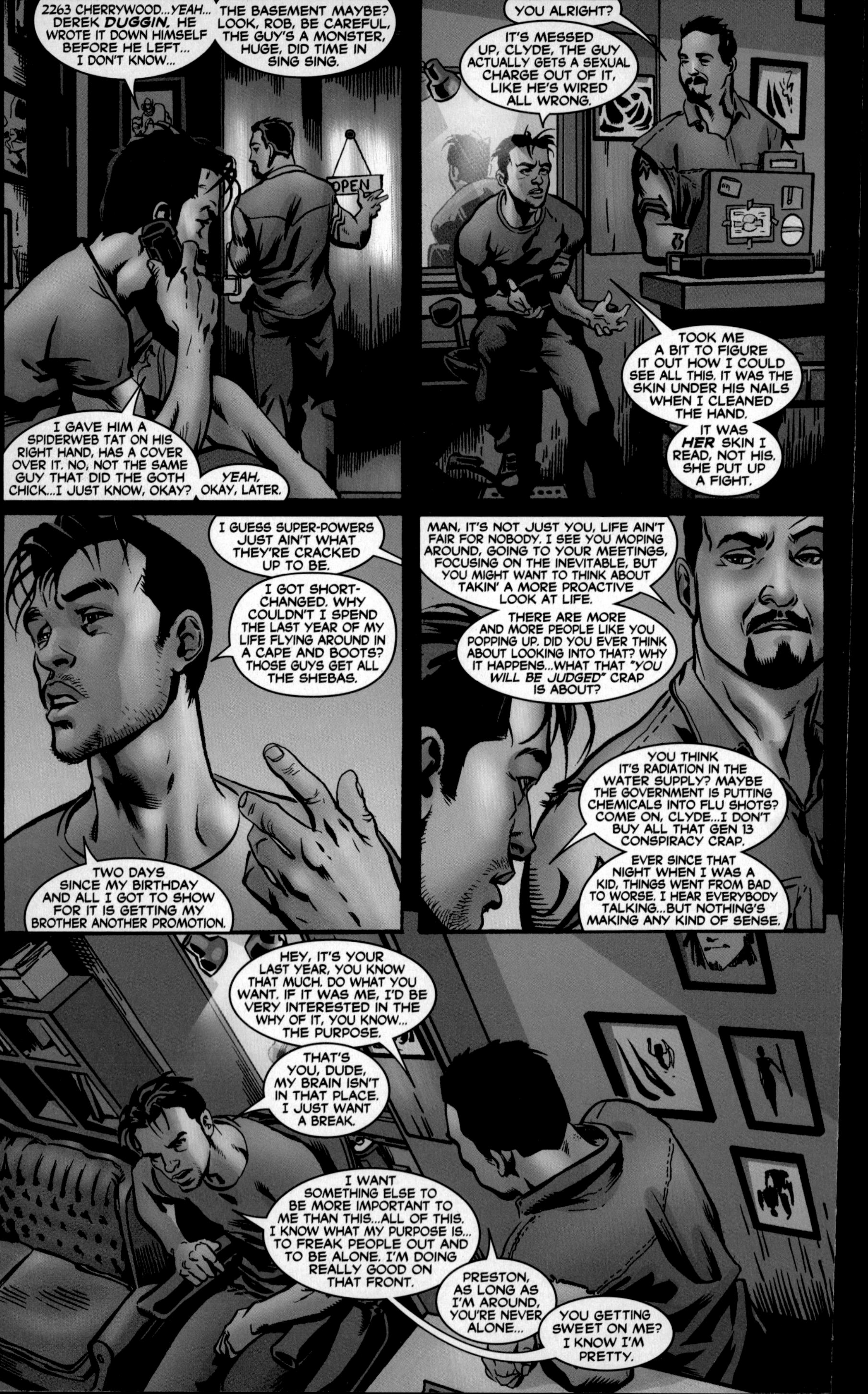
2263 CHERRYWOOD...YEAH... DEREK DUGGIN. HE WROTE IT DOWN HIMSELF BEFORE HE LEFT... I DON'T KNOW...
THE BASEMENT MAYBE? LOOK, ROB, BE CAREFUL, THE GUY'S A MONSTER, HUGE, DID TIME IN SING SING.
OPEN
I GAVE HIM A SPIDERWEB TAT ON HIS RIGHT HAND, HAS A COVER OVER IT. NO, NOT THE SAME GUY THAT DID THE GOTH CHICK...I JUST KNOW, OKAY?
YEAH, OKAY, LATER.
YOU ALRIGHT?
IT'S MESSED UP, CLYDE, THE GUY ACTUALLY GETS A SEXUAL CHARGE OUT OF IT, LIKE HE'S WIRED ALL WRONG.
TOOK ME A BIT TO FIGURE IT OUT HOW I COULD SEE ALL THIS. IT WAS THE SKIN UNDER HIS NAILS WHEN I CLEANED THE HAND.
IT WAS HER SKIN I READ, NOT HIS. SHE PUT UP A FIGHT.
I GUESS SUPER-POWERS JUST AIN'T WHAT THEY'RE CRACKED UP TO BE.
I GOT SHORT-CHANGED. WHY COULDN'T I SPEND THE LAST YEAR OF MY LIFE FLYING AROUND IN A CAPE AND BOOTS? THOSE GUYS GET ALL THE SHEBAS.
TWO DAYS SINCE MY BIRTHDAY AND ALL I GOT TO SHOW FOR IT IS GETTING MY BROTHER ANOTHER PROMOTION.
MAN, IT'S NOT JUST YOU, LIFE AIN'T FAIR FOR NOBODY. I SEE YOU MOPING AROUND, GOING TO YOUR MEETINGS, FOCUSING ON THE INEVITABLE, BUT YOU MIGHT WANT TO THINK ABOUT TAKIN' A MORE PROACTIVE LOOK AT LIFE.
THERE ARE MORE AND MORE PEOPLE LIKE YOU POPPING UP. DID YOU EVER THINK ABOUT LOOKING INTO THAT? WHY IT HAPPENS...WHAT THAT "YOU WILL BE JUDGED" CRAP IS ABOUT?
YOU THINK IT'S RADIATION IN THE WATER SUPPLY? MAYBE THE GOVERNMENT IS PUTTING CHEMICALS INTO FLU SHOTS? COME ON, CLYDE...I DON'T BUY ALL THAT GEN 13 CONSPIRACY CRAP.
EVER SINCE THAT NIGHT WHEN I WAS A KID, THINGS WENT FROM BAD TO WORSE. I HEAR EVERYBODY TALKING...BUT NOTHING'S MAKING ANY KIND OF SENSE.
HEY, IT'S YOUR LAST YEAR, YOU KNOW THAT MUCH. DO WHAT YOU WANT. IF IT WAS ME, I'D BE VERY INTERESTED IN THE WHY OF IT, YOU KNOW... THE PURPOSE.
THAT'S YOU, DUDE, MY BRAIN ISN'T IN THAT PLACE. I JUST WANT A BREAK.
I WANT SOMETHING ELSE TO BE MORE IMPORTANT TO ME THAN THIS...ALL OF THIS. I KNOW WHAT MY PURPOSE IS... TO FREAK PEOPLE OUT AND TO BE ALONE. I'M DOING REALLY GOOD ON THAT FRONT.
PRESTON, AS LONG AS I'M AROUND, YOU'RE NEVER ALONE...
YOU GETTING SWEET ON ME? I KNOW I'M PRETTY.

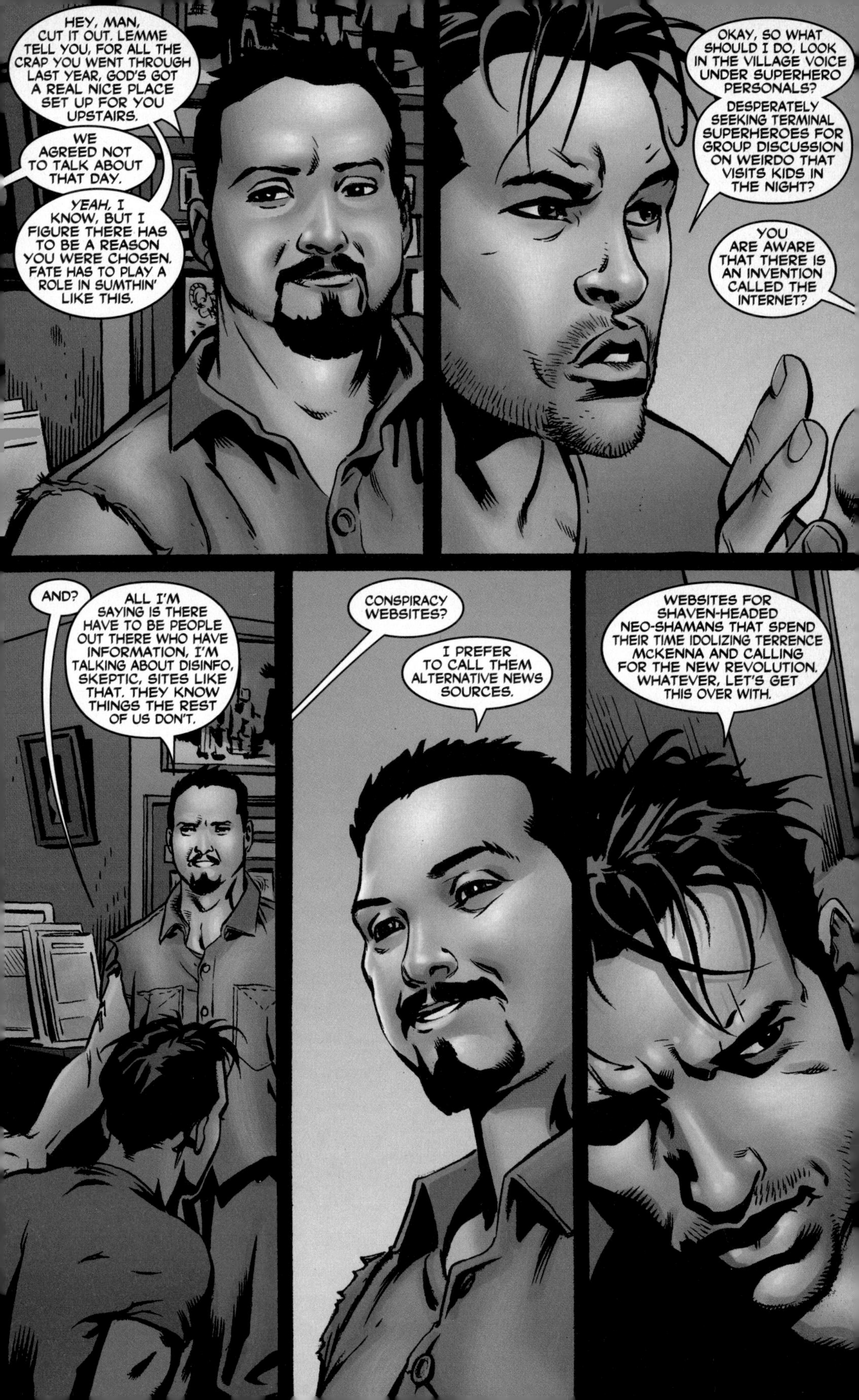
HEY, MAN, CUT IT OUT. LEMME TELL YOU, FOR ALL THE CRAP YOU WENT THROUGH LAST YEAR, GOD'S GOT A REAL NICE PLACE SET UP FOR YOU UPSTAIRS.
WE AGREED NOT TO TALK ABOUT THAT DAY.
YEAH, I KNOW, BUT I FIGURE THERE HAS TO BE A REASON YOU WERE CHOSEN. FATE HAS TO PLAY A ROLE IN SUMTHIN' LIKE THIS.
OKAY, SO WHAT SHOULD I DO, LOOK IN THE VILLAGE VOICE UNDER SUPERHERO PERSONALS?
DESPERATELY SEEKING TERMINAL SUPERHEROES FOR GROUP DISCUSSION ON WEIRDO THAT VISITS KIDS IN THE NIGHT?
YOU ARE AWARE THAT THERE IS AN INVENTION CALLED THE INTERNET?
AND?
ALL I'M SAYING IS THERE HAVE TO BE PEOPLE OUT THERE WHO HAVE INFORMATION, I'M TALKING ABOUT DISINFO, SKEPTIC, SITES LIKE THAT. THEY KNOW THINGS THE REST OF US DON'T.
CONSPIRACY WEBSITES?
I PREFER TO CALL THEM ALTERNATIVE NEWS SOURCES.
WEBSITES FOR SHAVEN-HEADED NEO-SHAMANS THAT SPEND THEIR TIME IDOLIZING TERRENCE McKENNA AND CALLING FOR THE NEW REVOLUTION. WHATEVER, LET'S GET THIS OVER WITH.

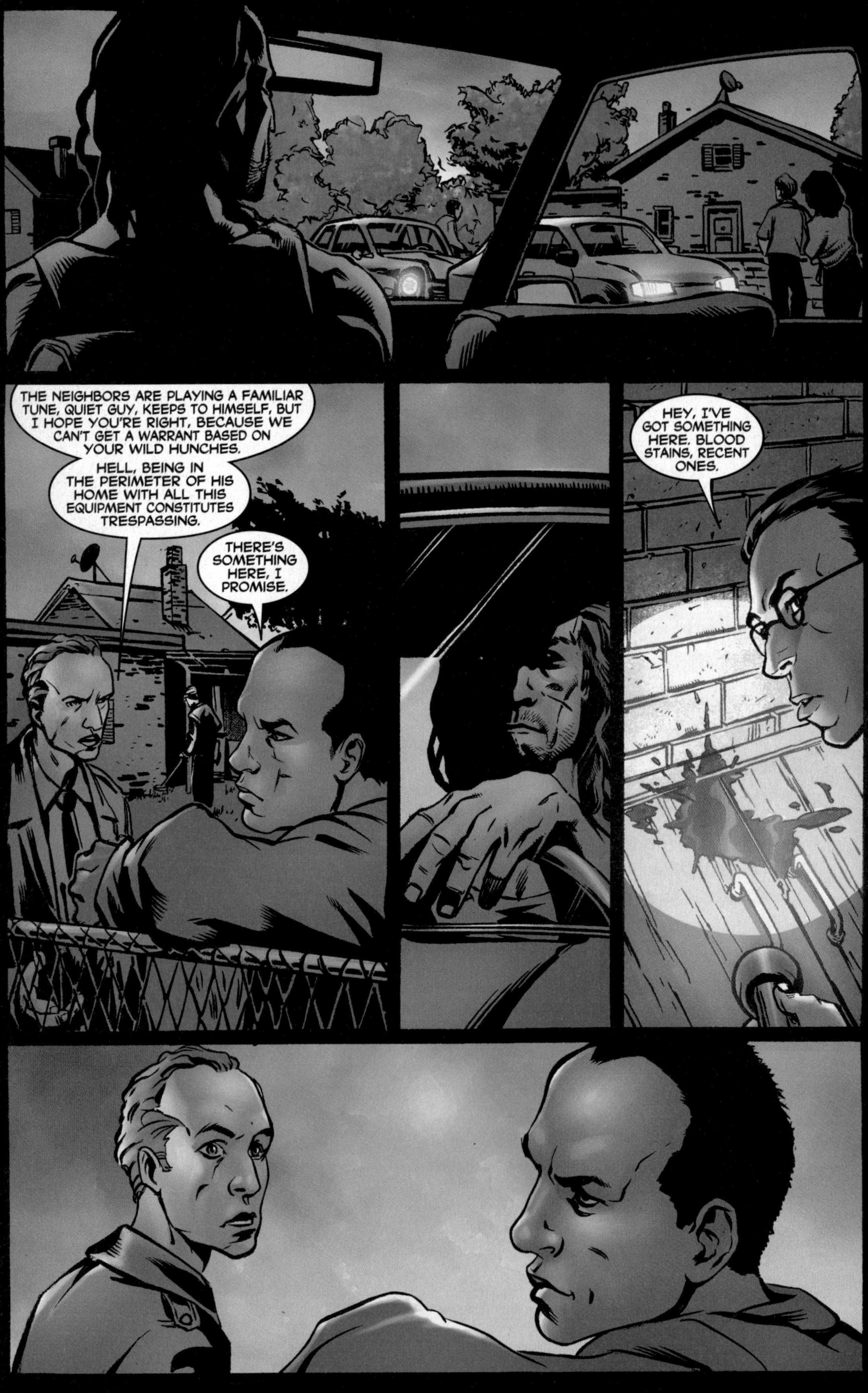
THE NEIGHBORS ARE PLAYING A FAMILIAR TUNE, QUIET GUY, KEEPS TO HIMSELF, BUT I HOPE YOU'RE RIGHT, BECAUSE WE CAN'T GET A WARRANT BASED ON YOUR WILD HUNCHES.
HELL, BEING IN THE PERIMETER OF HIS HOME WITH ALL THIS EQUIPMENT CONSTITUTES TRESPASSING.
THERE'S SOMETHING HERE, I PROMISE.
HEY, I'VE GOT SOMETHING HERE. BLOOD STAINS, RECENT ONES.

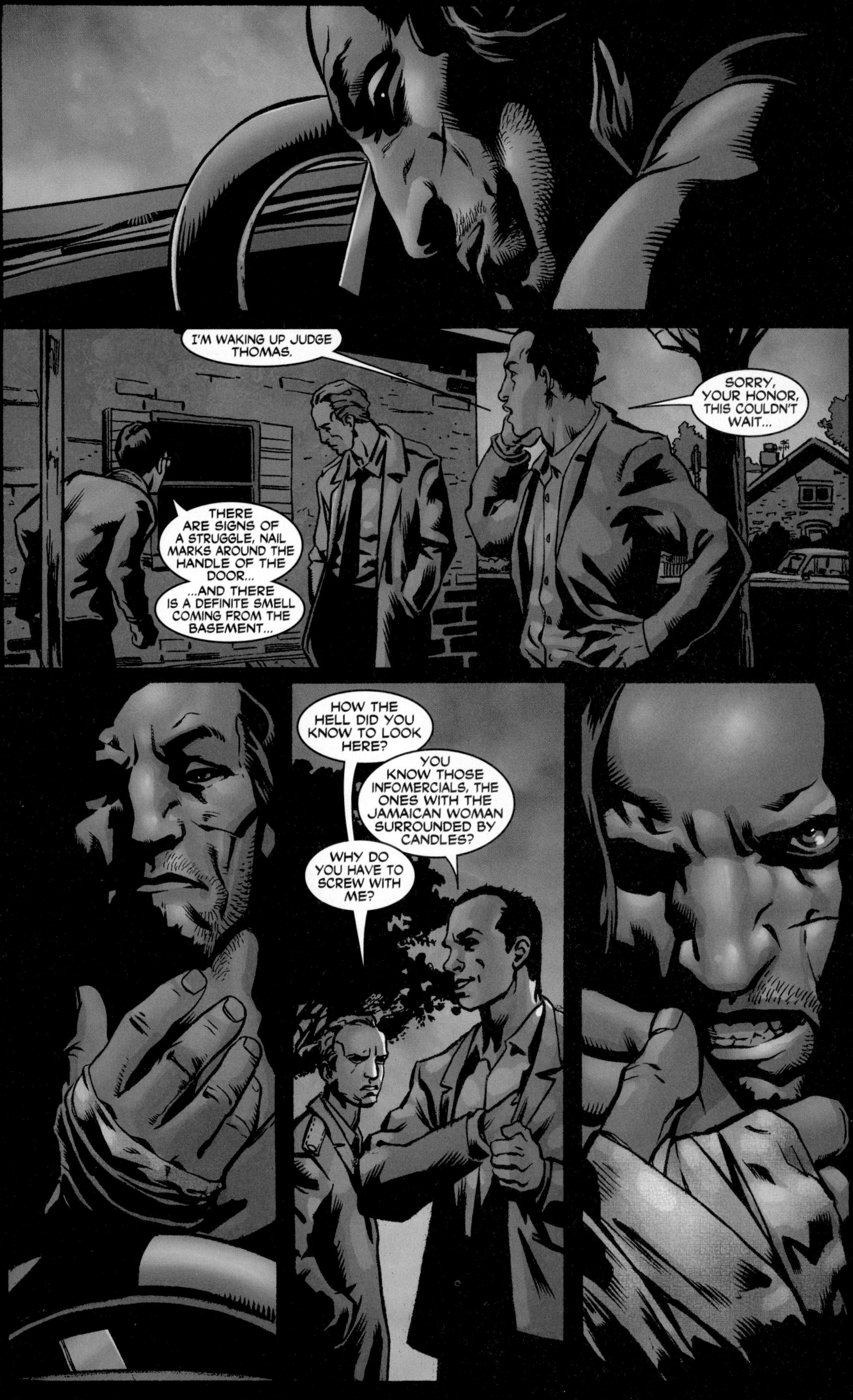
I'M WAKING UP JUDGE THOMAS.
SORRY, YOUR HONOR, THIS COULDN'T WAIT...
THERE ARE SIGNS OF A STRUGGLE, NAIL MARKS AROUND THE HANDLE OF THE DOOR...
...AND THERE IS A DEFINITE SMELL COMING FROM THE BASEMENT...
HOW THE HELL DID YOU KNOW TO LOOK HERE?
YOU KNOW THOSE INFOMERCIALS, THE ONES WITH THE JAMAICAN WOMAN SURROUNDED BY CANDLES?
WHY DO YOU HAVE TO SCREW WITH ME?

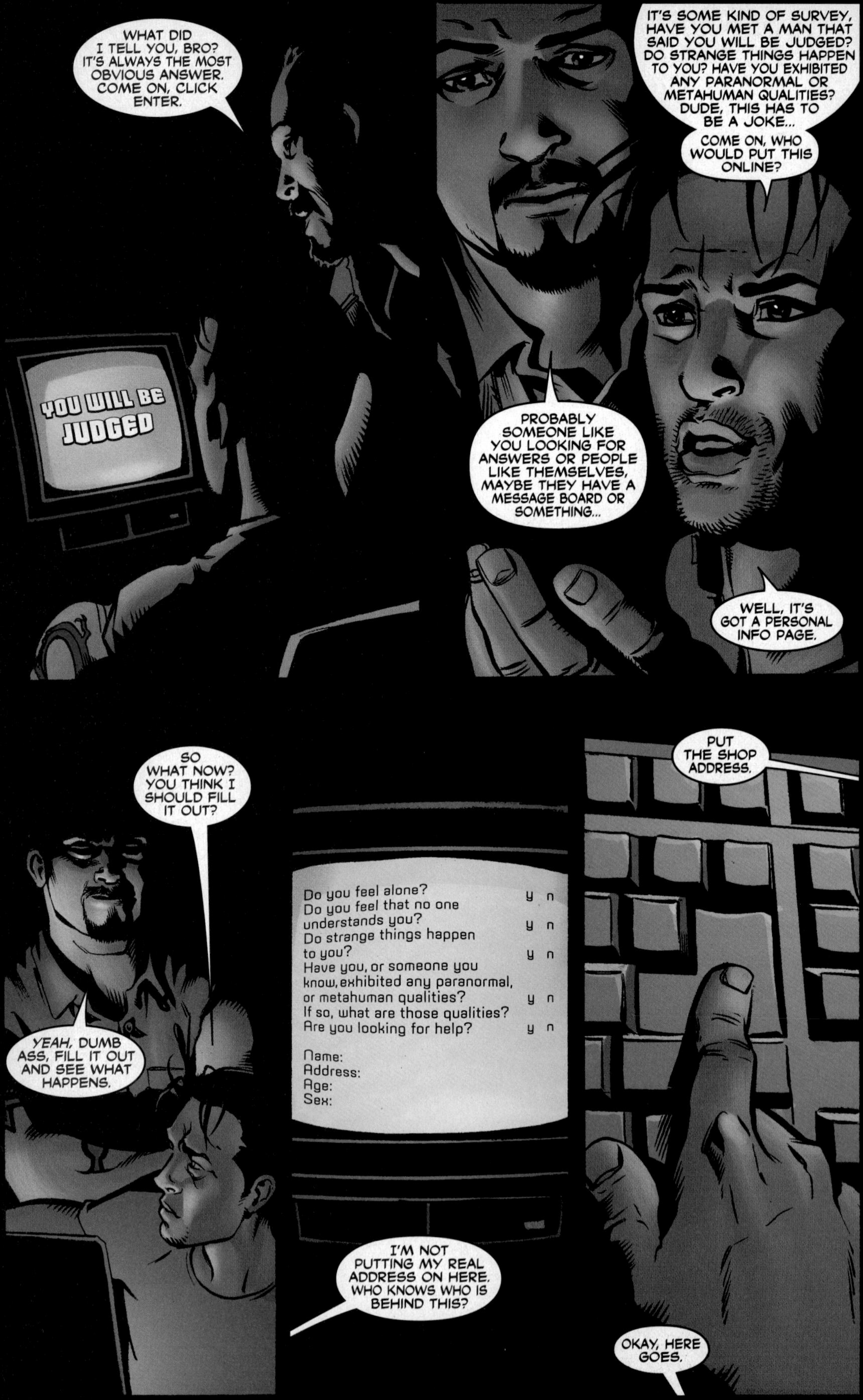
WHAT DID I TELL YOU, BRO? IT'S ALWAYS THE MOST OBVIOUS ANSWER. COME ON, CLICK ENTER.
YOU WILL BE JUDGED
IT'S SOME KIND OF SURVEY, HAVE YOU MET A MAN THAT SAID YOU WILL BE JUDGED? DO STRANGE THINGS HAPPEN TO YOU? HAVE YOU EXHIBITED ANY PARANORMAL OR METAHUMAN QUALITIES? DUDE, THIS HAS TO BE A JOKE...
COME ON, WHO WOULD PUT THIS ONLINE?
PROBABLY SOMEONE LIKE YOU LOOKING FOR ANSWERS OR PEOPLE LIKE THEMSELVES, MAYBE THEY HAVE A MESSAGE BOARD OR SOMETHING...
WELL, IT'S GOT A PERSONAL INFO PAGE.
SO WHAT NOW? YOU THINK I SHOULD FILL IT OUT?
YEAH, DUMB ASS, FILL IT OUT AND SEE WHAT HAPPENS.
Do you feel alone? y n
Do you feel that no one understands you? y n
Do strange things happen to you? y n
Have you, or someone you know, exhibited any paranormal, or metahuman qualities? y n
If so, what are those qualities?
Are you looking for help? y n
Name:
Address:
Age:
Sex:
I'M NOT PUTTING MY REAL ADDRESS ON HERE. WHO KNOWS WHO IS BEHIND THIS?
PUT THE SHOP ADDRESS.
OKAY, HERE GOES.

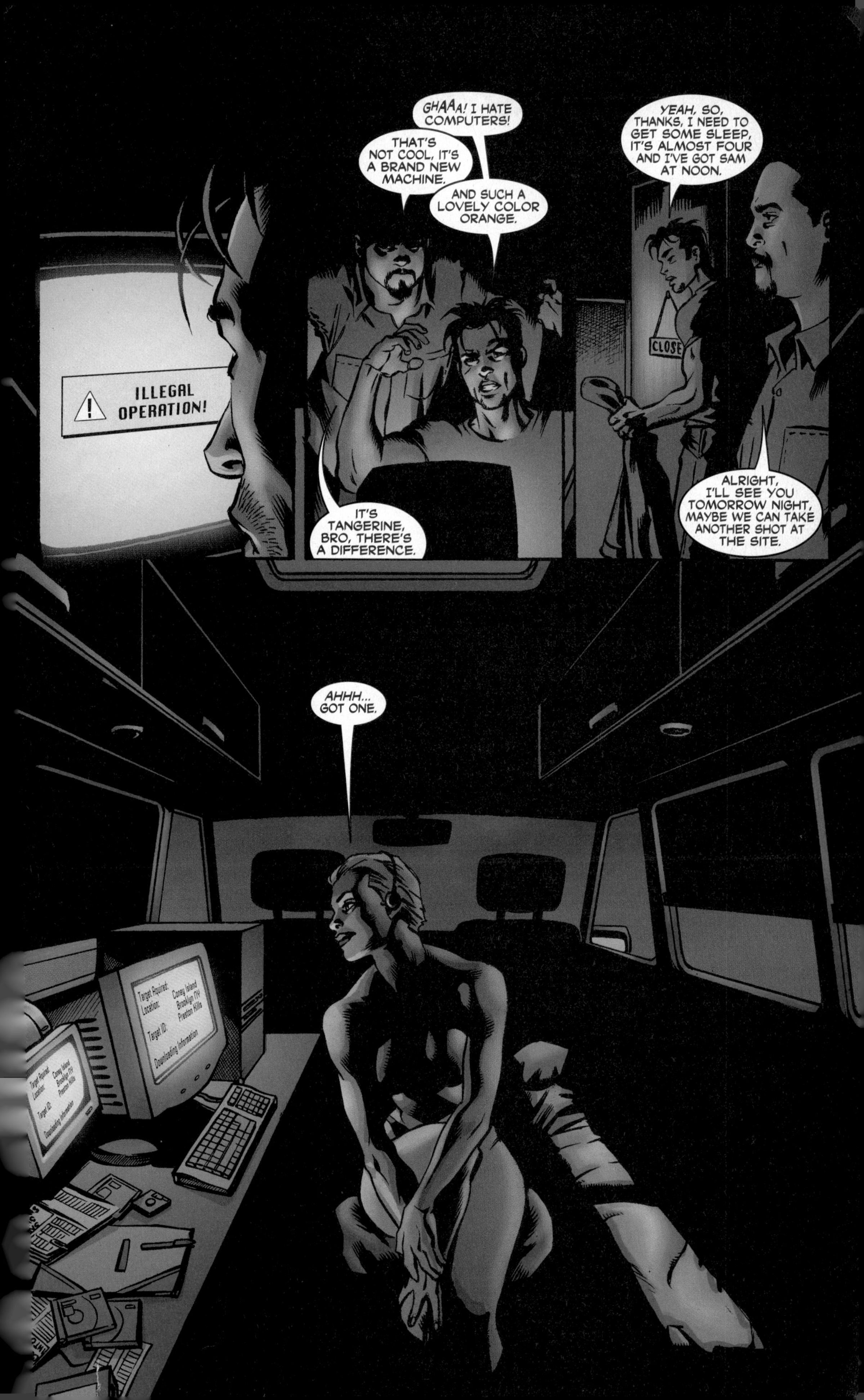
ILLEGAL OPERATION!
GHAAA! I HATE COMPUTERS!
THAT'S NOT COOL, IT'S A BRAND NEW MACHINE.
AND SUCH A LOVELY COLOR ORANGE.
IT'S TANGERINE, BRO, THERE'S A DIFFERENCE.
YEAH, SO, THANKS, I NEED TO GET SOME SLEEP, IT'S ALMOST FOUR AND I'VE GOT SAM AT NOON.
CLOSE
ALRIGHT, I'LL SEE YOU TOMORROW NIGHT, MAYBE WE CAN TAKE ANOTHER SHOT AT THE SITE.
AHHH... GOT ONE.
Target Aquired: Coney Island
Location: Brooklyn NY
Target ID: Preston Hills
Downloading Information

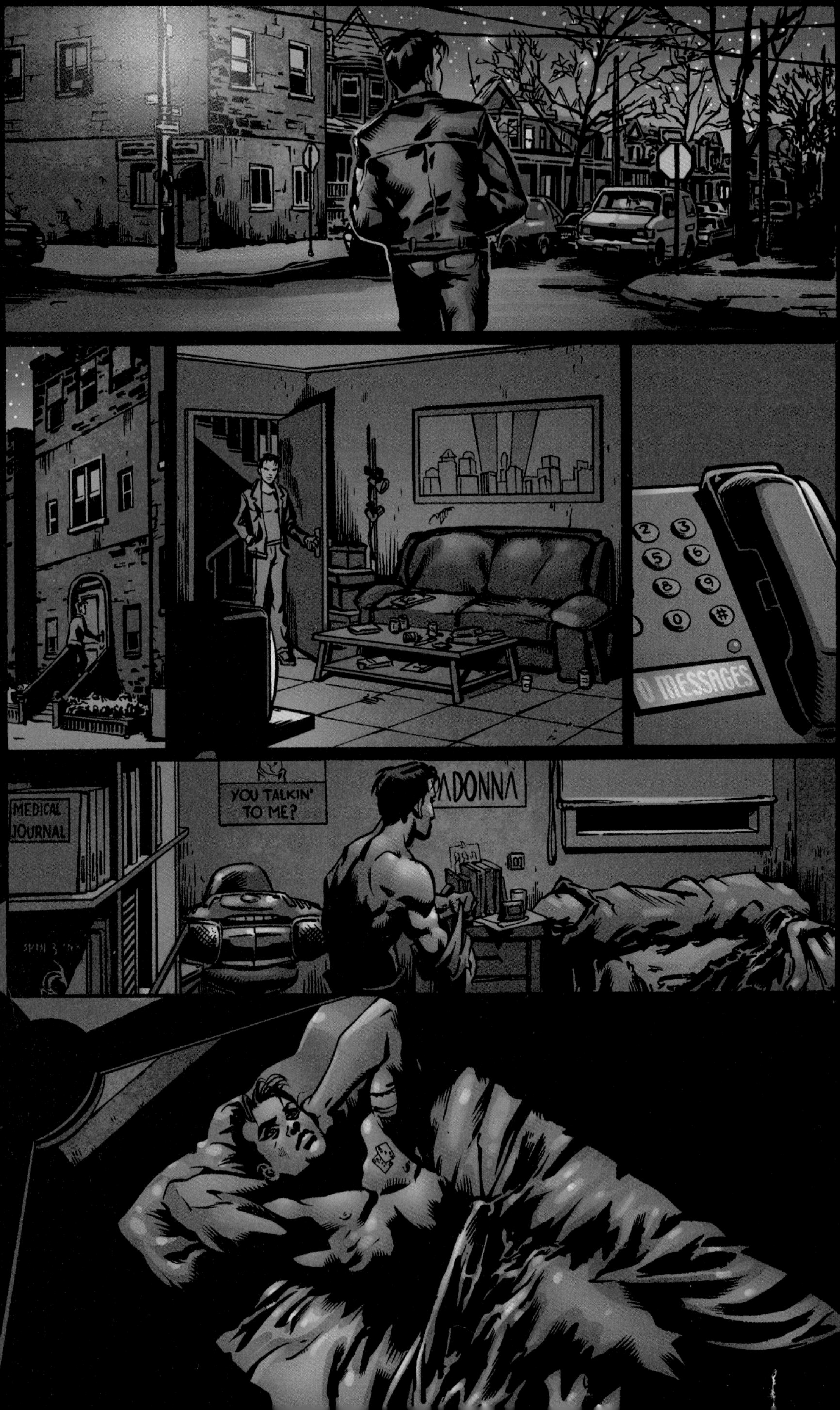
0 MESSAGES
YOU TALKIN' TO ME?
MEDICAL JOURNAL

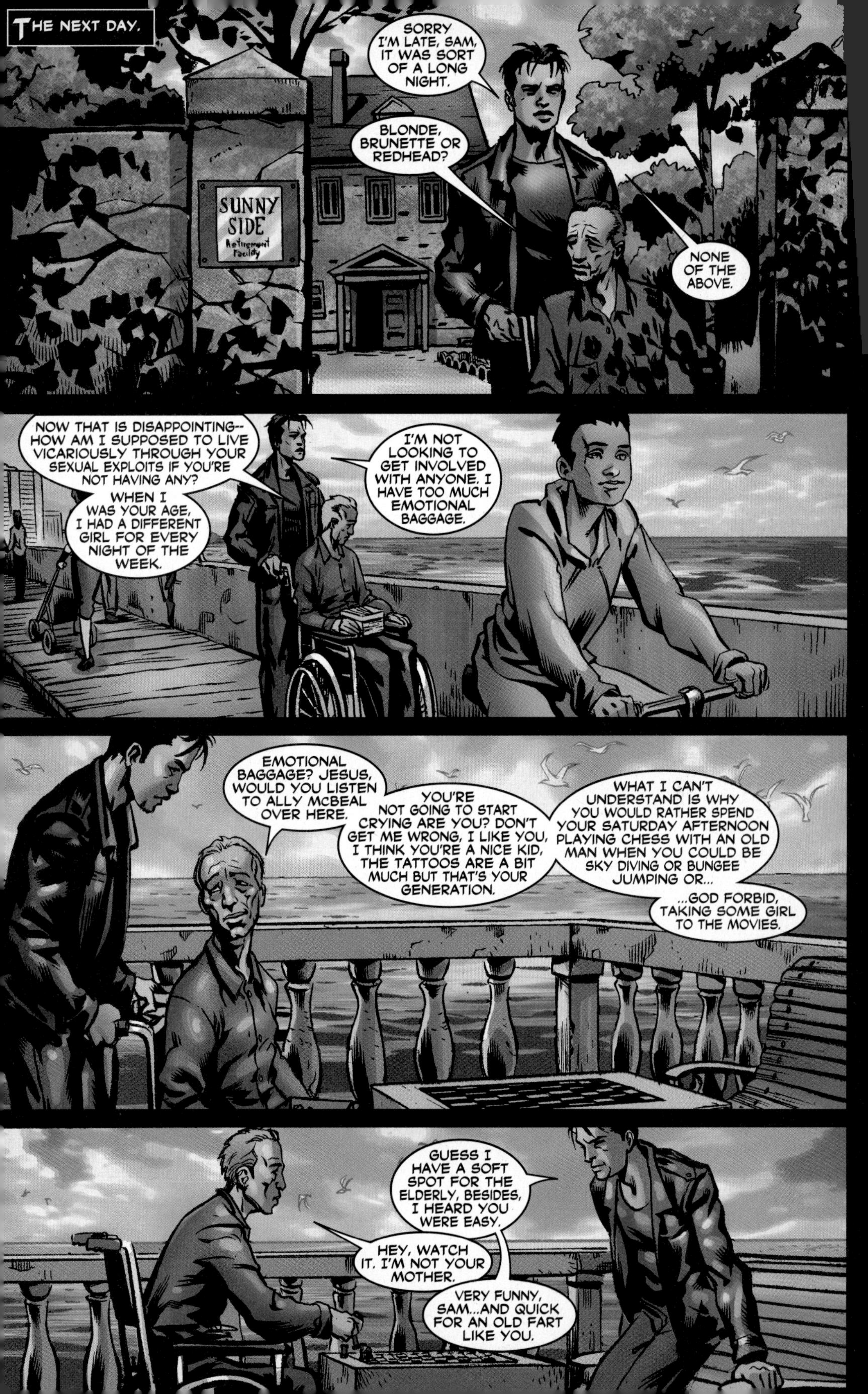
THE NEXT DAY.
SORRY I'M LATE, SAM, IT WAS SORT OF A LONG NIGHT.
BLONDE, BRUNETTE OR REDHEAD?
NONE OF THE ABOVE.
SUNNY SIDE Retirement Facility
NOW THAT IS DISAPPOINTING-- HOW AM I SUPPOSED TO LIVE VICARIOUSLY THROUGH YOUR SEXUAL EXPLOITS IF YOU'RE NOT HAVING ANY?
WHEN I WAS YOUR AGE, I HAD A DIFFERENT GIRL FOR EVERY NIGHT OF THE WEEK.
I'M NOT LOOKING TO GET INVOLVED WITH ANYONE. I HAVE TOO MUCH EMOTIONAL BAGGAGE.
EMOTIONAL BAGGAGE? JESUS, WOULD YOU LISTEN TO ALLY McBEAL OVER HERE.
YOU'RE NOT GOING TO START CRYING ARE YOU? DON'T GET ME WRONG, I LIKE YOU, I THINK YOU'RE A NICE KID, THE TATTOOS ARE A BIT MUCH BUT THAT'S YOUR GENERATION.
WHAT I CAN'T UNDERSTAND IS WHY YOU WOULD RATHER SPEND YOUR SATURDAY AFTERNOON PLAYING CHESS WITH AN OLD MAN WHEN YOU COULD BE SKY DIVING OR BUNGEE JUMPING OR...
...GOD FORBID, TAKING SOME GIRL TO THE MOVIES.
GUESS I HAVE A SOFT SPOT FOR THE ELDERLY, BESIDES, I HEARD YOU WERE EASY.
HEY, WATCH IT. I'M NOT YOUR MOTHER.
VERY FUNNY, SAM...AND QUICK FOR AN OLD FART LIKE YOU.

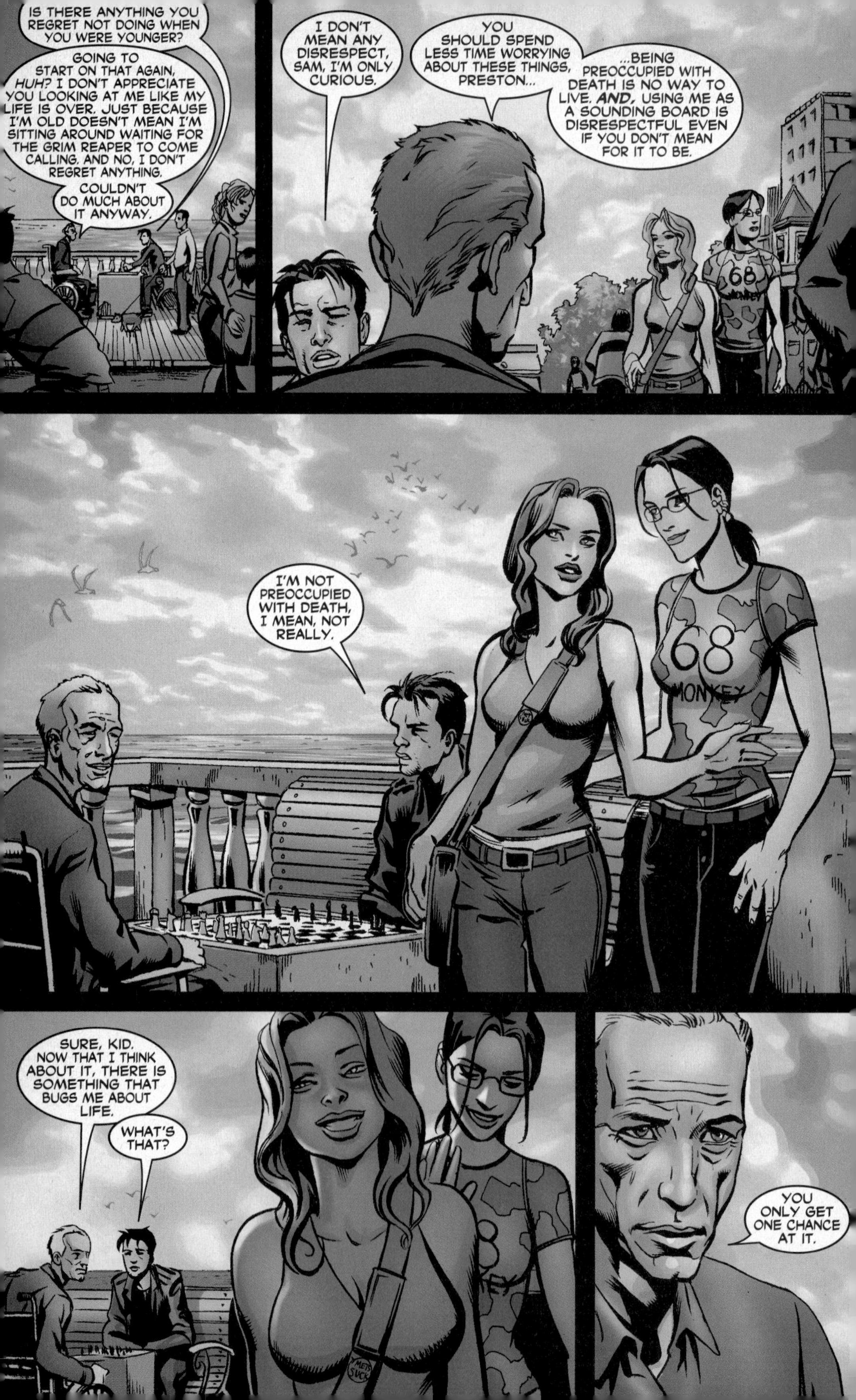

IS THERE ANYTHING YOU REGRET NOT DOING WHEN YOU WERE YOUNGER?
GOING TO START ON THAT AGAIN, *HUH?* I DON'T APPRECIATE YOU LOOKING AT ME LIKE MY LIFE IS OVER. JUST BECAUSE I'M OLD DOESN'T MEAN I'M SITTING AROUND WAITING FOR THE GRIM REAPER TO COME CALLING. AND NO, I DON'T REGRET ANYTHING.
COULDN'T DO MUCH ABOUT IT ANYWAY.
I DON'T MEAN ANY DISRESPECT, SAM, I'M ONLY CURIOUS.
YOU SHOULD SPEND LESS TIME WORRYING ABOUT THESE THINGS, PRESTON...
...BEING PREOCCUPIED WITH DEATH IS NO WAY TO LIVE. **AND,** USING ME AS A SOUNDING BOARD IS DISRESPECTFUL EVEN IF YOU DON'T MEAN FOR IT TO BE.
68 MONKEY
I'M NOT PREOCCUPIED WITH DEATH, I MEAN, NOT REALLY.
68 MONKEY
SURE, KID. NOW THAT I THINK ABOUT IT, THERE IS SOMETHING THAT BUGS ME ABOUT LIFE.
WHAT'S THAT?
YOU ONLY GET ONE CHANCE AT IT.

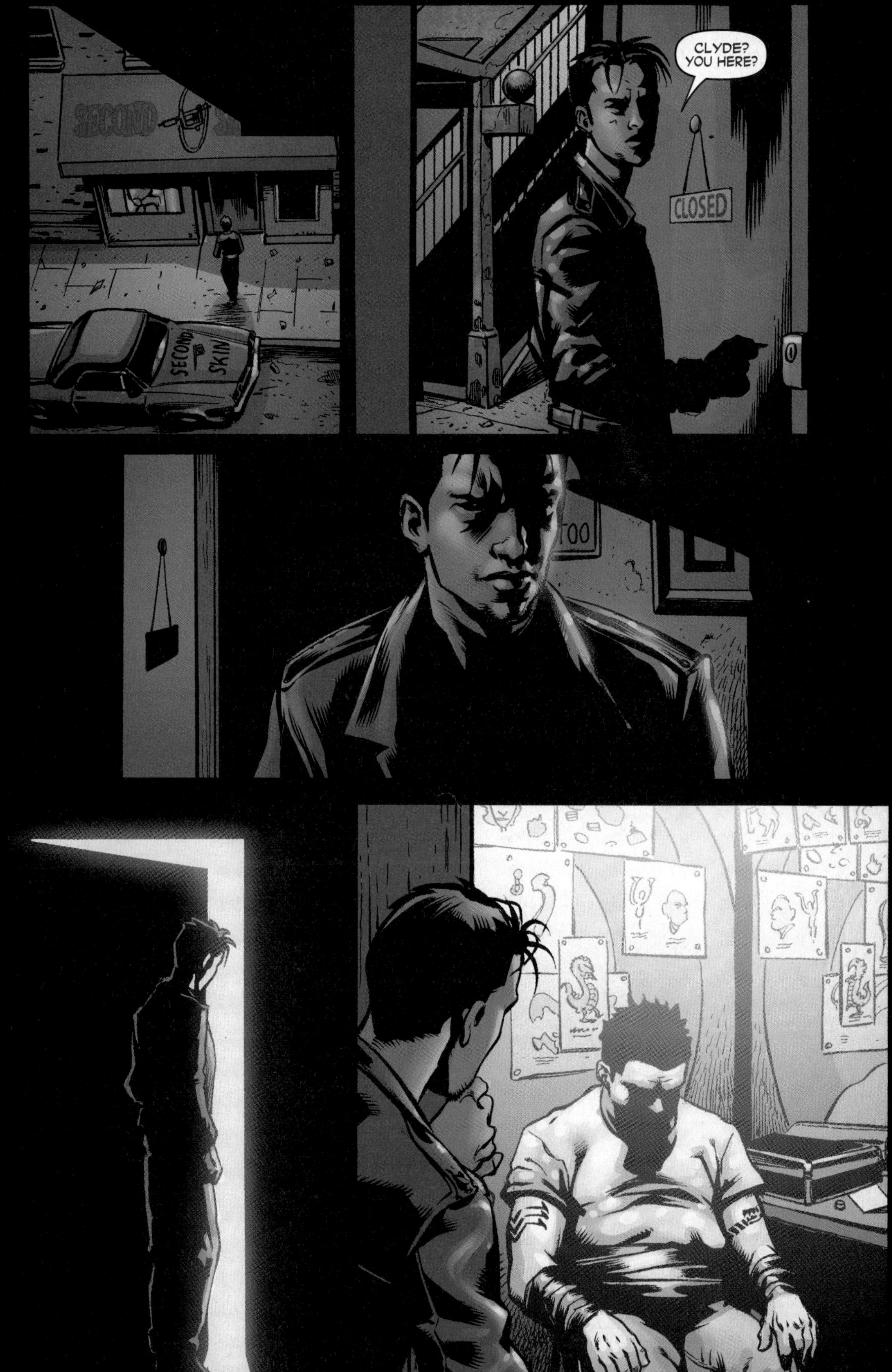
SECOND SKIN
CLYDE?
YOU HERE?
CLOSED
SECOND SKIN

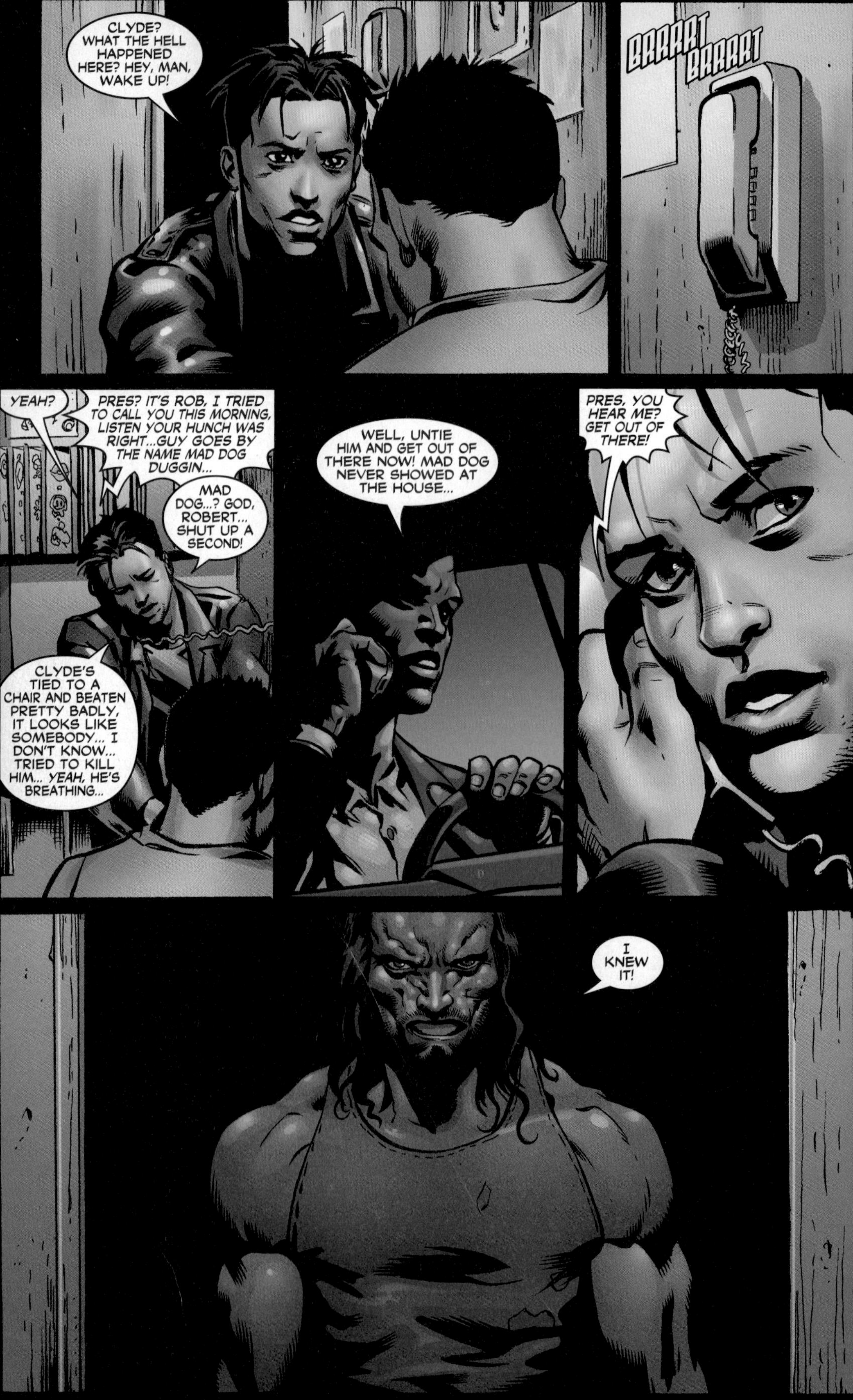
CLYDE? WHAT THE HELL HAPPENED HERE? HEY, MAN, WAKE UP!
BRRRRT BRRRRT
YEAH?
PRES? IT'S ROB, I TRIED TO CALL YOU THIS MORNING, LISTEN YOUR HUNCH WAS RIGHT...GUY GOES BY THE NAME MAD DOG DUGGIN...
MAD DOG...? GOD, ROBERT... SHUT UP A SECOND!
CLYDE'S TIED TO A CHAIR AND BEATEN PRETTY BADLY, IT LOOKS LIKE SOMEBODY... I DON'T KNOW... TRIED TO KILL HIM... YEAH, HE'S BREATHING...
WELL, UNTIE HIM AND GET OUT OF THERE NOW! MAD DOG NEVER SHOWED AT THE HOUSE...
PRES, YOU HEAR ME? GET OUT OF THERE!
I KNEW IT!

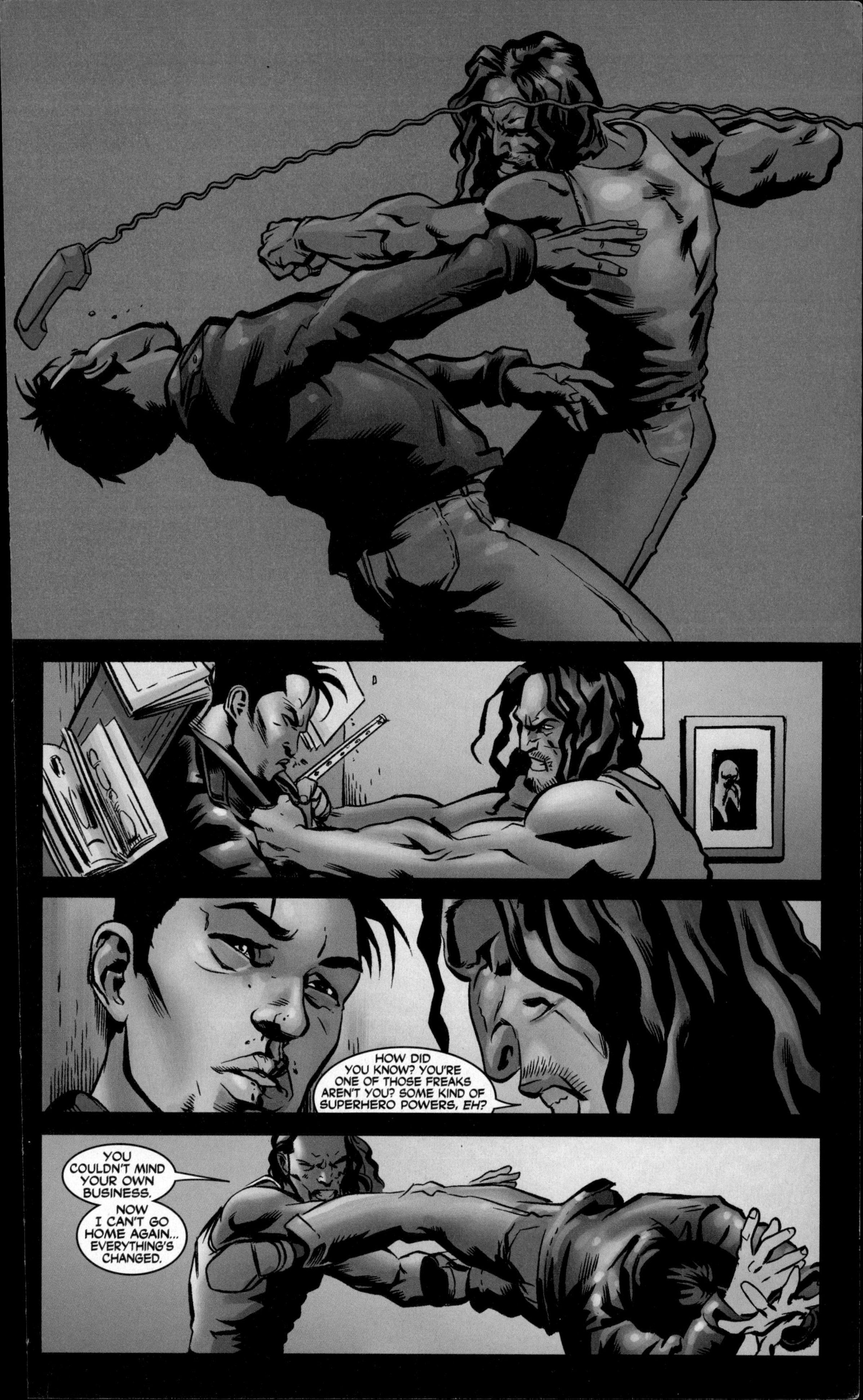
HOW DID YOU KNOW? YOU'RE ONE OF THOSE FREAKS AREN'T YOU? SOME KIND OF SUPERHERO POWERS, *EH?*
YOU COULDN'T MIND YOUR OWN BUSINESS.
NOW I CAN'T GO HOME AGAIN... EVERYTHING'S CHANGED.

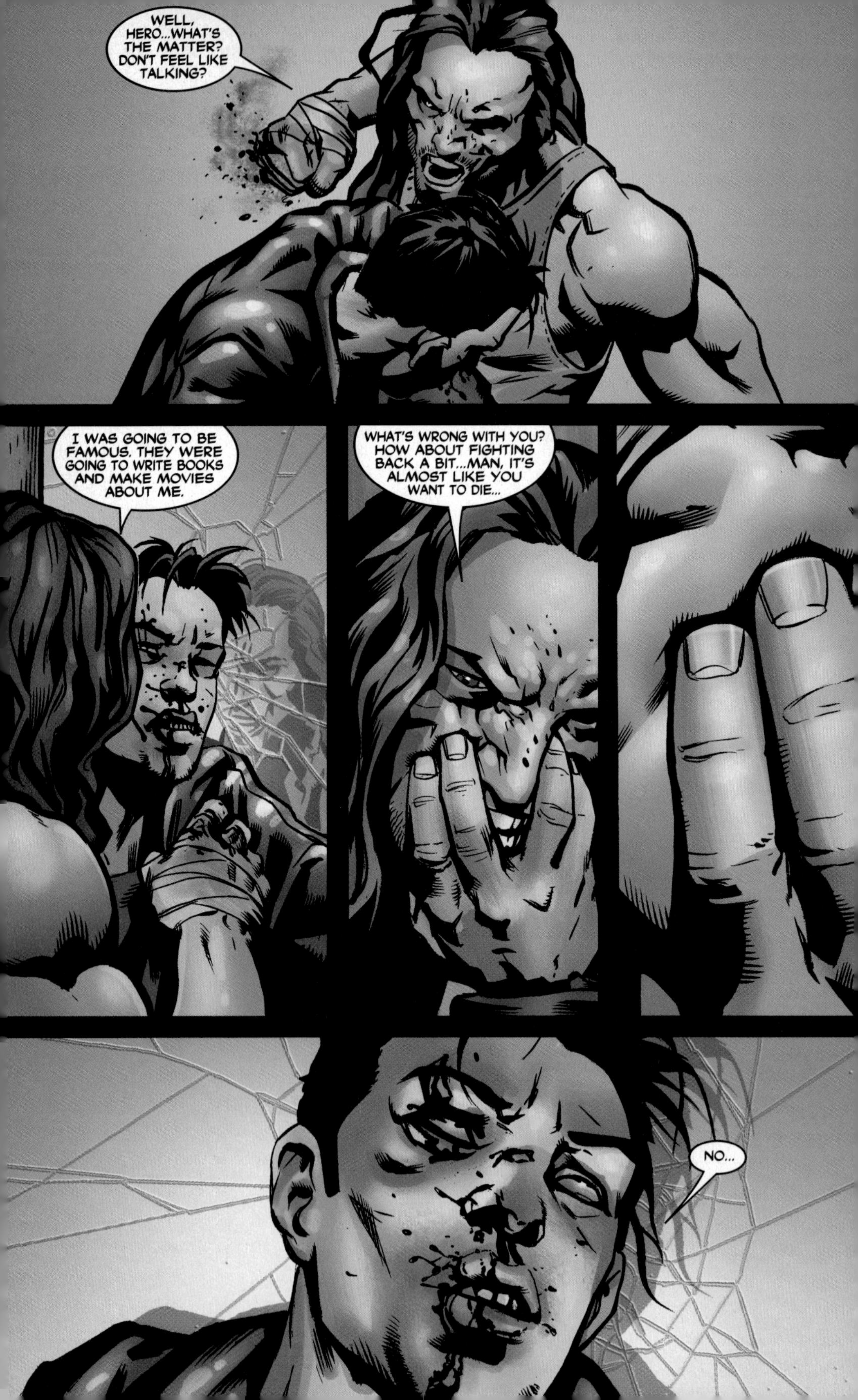
WELL, HERO...WHAT'S THE MATTER? DON'T FEEL LIKE TALKING?
I WAS GOING TO BE FAMOUS. THEY WERE GOING TO WRITE BOOKS AND MAKE MOVIES ABOUT ME.
WHAT'S WRONG WITH YOU? HOW ABOUT FIGHTING BACK A BIT...MAN, IT'S ALMOST LIKE YOU WANT TO DIE...
NO...

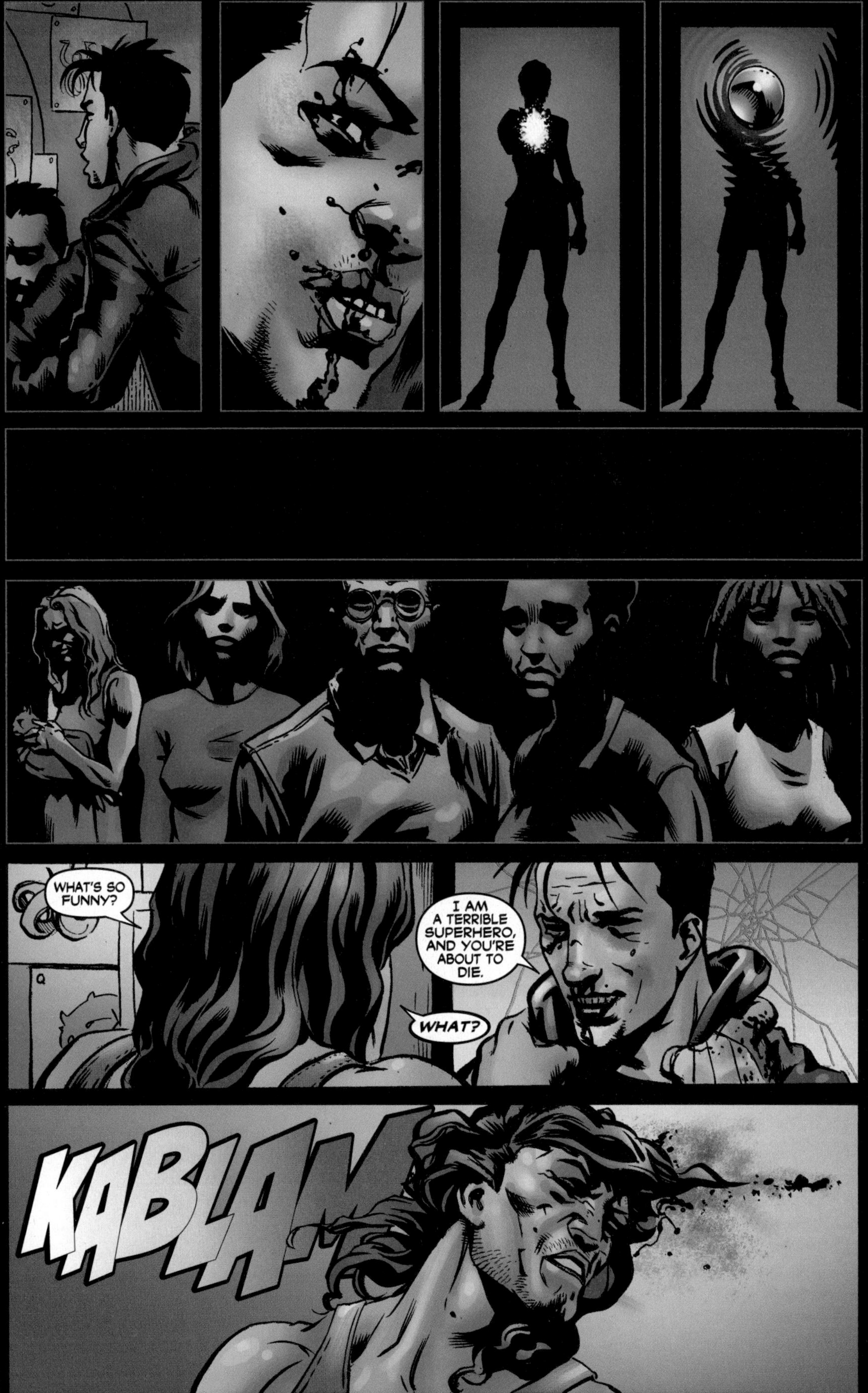
WHAT'S SO FUNNY?
I AM A TERRIBLE SUPERHERO, AND YOU'RE ABOUT TO DIE.
WHAT?
KABLAM

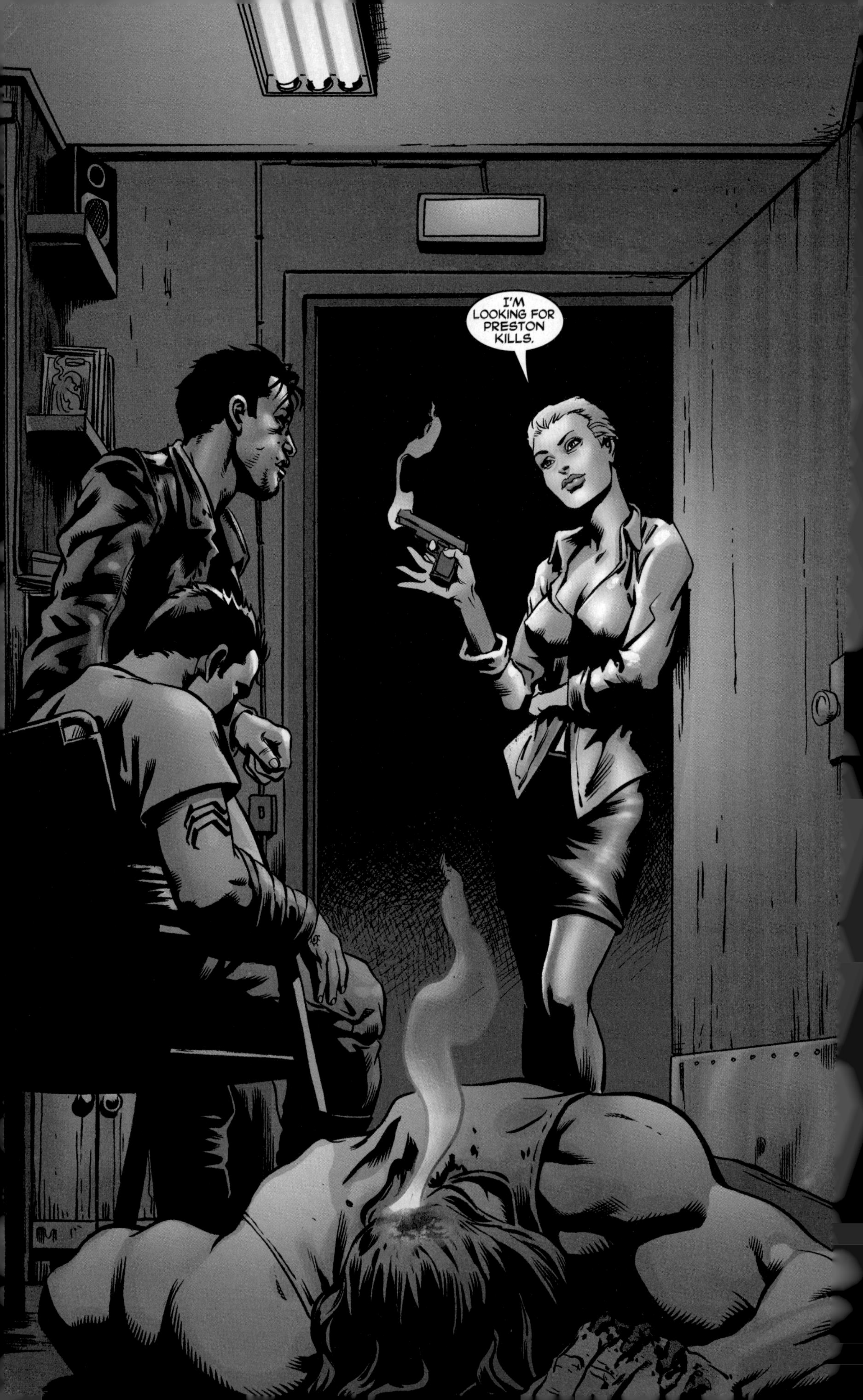
I'M LOOKING FOR PRESTON KILLS.

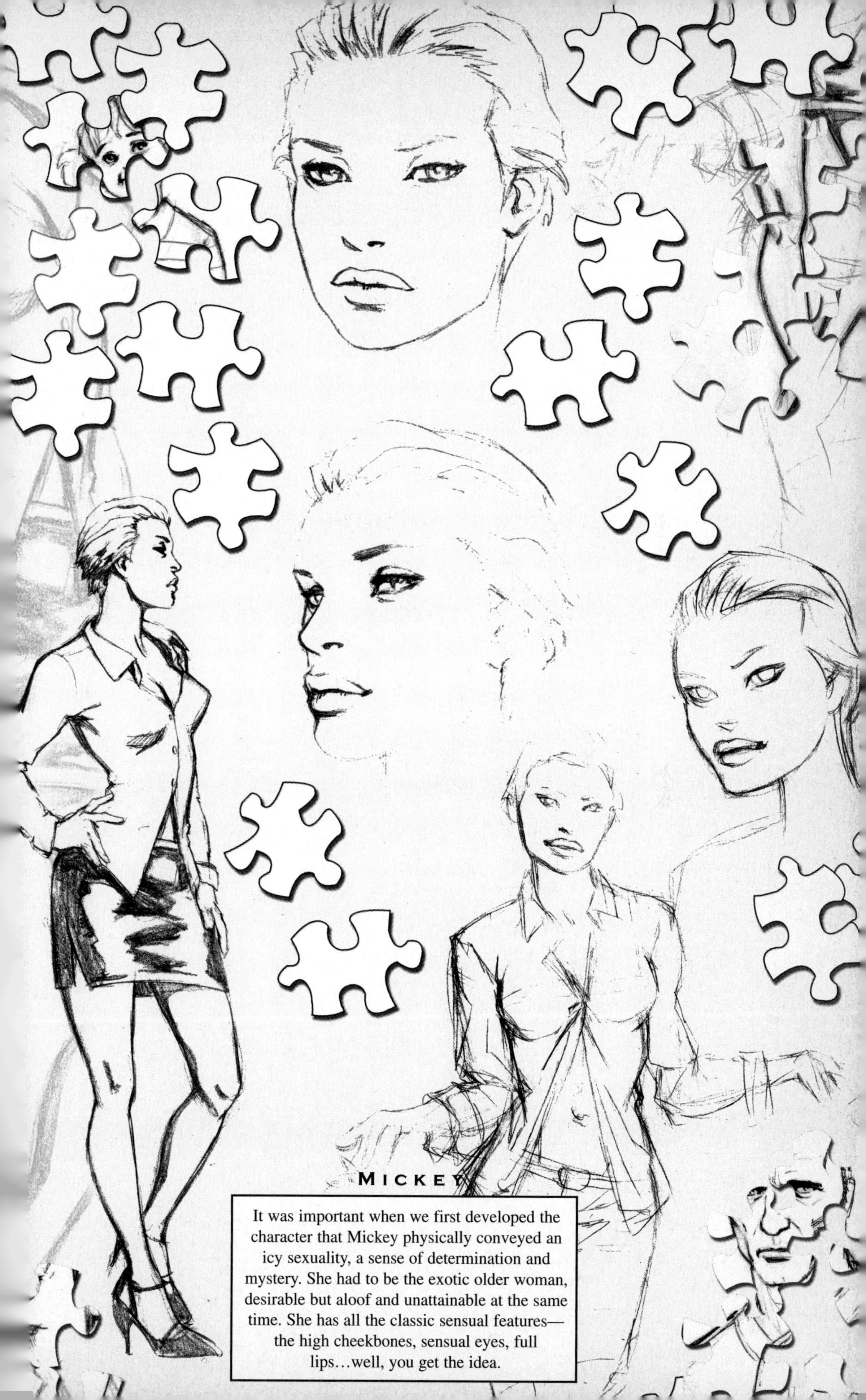

MICKEY

It was important when we first developed the character that Mickey physically conveyed an icy sexuality, a sense of determination and mystery. She had to be the exotic older woman, desirable but aloof and unattainable at the same time. She has all the classic sensual features—the high cheekbones, sensual eyes, full lips…well, you get the idea.

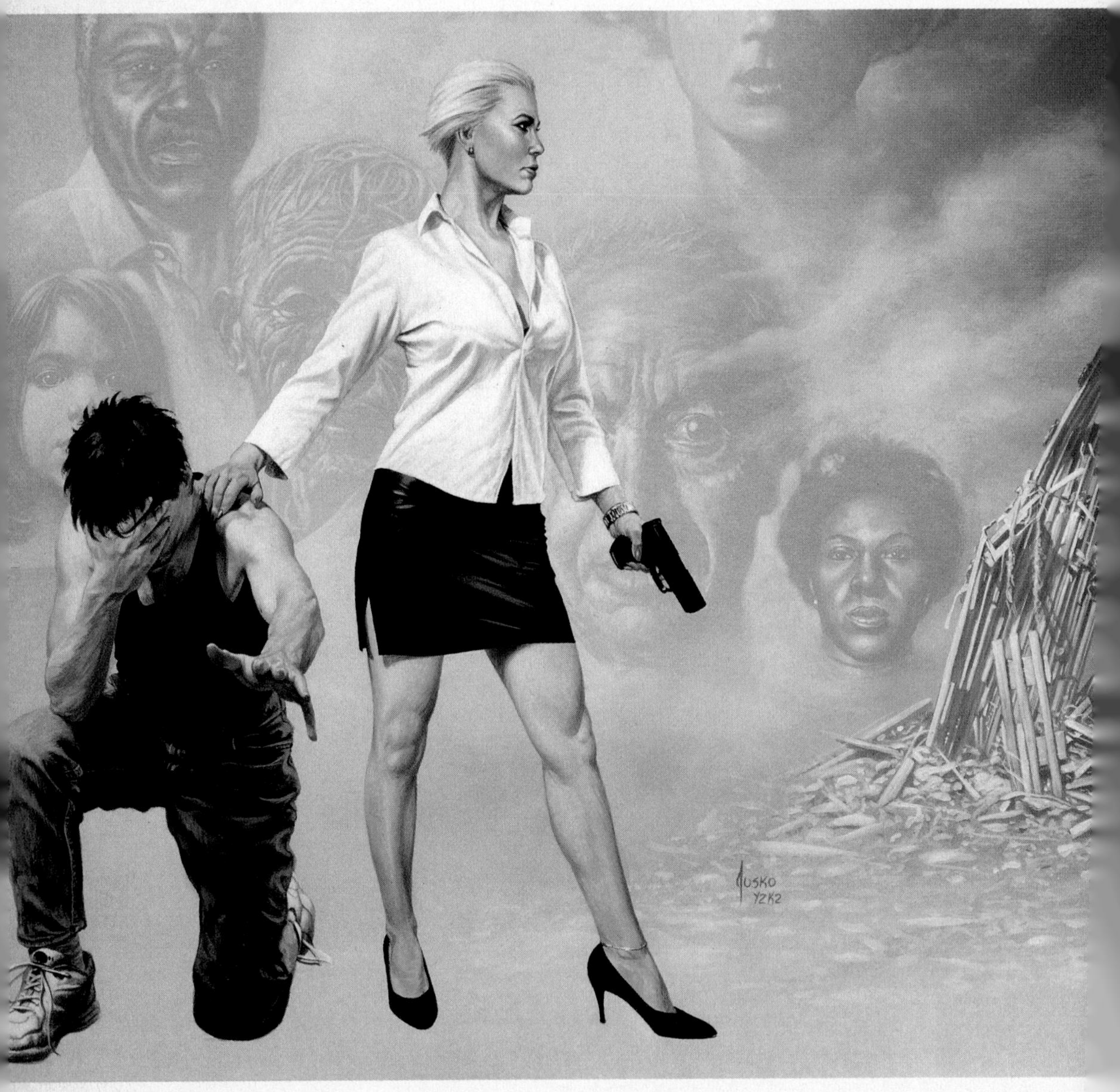
JUSKO
Y2K2

I Like to Wear Sheep's Clothing

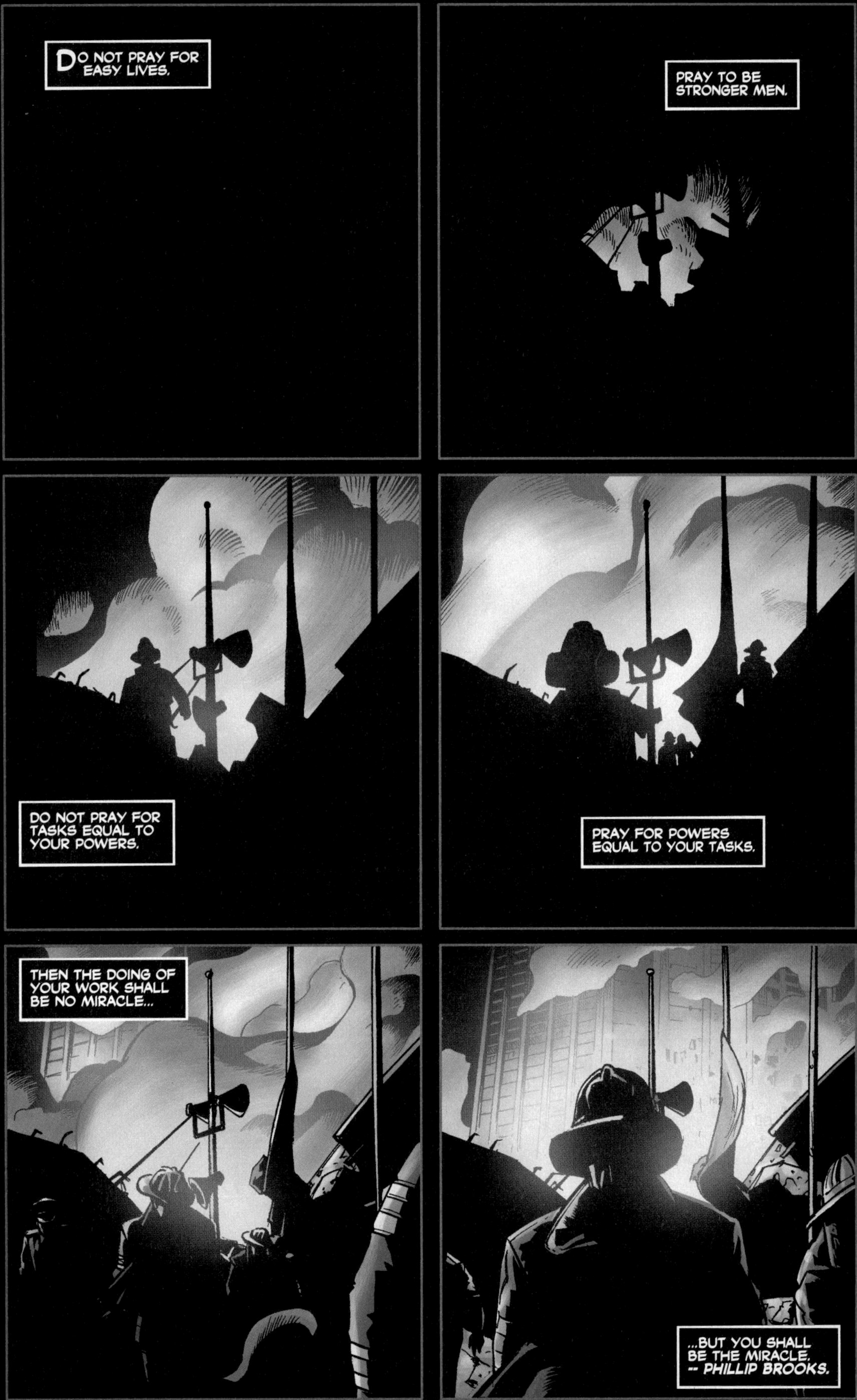
DO NOT PRAY FOR EASY LIVES.
PRAY TO BE STRONGER MEN.
DO NOT PRAY FOR TASKS EQUAL TO YOUR POWERS.
PRAY FOR POWERS EQUAL TO YOUR TASKS.
THEN THE DOING OF YOUR WORK SHALL BE NO MIRACLE...
...BUT YOU SHALL BE THE MIRACLE.
-- PHILLIP BROOKS.

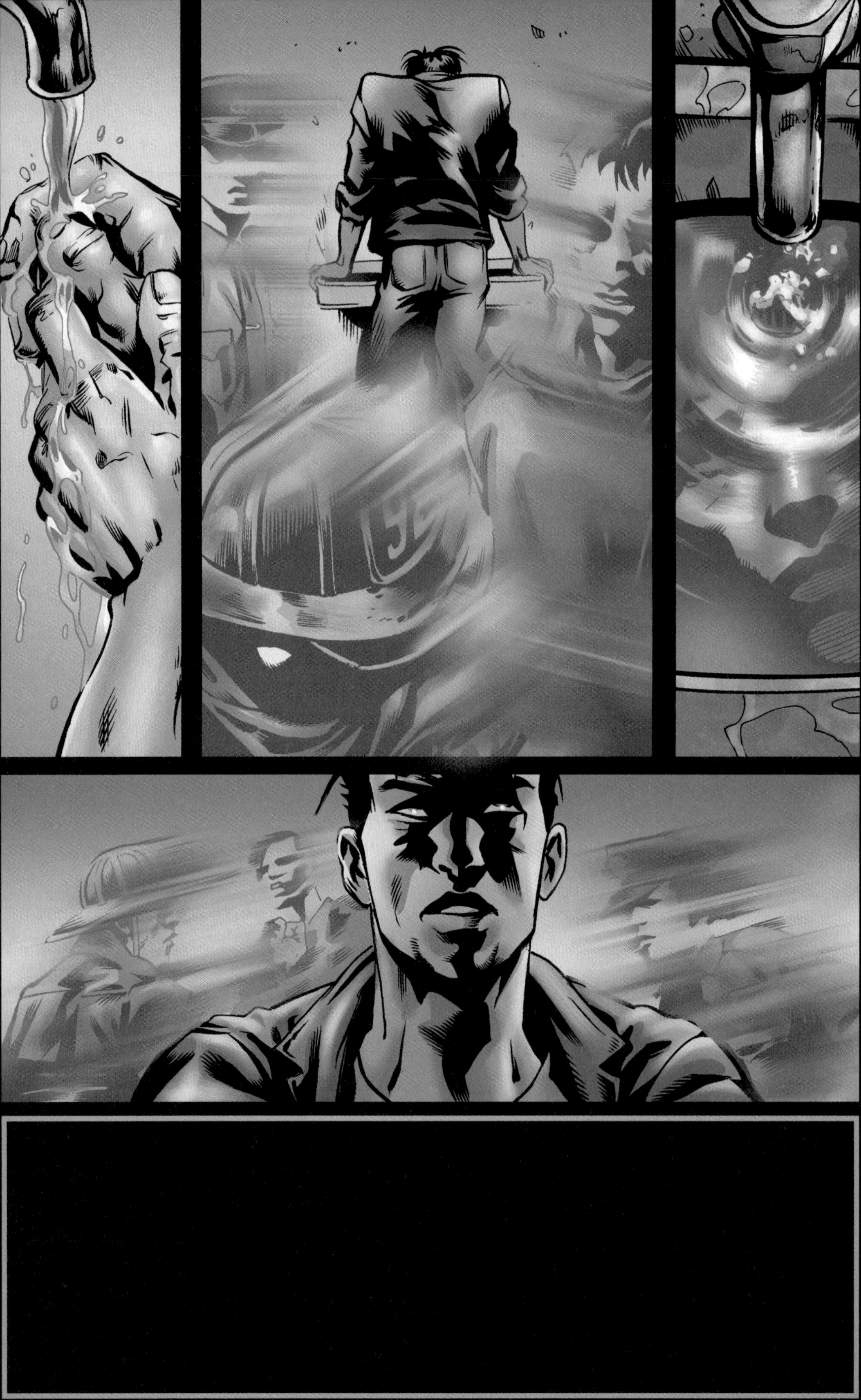

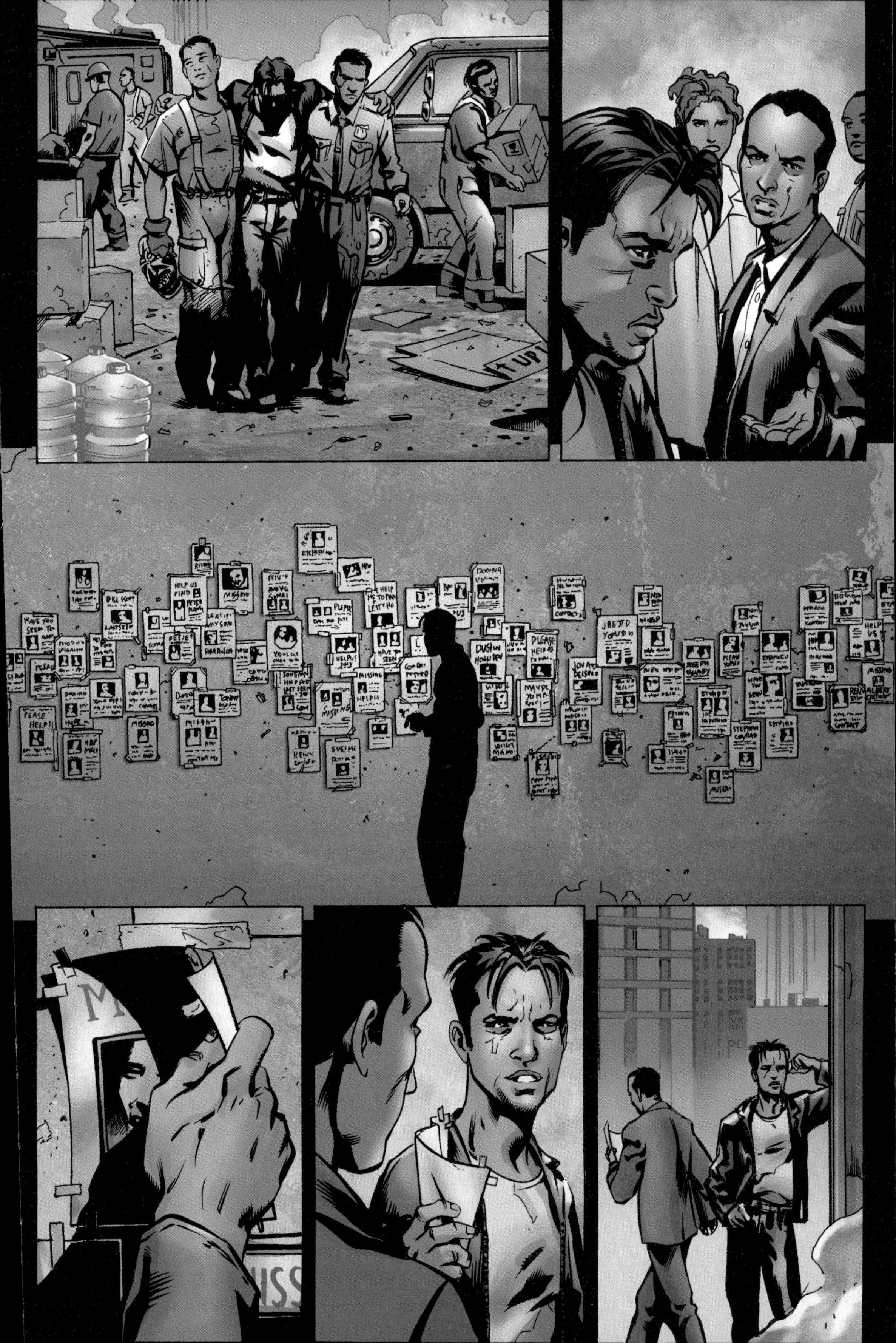

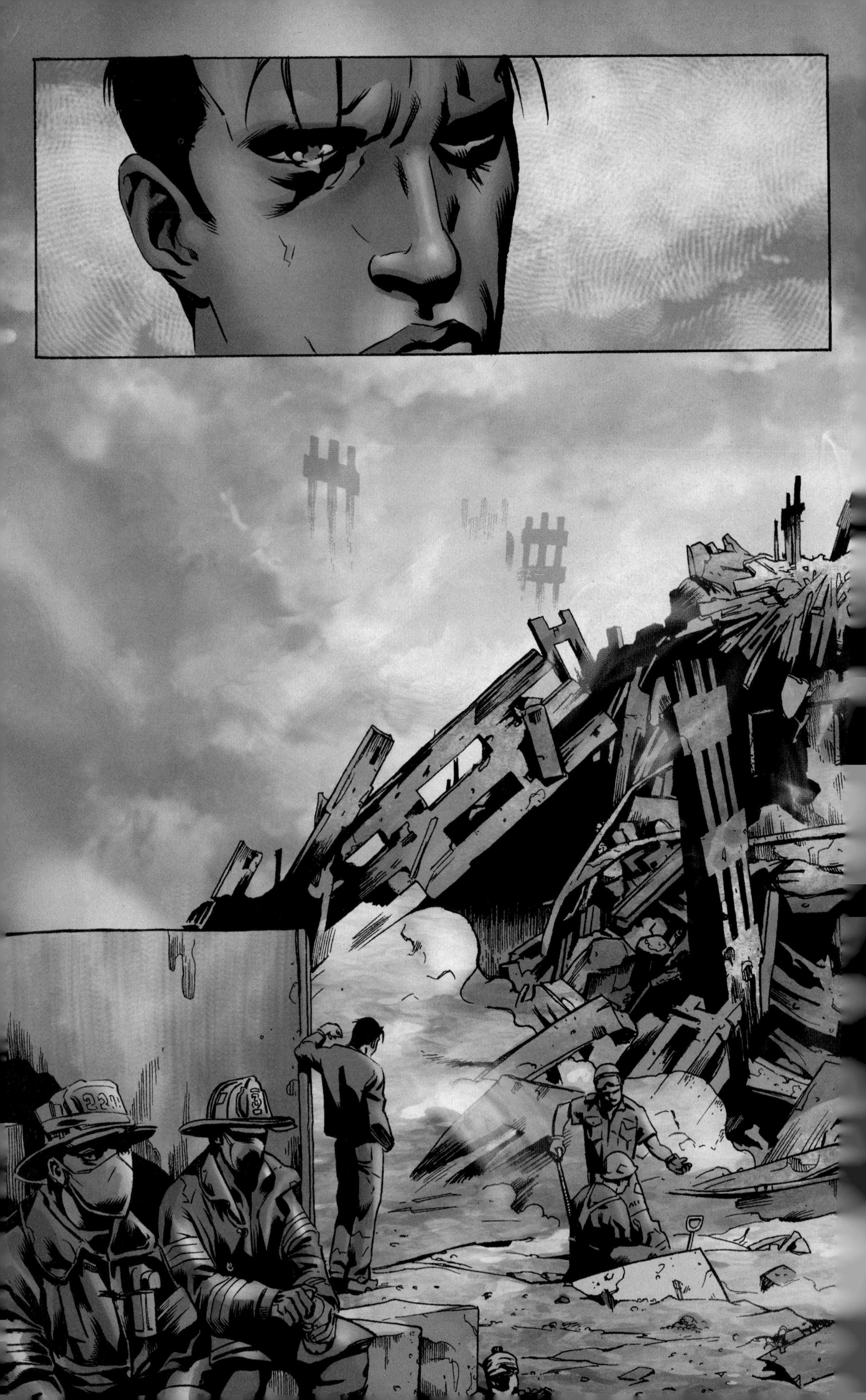

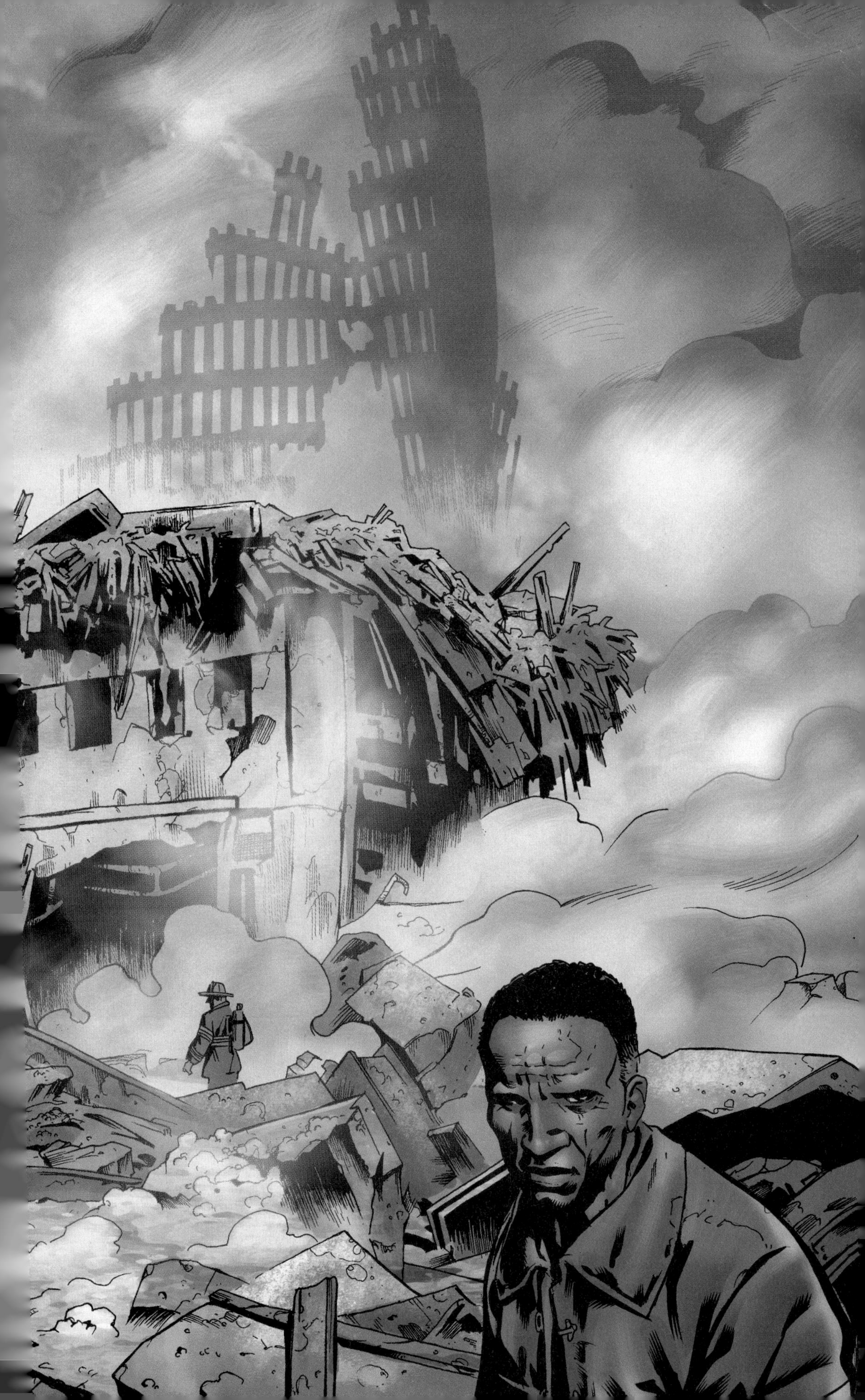

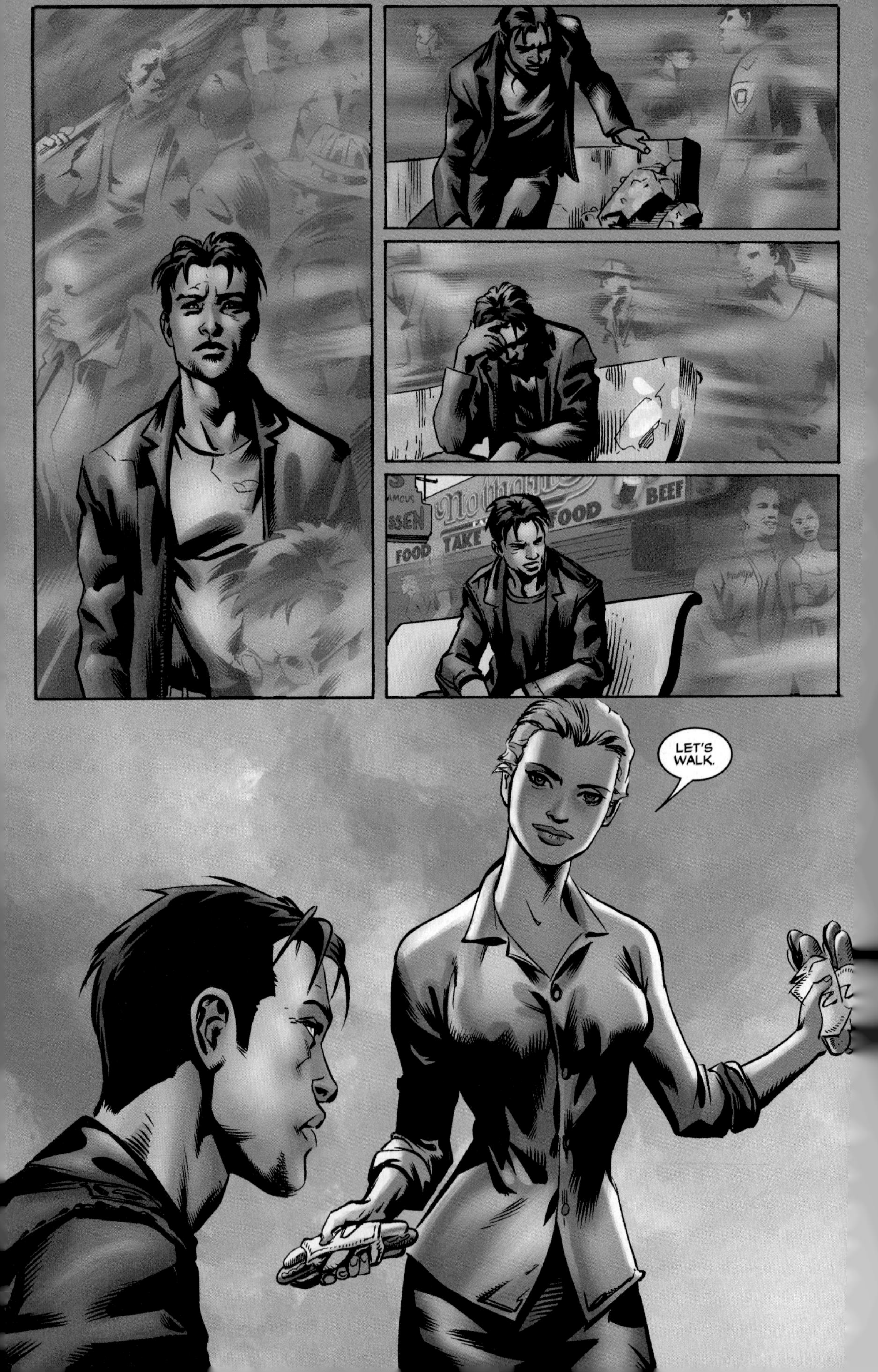
FAMOUS
SSEN
FOOD
TAKE
FOOD
BEEF
LET'S WALK.

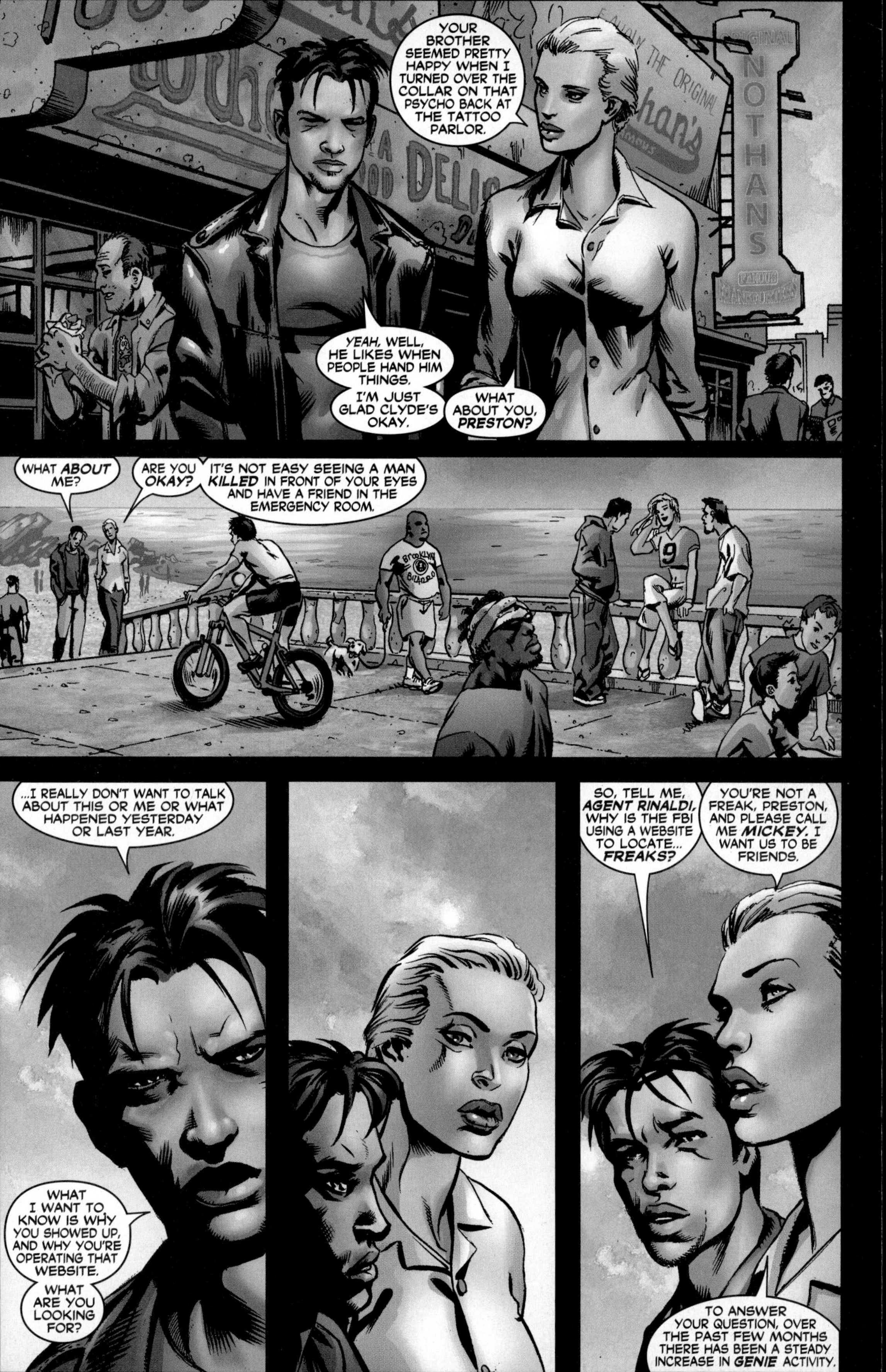
YOUR BROTHER SEEMED PRETTY HAPPY WHEN I TURNED OVER THE COLLAR ON THAT PSYCHO BACK AT THE TATTOO PARLOR.
YEAH, WELL, HE LIKES WHEN PEOPLE HAND HIM THINGS.
I'M JUST GLAD CLYDE'S OKAY.
WHAT ABOUT YOU, PRESTON?
WHAT ABOUT ME?
ARE YOU OKAY?
IT'S NOT EASY SEEING A MAN KILLED IN FRONT OF YOUR EYES AND HAVE A FRIEND IN THE EMERGENCY ROOM.
...I REALLY DON'T WANT TO TALK ABOUT THIS OR ME OR WHAT HAPPENED YESTERDAY OR LAST YEAR.
WHAT I WANT TO KNOW IS WHY YOU SHOWED UP, AND WHY YOU'RE OPERATING THAT WEBSITE.
WHAT ARE YOU LOOKING FOR?
SO, TELL ME, AGENT RINALDI, WHY IS THE FBI USING A WEBSITE TO LOCATE... FREAKS?
YOU'RE NOT A FREAK, PRESTON, AND PLEASE CALL ME MICKEY. I WANT US TO BE FRIENDS.
TO ANSWER YOUR QUESTION, OVER THE PAST FEW MONTHS THERE HAS BEEN A STEADY INCREASE IN GENIE ACTIVITY.

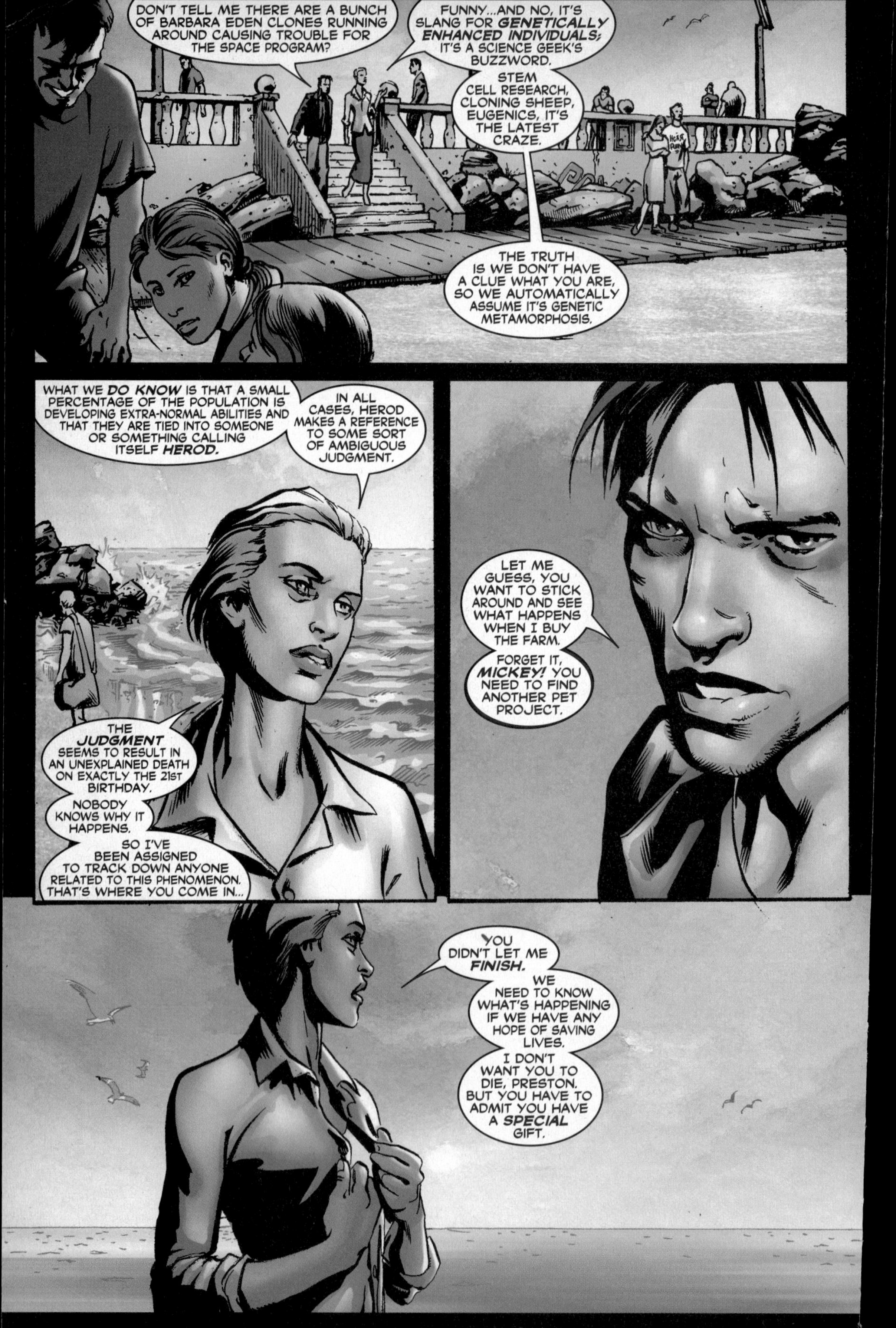
DON'T TELL ME THERE ARE A BUNCH OF BARBARA EDEN CLONES RUNNING AROUND CAUSING TROUBLE FOR THE SPACE PROGRAM?
FUNNY...AND NO, IT'S SLANG FOR GENETICALLY ENHANCED INDIVIDUALS; IT'S A SCIENCE GEEK'S BUZZWORD.
STEM CELL RESEARCH, CLONING SHEEP, EUGENICS, IT'S THE LATEST CRAZE.
THE TRUTH IS WE DON'T HAVE A CLUE WHAT YOU ARE, SO WE AUTOMATICALLY ASSUME IT'S GENETIC METAMORPHOSIS.
WHAT WE DO KNOW IS THAT A SMALL PERCENTAGE OF THE POPULATION IS DEVELOPING EXTRA-NORMAL ABILITIES AND THAT THEY ARE TIED INTO SOMEONE OR SOMETHING CALLING ITSELF HEROD.
IN ALL CASES, HEROD MAKES A REFERENCE TO SOME SORT OF AMBIGUOUS JUDGMENT.
THE JUDGMENT SEEMS TO RESULT IN AN UNEXPLAINED DEATH ON EXACTLY THE 21ST BIRTHDAY.
NOBODY KNOWS WHY IT HAPPENS.
SO I'VE BEEN ASSIGNED TO TRACK DOWN ANYONE RELATED TO THIS PHENOMENON. THAT'S WHERE YOU COME IN...
LET ME GUESS, YOU WANT TO STICK AROUND AND SEE WHAT HAPPENS WHEN I BUY THE FARM.
FORGET IT, MICKEY! YOU NEED TO FIND ANOTHER PET PROJECT.
YOU DIDN'T LET ME FINISH.
WE NEED TO KNOW WHAT'S HAPPENING IF WE HAVE ANY HOPE OF SAVING LIVES.
I DON'T WANT YOU TO DIE, PRESTON. BUT YOU HAVE TO ADMIT YOU HAVE A SPECIAL GIFT.

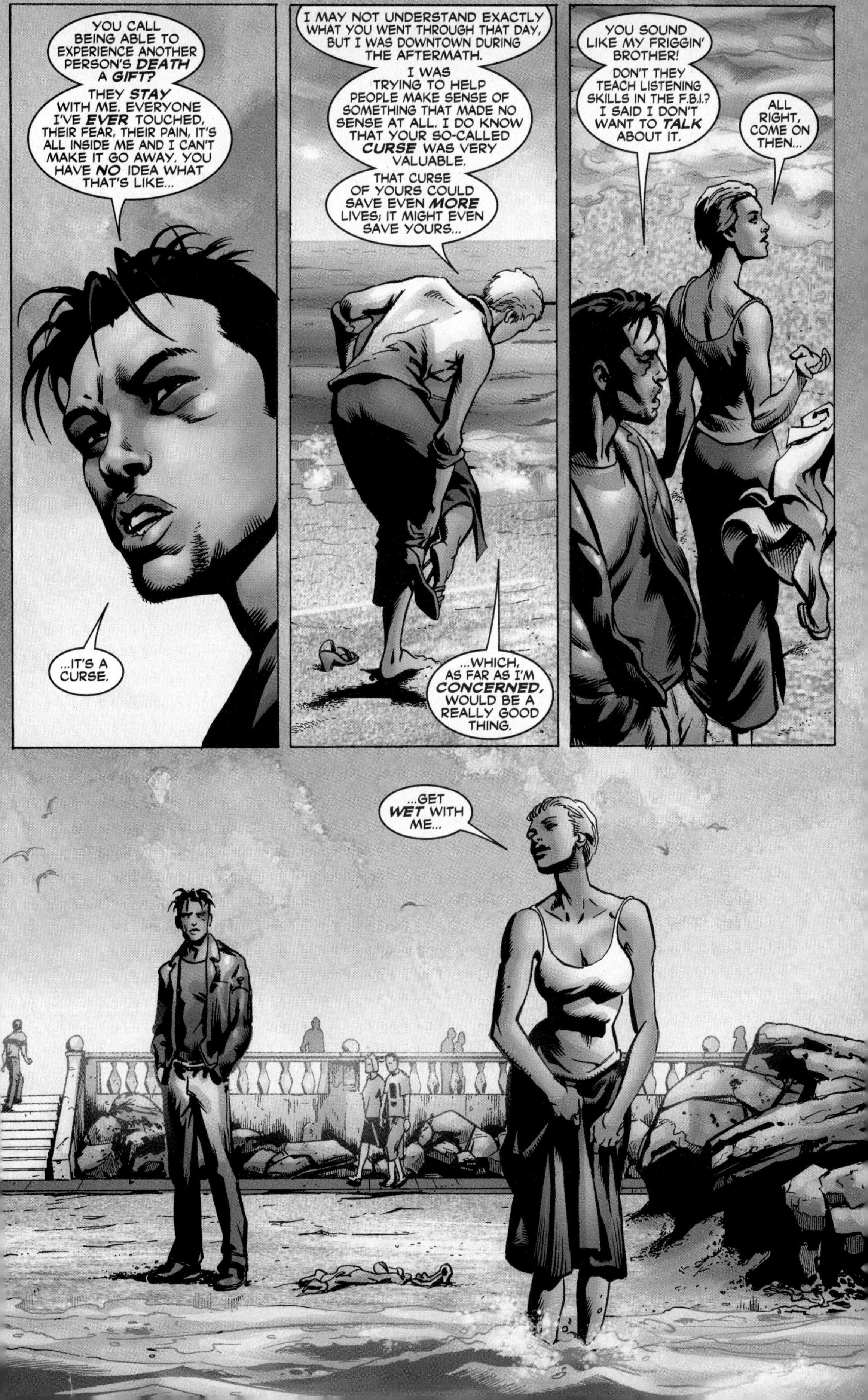
YOU CALL BEING ABLE TO EXPERIENCE ANOTHER PERSON'S DEATH A GIFT?
THEY STAY WITH ME. EVERYONE I'VE EVER TOUCHED, THEIR FEAR, THEIR PAIN, IT'S ALL INSIDE ME AND I CAN'T MAKE IT GO AWAY. YOU HAVE NO IDEA WHAT THAT'S LIKE...
...IT'S A CURSE.
I MAY NOT UNDERSTAND EXACTLY WHAT YOU WENT THROUGH THAT DAY, BUT I WAS DOWNTOWN DURING THE AFTERMATH.
I WAS TRYING TO HELP PEOPLE MAKE SENSE OF SOMETHING THAT MADE NO SENSE AT ALL. I DO KNOW THAT YOUR SO-CALLED CURSE WAS VERY VALUABLE.
THAT CURSE OF YOURS COULD SAVE EVEN MORE LIVES; IT MIGHT EVEN SAVE YOURS...
...WHICH, AS FAR AS I'M CONCERNED, WOULD BE A REALLY GOOD THING.
YOU SOUND LIKE MY FRIGGIN' BROTHER!
DON'T THEY TEACH LISTENING SKILLS IN THE F.B.I.? I SAID I DON'T WANT TO TALK ABOUT IT.
ALL RIGHT, COME ON THEN...
...GET WET WITH ME...

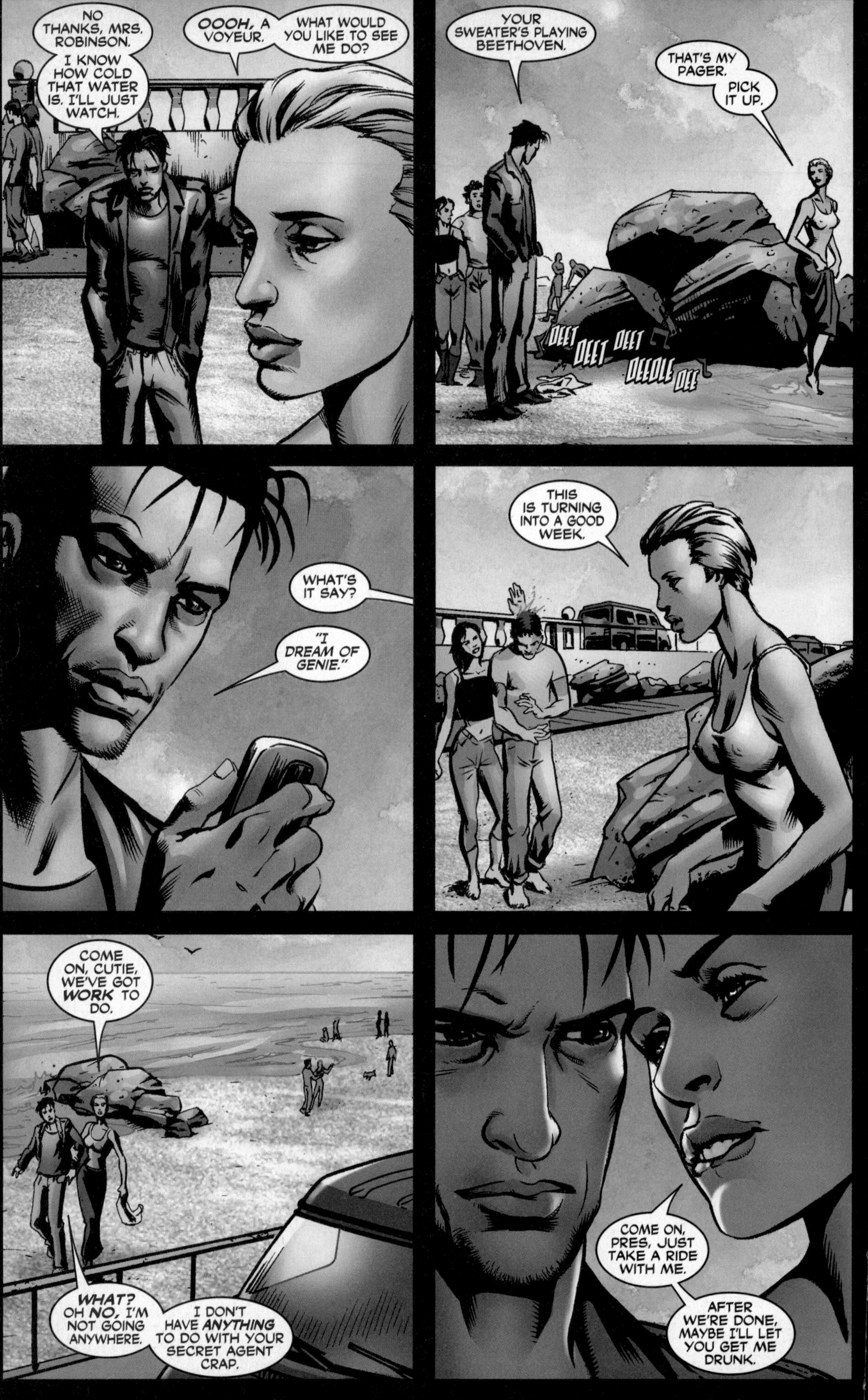

NO THANKS, MRS. ROBINSON.
I KNOW HOW COLD THAT WATER IS. I'LL JUST WATCH.
OOOH, A VOYEUR.
WHAT WOULD YOU LIKE TO SEE ME DO?
YOUR SWEATER'S PLAYING BEETHOVEN.
THAT'S MY PAGER.
PICK IT UP.
DEET DEET DEET DEEDLE DEE
WHAT'S IT SAY?
"I DREAM OF GENIE."
THIS IS TURNING INTO A GOOD WEEK.
COME ON, CUTIE, WE'VE GOT WORK TO DO.
WHAT? OH NO, I'M NOT GOING ANYWHERE.
I DON'T HAVE ANYTHING TO DO WITH YOUR SECRET AGENT CRAP.
COME ON, PRES, JUST TAKE A RIDE WITH ME.
AFTER WE'RE DONE, MAYBE I'LL LET YOU GET ME DRUNK.

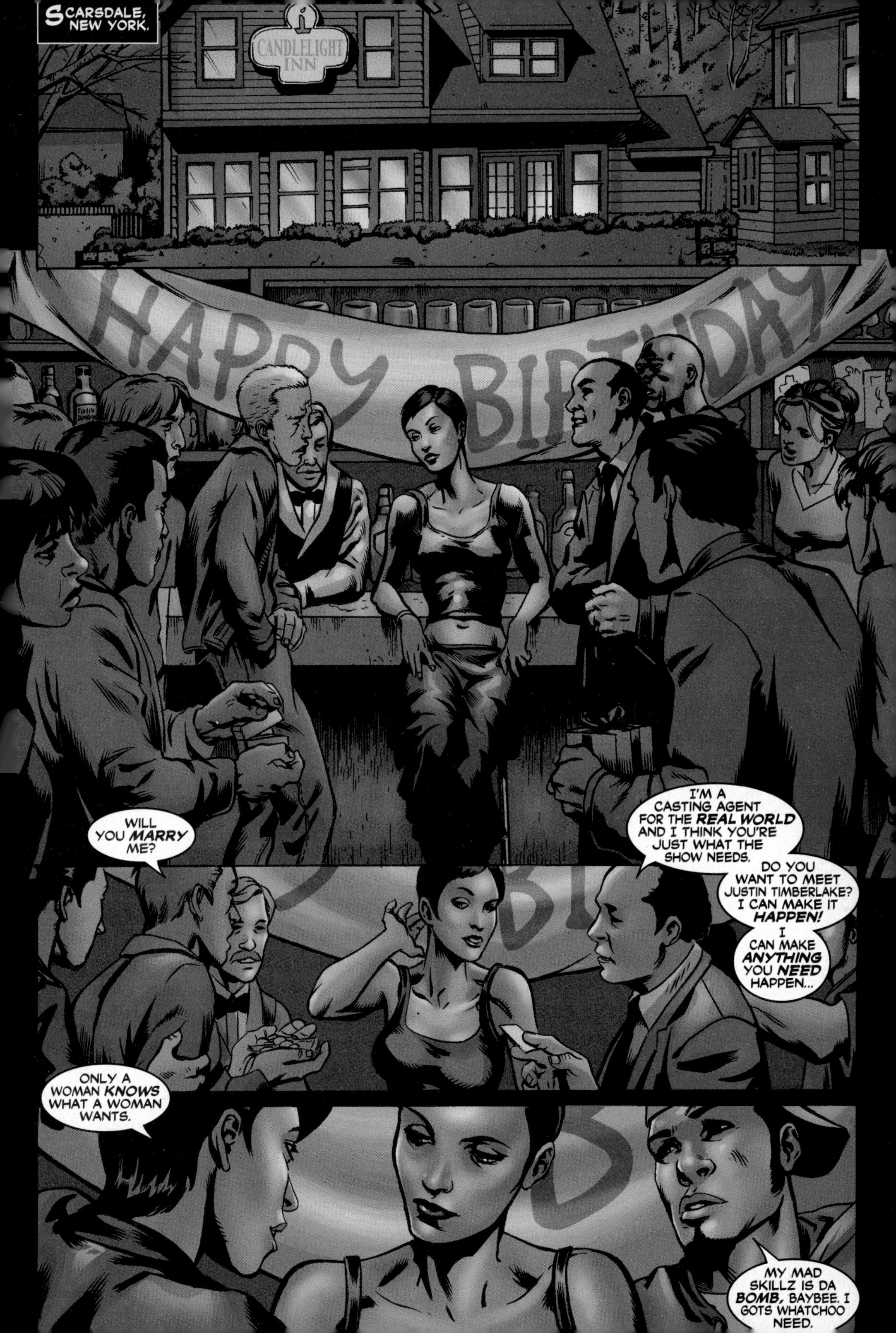
SCARSDALE, NEW YORK.
CANDLELIGHT INN
HAPPY BIRTHDAY
WILL YOU MARRY ME?
I'M A CASTING AGENT FOR THE REAL WORLD AND I THINK YOU'RE JUST WHAT THE SHOW NEEDS.
DO YOU WANT TO MEET JUSTIN TIMBERLAKE? I CAN MAKE IT HAPPEN!
I CAN MAKE ANYTHING YOU NEED HAPPEN...
ONLY A WOMAN KNOWS WHAT A WOMAN WANTS.
MY MAD SKILLZ IS DA BOMB, BAYBEE. I GOTS WHATCHOO NEED.

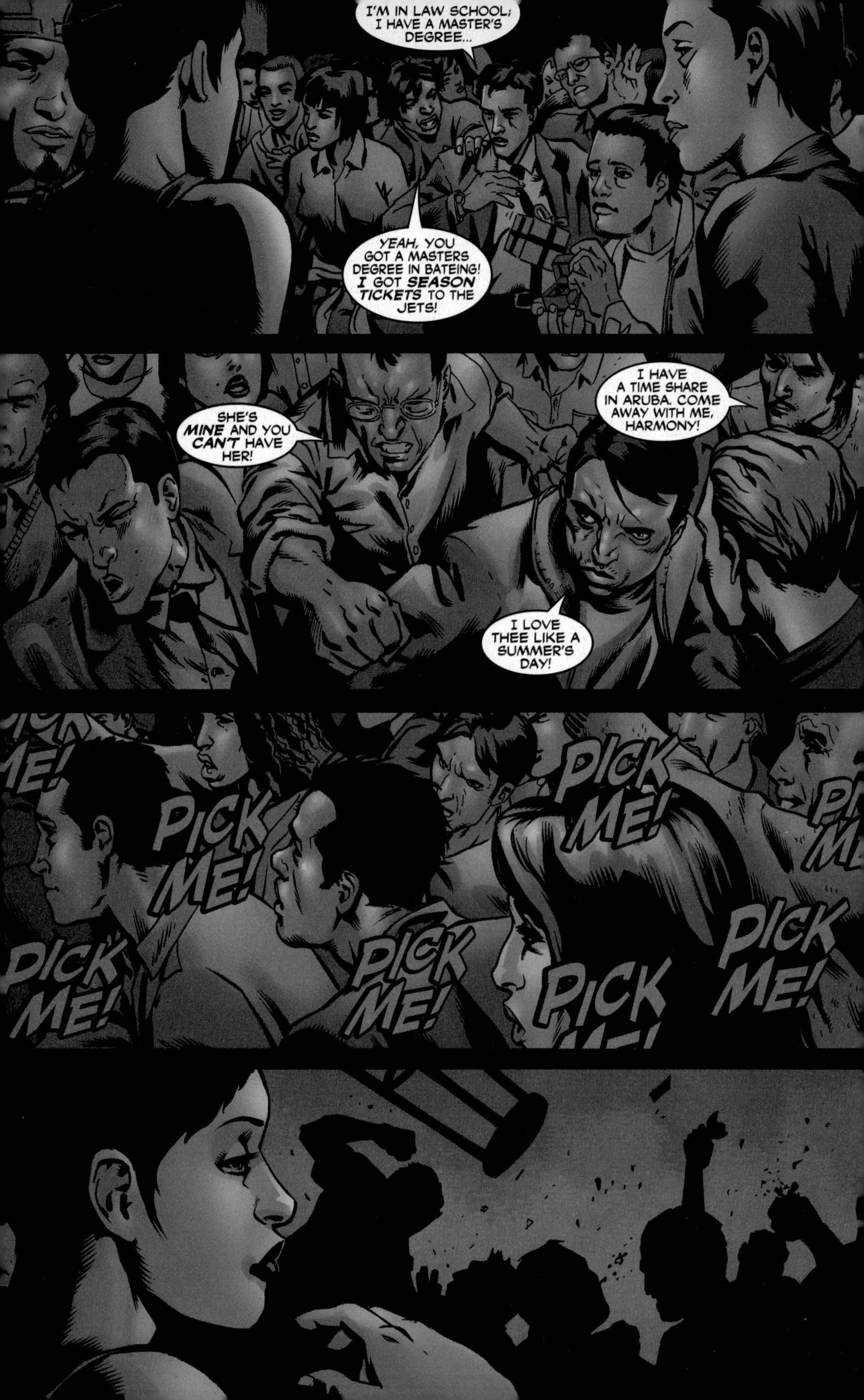
I'M IN LAW SCHOOL; I HAVE A MASTER'S DEGREE...
YEAH, YOU GOT A MASTERS DEGREE IN BATEING! I GOT SEASON TICKETS TO THE JETS!
SHE'S MINE AND YOU CAN'T HAVE HER!
I HAVE A TIME SHARE IN ARUBA. COME AWAY WITH ME, HARMONY!
I LOVE THEE LIKE A SUMMER'S DAY!
PICK ME!
PICK ME!
PICK ME!
PICK ME!
PICK ME!
PICK ME!

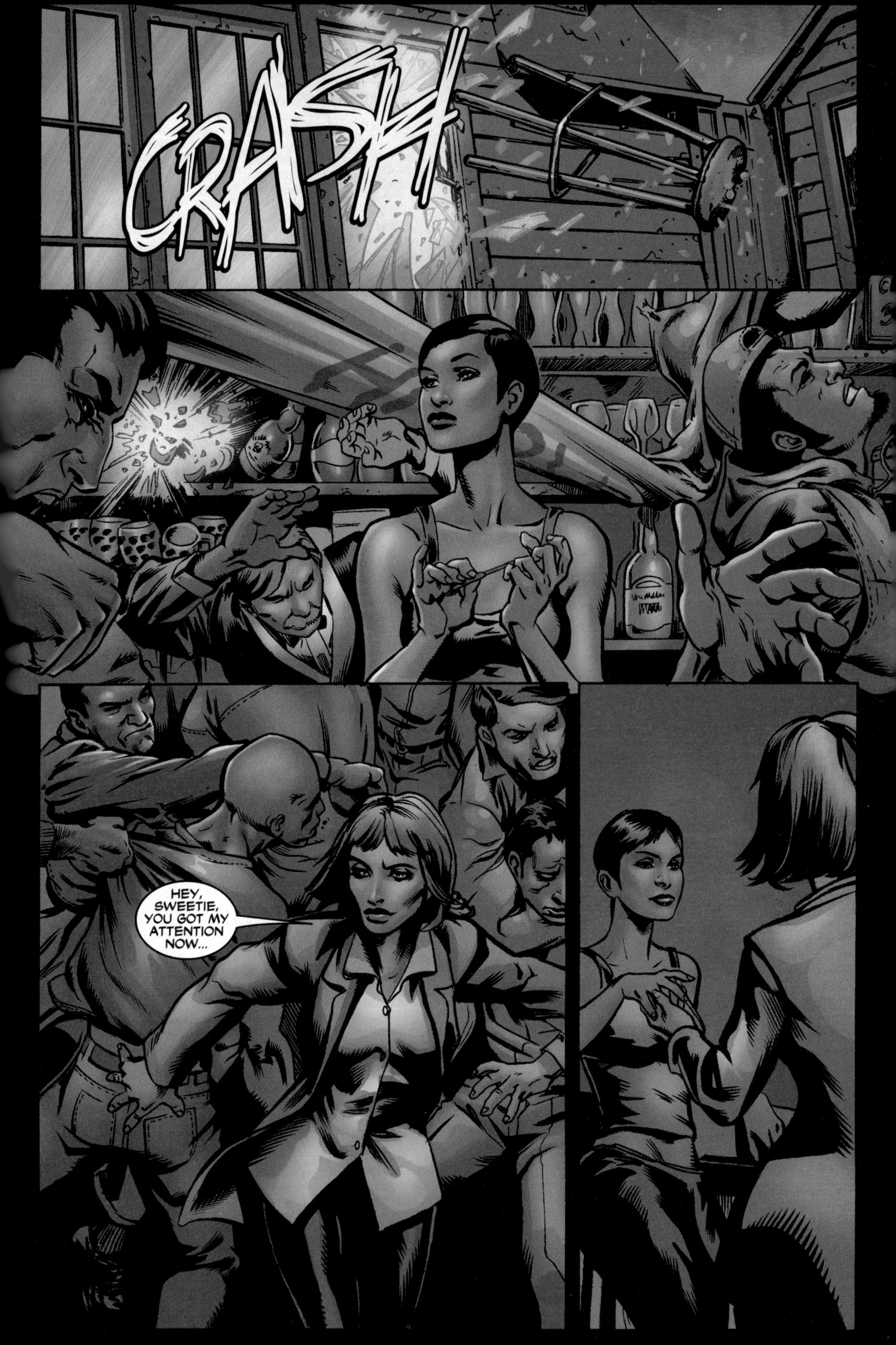
CRASH
HEY, SWEETIE, YOU GOT MY ATTENTION NOW...

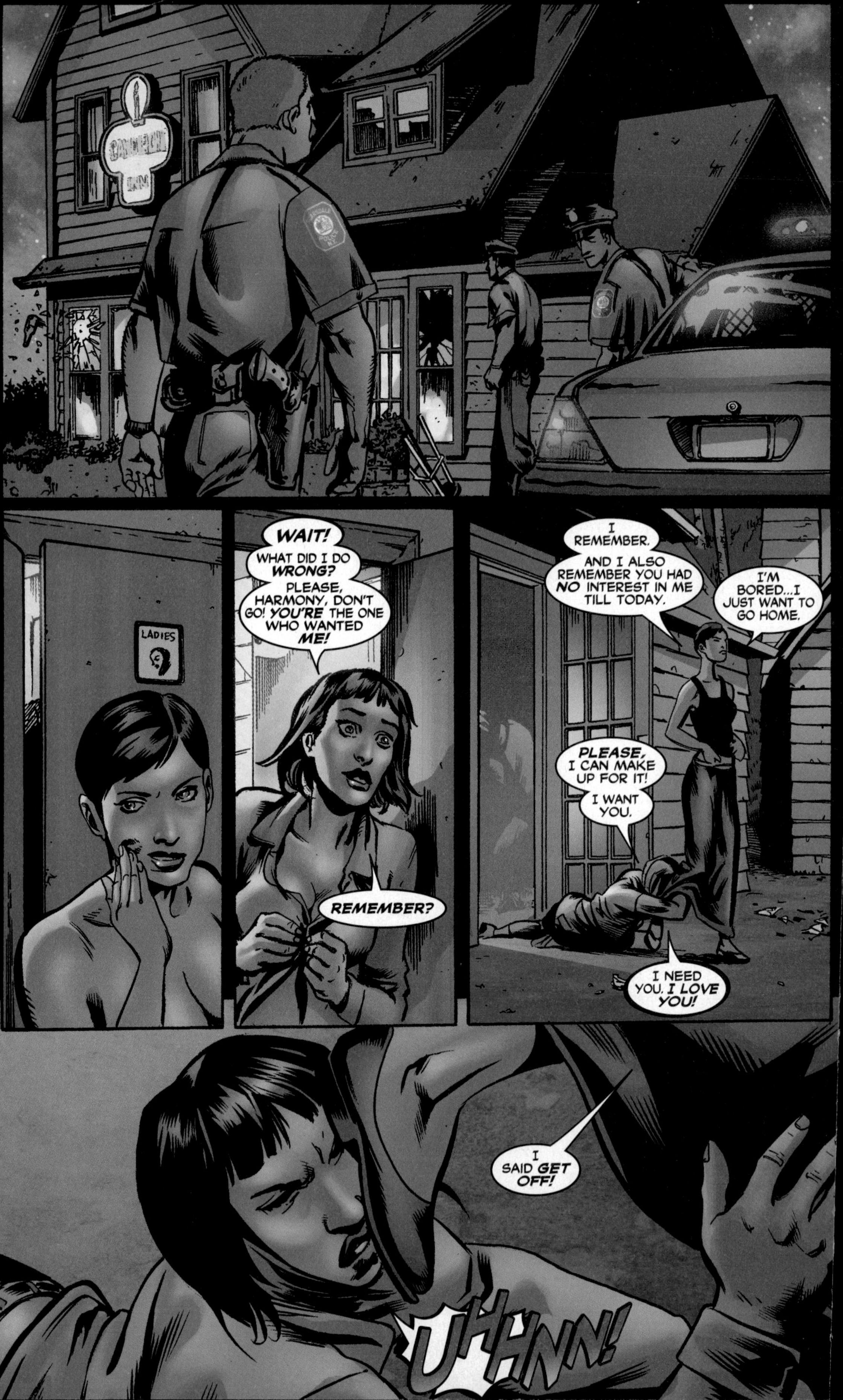

LADIES
WAIT! WHAT DID I DO WRONG? PLEASE, HARMONY, DON'T GO! YOU'RE THE ONE WHO WANTED ME!
REMEMBER?
I REMEMBER.
AND I ALSO REMEMBER YOU HAD NO INTEREST IN ME TILL TODAY.
I'M BORED...I JUST WANT TO GO HOME.
PLEASE, I CAN MAKE UP FOR IT!
I WANT YOU.
I NEED YOU. I LOVE YOU!
I SAID GET OFF!
UHHNN!

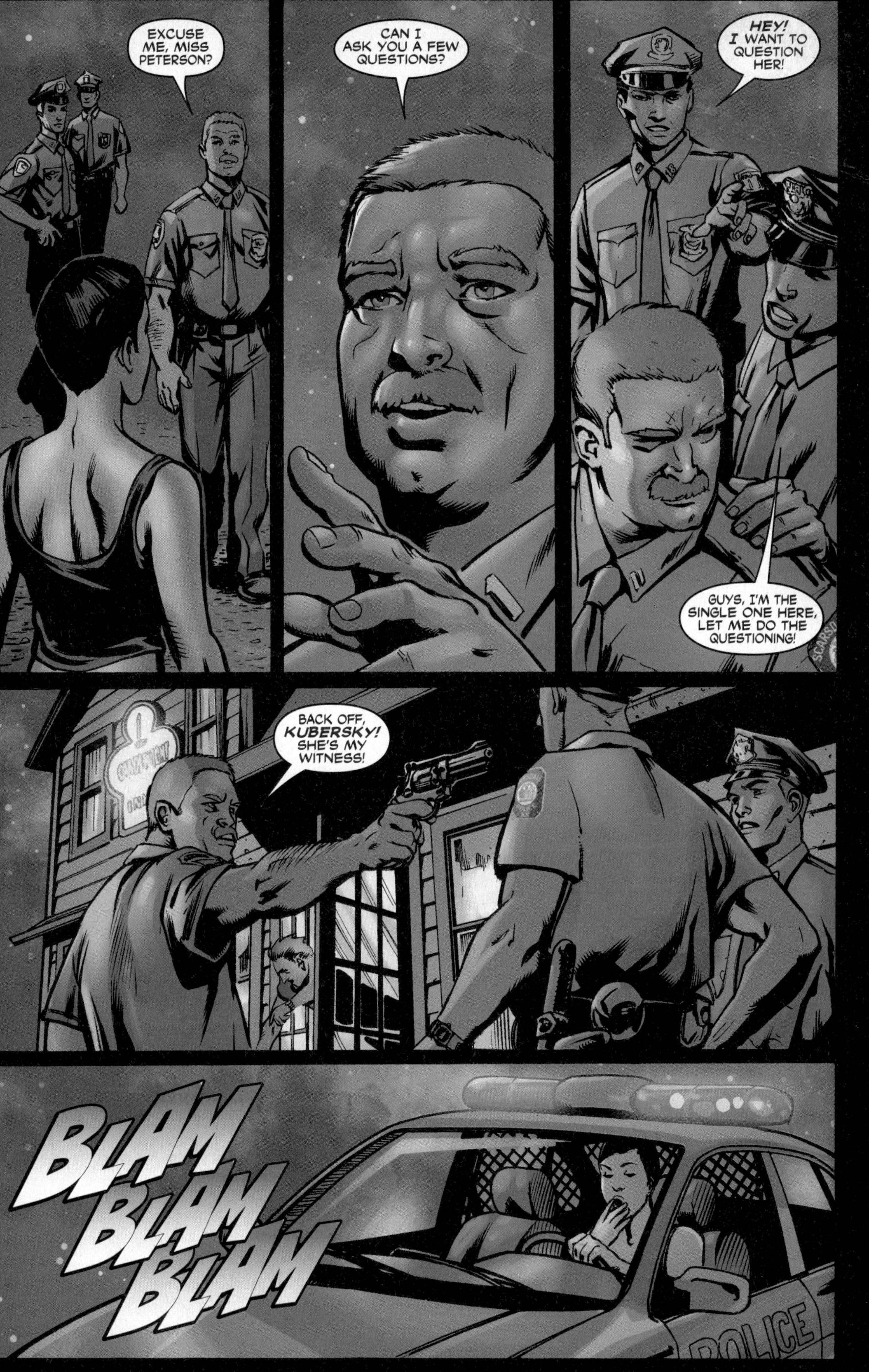
EXCUSE ME, MISS PETERSON?
CAN I ASK YOU A FEW QUESTIONS?
HEY! I WANT TO QUESTION HER!
GUYS, I'M THE SINGLE ONE HERE, LET ME DO THE QUESTIONING!
BACK OFF, KUBERSKY! SHE'S MY WITNESS!
BLAM BLAM BLAM
POLICE

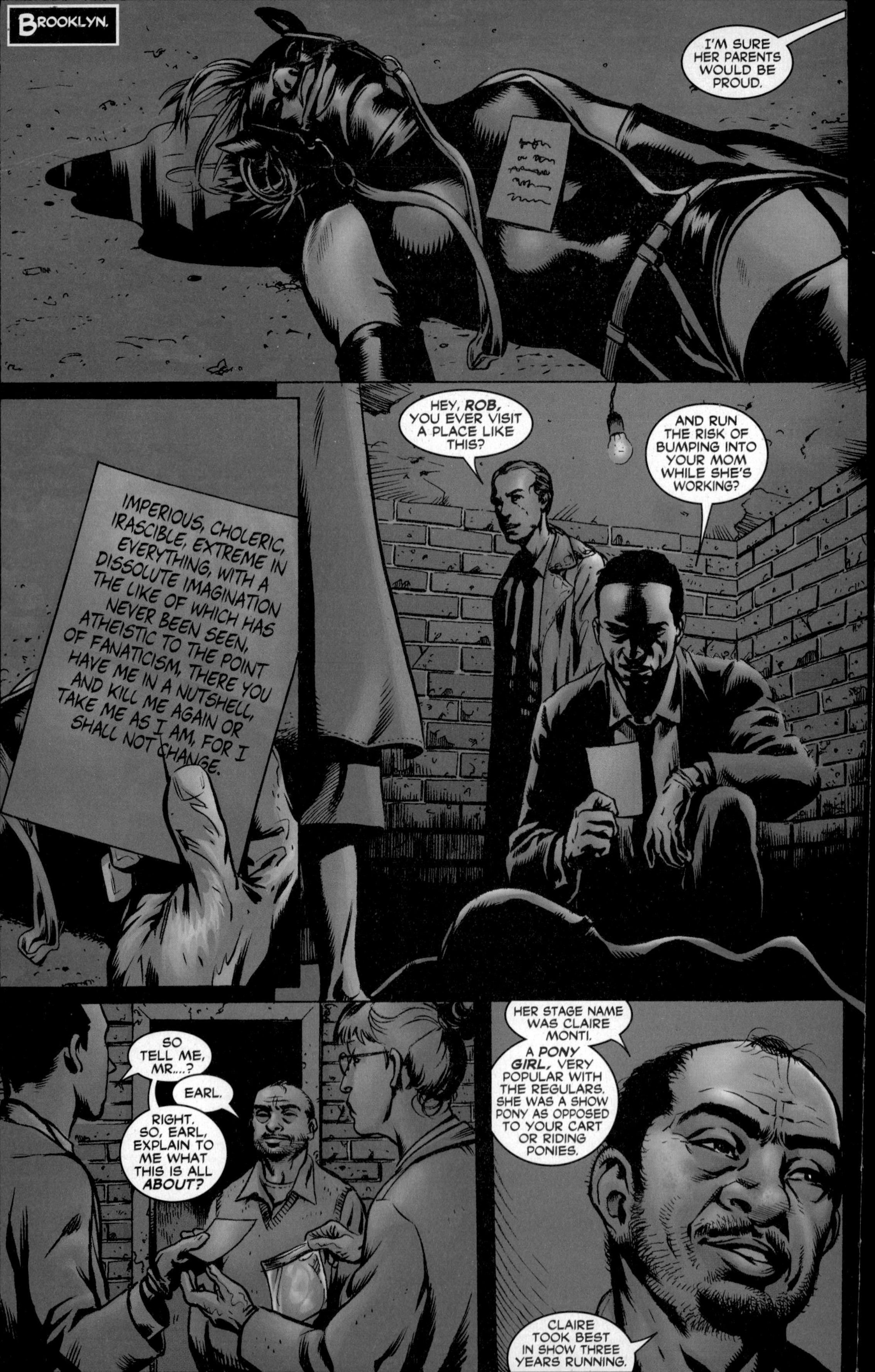
BROOKLYN.
I'M SURE HER PARENTS WOULD BE PROUD.
IMPERIOUS, CHOLERIC, IRASCIBLE, EXTREME IN EVERYTHING, WITH A DISSOLUTE IMAGINATION THE LIKE OF WHICH HAS NEVER BEEN SEEN, ATHEISTIC TO THE POINT OF FANATICISM, THERE YOU HAVE ME IN A NUTSHELL, AND KILL ME AGAIN OR TAKE ME AS I AM, FOR I SHALL NOT CHANGE.
HEY, ROB, YOU EVER VISIT A PLACE LIKE THIS?
AND RUN THE RISK OF BUMPING INTO YOUR MOM WHILE SHE'S WORKING?
SO TELL ME, MR....?
EARL.
RIGHT. SO, EARL, EXPLAIN TO ME WHAT THIS IS ALL ABOUT?
HER STAGE NAME WAS CLAIRE MONTI.
A PONY GIRL, VERY POPULAR WITH THE REGULARS. SHE WAS A SHOW PONY AS OPPOSED TO YOUR CART OR RIDING PONIES.
CLAIRE TOOK BEST IN SHOW THREE YEARS RUNNING.

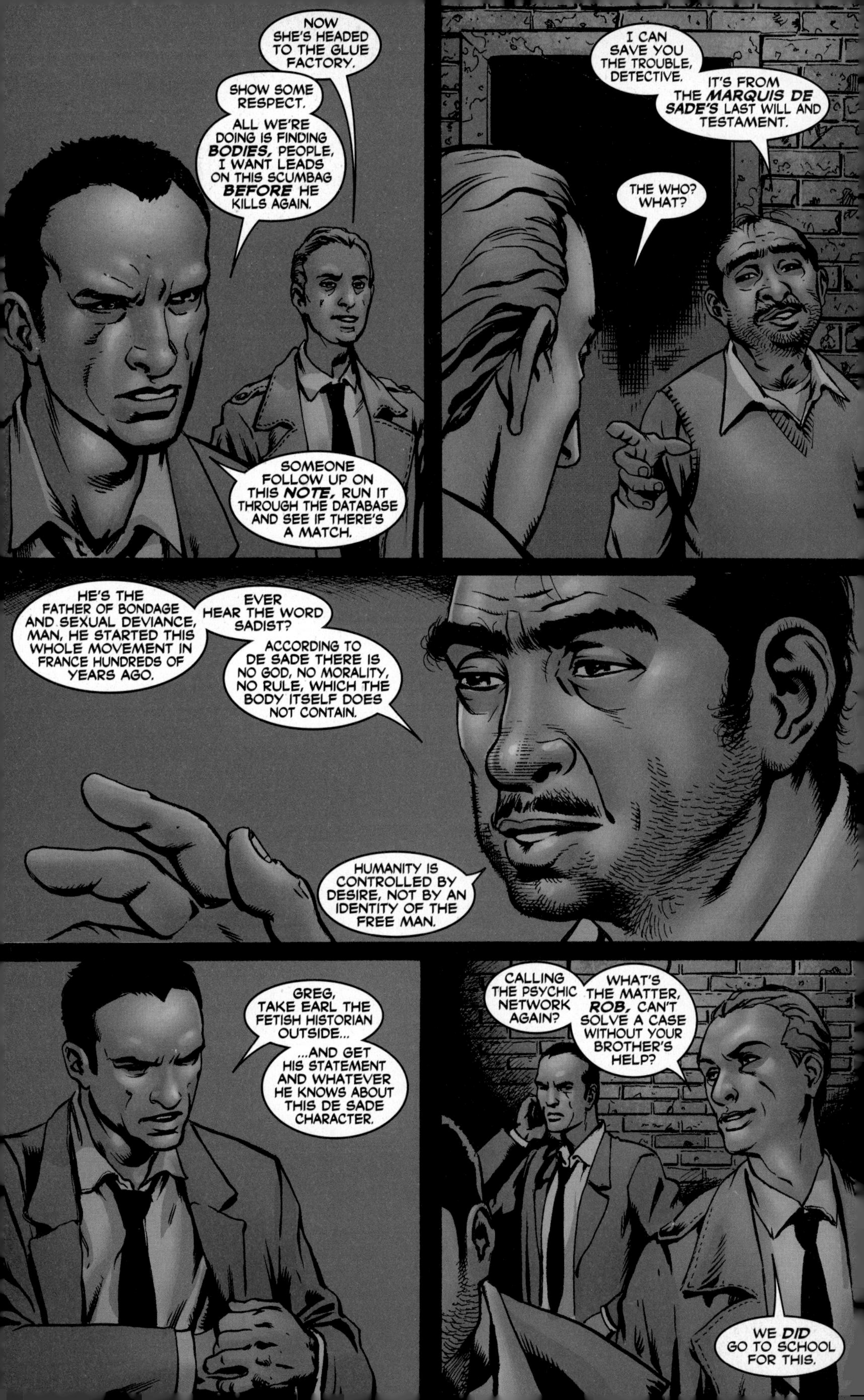
NOW SHE'S HEADED TO THE GLUE FACTORY.
SHOW SOME RESPECT.
ALL WE'RE DOING IS FINDING **BODIES,** PEOPLE, I WANT LEADS ON THIS SCUMBAG **BEFORE** HE KILLS AGAIN.
SOMEONE FOLLOW UP ON THIS **NOTE,** RUN IT THROUGH THE DATABASE AND SEE IF THERE'S A MATCH.
I CAN SAVE YOU THE TROUBLE, DETECTIVE.
IT'S FROM THE **MARQUIS DE SADE'S** LAST WILL AND TESTAMENT.
THE WHO? WHAT?
HE'S THE FATHER OF BONDAGE AND SEXUAL DEVIANCE, MAN, HE STARTED THIS WHOLE MOVEMENT IN FRANCE HUNDREDS OF YEARS AGO.
EVER HEAR THE WORD SADIST?
ACCORDING TO DE SADE THERE IS NO GOD, NO MORALITY, NO RULE, WHICH THE BODY ITSELF DOES NOT CONTAIN.
HUMANITY IS CONTROLLED BY DESIRE, NOT BY AN IDENTITY OF THE FREE MAN.
GREG, TAKE EARL THE FETISH HISTORIAN OUTSIDE...
...AND GET HIS STATEMENT AND WHATEVER HE KNOWS ABOUT THIS DE SADE CHARACTER.
CALLING THE PSYCHIC NETWORK AGAIN?
WHAT'S THE MATTER, **ROB,** CAN'T SOLVE A CASE WITHOUT YOUR BROTHER'S HELP?
WE **DID** GO TO SCHOOL FOR THIS.

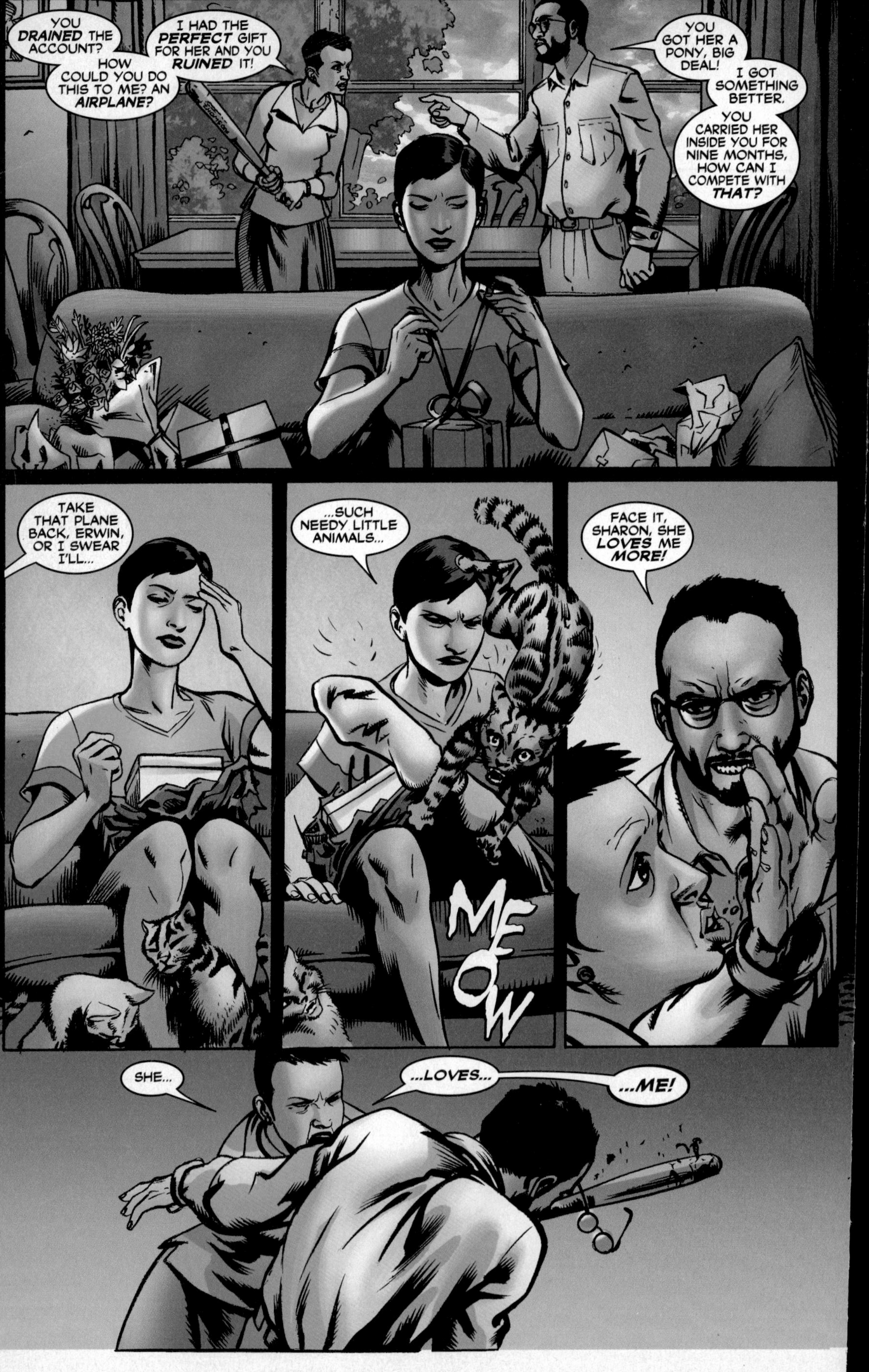
YOU DRAINED THE ACCOUNT? HOW COULD YOU DO THIS TO ME? AN AIRPLANE?
I HAD THE PERFECT GIFT FOR HER AND YOU RUINED IT!
YOU GOT HER A PONY, BIG DEAL!
I GOT SOMETHING BETTER.
YOU CARRIED HER INSIDE YOU FOR NINE MONTHS, HOW CAN I COMPETE WITH THAT?
TAKE THAT PLANE BACK, ERWIN, OR I SWEAR I'LL...
...SUCH NEEDY LITTLE ANIMALS...
MEOW
FACE IT, SHARON, SHE LOVES ME MORE!
SHE...
...LOVES...
...ME!

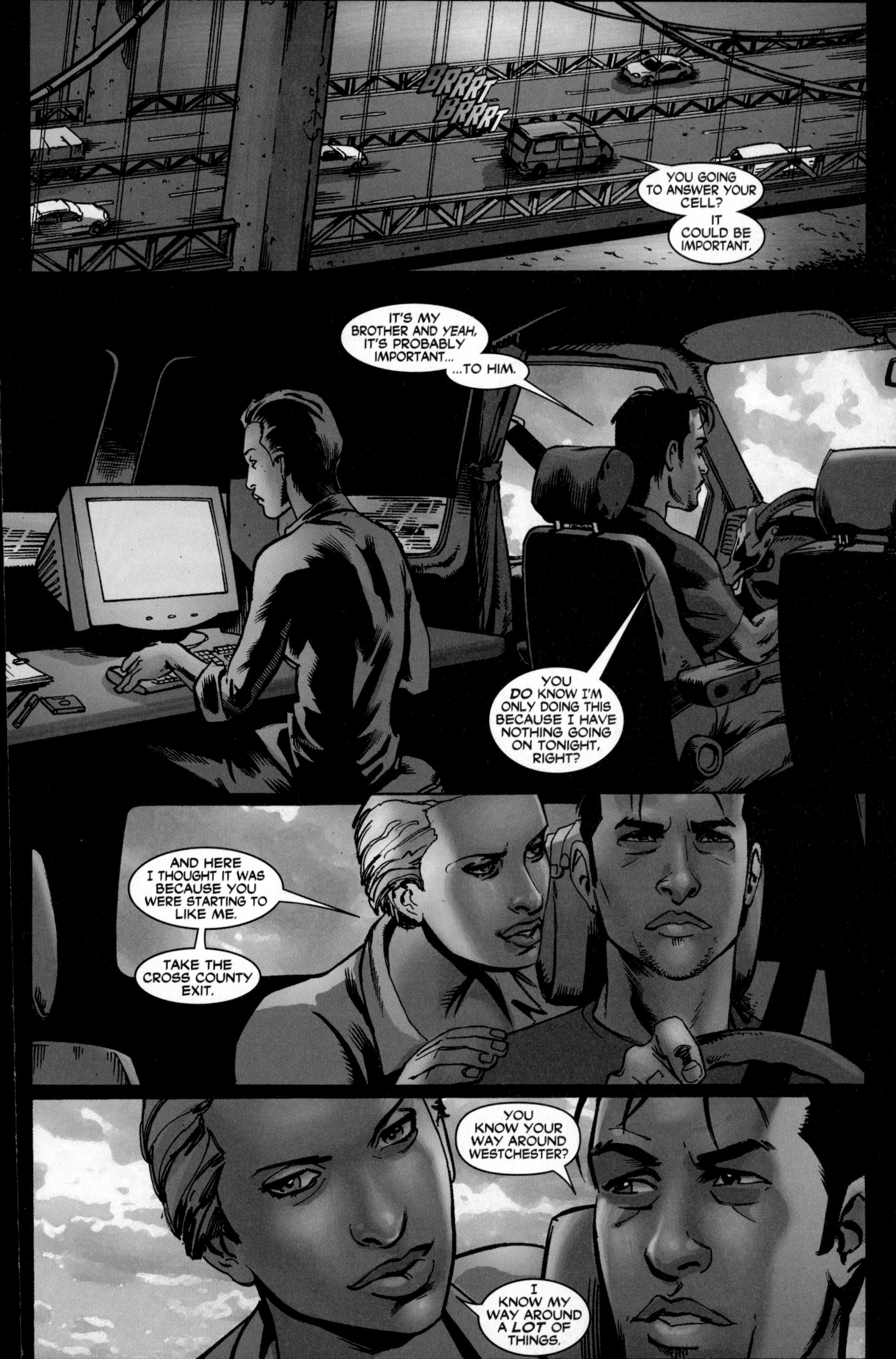
BRRRT
BRRRT
YOU GOING TO ANSWER YOUR CELL?
IT COULD BE IMPORTANT.
IT'S MY BROTHER AND YEAH, IT'S PROBABLY IMPORTANT...
...TO HIM.
YOU DO KNOW I'M ONLY DOING THIS BECAUSE I HAVE NOTHING GOING ON TONIGHT, RIGHT?
AND HERE I THOUGHT IT WAS BECAUSE YOU WERE STARTING TO LIKE ME.
TAKE THE CROSS COUNTY EXIT.
YOU KNOW YOUR WAY AROUND WESTCHESTER?
I KNOW MY WAY AROUND A LOT OF THINGS.

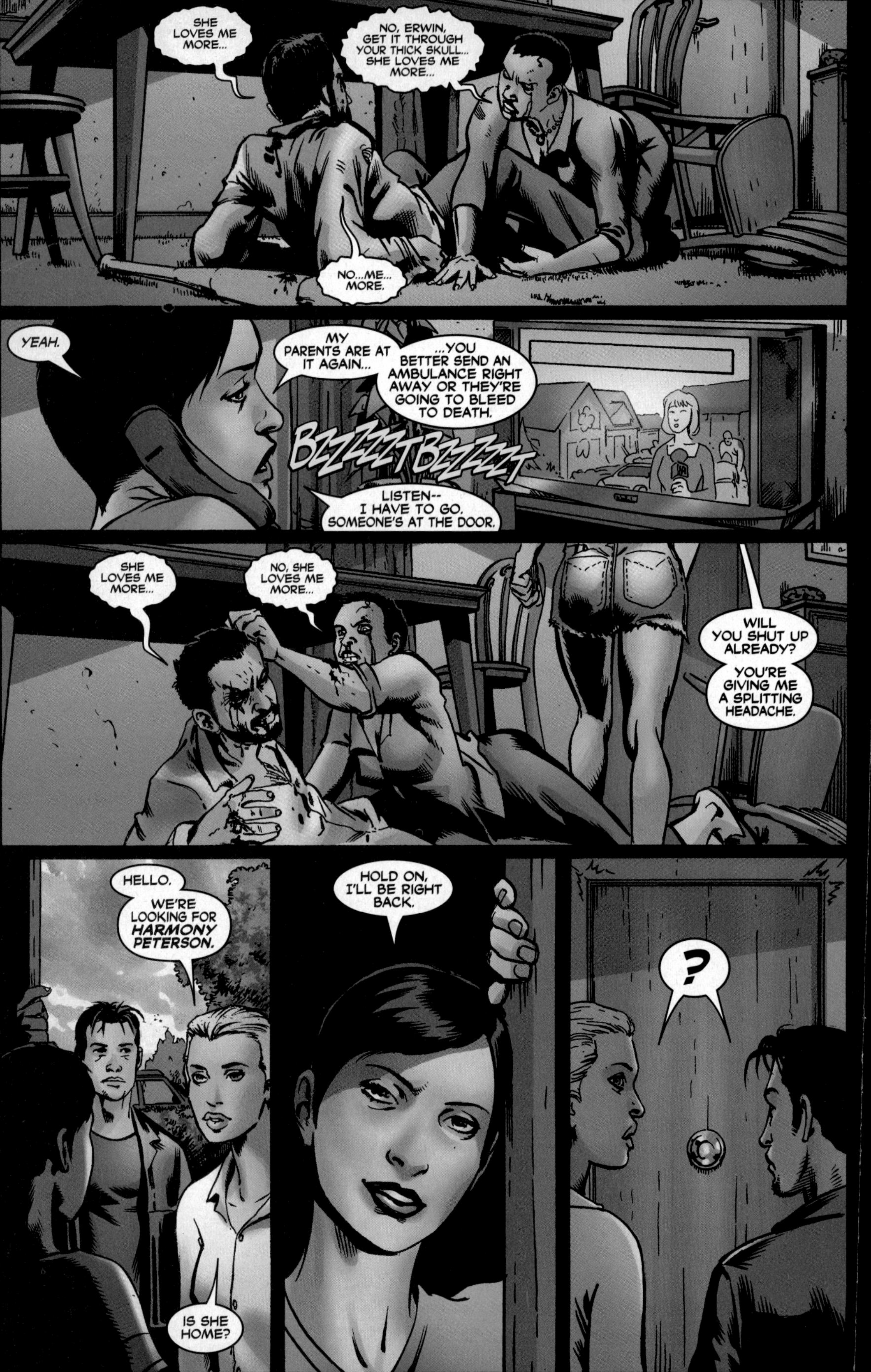
SHE LOVES ME MORE...
NO, ERWIN, GET IT THROUGH YOUR THICK SKULL... SHE LOVES ME MORE...
NO...ME... MORE.
YEAH.
MY PARENTS ARE AT IT AGAIN...
...YOU BETTER SEND AN AMBULANCE RIGHT AWAY OR THEY'RE GOING TO BLEED TO DEATH.
BZZZZZTBZZZZZT
LISTEN-- I HAVE TO GO. SOMEONE'S AT THE DOOR.
SHE LOVES ME MORE...
NO, SHE LOVES ME MORE...
WILL YOU SHUT UP ALREADY?
YOU'RE GIVING ME A SPLITTING HEADACHE.
HELLO.
WE'RE LOOKING FOR HARMONY PETERSON.
IS SHE HOME?
HOLD ON, I'LL BE RIGHT BACK.
?

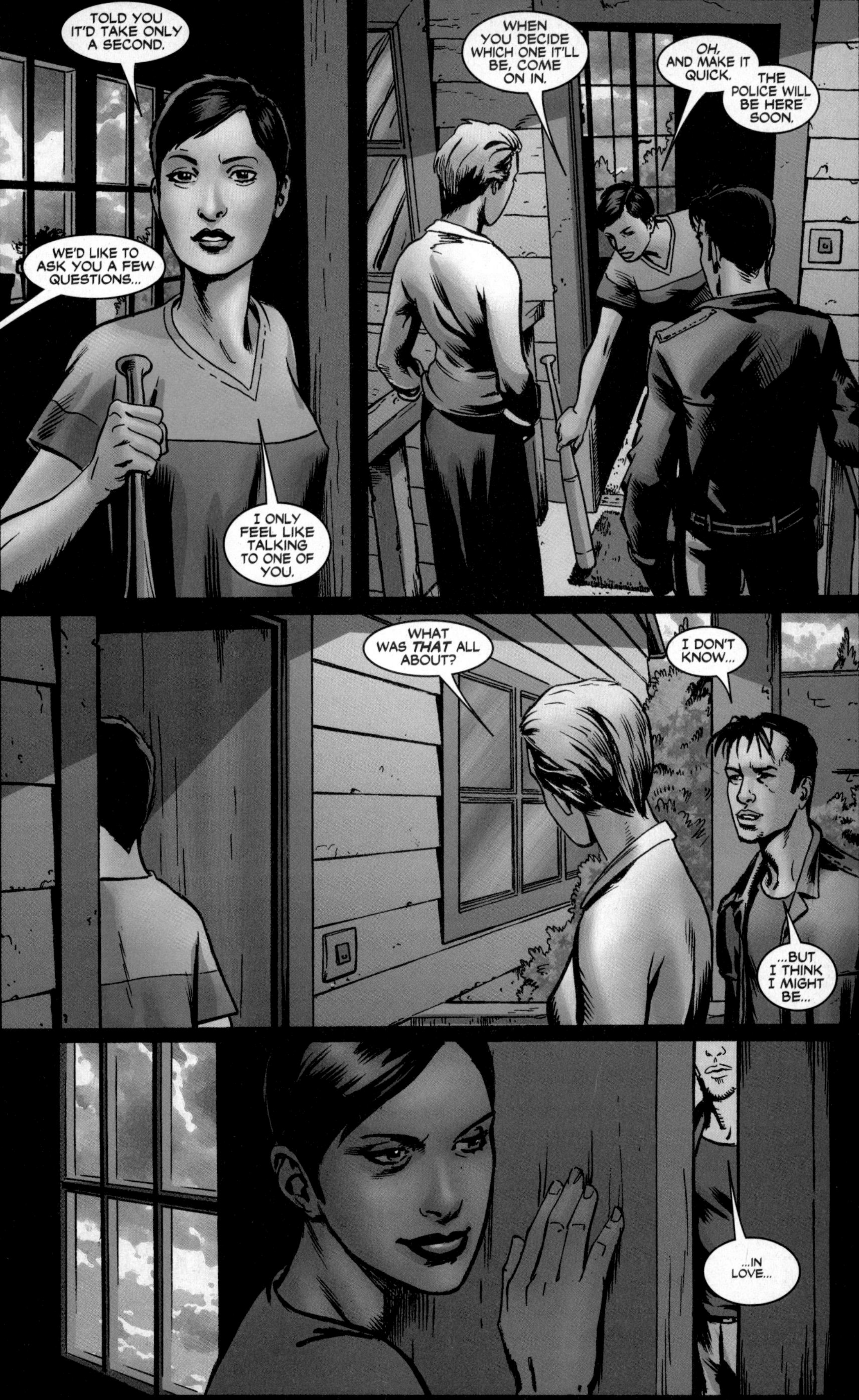

TOLD YOU IT'D TAKE ONLY A SECOND.
WE'D LIKE TO ASK YOU A FEW QUESTIONS...
I ONLY FEEL LIKE TALKING TO ONE OF YOU.
WHEN YOU DECIDE WHICH ONE IT'LL BE, COME ON IN.
OH, AND MAKE IT QUICK.
THE POLICE WILL BE HERE SOON.
WHAT WAS THAT ALL ABOUT?
I DON'T KNOW...
...BUT I THINK I MIGHT BE...
...IN LOVE...

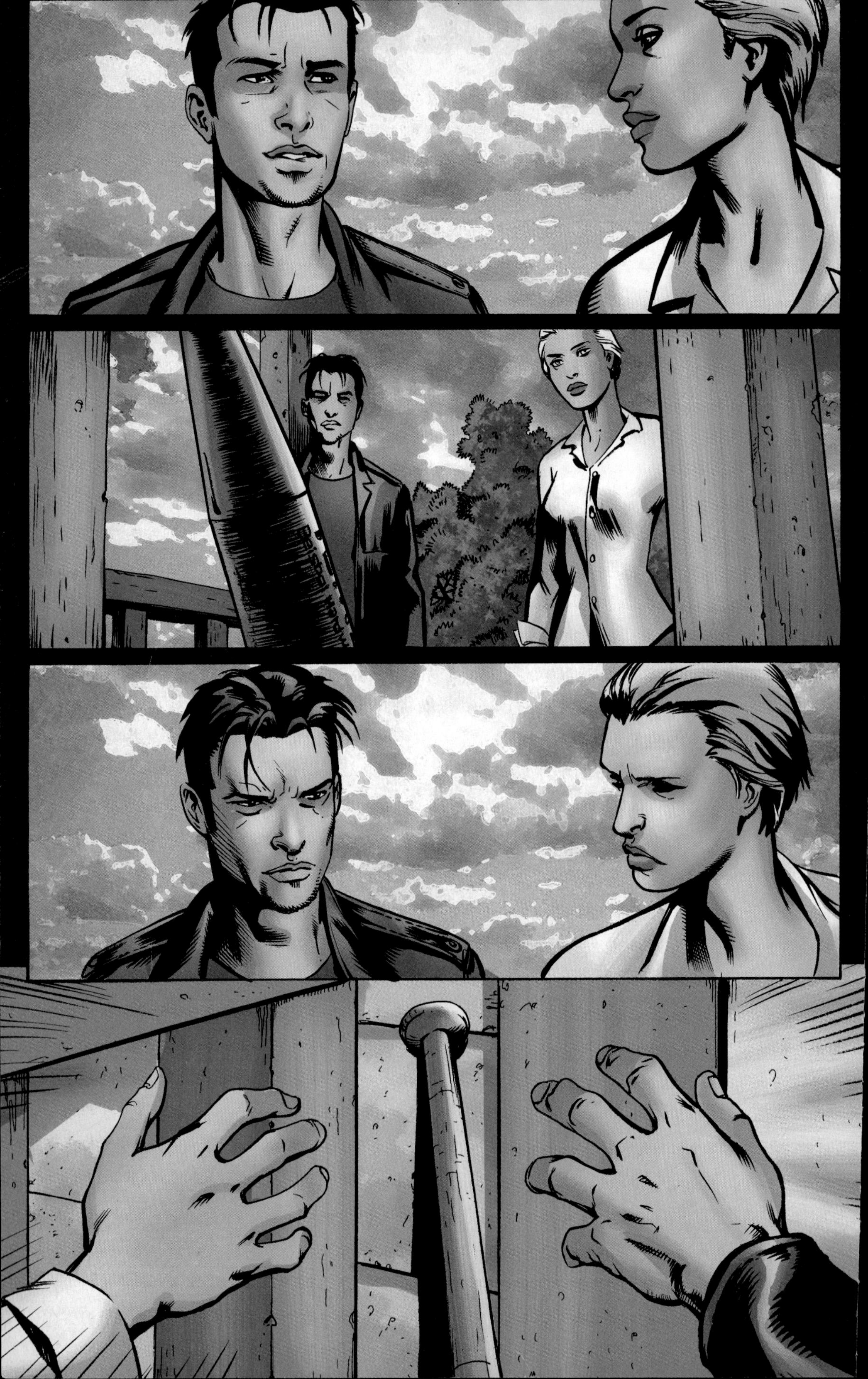

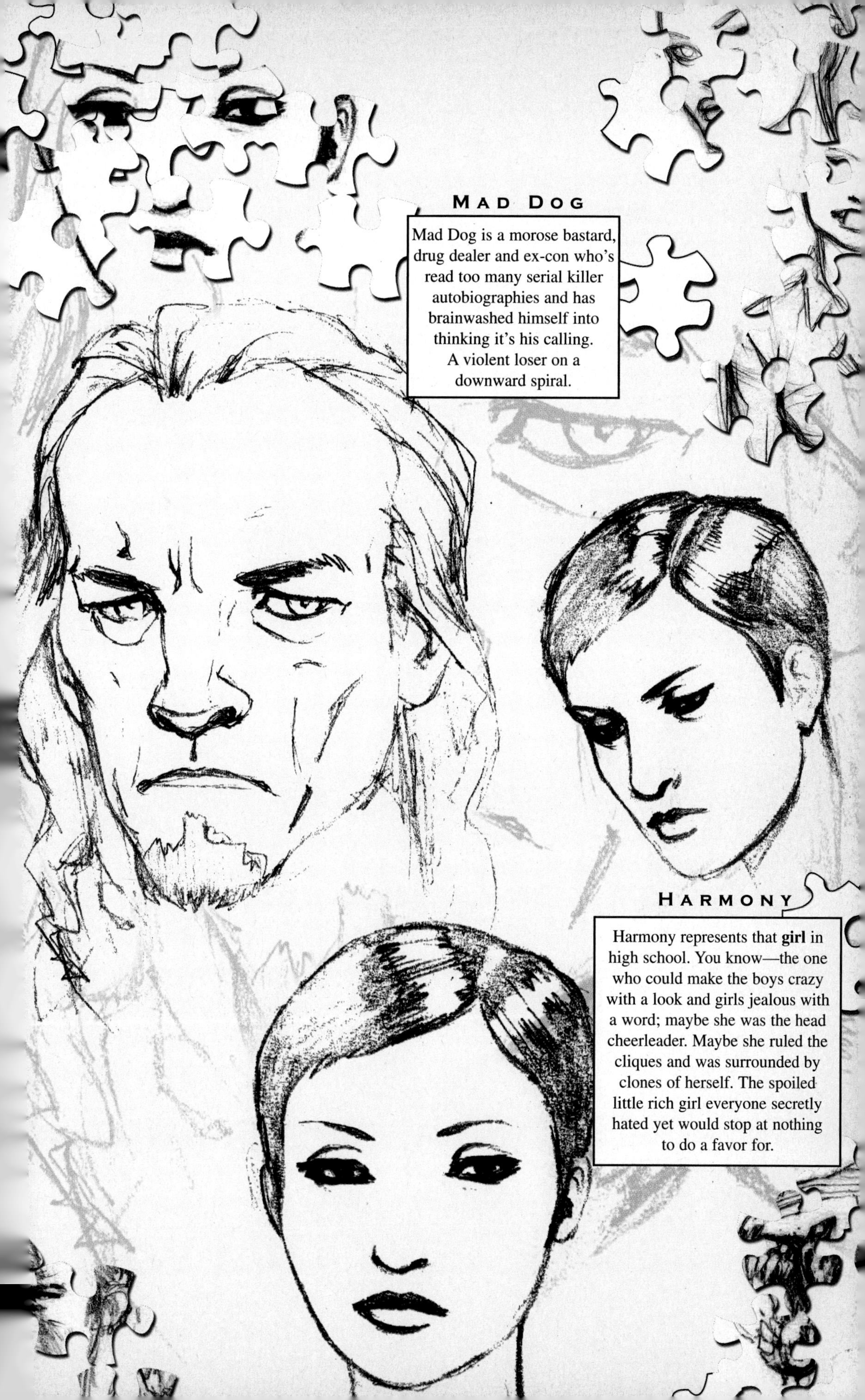

MAD DOG

Mad Dog is a morose bastard, drug dealer and ex-con who's read too many serial killer autobiographies and has brainwashed himself into thinking it's his calling. A violent loser on a downward spiral.

HARMONY

Harmony represents that **girl** in high school. You know—the one who could make the boys crazy with a look and girls jealous with a word; maybe she was the head cheerleader. Maybe she ruled the cliques and was surrounded by clones of herself. The spoiled little rich girl everyone secretly hated yet would stop at nothing to do a favor for.

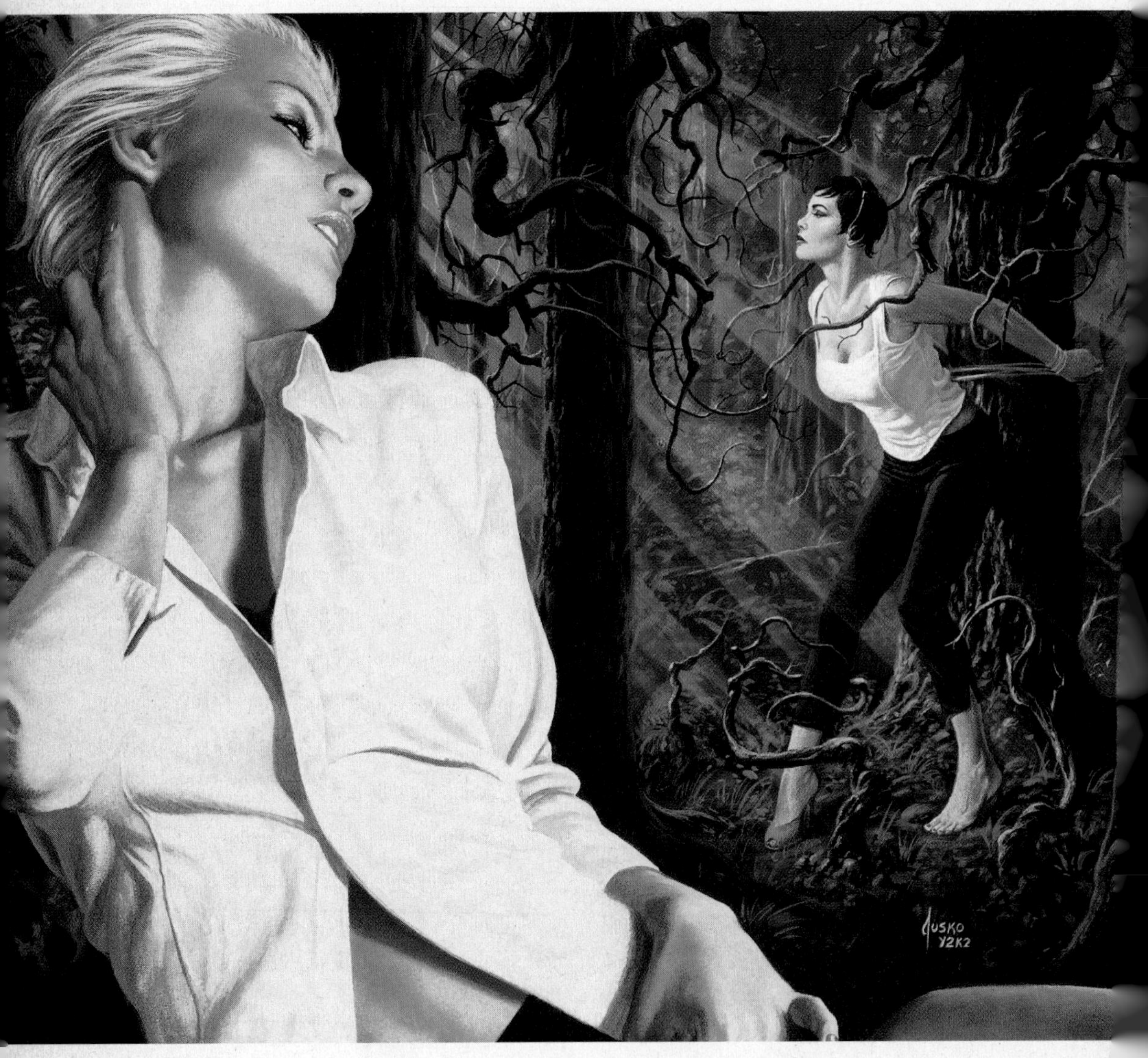
JUSKO
Y2K2

I'M NOT SICK, BUT I'M NOT WELL

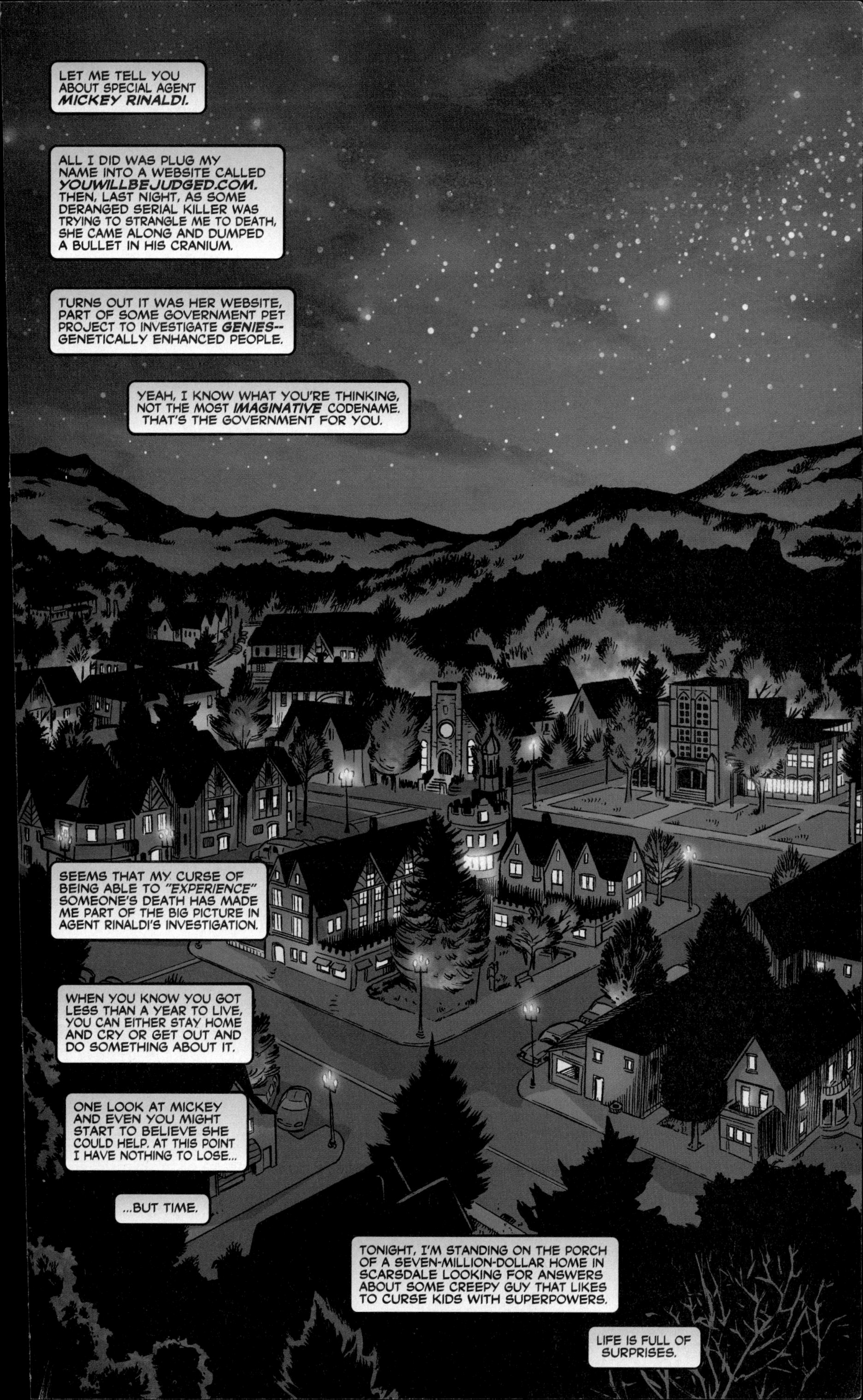
LET ME TELL YOU ABOUT SPECIAL AGENT MICKEY RINALDI.
ALL I DID WAS PLUG MY NAME INTO A WEBSITE CALLED YOUWILLBEJUDGED.COM. THEN, LAST NIGHT, AS SOME DERANGED SERIAL KILLER WAS TRYING TO STRANGLE ME TO DEATH, SHE CAME ALONG AND DUMPED A BULLET IN HIS CRANIUM.
TURNS OUT IT WAS HER WEBSITE, PART OF SOME GOVERNMENT PET PROJECT TO INVESTIGATE GENIES-- GENETICALLY ENHANCED PEOPLE.
YEAH, I KNOW WHAT YOU'RE THINKING, NOT THE MOST IMAGINATIVE CODENAME. THAT'S THE GOVERNMENT FOR YOU.
SEEMS THAT MY CURSE OF BEING ABLE TO "EXPERIENCE" SOMEONE'S DEATH HAS MADE ME PART OF THE BIG PICTURE IN AGENT RINALDI'S INVESTIGATION.
WHEN YOU KNOW YOU GOT LESS THAN A YEAR TO LIVE, YOU CAN EITHER STAY HOME AND CRY OR GET OUT AND DO SOMETHING ABOUT IT.
ONE LOOK AT MICKEY AND EVEN YOU MIGHT START TO BELIEVE SHE COULD HELP. AT THIS POINT I HAVE NOTHING TO LOSE...
...BUT TIME.
TONIGHT, I'M STANDING ON THE PORCH OF A SEVEN-MILLION-DOLLAR HOME IN SCARSDALE LOOKING FOR ANSWERS ABOUT SOME CREEPY GUY THAT LIKES TO CURSE KIDS WITH SUPERPOWERS.
LIFE IS FULL OF SURPRISES.

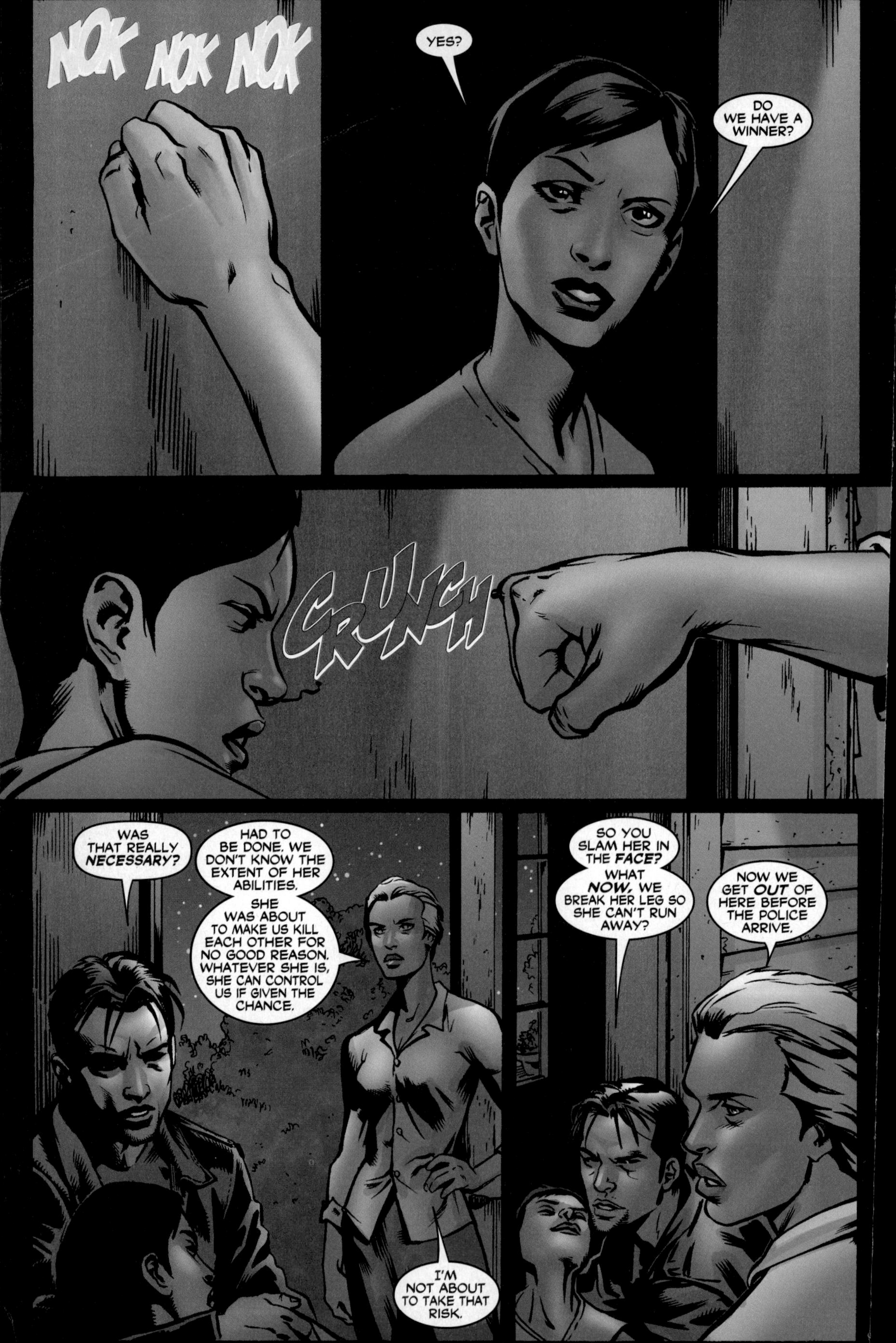
NOK NOK NOK
YES?
DO WE HAVE A WINNER?
CRUNCH
WAS THAT REALLY NECESSARY?
HAD TO BE DONE. WE DON'T KNOW THE EXTENT OF HER ABILITIES.
SHE WAS ABOUT TO MAKE US KILL EACH OTHER FOR NO GOOD REASON. WHATEVER SHE IS, SHE CAN CONTROL US IF GIVEN THE CHANCE.
I'M NOT ABOUT TO TAKE THAT RISK.
SO YOU SLAM HER IN THE FACE?
WHAT NOW, WE BREAK HER LEG SO SHE CAN'T RUN AWAY?
NOW WE GET OUT OF HERE BEFORE THE POLICE ARRIVE.

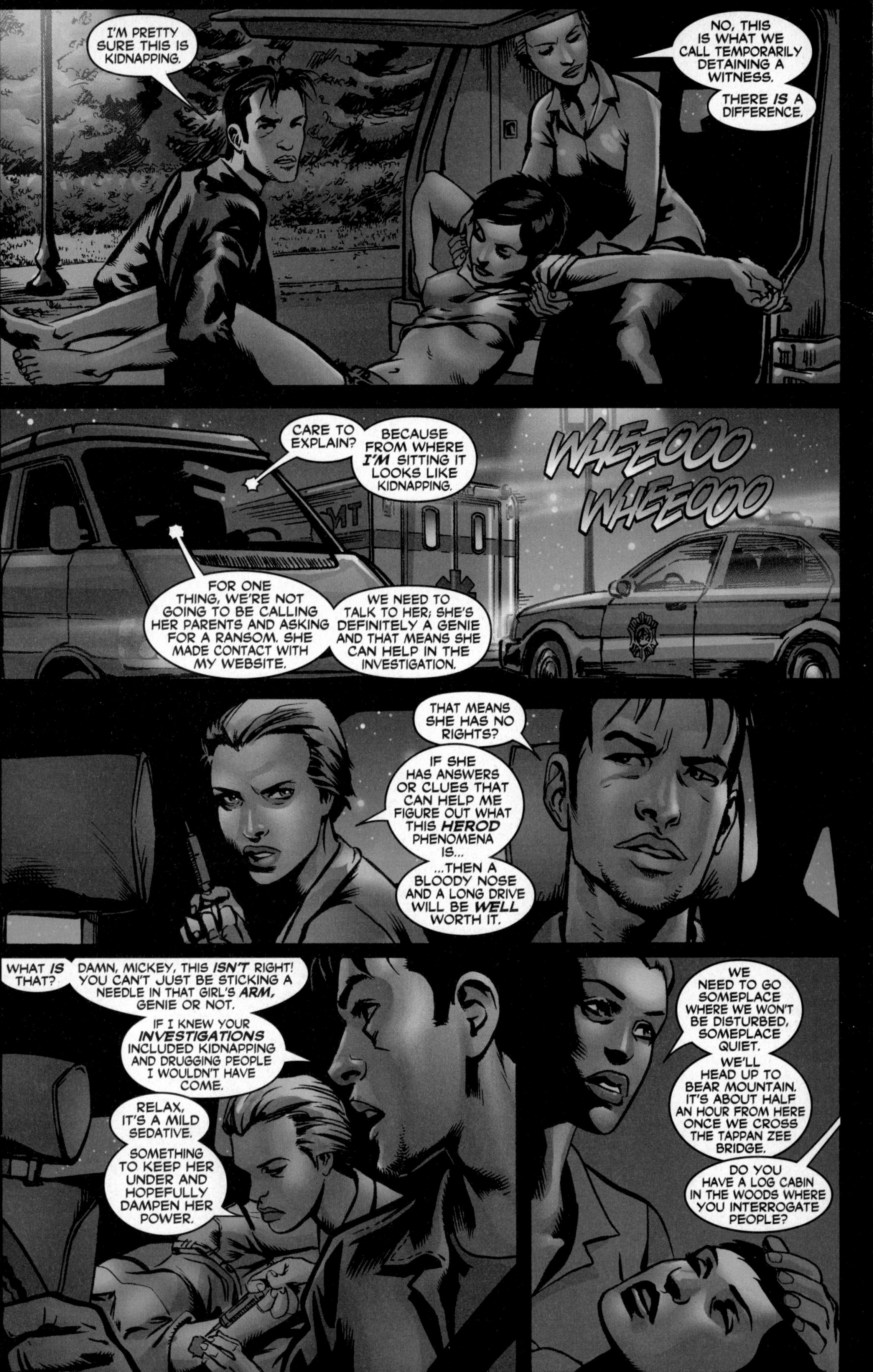

I'M PRETTY SURE THIS IS KIDNAPPING.
NO, THIS IS WHAT WE CALL TEMPORARILY DETAINING A WITNESS.
THERE *IS* A DIFFERENCE.
CARE TO EXPLAIN?
BECAUSE FROM WHERE *I'M* SITTING IT LOOKS LIKE KIDNAPPING.
WHEEOOO WHEEOOO
FOR ONE THING, WE'RE NOT GOING TO BE CALLING HER PARENTS AND ASKING FOR A RANSOM. SHE MADE CONTACT WITH MY WEBSITE.
WE NEED TO TALK TO HER; SHE'S DEFINITELY A GENIE AND THAT MEANS SHE CAN HELP IN THE INVESTIGATION.
THAT MEANS SHE HAS NO RIGHTS?
IF SHE HAS ANSWERS OR CLUES THAT CAN HELP ME FIGURE OUT WHAT THIS *HEROD* PHENOMENA IS...
...THEN A BLOODY NOSE AND A LONG DRIVE WILL BE *WELL* WORTH IT.
WHAT *IS* THAT?
DAMN, MICKEY, THIS *ISN'T* RIGHT! YOU CAN'T JUST BE STICKING A NEEDLE IN THAT GIRL'S *ARM*, GENIE OR NOT.
IF I KNEW YOUR *INVESTIGATIONS* INCLUDED KIDNAPPING AND DRUGGING PEOPLE I WOULDN'T HAVE COME.
RELAX, IT'S A MILD SEDATIVE.
SOMETHING TO KEEP HER UNDER AND HOPEFULLY DAMPEN HER POWER.
WE NEED TO GO SOMEPLACE WHERE WE WON'T BE DISTURBED, SOMEPLACE QUIET.
WE'LL HEAD UP TO BEAR MOUNTAIN. IT'S ABOUT HALF AN HOUR FROM HERE ONCE WE CROSS THE TAPPAN ZEE BRIDGE.
DO YOU HAVE A LOG CABIN IN THE WOODS WHERE YOU INTERROGATE PEOPLE?

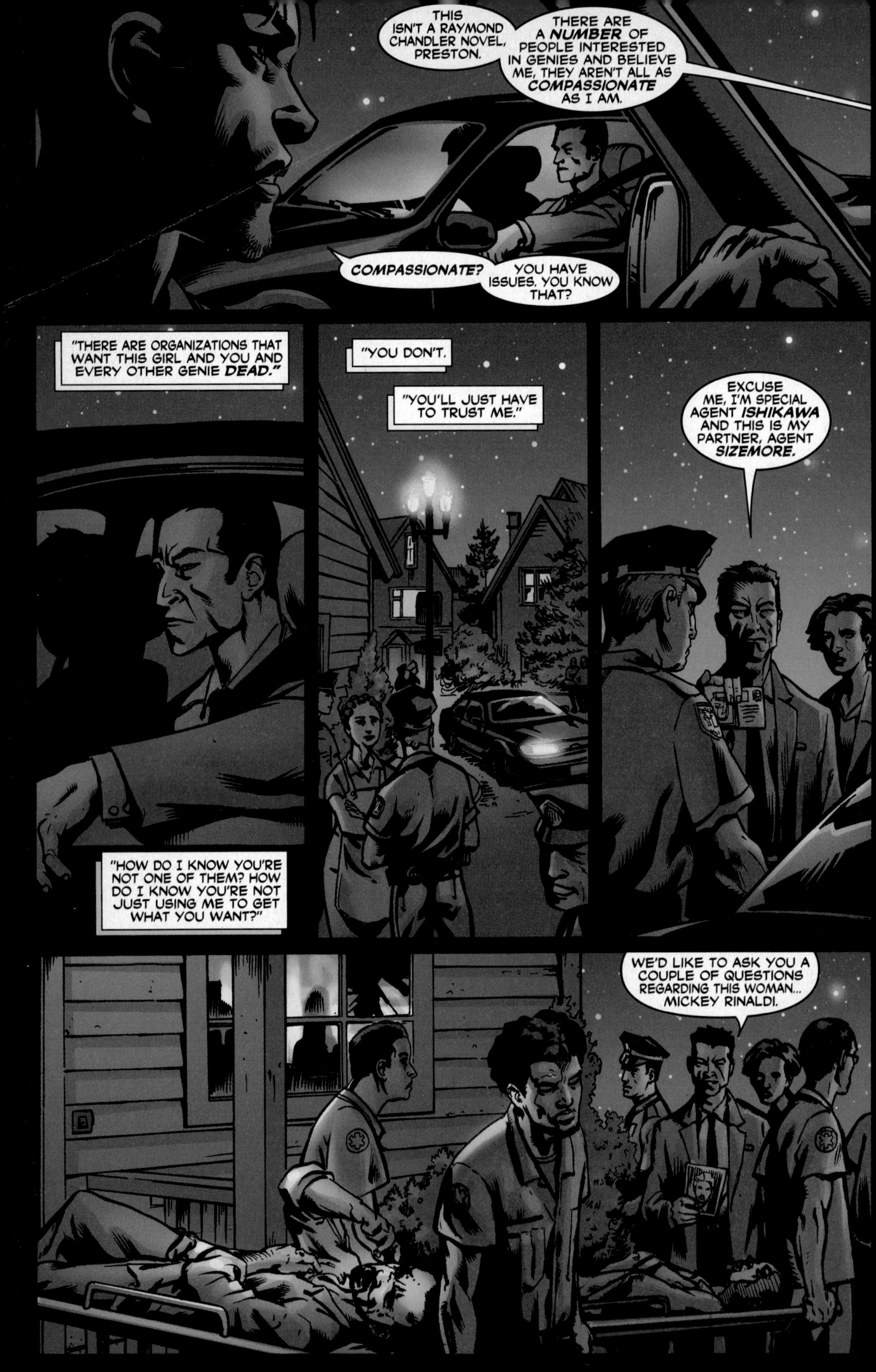

THIS ISN'T A RAYMOND CHANDLER NOVEL, PRESTON.
THERE ARE A **NUMBER** OF PEOPLE INTERESTED IN GENIES AND BELIEVE ME, THEY AREN'T ALL AS ***COMPASSIONATE*** AS I AM.
COMPASSIONATE?
YOU HAVE ISSUES, YOU KNOW THAT?
"THERE ARE ORGANIZATIONS THAT WANT THIS GIRL AND YOU AND EVERY OTHER GENIE ***DEAD.***"
"HOW DO I KNOW YOU'RE NOT ONE OF THEM? HOW DO I KNOW YOU'RE NOT JUST USING ME TO GET WHAT YOU WANT?"
"YOU DON'T.
"YOU'LL JUST HAVE TO TRUST ME."
EXCUSE ME, I'M SPECIAL AGENT ***ISHIKAWA*** AND THIS IS MY PARTNER, AGENT ***SIZEMORE.***
WE'D LIKE TO ASK YOU A COUPLE OF QUESTIONS REGARDING THIS WOMAN... MICKEY RINALDI.

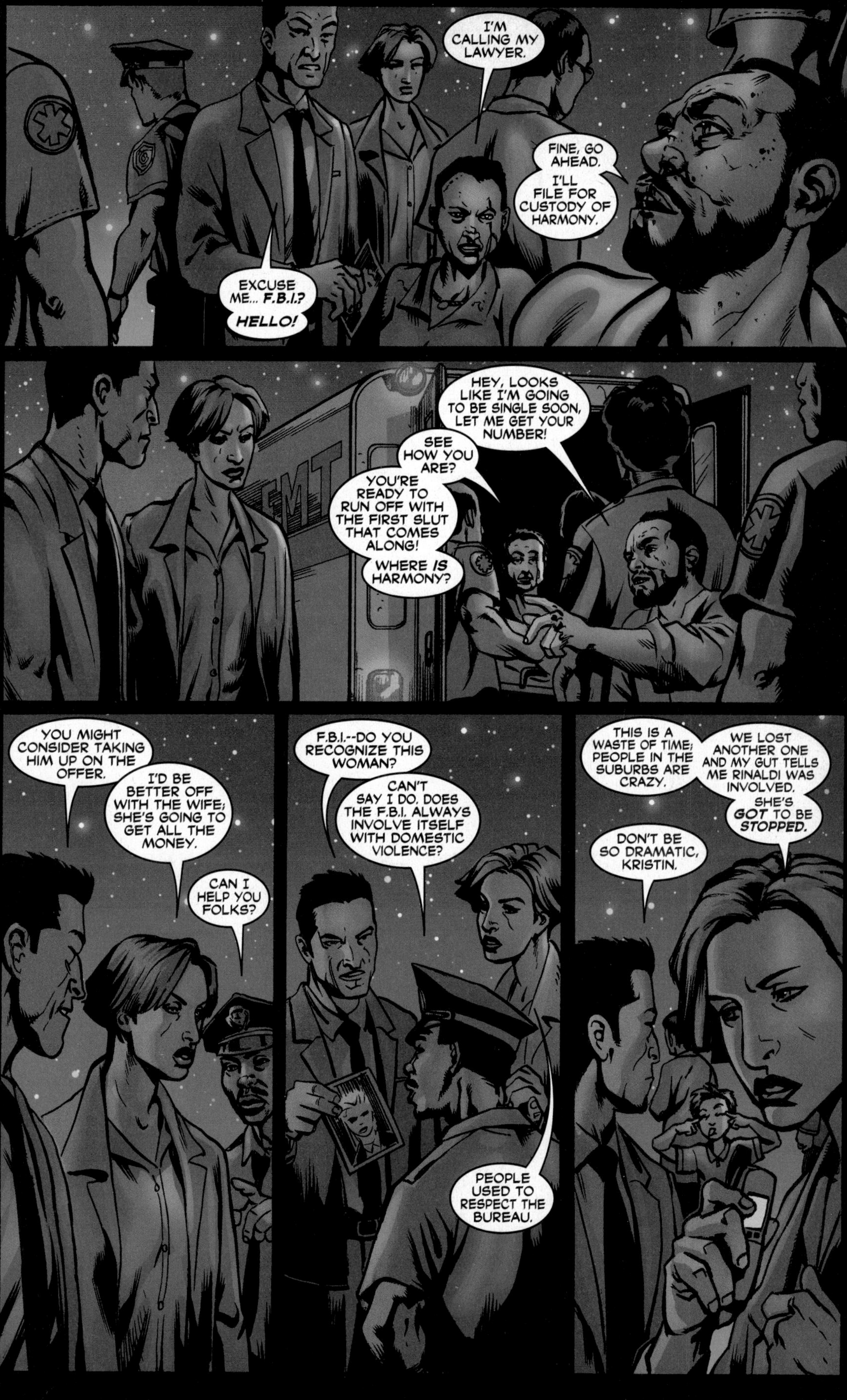
I'M CALLING MY LAWYER.
FINE, GO AHEAD. I'LL FILE FOR CUSTODY OF HARMONY.
EXCUSE ME... F.B.I.? HELLO!
HEY, LOOKS LIKE I'M GOING TO BE SINGLE SOON, LET ME GET YOUR NUMBER!
SEE HOW YOU ARE? YOU'RE READY TO RUN OFF WITH THE FIRST SLUT THAT COMES ALONG!
WHERE IS HARMONY?
EMT
YOU MIGHT CONSIDER TAKING HIM UP ON THE OFFER.
I'D BE BETTER OFF WITH THE WIFE; SHE'S GOING TO GET ALL THE MONEY.
CAN I HELP YOU FOLKS?
F.B.I.--DO YOU RECOGNIZE THIS WOMAN?
CAN'T SAY I DO. DOES THE F.B.I. ALWAYS INVOLVE ITSELF WITH DOMESTIC VIOLENCE?
PEOPLE USED TO RESPECT THE BUREAU.
THIS IS A WASTE OF TIME; PEOPLE IN THE SUBURBS ARE CRAZY.
WE LOST ANOTHER ONE AND MY GUT TELLS ME RINALDI WAS INVOLVED.
SHE'S GOT TO BE STOPPED.
DON'T BE SO DRAMATIC, KRISTIN.

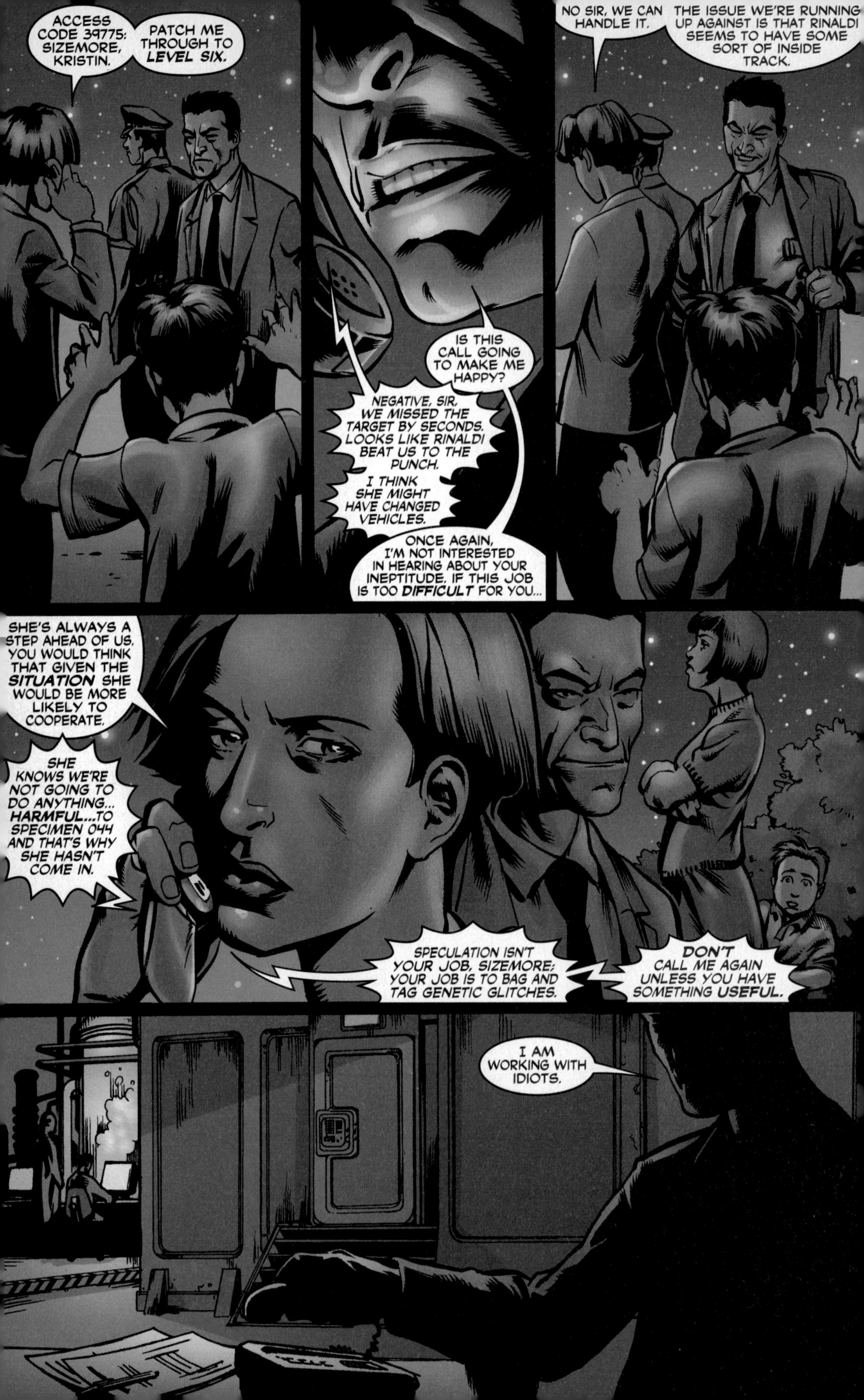
ACCESS CODE 39775: SIZEMORE, KRISTIN.
PATCH ME THROUGH TO LEVEL SIX.
IS THIS CALL GOING TO MAKE ME HAPPY?
NEGATIVE, SIR. WE MISSED THE TARGET BY SECONDS. LOOKS LIKE RINALDI BEAT US TO THE PUNCH.
I THINK SHE MIGHT HAVE CHANGED VEHICLES.
ONCE AGAIN, I'M NOT INTERESTED IN HEARING ABOUT YOUR INEPTITUDE. IF THIS JOB IS TOO DIFFICULT FOR YOU...
NO SIR, WE CAN HANDLE IT.
THE ISSUE WE'RE RUNNING UP AGAINST IS THAT RINALDI SEEMS TO HAVE SOME SORT OF INSIDE TRACK.
SHE'S ALWAYS A STEP AHEAD OF US. YOU WOULD THINK THAT GIVEN THE SITUATION SHE WOULD BE MORE LIKELY TO COOPERATE.
SHE KNOWS WE'RE NOT GOING TO DO ANYTHING... HARMFUL...TO SPECIMEN 044 AND THAT'S WHY SHE HASN'T COME IN.
SPECULATION ISN'T YOUR JOB, SIZEMORE; YOUR JOB IS TO BAG AND TAG GENETIC GLITCHES.
DON'T CALL ME AGAIN UNLESS YOU HAVE SOMETHING USEFUL.
I AM WORKING WITH IDIOTS.

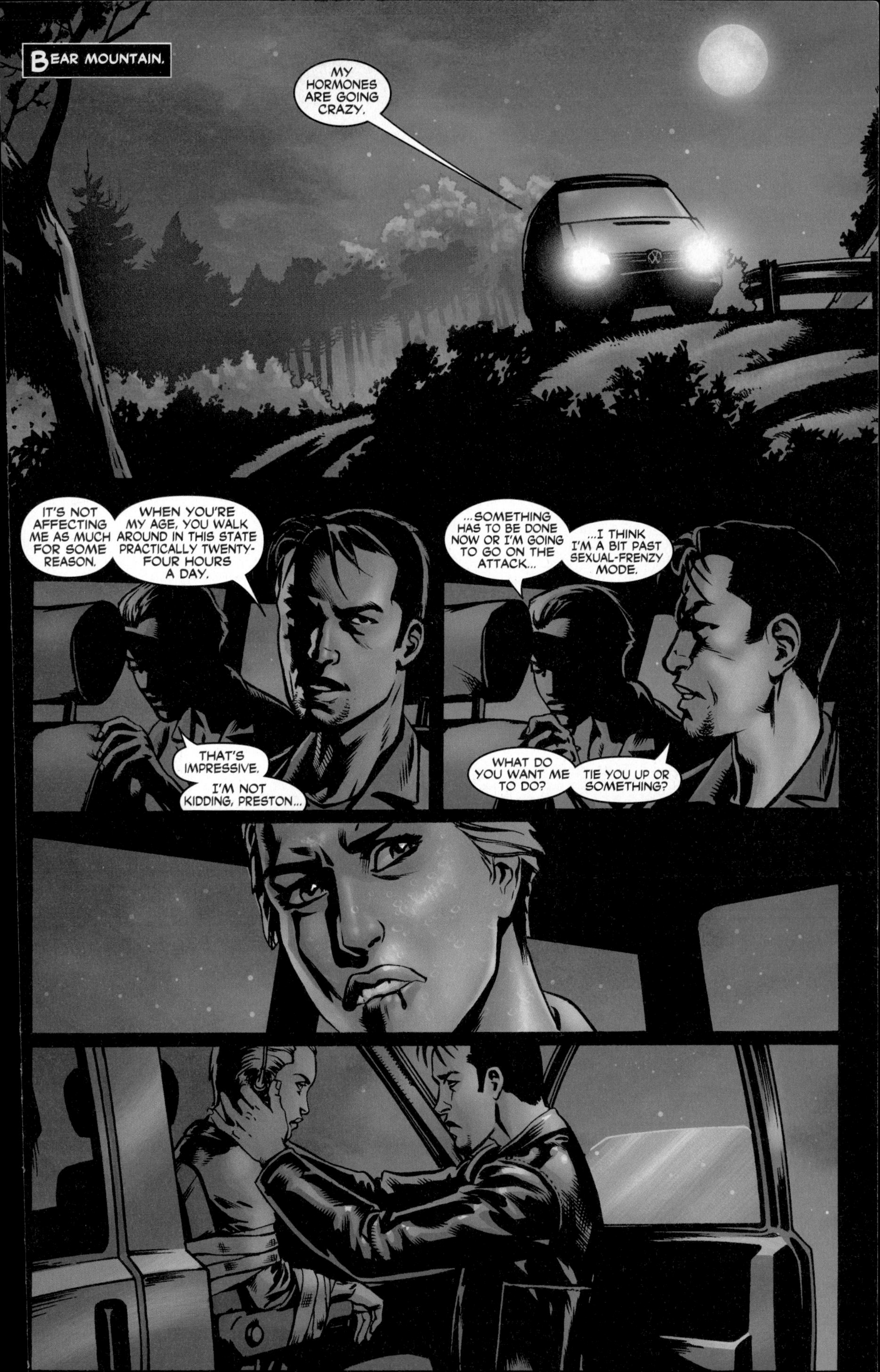
BEAR MOUNTAIN.
MY HORMONES ARE GOING CRAZY.
IT'S NOT AFFECTING ME AS MUCH FOR SOME REASON.
WHEN YOU'RE MY AGE, YOU WALK AROUND IN THIS STATE PRACTICALLY TWENTY-FOUR HOURS A DAY.
THAT'S IMPRESSIVE.
I'M NOT KIDDING, PRESTON...
...SOMETHING HAS TO BE DONE NOW OR I'M GOING TO GO ON THE ATTACK...
...I THINK I'M A BIT PAST SEXUAL-FRENZY MODE.
WHAT DO YOU WANT ME TO DO?
TIE YOU UP OR SOMETHING?

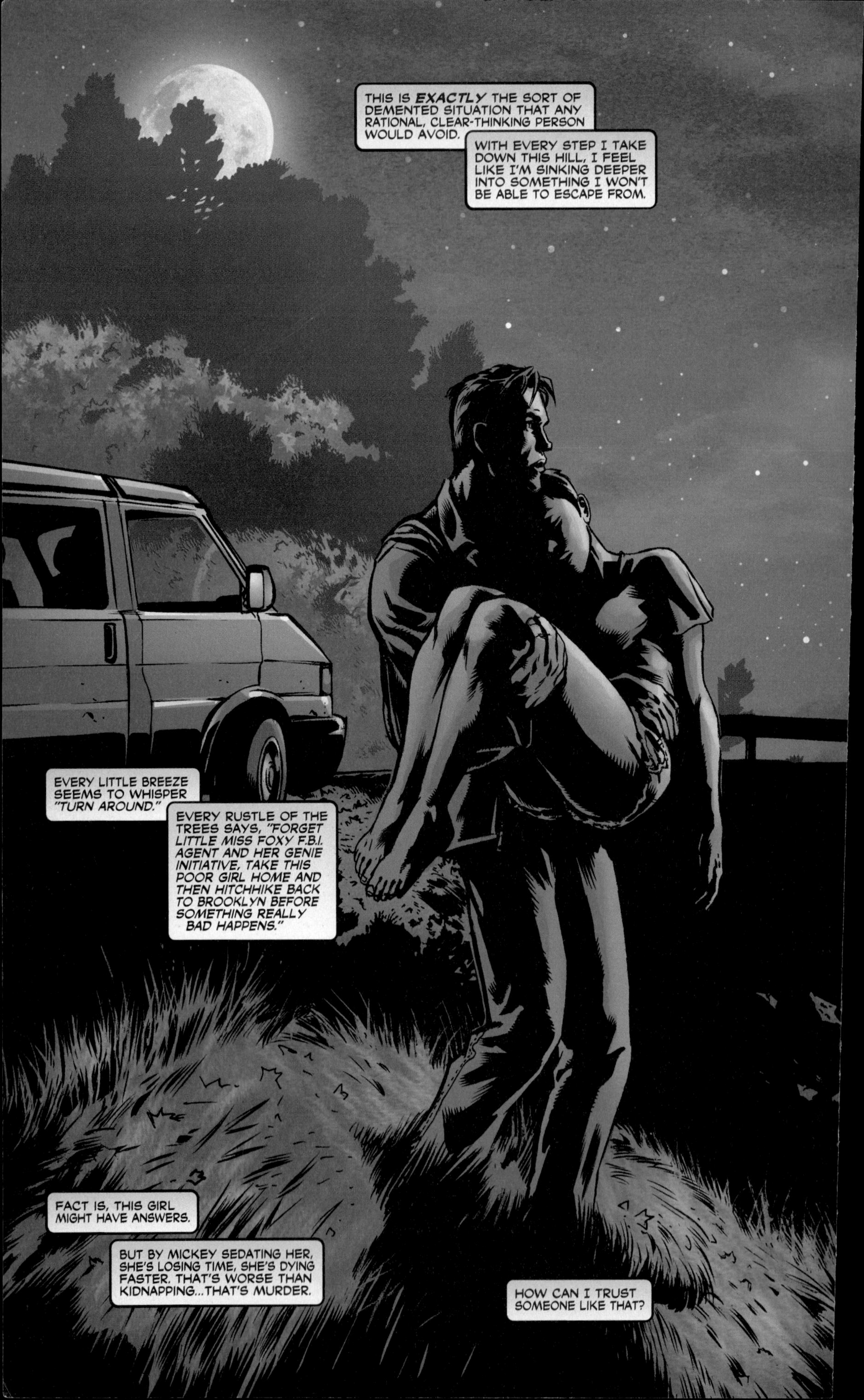
THIS IS *EXACTLY* THE SORT OF DEMENTED SITUATION THAT ANY RATIONAL, CLEAR-THINKING PERSON WOULD AVOID.
WITH EVERY STEP I TAKE DOWN THIS HILL, I FEEL LIKE I'M SINKING DEEPER INTO SOMETHING I WON'T BE ABLE TO ESCAPE FROM.
EVERY LITTLE BREEZE SEEMS TO WHISPER *"TURN AROUND."*
EVERY RUSTLE OF THE TREES SAYS, *"FORGET LITTLE MISS FOXY F.B.I. AGENT AND HER GENIE INITIATIVE, TAKE THIS POOR GIRL HOME AND THEN HITCHHIKE BACK TO BROOKLYN BEFORE SOMETHING REALLY BAD HAPPENS."*
FACT IS, THIS GIRL MIGHT HAVE ANSWERS.
BUT BY MICKEY SEDATING HER, SHE'S LOSING TIME, SHE'S DYING FASTER. THAT'S WORSE THAN KIDNAPPING...THAT'S MURDER.
HOW CAN I TRUST SOMEONE LIKE THAT?

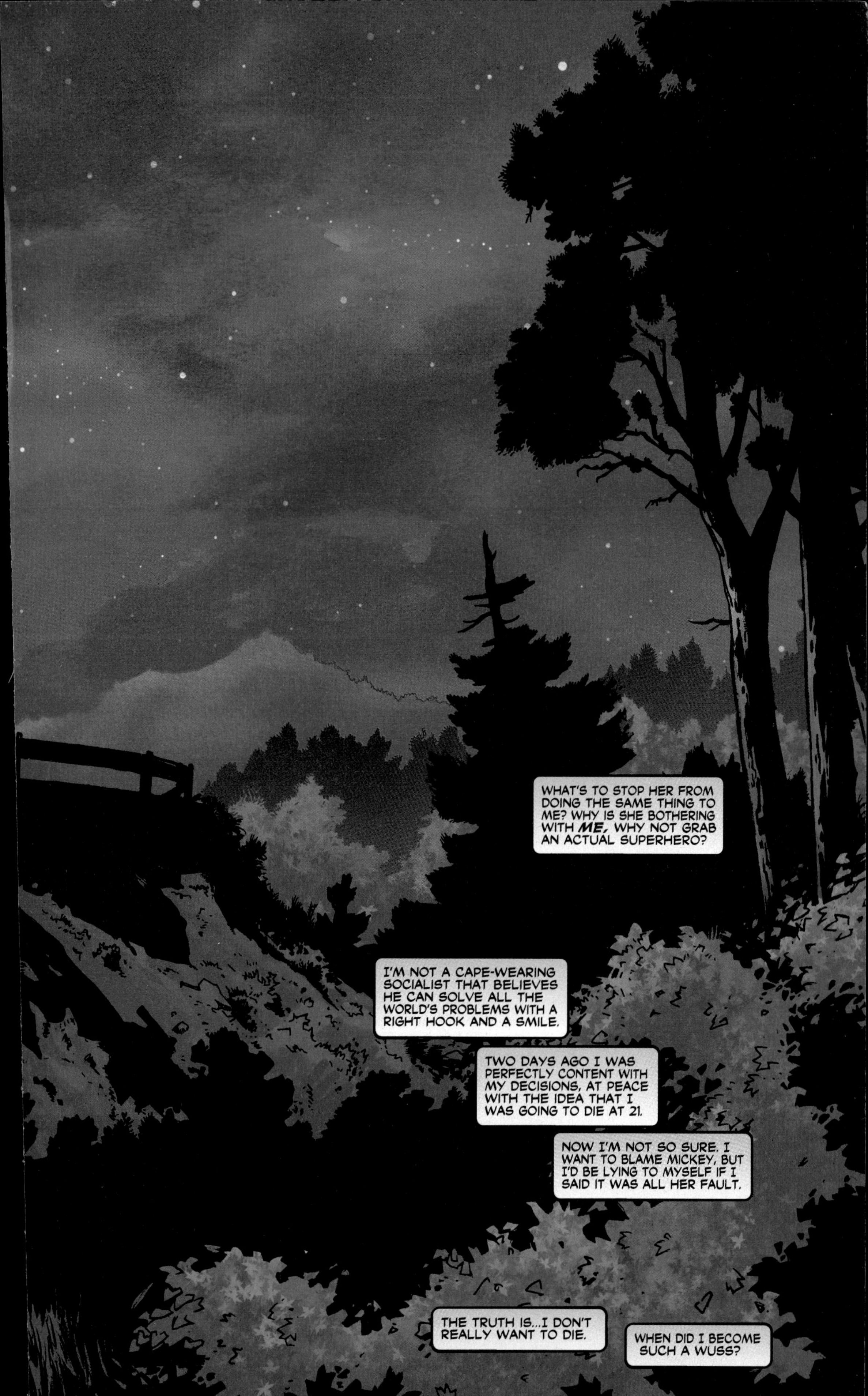
WHAT'S TO STOP HER FROM DOING THE SAME THING TO ME? WHY IS SHE BOTHERING WITH ME, WHY NOT GRAB AN ACTUAL SUPERHERO?
I'M NOT A CAPE-WEARING SOCIALIST THAT BELIEVES HE CAN SOLVE ALL THE WORLD'S PROBLEMS WITH A RIGHT HOOK AND A SMILE.
TWO DAYS AGO I WAS PERFECTLY CONTENT WITH MY DECISIONS, AT PEACE WITH THE IDEA THAT I WAS GOING TO DIE AT 21.
NOW I'M NOT SO SURE. I WANT TO BLAME MICKEY, BUT I'D BE LYING TO MYSELF IF I SAID IT WAS ALL HER FAULT.
THE TRUTH IS...I DON'T REALLY WANT TO DIE.
WHEN DID I BECOME SUCH A WUSS?

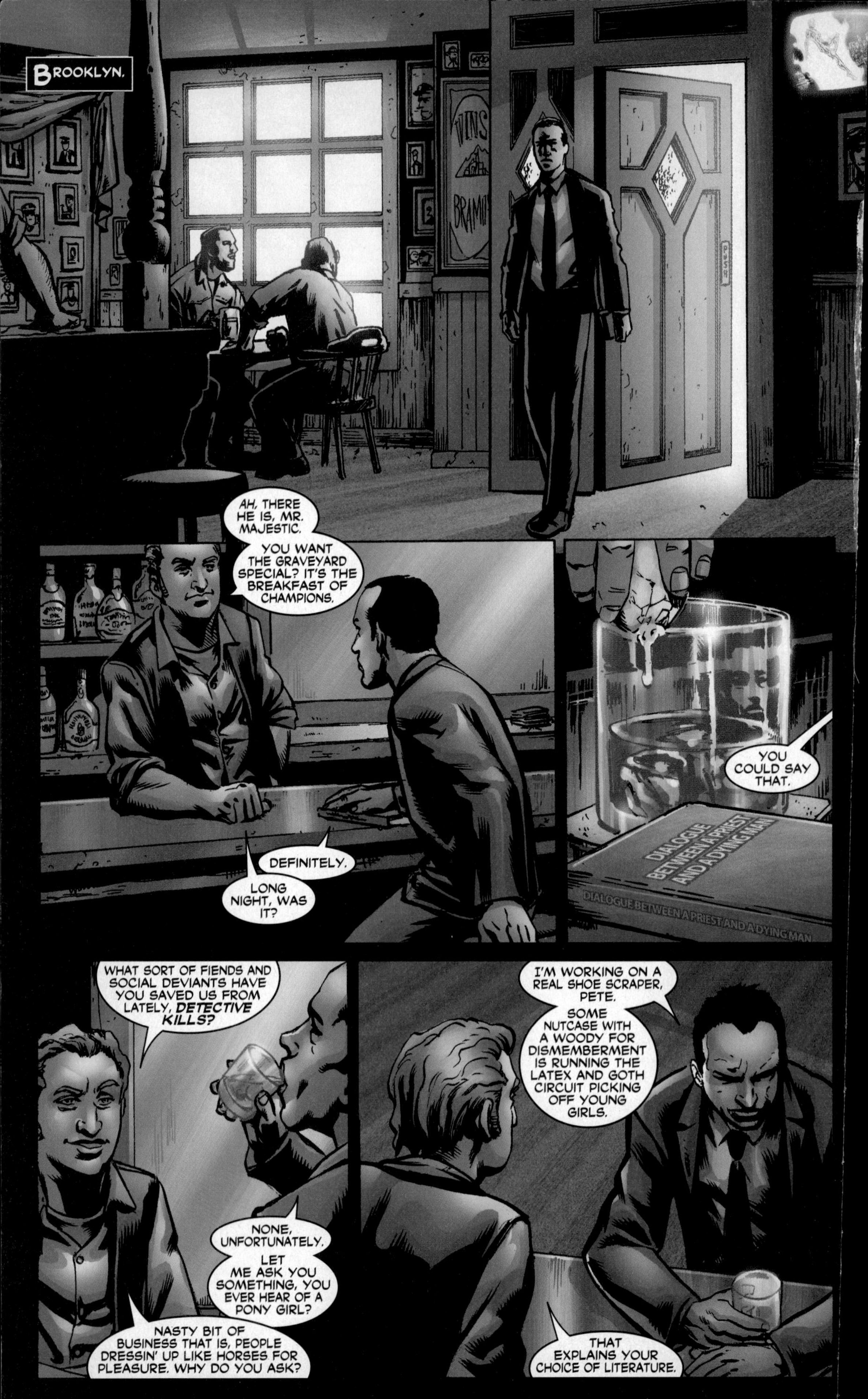

BROOKLYN.
AH, THERE HE IS, MR. MAJESTIC.
YOU WANT THE GRAVEYARD SPECIAL? IT'S THE BREAKFAST OF CHAMPIONS.
DEFINITELY.
LONG NIGHT, WAS IT?
YOU COULD SAY THAT.
DIALOGUE BETWEEN A PRIEST AND A DYING MAN
DIALOGUE BETWEEN A PRIEST AND A DYING MAN
WHAT SORT OF FIENDS AND SOCIAL DEVIANTS HAVE YOU SAVED US FROM LATELY, DETECTIVE KILLS?
NONE, UNFORTUNATELY.
LET ME ASK YOU SOMETHING, YOU EVER HEAR OF A PONY GIRL?
NASTY BIT OF BUSINESS THAT IS, PEOPLE DRESSIN' UP LIKE HORSES FOR PLEASURE. WHY DO YOU ASK?
I'M WORKING ON A REAL SHOE SCRAPER, PETE.
SOME NUTCASE WITH A WOODY FOR DISMEMBERMENT IS RUNNING THE LATEX AND GOTH CIRCUIT PICKING OFF YOUNG GIRLS.
THAT EXPLAINS YOUR CHOICE OF LITERATURE.

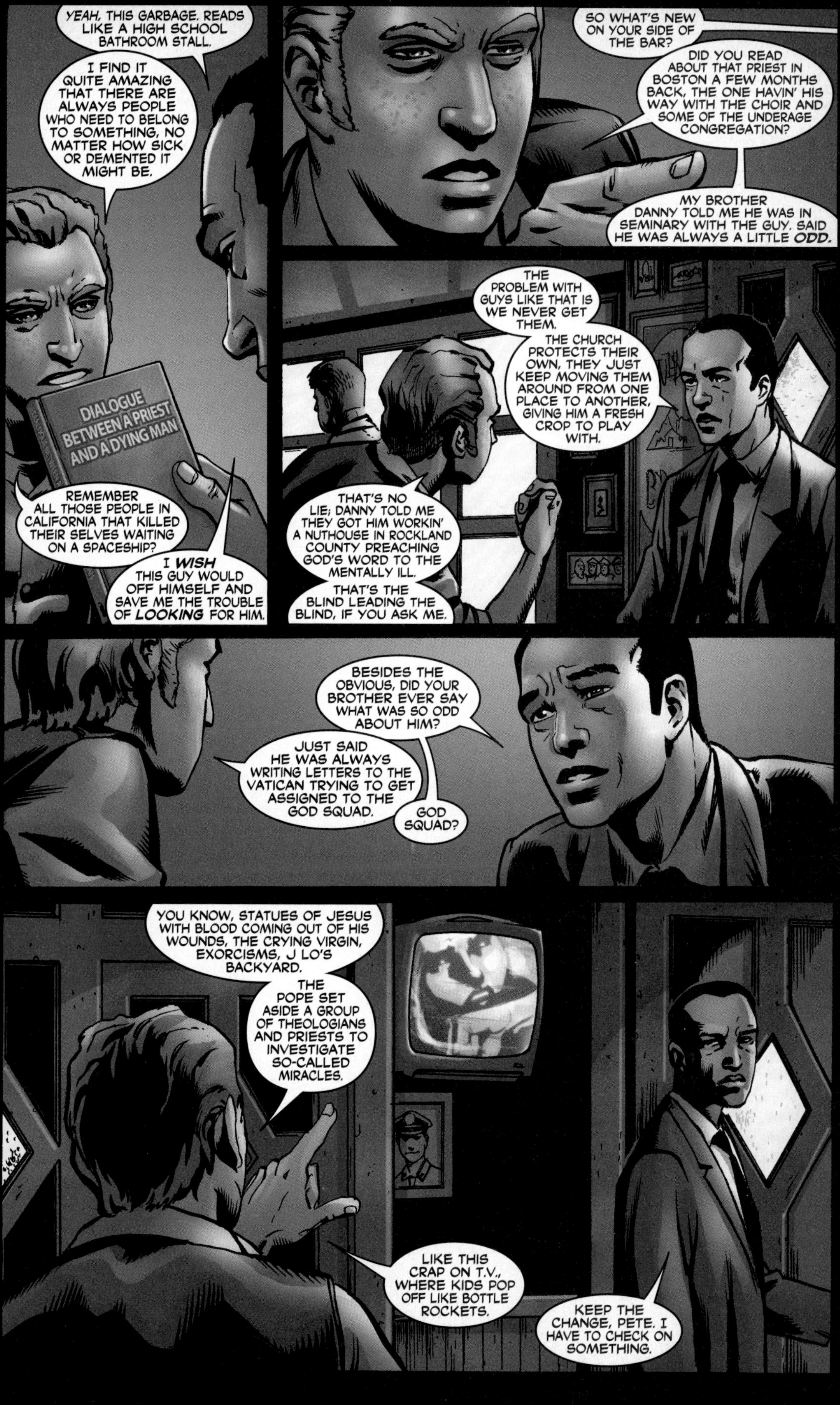
YEAH, THIS GARBAGE. READS LIKE A HIGH SCHOOL BATHROOM STALL.
I FIND IT QUITE AMAZING THAT THERE ARE ALWAYS PEOPLE WHO NEED TO BELONG TO SOMETHING, NO MATTER HOW SICK OR DEMENTED IT MIGHT BE.
DIALOGUE BETWEEN A PRIEST AND A DYING MAN
REMEMBER ALL THOSE PEOPLE IN CALIFORNIA THAT KILLED THEIR SELVES WAITING ON A SPACESHIP?
I WISH THIS GUY WOULD OFF HIMSELF AND SAVE ME THE TROUBLE OF LOOKING FOR HIM.
SO WHAT'S NEW ON YOUR SIDE OF THE BAR?
DID YOU READ ABOUT THAT PRIEST IN BOSTON A FEW MONTHS BACK, THE ONE HAVIN' HIS WAY WITH THE CHOIR AND SOME OF THE UNDERAGE CONGREGATION?
MY BROTHER DANNY TOLD ME HE WAS IN SEMINARY WITH THE GUY. SAID HE WAS ALWAYS A LITTLE ODD.
THE PROBLEM WITH GUYS LIKE THAT IS WE NEVER GET THEM.
THE CHURCH PROTECTS THEIR OWN, THEY JUST KEEP MOVING THEM AROUND FROM ONE PLACE TO ANOTHER, GIVING HIM A FRESH CROP TO PLAY WITH.
THAT'S NO LIE; DANNY TOLD ME THEY GOT HIM WORKIN' A NUTHOUSE IN ROCKLAND COUNTY PREACHING GOD'S WORD TO THE MENTALLY ILL.
THAT'S THE BLIND LEADING THE BLIND, IF YOU ASK ME.
BESIDES THE OBVIOUS, DID YOUR BROTHER EVER SAY WHAT WAS SO ODD ABOUT HIM?
JUST SAID HE WAS ALWAYS WRITING LETTERS TO THE VATICAN TRYING TO GET ASSIGNED TO THE GOD SQUAD.
GOD SQUAD?
YOU KNOW, STATUES OF JESUS WITH BLOOD COMING OUT OF HIS WOUNDS, THE CRYING VIRGIN, EXORCISMS, J LO'S BACKYARD.
THE POPE SET ASIDE A GROUP OF THEOLOGIANS AND PRIESTS TO INVESTIGATE SO-CALLED MIRACLES.
LIKE THIS CRAP ON T.V., WHERE KIDS POP OFF LIKE BOTTLE ROCKETS.
KEEP THE CHANGE, PETE. I HAVE TO CHECK ON SOMETHING.

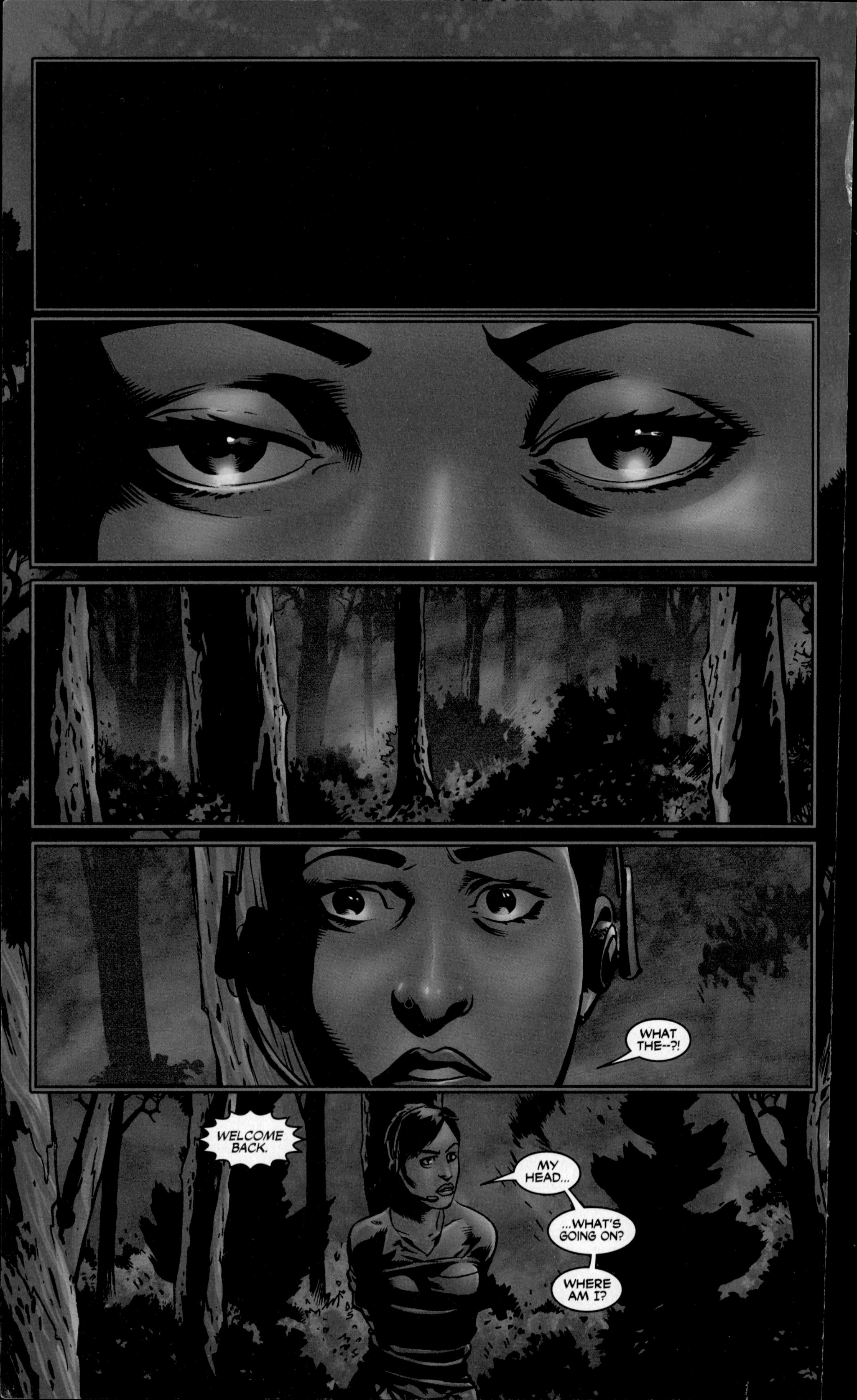
WHAT THE--?!
WELCOME BACK.
MY HEAD...
...WHAT'S GOING ON?
WHERE AM I?

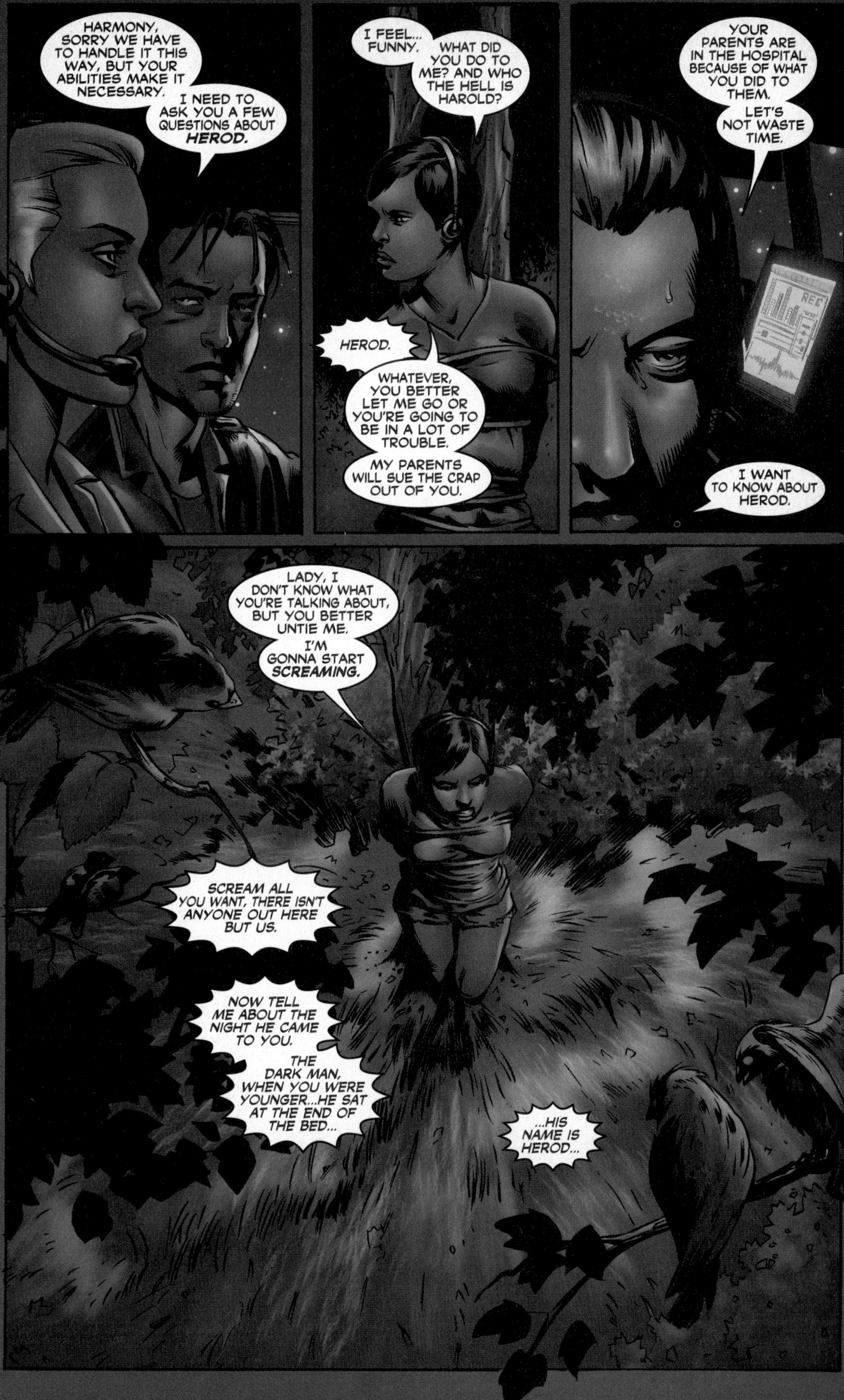
HARMONY, SORRY WE HAVE TO HANDLE IT THIS WAY, BUT YOUR ABILITIES MAKE IT NECESSARY.
I NEED TO ASK YOU A FEW QUESTIONS ABOUT HEROD.
I FEEL... FUNNY.
WHAT DID YOU DO TO ME? AND WHO THE HELL IS HAROLD?
HEROD.
WHATEVER, YOU BETTER LET ME GO OR YOU'RE GOING TO BE IN A LOT OF TROUBLE.
MY PARENTS WILL SUE THE CRAP OUT OF YOU.
YOUR PARENTS ARE IN THE HOSPITAL BECAUSE OF WHAT YOU DID TO THEM.
LET'S NOT WASTE TIME.
REC
I WANT TO KNOW ABOUT HEROD.
LADY, I DON'T KNOW WHAT YOU'RE TALKING ABOUT, BUT YOU BETTER UNTIE ME.
I'M GONNA START SCREAMING.
SCREAM ALL YOU WANT, THERE ISN'T ANYONE OUT HERE BUT US.
NOW TELL ME ABOUT THE NIGHT HE CAME TO YOU.
THE DARK MAN, WHEN YOU WERE YOUNGER...HE SAT AT THE END OF THE BED...
...HIS NAME IS HEROD...

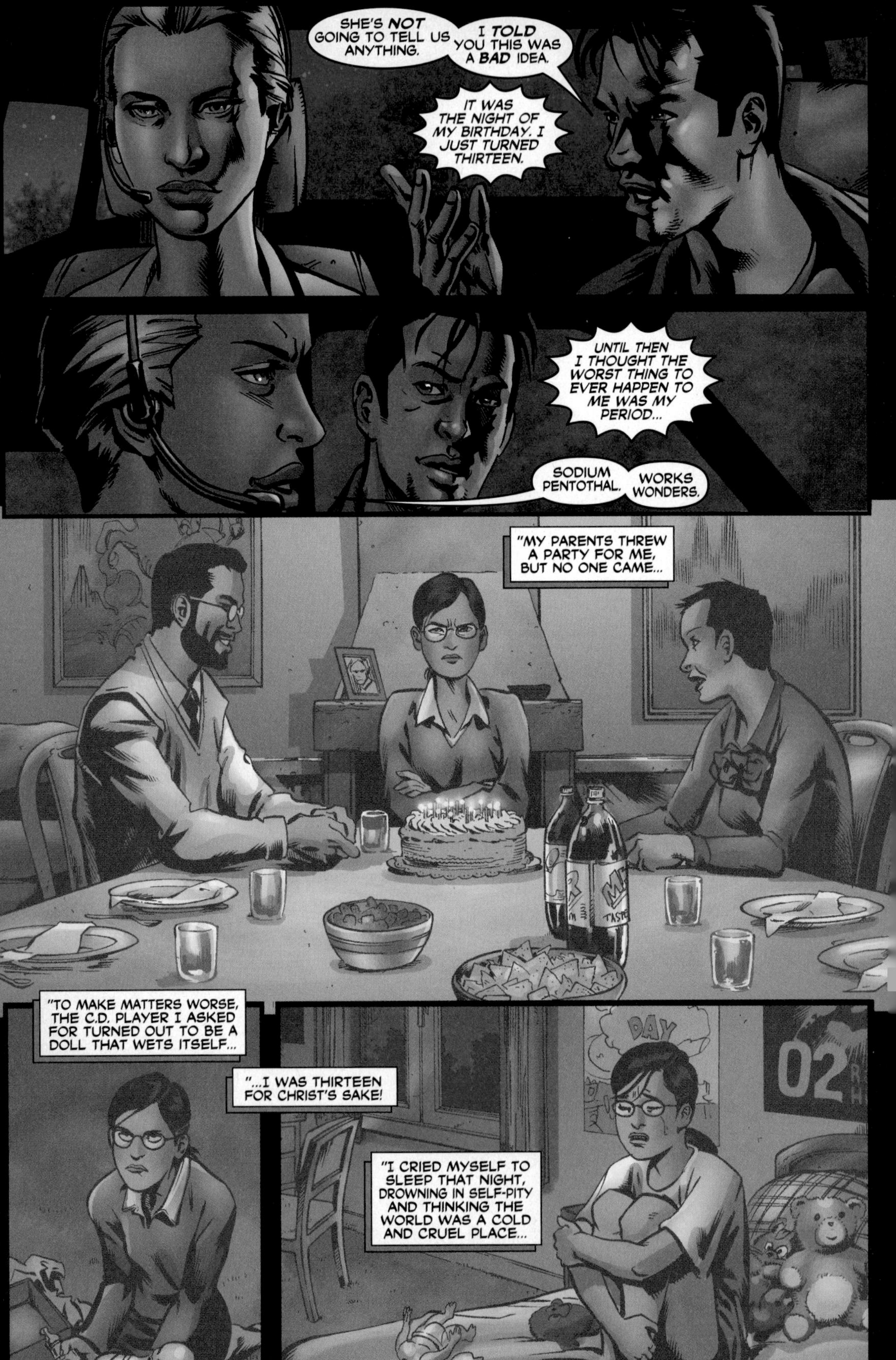
SHE'S NOT GOING TO TELL US ANYTHING.
I TOLD YOU THIS WAS A BAD IDEA.
IT WAS THE NIGHT OF MY BIRTHDAY. I JUST TURNED THIRTEEN.
UNTIL THEN I THOUGHT THE WORST THING TO EVER HAPPEN TO ME WAS MY PERIOD...
SODIUM PENTOTHAL.
WORKS WONDERS.
"MY PARENTS THREW A PARTY FOR ME, BUT NO ONE CAME...
"TO MAKE MATTERS WORSE, THE C.D. PLAYER I ASKED FOR TURNED OUT TO BE A DOLL THAT WETS ITSELF...
"...I WAS THIRTEEN FOR CHRIST'S SAKE!
"I CRIED MYSELF TO SLEEP THAT NIGHT, DROWNING IN SELF-PITY AND THINKING THE WORLD WAS A COLD AND CRUEL PLACE...

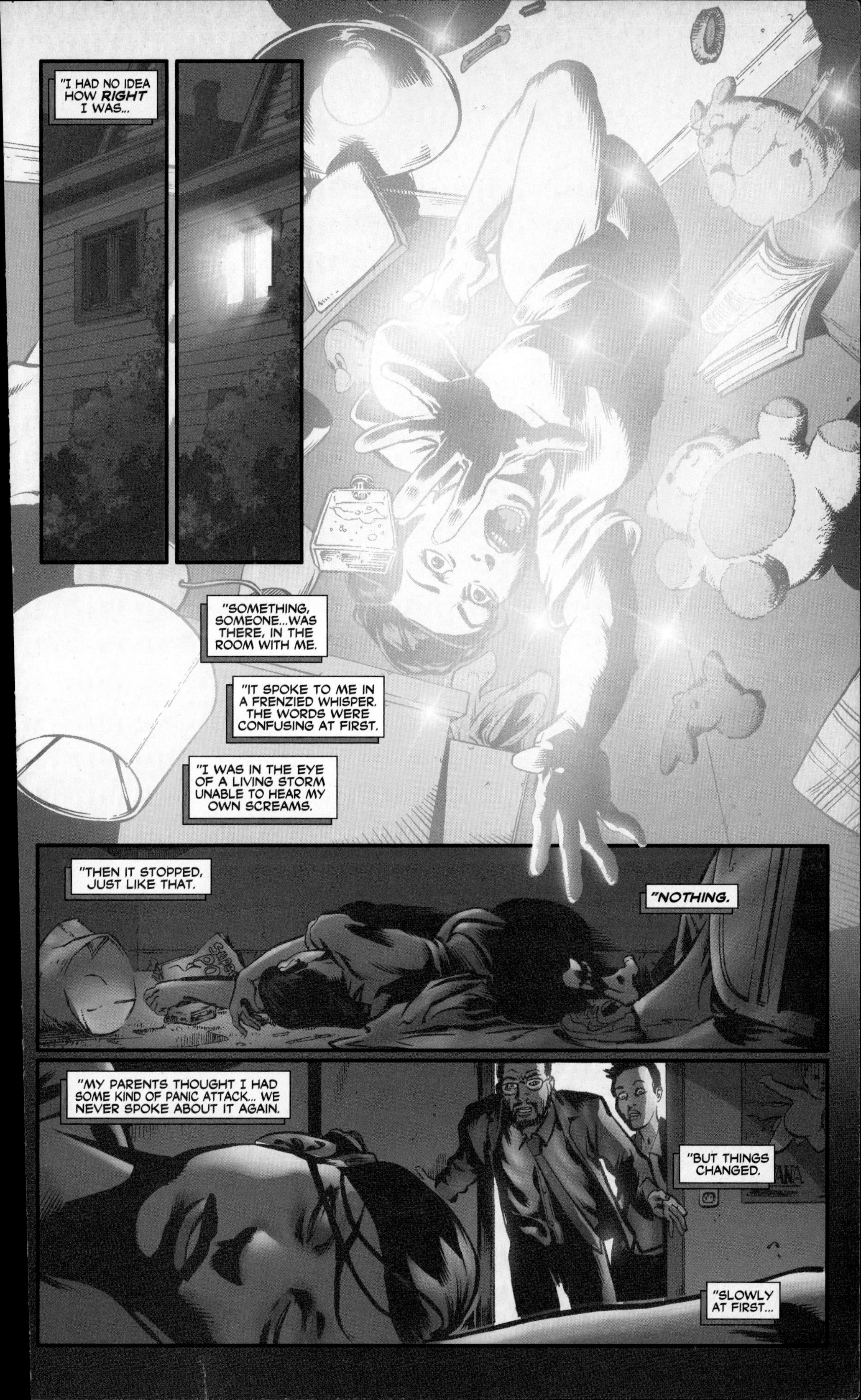
"I HAD NO IDEA HOW **RIGHT** I WAS...
"SOMETHING, SOMEONE...WAS THERE, IN THE ROOM WITH ME.
"IT SPOKE TO ME IN A FRENZIED WHISPER. THE WORDS WERE CONFUSING AT FIRST.
"I WAS IN THE EYE OF A LIVING STORM UNABLE TO HEAR MY OWN SCREAMS.
"THEN IT STOPPED, JUST LIKE THAT.
"NOTHING.
"MY PARENTS THOUGHT I HAD SOME KIND OF PANIC ATTACK... WE NEVER SPOKE ABOUT IT AGAIN.
"BUT THINGS CHANGED.
"SLOWLY AT FIRST...

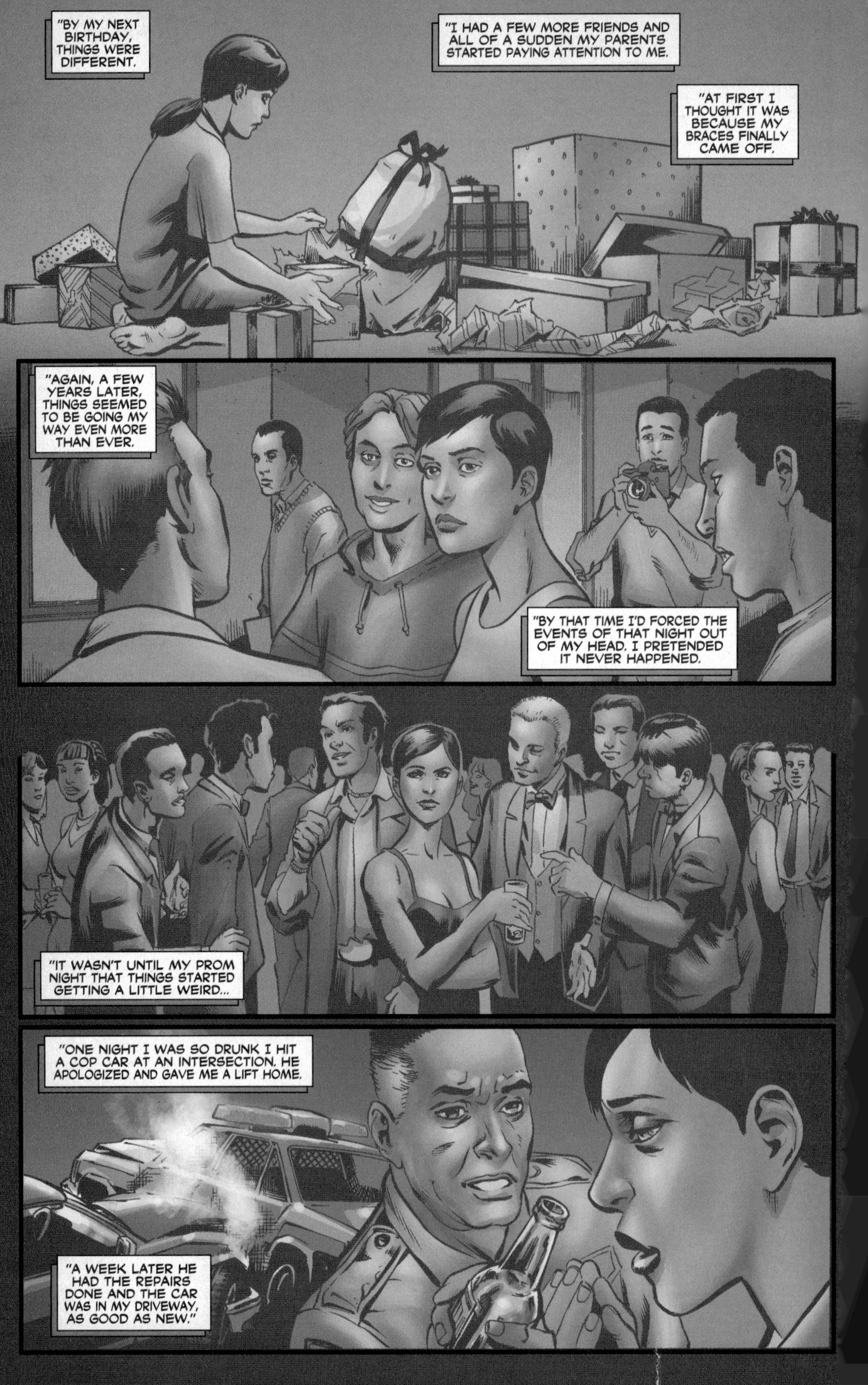
"BY MY NEXT BIRTHDAY, THINGS WERE DIFFERENT.
"I HAD A FEW MORE FRIENDS AND ALL OF A SUDDEN MY PARENTS STARTED PAYING ATTENTION TO ME.
"AT FIRST I THOUGHT IT WAS BECAUSE MY BRACES FINALLY CAME OFF.
"AGAIN, A FEW YEARS LATER, THINGS SEEMED TO BE GOING MY WAY EVEN MORE THAN EVER.
"BY THAT TIME I'D FORCED THE EVENTS OF THAT NIGHT OUT OF MY HEAD. I PRETENDED IT NEVER HAPPENED.
"IT WASN'T UNTIL MY PROM NIGHT THAT THINGS STARTED GETTING A LITTLE WEIRD...
"ONE NIGHT I WAS SO DRUNK I HIT A COP CAR AT AN INTERSECTION. HE APOLOGIZED AND GAVE ME A LIFT HOME.
"A WEEK LATER HE HAD THE REPAIRS DONE AND THE CAR WAS IN MY DRIVEWAY, AS GOOD AS NEW."

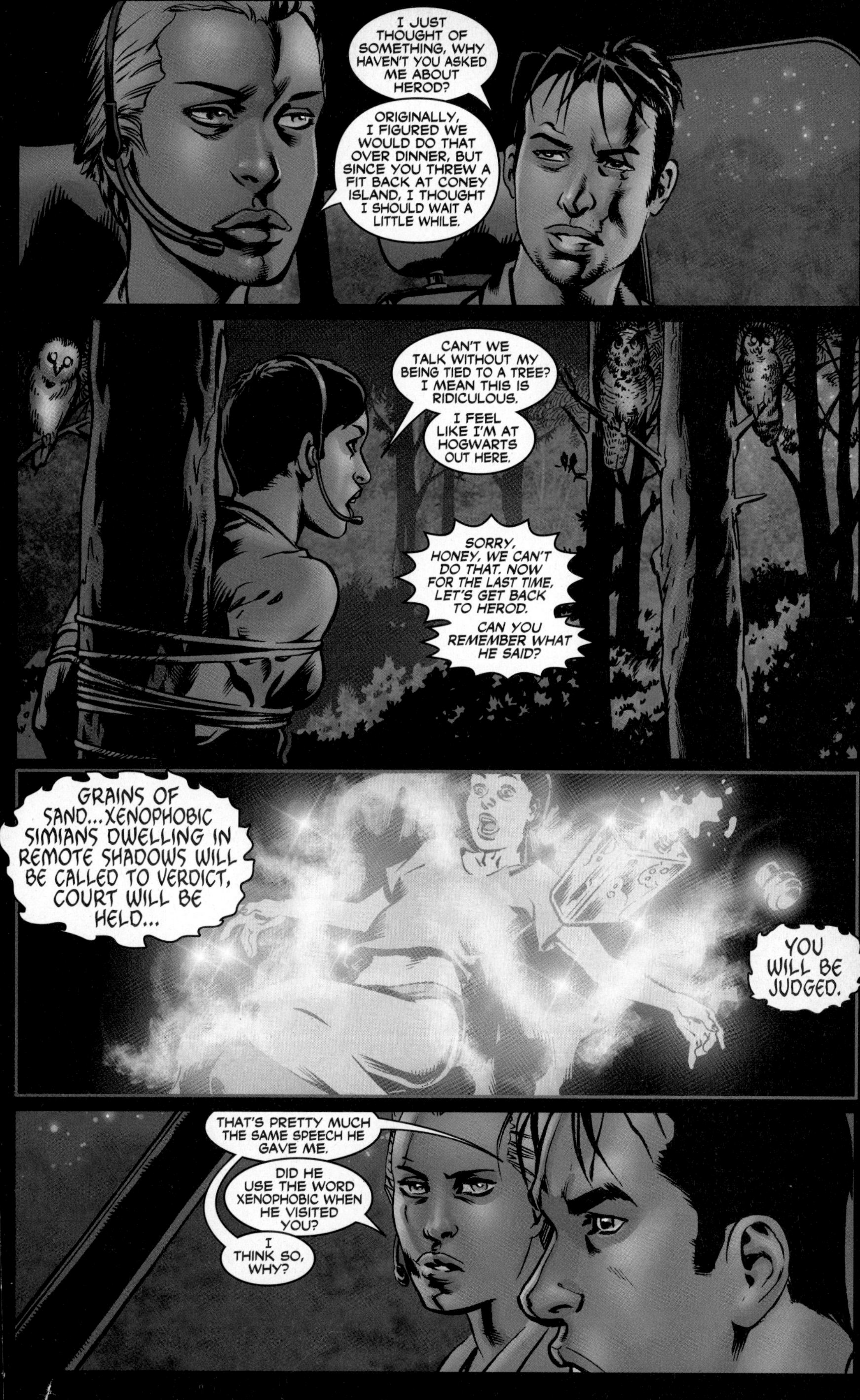

I JUST THOUGHT OF SOMETHING, WHY HAVEN'T YOU ASKED ME ABOUT HEROD?
ORIGINALLY, I FIGURED WE WOULD DO THAT OVER DINNER, BUT SINCE YOU THREW A FIT BACK AT CONEY ISLAND, I THOUGHT I SHOULD WAIT A LITTLE WHILE.
CAN'T WE TALK WITHOUT MY BEING TIED TO A TREE? I MEAN THIS IS RIDICULOUS.
I FEEL LIKE I'M AT HOGWARTS OUT HERE.
SORRY, HONEY, WE CAN'T DO THAT. NOW FOR THE LAST TIME, LET'S GET BACK TO HEROD.
CAN YOU REMEMBER WHAT HE SAID?
GRAINS OF SAND...XENOPHOBIC SIMIANS DWELLING IN REMOTE SHADOWS WILL BE CALLED TO VERDICT, COURT WILL BE HELD...
YOU WILL BE JUDGED.
THAT'S PRETTY MUCH THE SAME SPEECH HE GAVE ME.
DID HE USE THE WORD XENOPHOBIC WHEN HE VISITED YOU?
I THINK SO, WHY?

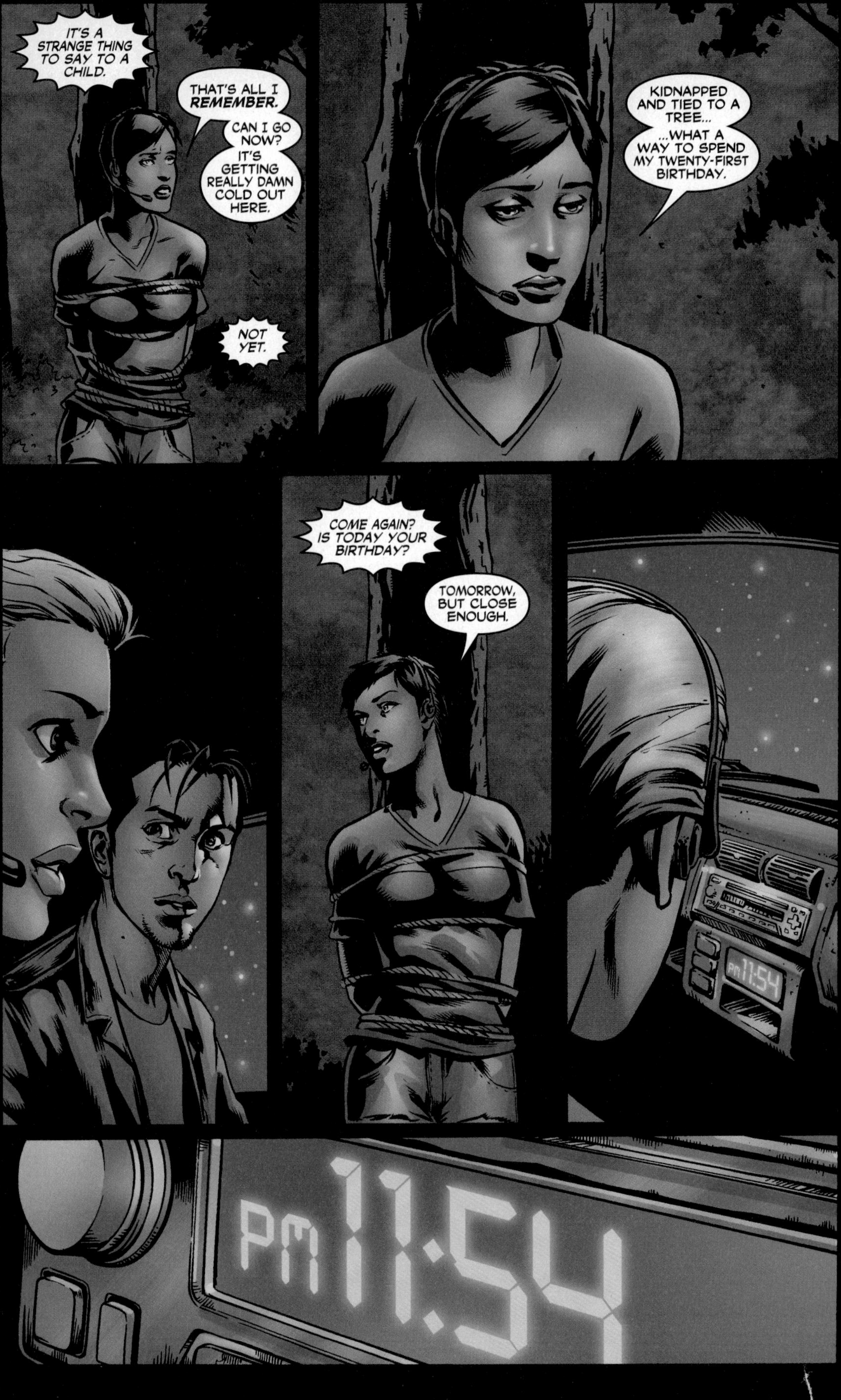
IT'S A STRANGE THING TO SAY TO A CHILD.
THAT'S ALL I REMEMBER.
CAN I GO NOW? IT'S GETTING REALLY DAMN COLD OUT HERE.
NOT YET.
KIDNAPPED AND TIED TO A TREE...
...WHAT A WAY TO SPEND MY TWENTY-FIRST BIRTHDAY.
COME AGAIN? IS TODAY YOUR BIRTHDAY?
TOMORROW, BUT CLOSE ENOUGH.
PM 11:54
PM 11:54

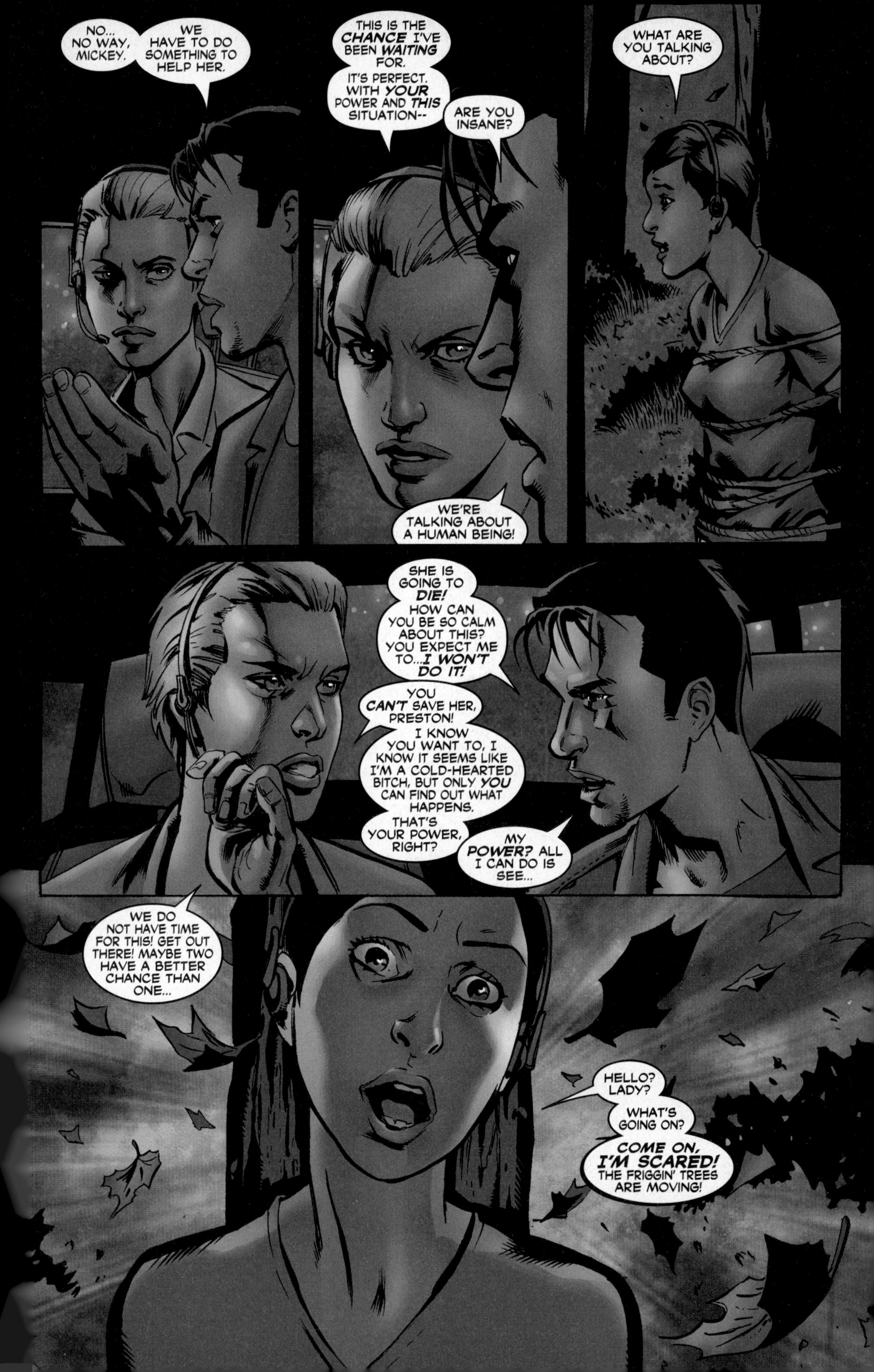
NO... NO WAY, MICKEY.
WE HAVE TO DO SOMETHING TO HELP HER.
THIS IS THE **CHANCE** I'VE BEEN **WAITING** FOR.
IT'S PERFECT. WITH **YOUR** POWER AND **THIS** SITUATION--
ARE YOU INSANE?
WE'RE TALKING ABOUT A HUMAN BEING!
WHAT ARE YOU TALKING ABOUT?
SHE IS GOING TO **DIE!**
HOW CAN YOU BE SO CALM ABOUT THIS? YOU EXPECT ME TO...**I WON'T DO IT!**
YOU **CAN'T** SAVE HER, PRESTON!
I KNOW YOU WANT TO, I KNOW IT SEEMS LIKE I'M A COLD-HEARTED BITCH, BUT ONLY **YOU** CAN FIND OUT WHAT HAPPENS.
THAT'S YOUR POWER, RIGHT?
MY **POWER?** ALL I CAN DO IS SEE...
WE DO NOT HAVE TIME FOR THIS! GET OUT THERE! MAYBE TWO HAVE A BETTER CHANCE THAN ONE...
HELLO? LADY?
WHAT'S GOING ON?
COME ON, I'M SCARED! THE FRIGGIN' TREES ARE MOVING!

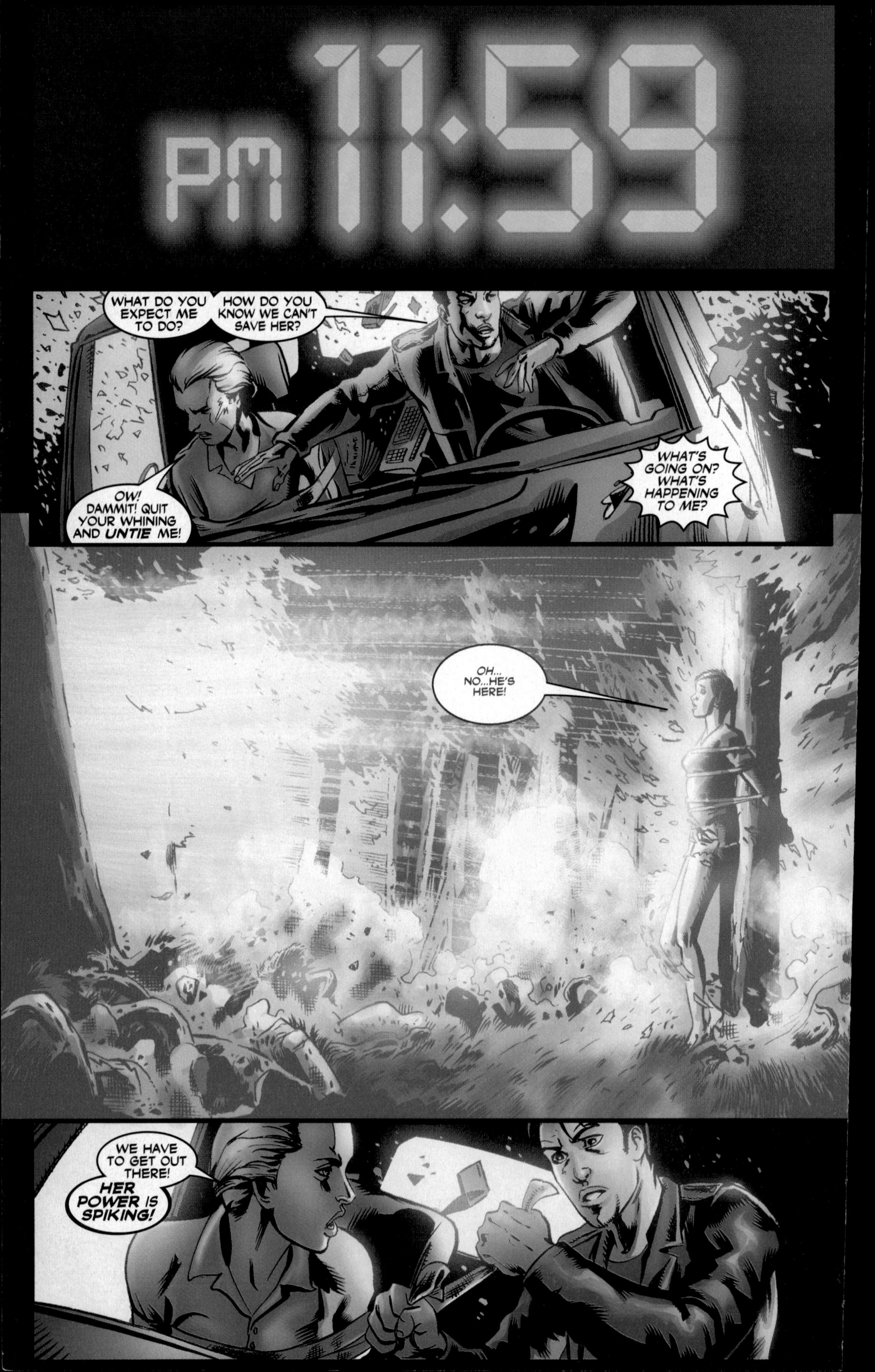
PM 11:59
WHAT DO YOU EXPECT ME TO DO?
HOW DO YOU KNOW WE CAN'T SAVE HER?
OW! DAMMIT! QUIT YOUR WHINING AND UNTIE ME!
WHAT'S GOING ON? WHAT'S HAPPENING TO ME?
OH... NO...HE'S HERE!
WE HAVE TO GET OUT THERE! HER POWER IS SPIKING!

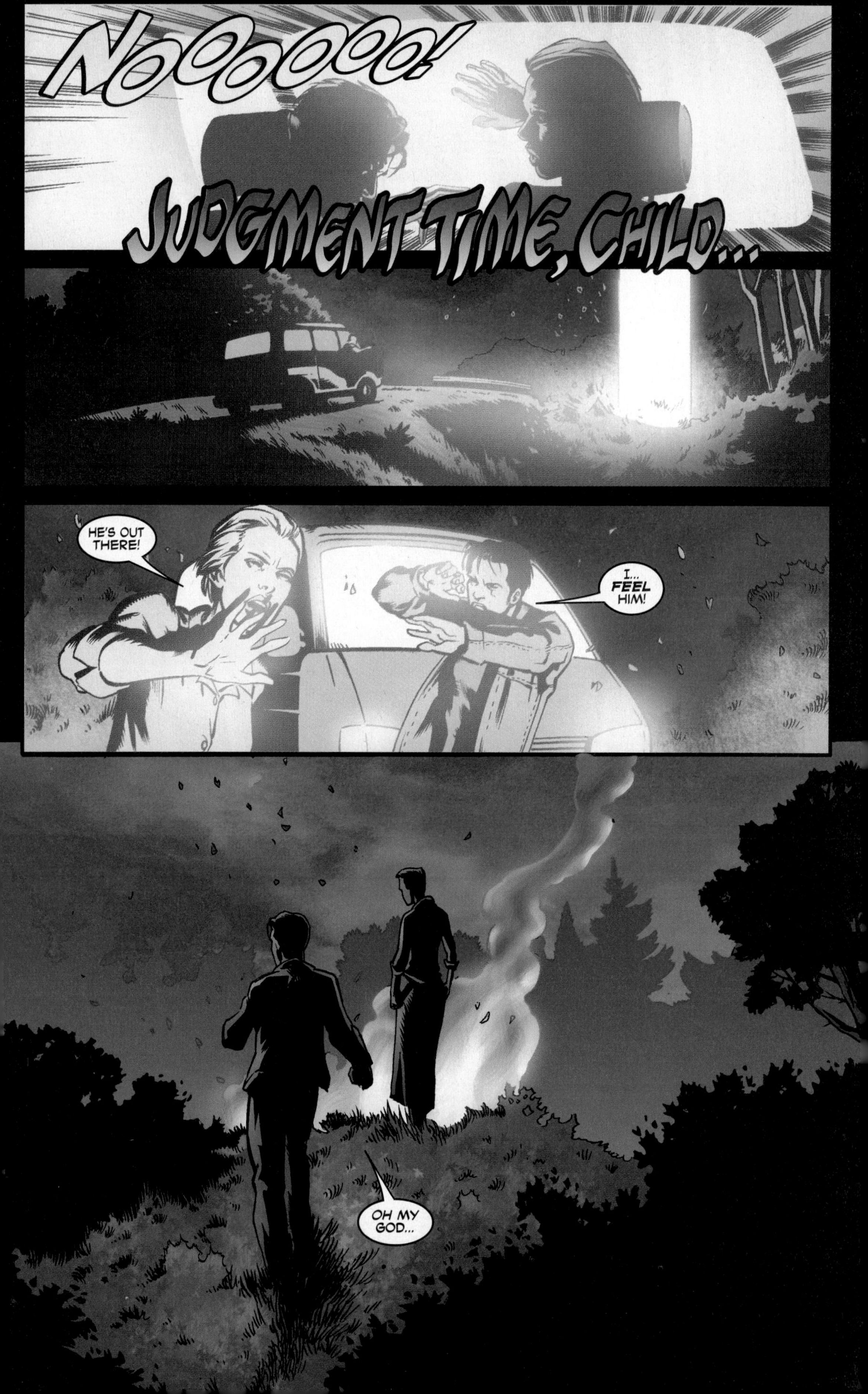
NOOOOOOO!
JUDGMENT TIME, CHILD...
HE'S OUT THERE!
I... FEEL HIM!
OH MY GOD...

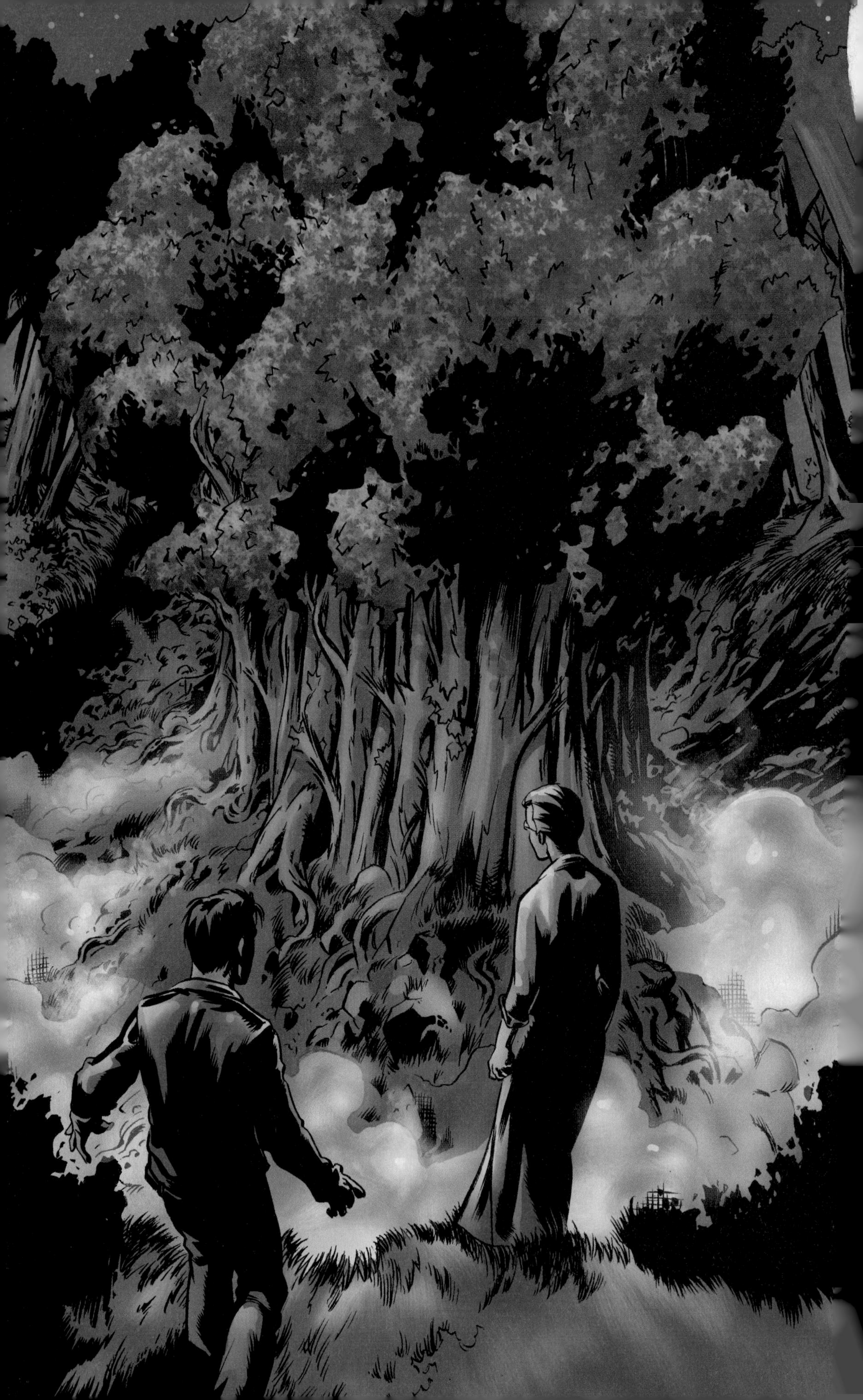

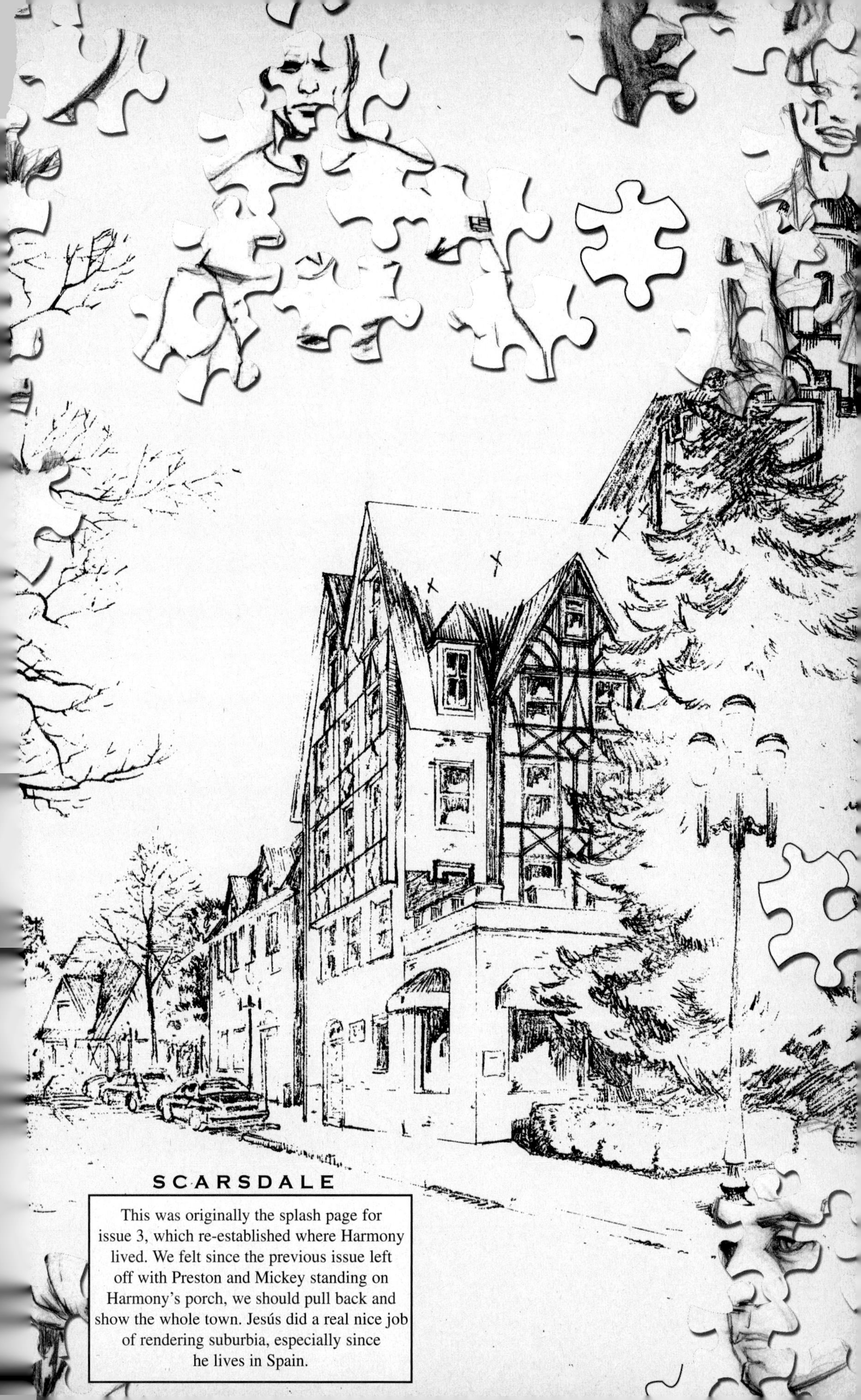

SCARSDALE

This was originally the splash page for issue 3, which re-established where Harmony lived. We felt since the previous issue left off with Preston and Mickey standing on Harmony's porch, we should pull back and show the whole town. Jesús did a real nice job of rendering suburbia, especially since he lives in Spain.

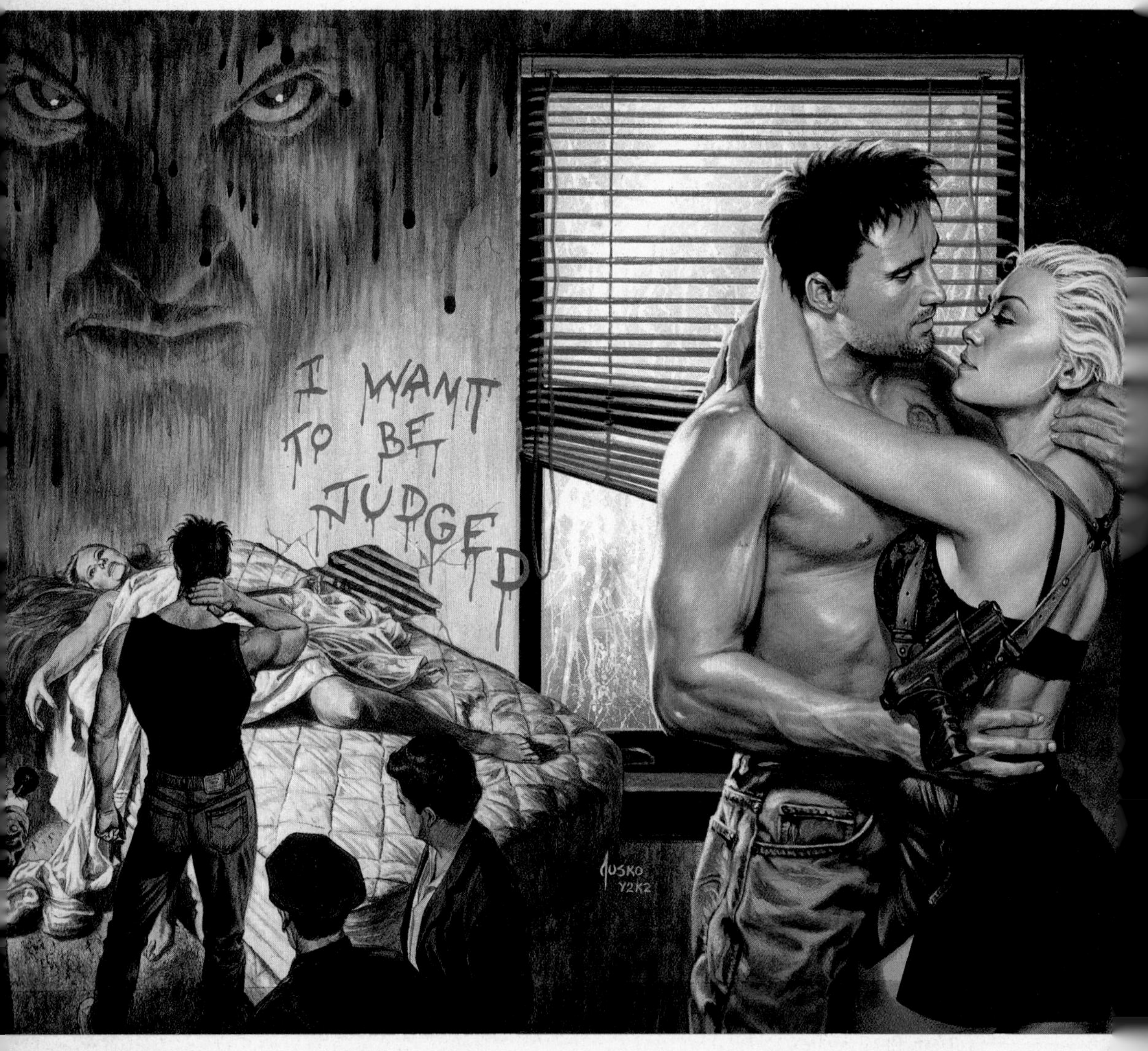
I WANT TO BE JUDGED
JUSKO Y2K2

DON'T STAND ALONE IN THESE STRANGEST OF TIMES

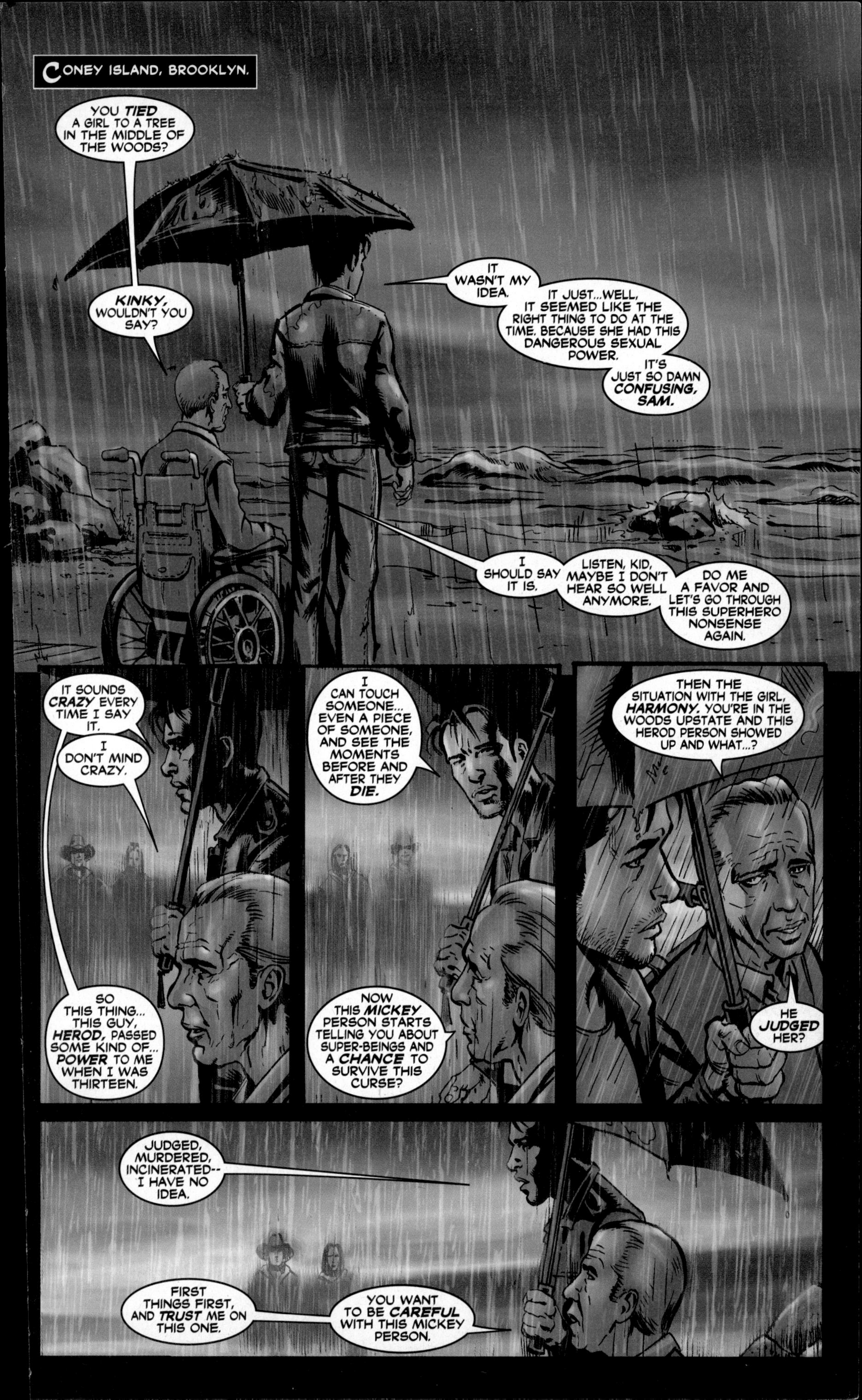
CONEY ISLAND, BROOKLYN.
YOU TIED A GIRL TO A TREE IN THE MIDDLE OF THE WOODS?
KINKY, WOULDN'T YOU SAY?
IT WASN'T MY IDEA.
IT JUST...WELL, IT SEEMED LIKE THE RIGHT THING TO DO AT THE TIME. BECAUSE SHE HAD THIS DANGEROUS SEXUAL POWER.
IT'S JUST SO DAMN CONFUSING, SAM.
I SHOULD SAY IT IS.
LISTEN, KID, MAYBE I DON'T HEAR SO WELL ANYMORE.
DO ME A FAVOR AND LET'S GO THROUGH THIS SUPERHERO NONSENSE AGAIN.
IT SOUNDS CRAZY EVERY TIME I SAY IT.
I DON'T MIND CRAZY.
SO THIS THING... THIS GUY, HEROD, PASSED SOME KIND OF... POWER TO ME WHEN I WAS THIRTEEN.
I CAN TOUCH SOMEONE... EVEN A PIECE OF SOMEONE, AND SEE THE MOMENTS BEFORE AND AFTER THEY DIE.
NOW THIS MICKEY PERSON STARTS TELLING YOU ABOUT SUPER-BEINGS AND A CHANCE TO SURVIVE THIS CURSE?
THEN THE SITUATION WITH THE GIRL, HARMONY. YOU'RE IN THE WOODS UPSTATE AND THIS HEROD PERSON SHOWED UP AND WHAT...?
HE JUDGED HER?
JUDGED, MURDERED, INCINERATED-- I HAVE NO IDEA.
FIRST THINGS FIRST, AND TRUST ME ON THIS ONE.
YOU WANT TO BE CAREFUL WITH THIS MICKEY PERSON.

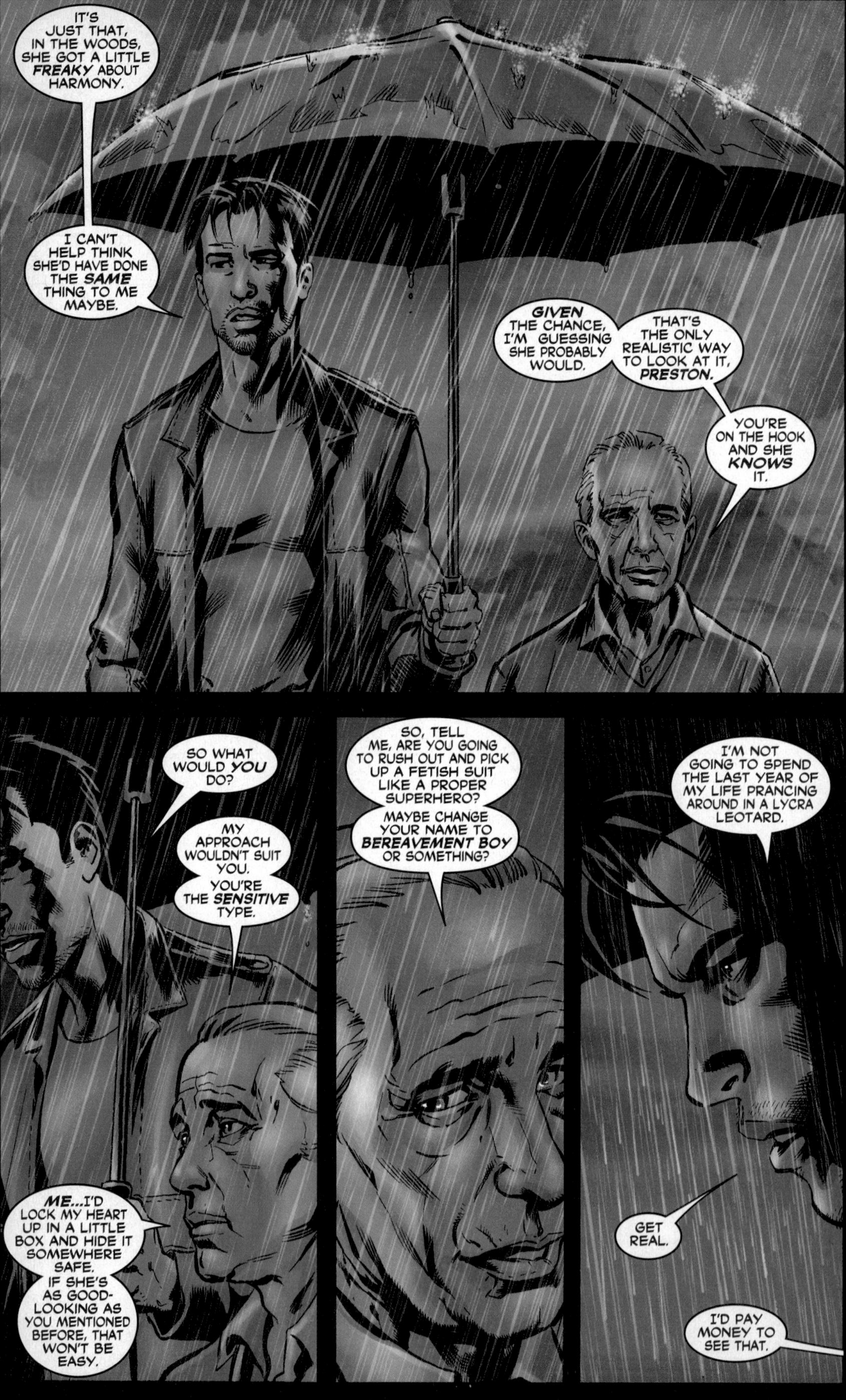
IT'S JUST THAT, IN THE WOODS, SHE GOT A LITTLE FREAKY ABOUT HARMONY.
I CAN'T HELP THINK SHE'D HAVE DONE THE SAME THING TO ME MAYBE.
GIVEN THE CHANCE, I'M GUESSING SHE PROBABLY WOULD.
THAT'S THE ONLY REALISTIC WAY TO LOOK AT IT, PRESTON.
YOU'RE ON THE HOOK AND SHE KNOWS IT.
SO WHAT WOULD YOU DO?
MY APPROACH WOULDN'T SUIT YOU. YOU'RE THE SENSITIVE TYPE.
ME...I'D LOCK MY HEART UP IN A LITTLE BOX AND HIDE IT SOMEWHERE SAFE.
IF SHE'S AS GOOD-LOOKING AS YOU MENTIONED BEFORE, THAT WON'T BE EASY.
SO, TELL ME, ARE YOU GOING TO RUSH OUT AND PICK UP A FETISH SUIT LIKE A PROPER SUPERHERO?
MAYBE CHANGE YOUR NAME TO BEREAVEMENT BOY OR SOMETHING?
I'M NOT GOING TO SPEND THE LAST YEAR OF MY LIFE PRANCING AROUND IN A LYCRA LEOTARD.
GET REAL.
I'D PAY MONEY TO SEE THAT.

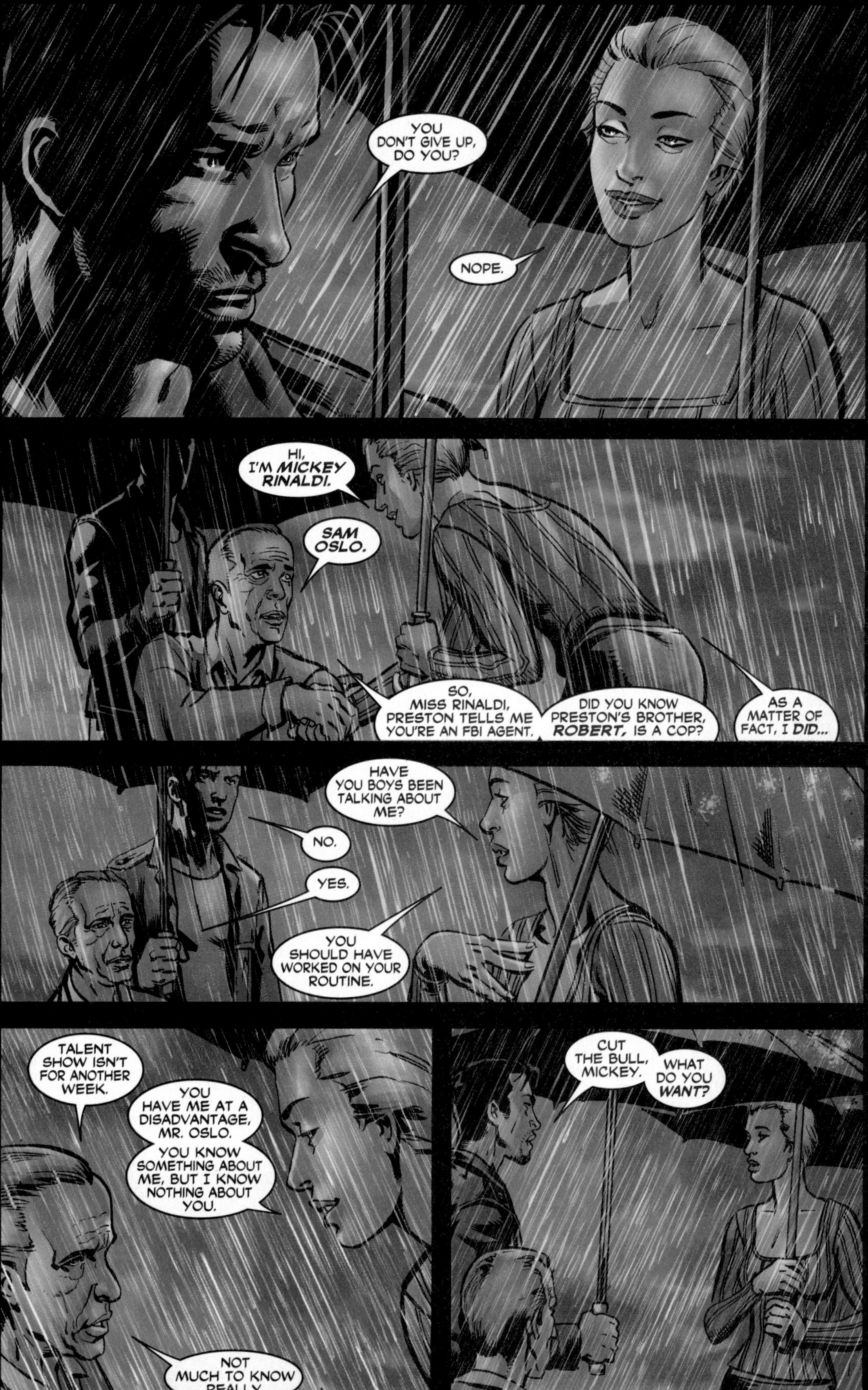
YOU DON'T GIVE UP, DO YOU?
NOPE.
HI, I'M MICKEY RINALDI.
SAM OSLO.
SO, MISS RINALDI, PRESTON TELLS ME YOU'RE AN FBI AGENT.
DID YOU KNOW PRESTON'S BROTHER, ROBERT, IS A COP?
AS A MATTER OF FACT, I DID...
HAVE YOU BOYS BEEN TALKING ABOUT ME?
NO.
YES.
YOU SHOULD HAVE WORKED ON YOUR ROUTINE.
TALENT SHOW ISN'T FOR ANOTHER WEEK.
YOU HAVE ME AT A DISADVANTAGE, MR. OSLO.
YOU KNOW SOMETHING ABOUT ME, BUT I KNOW NOTHING ABOUT YOU.
NOT MUCH TO KNOW REALLY.
CUT THE BULL, MICKEY.
WHAT DO YOU WANT?

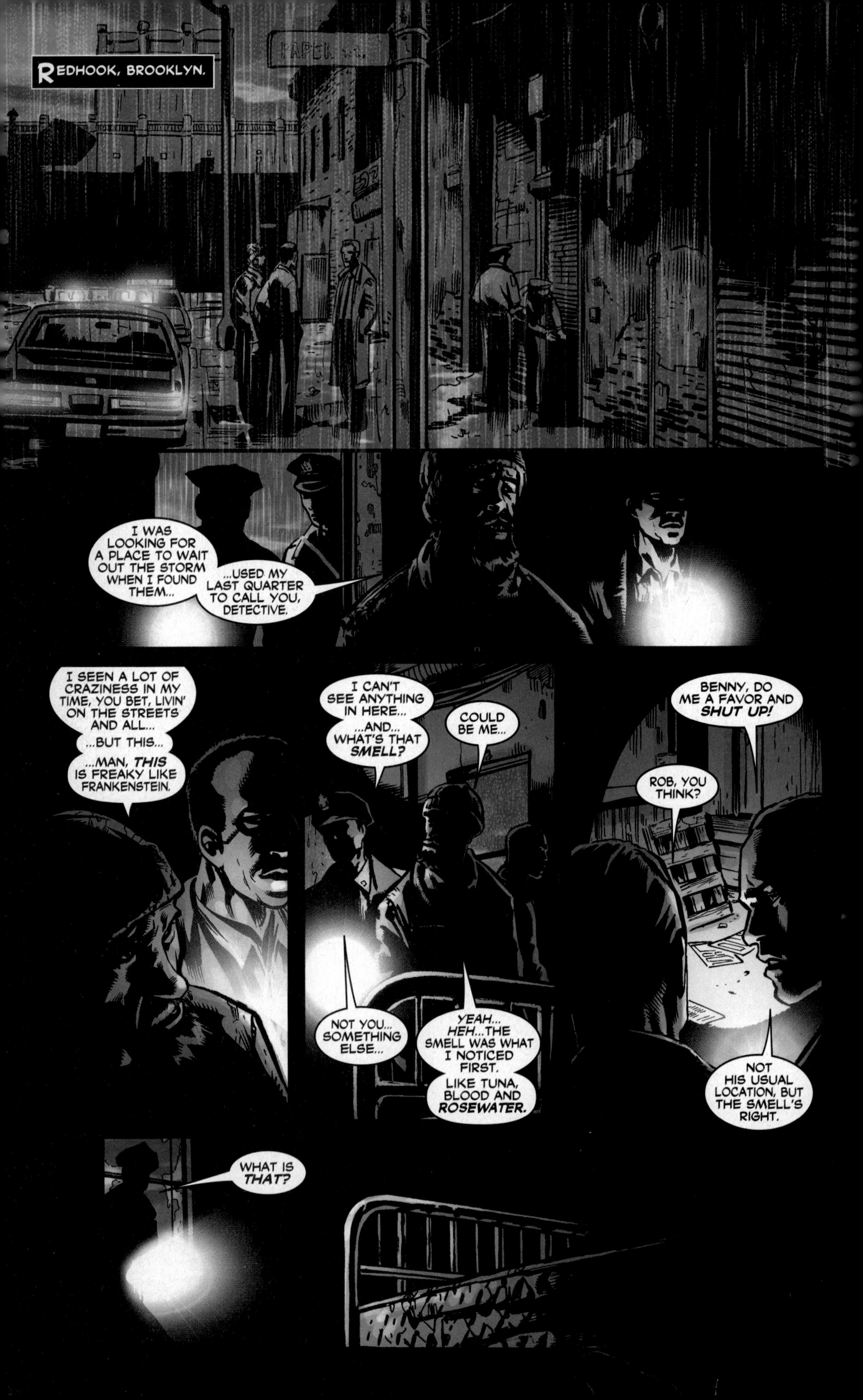
REDHOOK, BROOKLYN.
PAPER
I WAS LOOKING FOR A PLACE TO WAIT OUT THE STORM WHEN I FOUND THEM...
...USED MY LAST QUARTER TO CALL YOU, DETECTIVE.
I SEEN A LOT OF CRAZINESS IN MY TIME, YOU BET, LIVIN' ON THE STREETS AND ALL...
...BUT THIS...
...MAN, *THIS* IS FREAKY LIKE FRANKENSTEIN.
I CAN'T SEE ANYTHING IN HERE...
...AND... WHAT'S THAT *SMELL?*
COULD BE ME...
NOT YOU... SOMETHING ELSE...
YEAH... HEH...THE SMELL WAS WHAT I NOTICED FIRST.
LIKE TUNA, BLOOD AND *ROSEWATER.*
BENNY, DO ME A FAVOR AND *SHUT UP!*
ROB, YOU THINK?
NOT HIS USUAL LOCATION, BUT THE SMELL'S RIGHT.
WHAT IS *THAT?*

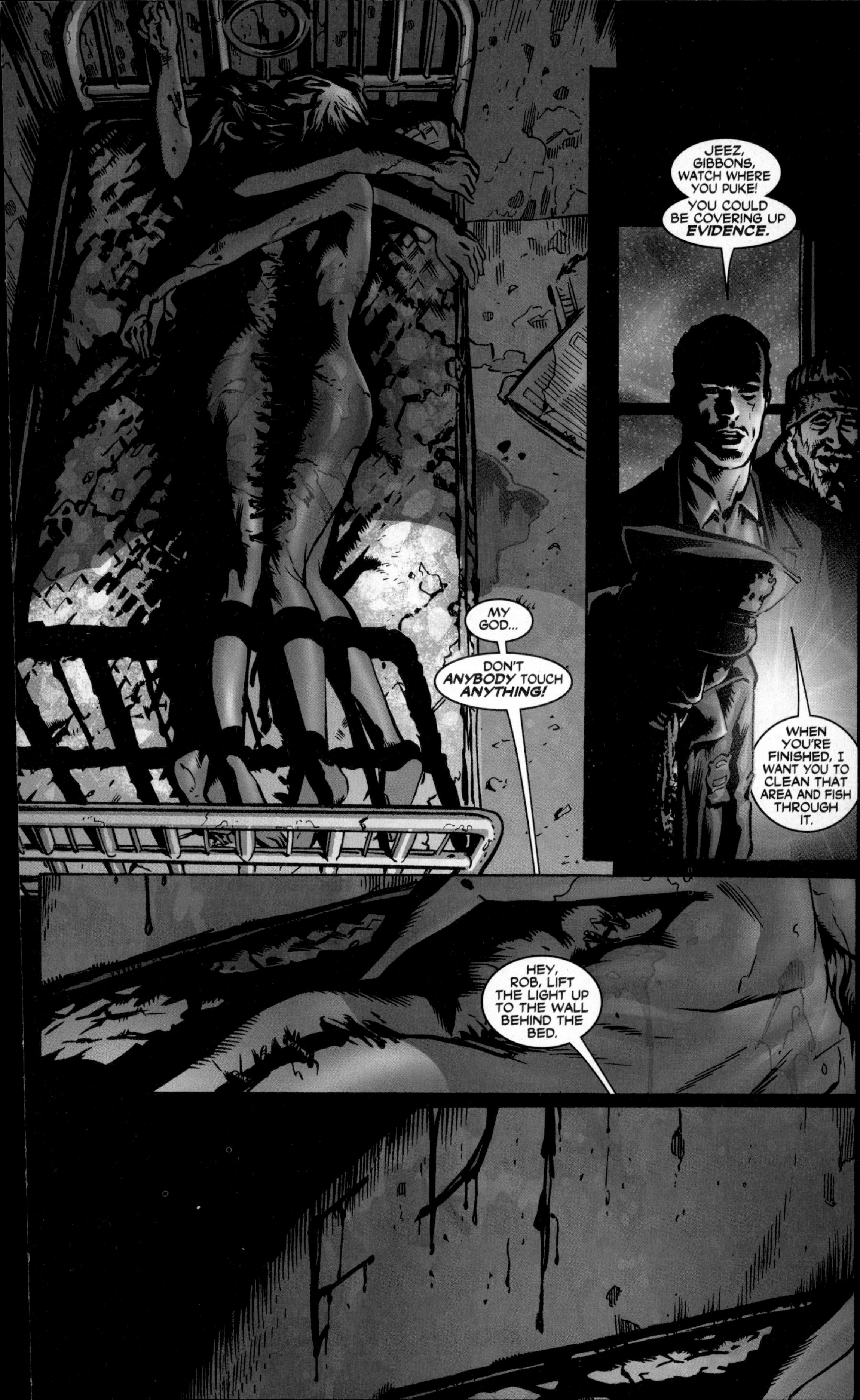
JEEZ, GIBBONS, WATCH WHERE YOU PUKE!
YOU COULD BE COVERING UP *EVIDENCE.*
MY GOD...
DON'T *ANYBODY* TOUCH *ANYTHING!*
WHEN YOU'RE FINISHED, I WANT YOU TO CLEAN THAT AREA AND FISH THROUGH IT.
HEY, ROB, LIFT THE LIGHT UP TO THE WALL BEHIND THE BED.

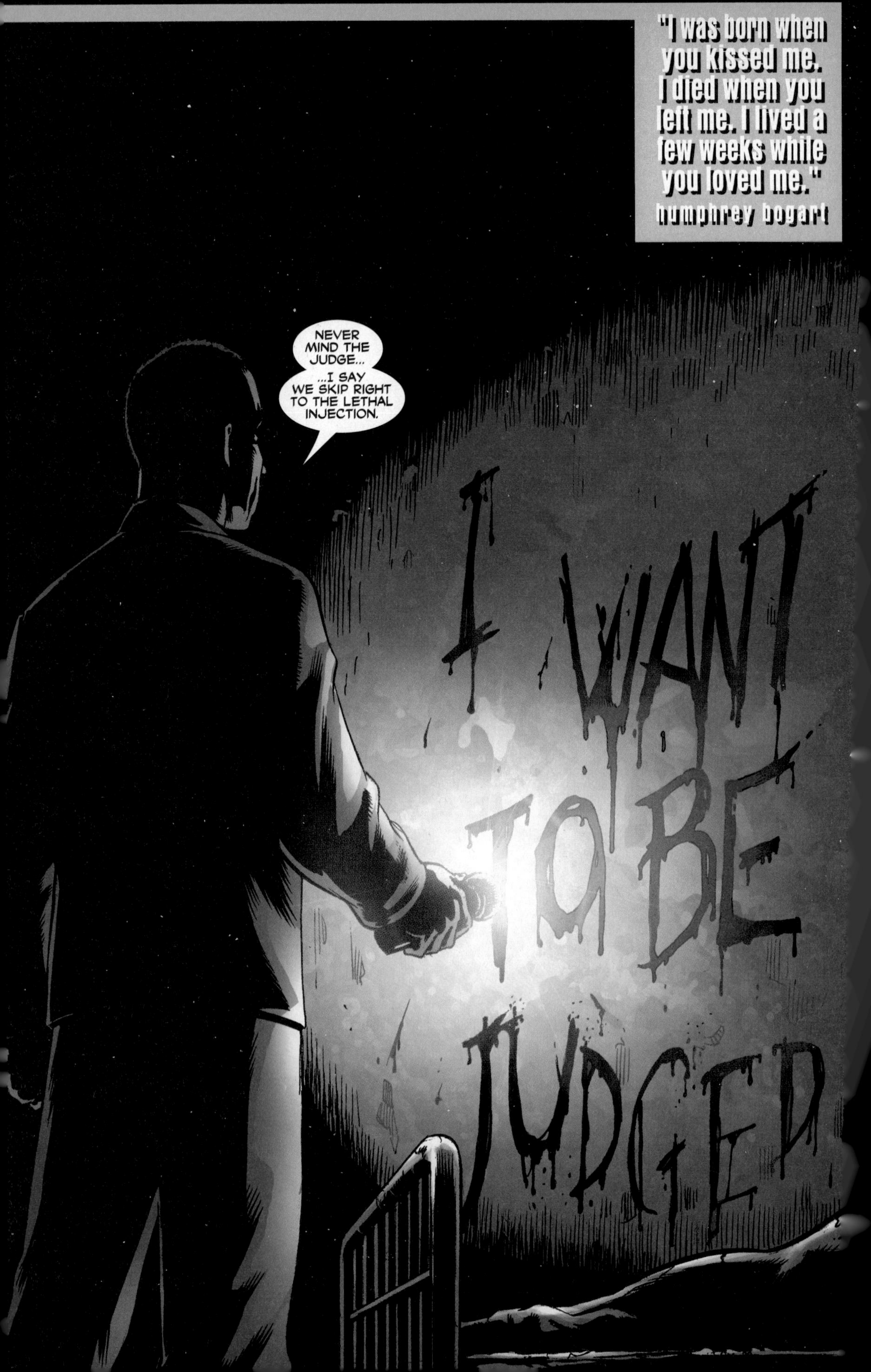
"I was born when you kissed me. I died when you left me. I lived a few weeks while you loved me."
humphrey bogart
NEVER MIND THE JUDGE... ...I SAY WE SKIP RIGHT TO THE LETHAL INJECTION.
I WANT TO BE JUDGED

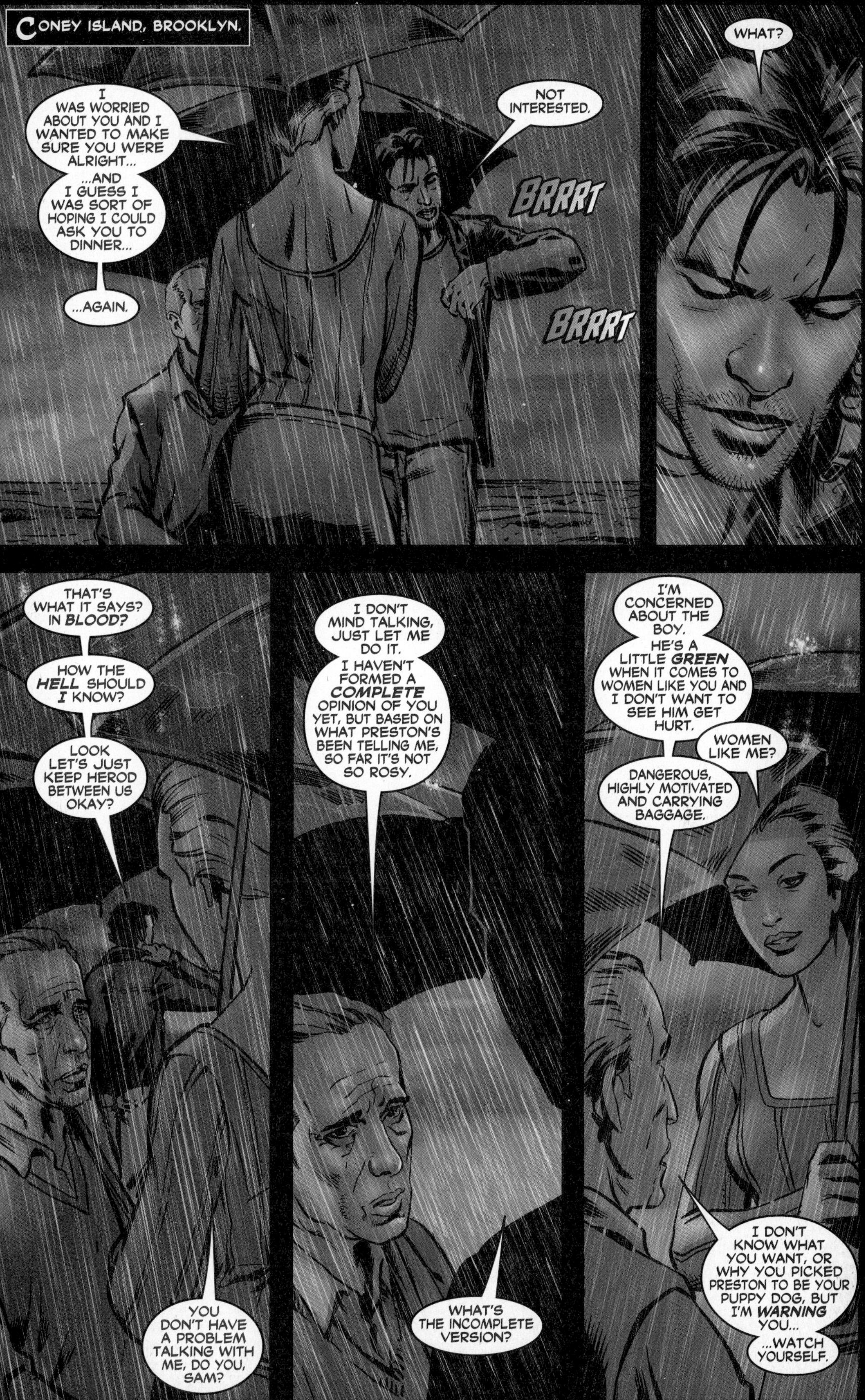
CONEY ISLAND, BROOKLYN.
I WAS WORRIED ABOUT YOU AND I WANTED TO MAKE SURE YOU WERE ALRIGHT...
...AND I GUESS I WAS SORT OF HOPING I COULD ASK YOU TO DINNER...
...AGAIN.
NOT INTERESTED.
BRRRT
BRRRT
WHAT?
THAT'S WHAT IT SAYS? IN BLOOD?
HOW THE HELL SHOULD I KNOW?
LOOK LET'S JUST KEEP HEROD BETWEEN US OKAY?
YOU DON'T HAVE A PROBLEM TALKING WITH ME, DO YOU, SAM?
I DON'T MIND TALKING, JUST LET ME DO IT.
I HAVEN'T FORMED A COMPLETE OPINION OF YOU YET, BUT BASED ON WHAT PRESTON'S BEEN TELLING ME, SO FAR IT'S NOT SO ROSY.
WHAT'S THE INCOMPLETE VERSION?
I'M CONCERNED ABOUT THE BOY.
HE'S A LITTLE GREEN WHEN IT COMES TO WOMEN LIKE YOU AND I DON'T WANT TO SEE HIM GET HURT.
WOMEN LIKE ME?
DANGEROUS, HIGHLY MOTIVATED AND CARRYING BAGGAGE.
I DON'T KNOW WHAT YOU WANT, OR WHY YOU PICKED PRESTON TO BE YOUR PUPPY DOG, BUT I'M WARNING YOU...
...WATCH YOURSELF.

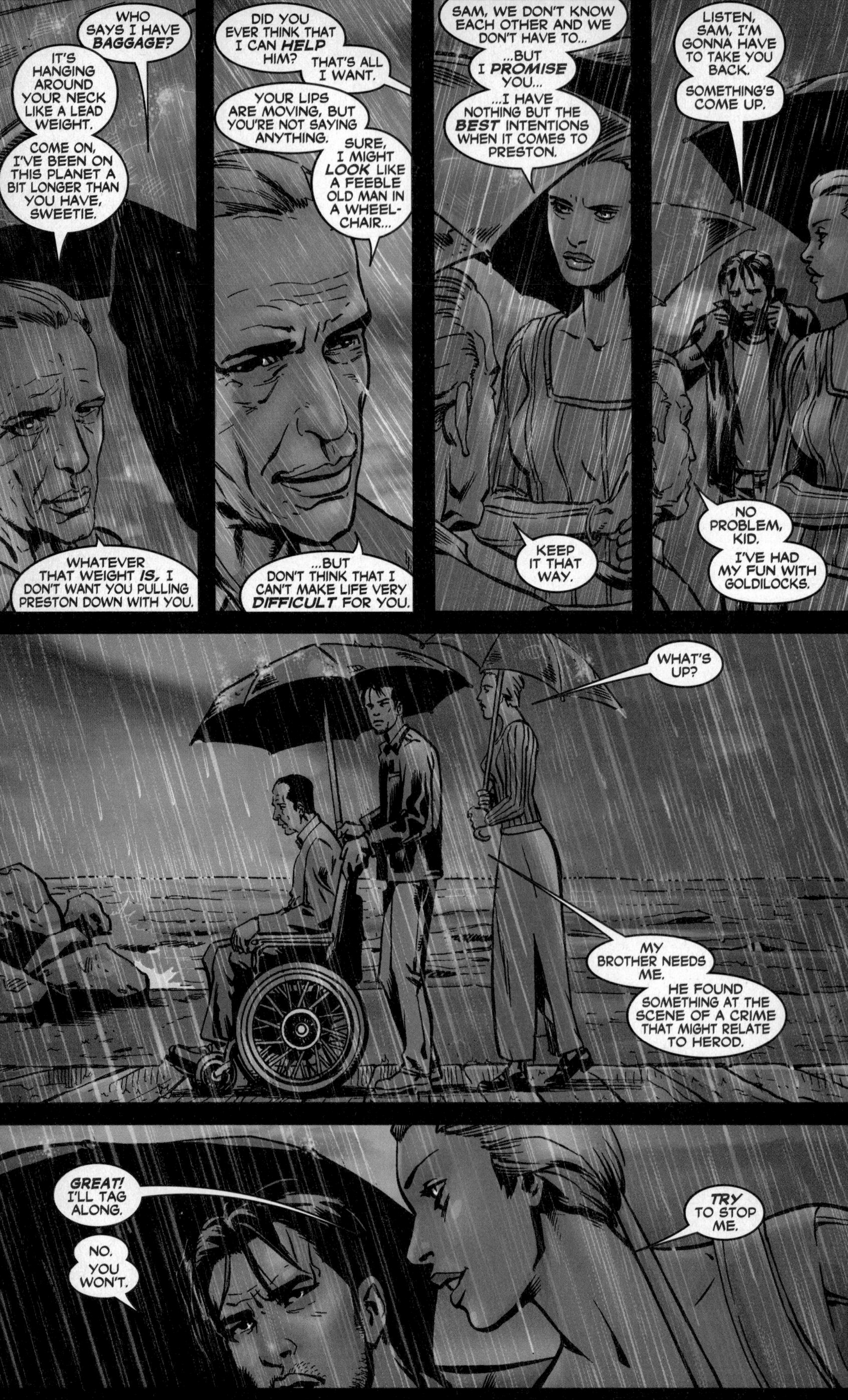
WHO SAYS I HAVE *BAGGAGE?*
IT'S HANGING AROUND YOUR NECK LIKE A LEAD WEIGHT.
COME ON, I'VE BEEN ON THIS PLANET A BIT LONGER THAN YOU HAVE, SWEETIE.
WHATEVER THAT WEIGHT *IS,* I DON'T WANT YOU PULLING PRESTON DOWN WITH YOU.
DID YOU EVER THINK THAT I CAN *HELP* HIM?
THAT'S ALL I WANT.
YOUR LIPS ARE MOVING, BUT YOU'RE NOT SAYING ANYTHING.
SURE, I MIGHT *LOOK* LIKE A FEEBLE OLD MAN IN A WHEEL-CHAIR...
...BUT DON'T THINK THAT I CAN'T MAKE LIFE VERY *DIFFICULT* FOR YOU.
SAM, WE DON'T KNOW EACH OTHER AND WE DON'T HAVE TO...
...BUT I *PROMISE* YOU...
...I HAVE NOTHING BUT THE *BEST* INTENTIONS WHEN IT COMES TO PRESTON.
KEEP IT THAT WAY.
LISTEN, SAM, I'M GONNA HAVE TO TAKE YOU BACK.
SOMETHING'S COME UP.
NO PROBLEM, KID.
I'VE HAD MY FUN WITH GOLDILOCKS.
WHAT'S UP?
MY BROTHER NEEDS ME.
HE FOUND SOMETHING AT THE SCENE OF A CRIME THAT MIGHT RELATE TO HEROD.
GREAT! I'LL TAG ALONG.
NO.
YOU WON'T.
TRY TO STOP ME.

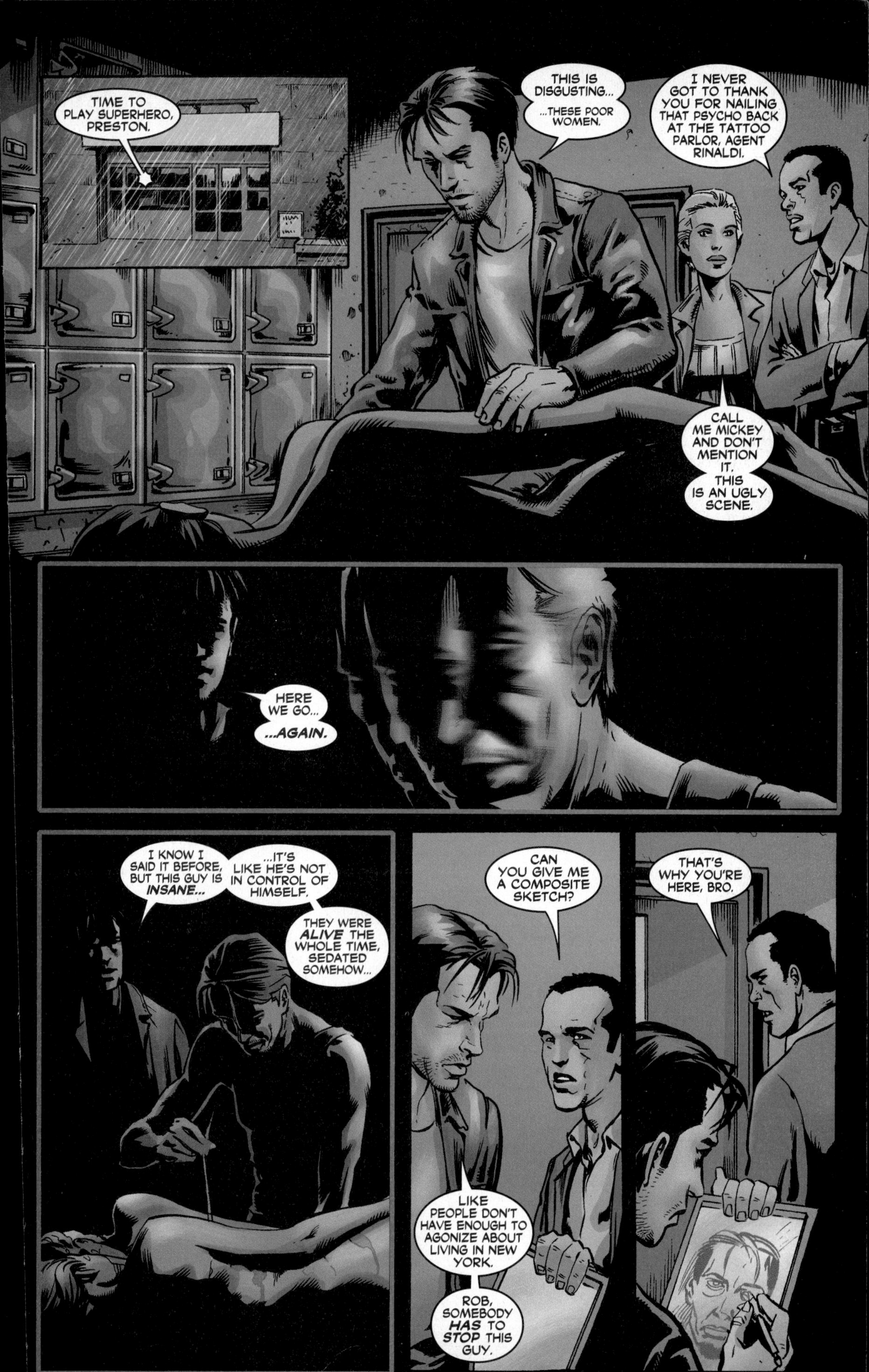
TIME TO PLAY SUPERHERO, PRESTON.
THIS IS DISGUSTING... ...THESE POOR WOMEN.
I NEVER GOT TO THANK YOU FOR NAILING THAT PSYCHO BACK AT THE TATTOO PARLOR, AGENT RINALDI.
CALL ME MICKEY AND DON'T MENTION IT. THIS IS AN UGLY SCENE.
HERE WE GO... ...AGAIN.
I KNOW I SAID IT BEFORE, BUT THIS GUY IS INSANE...
...IT'S LIKE HE'S NOT IN CONTROL OF HIMSELF.
THEY WERE ALIVE THE WHOLE TIME, SEDATED SOMEHOW...
CAN YOU GIVE ME A COMPOSITE SKETCH?
LIKE PEOPLE DON'T HAVE ENOUGH TO AGONIZE ABOUT LIVING IN NEW YORK.
ROB, SOMEBODY HAS TO STOP THIS GUY.
THAT'S WHY YOU'RE HERE, BRO.

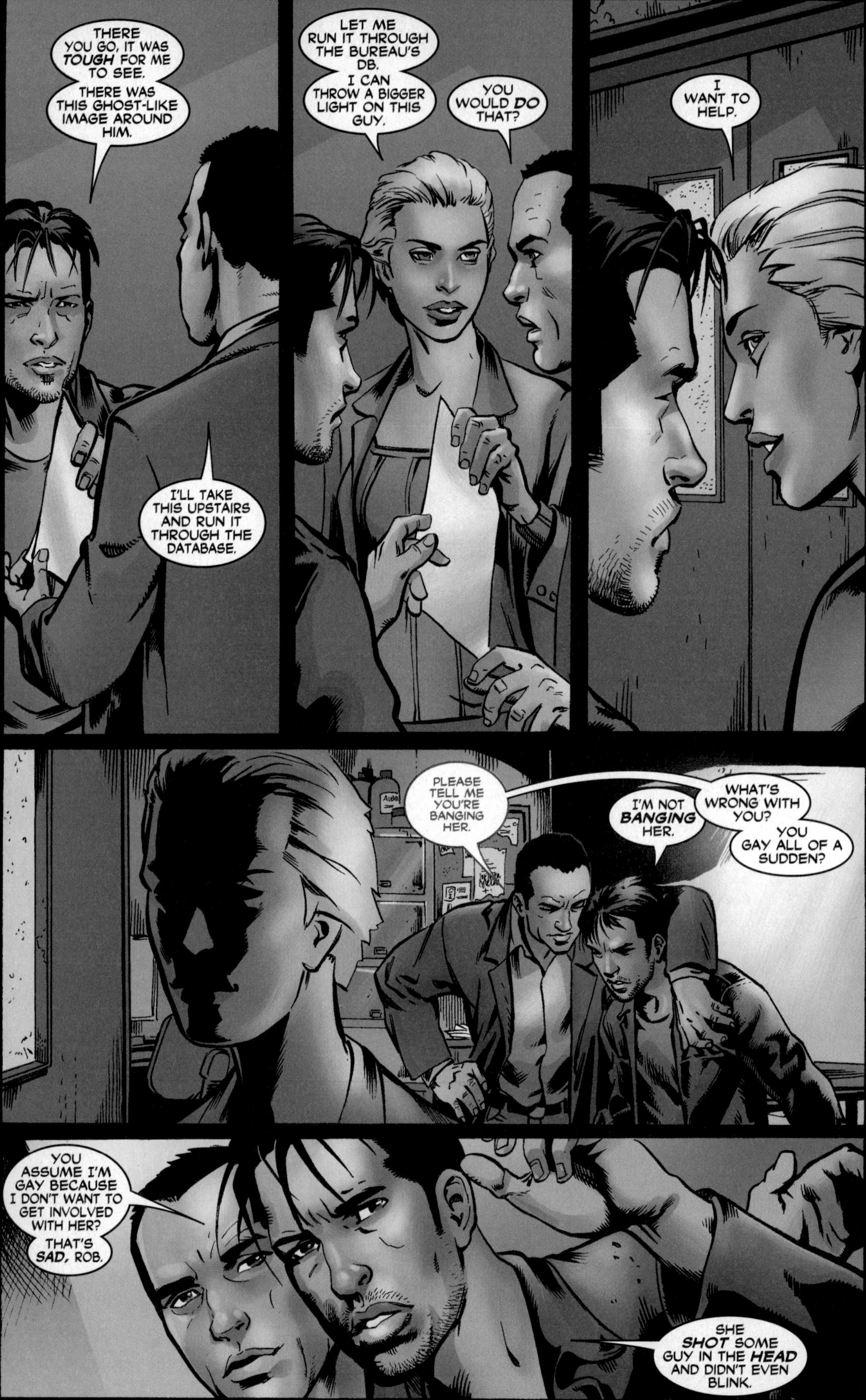
THERE YOU GO, IT WAS TOUGH FOR ME TO SEE.
THERE WAS THIS GHOST-LIKE IMAGE AROUND HIM.
I'LL TAKE THIS UPSTAIRS AND RUN IT THROUGH THE DATABASE.
LET ME RUN IT THROUGH THE BUREAU'S DB.
I CAN THROW A BIGGER LIGHT ON THIS GUY.
YOU WOULD DO THAT?
I WANT TO HELP.
PLEASE TELL ME YOU'RE BANGING HER.
I'M NOT BANGING HER.
WHAT'S WRONG WITH YOU?
YOU GAY ALL OF A SUDDEN?
YOU ASSUME I'M GAY BECAUSE I DON'T WANT TO GET INVOLVED WITH HER?
THAT'S SAD, ROB.
SHE SHOT SOME GUY IN THE HEAD AND DIDN'T EVEN BLINK.

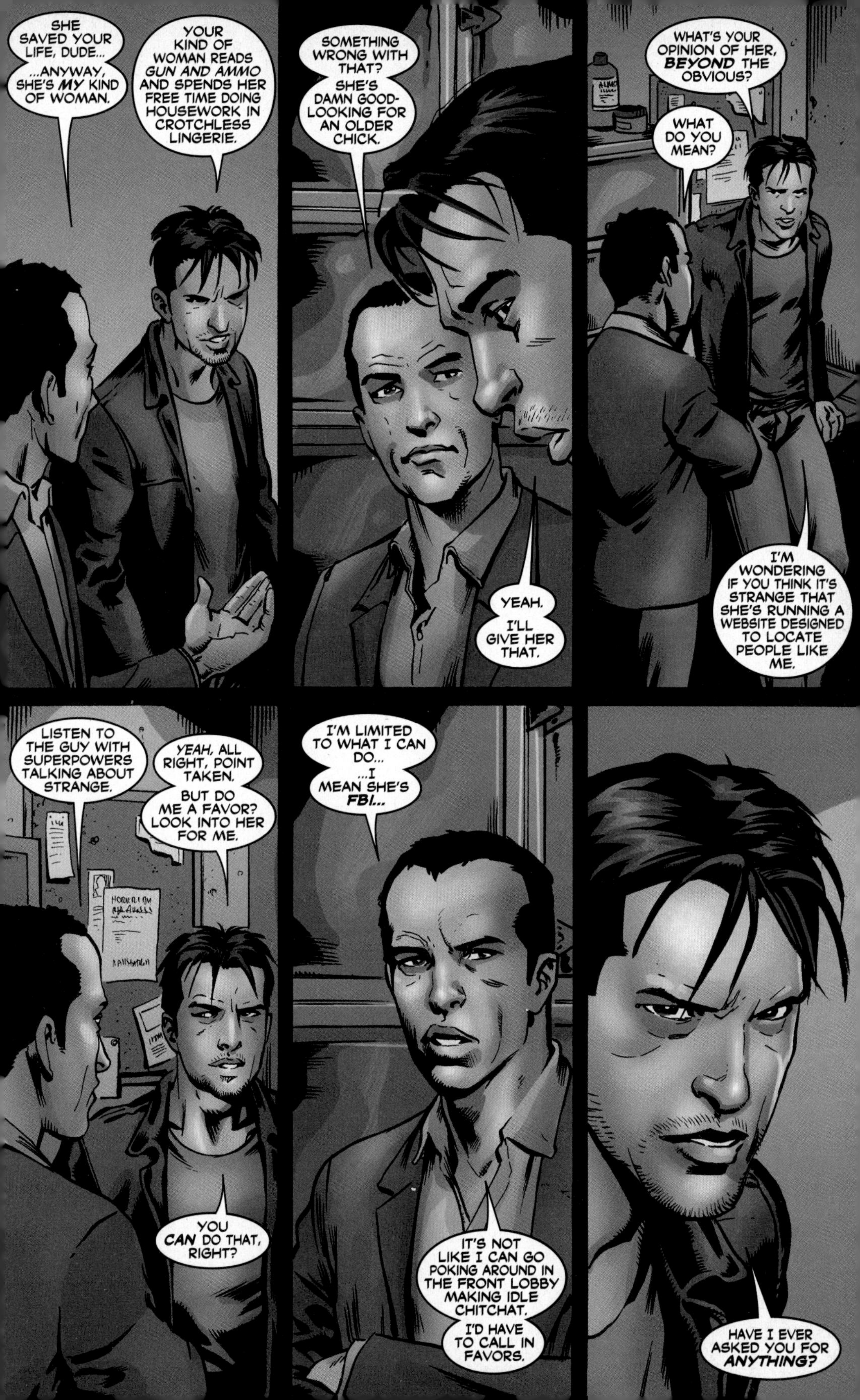
SHE SAVED YOUR LIFE, DUDE...
...ANYWAY, SHE'S MY KIND OF WOMAN.
YOUR KIND OF WOMAN READS GUN AND AMMO AND SPENDS HER FREE TIME DOING HOUSEWORK IN CROTCHLESS LINGERIE.
SOMETHING WRONG WITH THAT?
SHE'S DAMN GOOD-LOOKING FOR AN OLDER CHICK.
YEAH, I'LL GIVE HER THAT.
WHAT'S YOUR OPINION OF HER, BEYOND THE OBVIOUS?
WHAT DO YOU MEAN?
I'M WONDERING IF YOU THINK IT'S STRANGE THAT SHE'S RUNNING A WEBSITE DESIGNED TO LOCATE PEOPLE LIKE ME.
LISTEN TO THE GUY WITH SUPERPOWERS TALKING ABOUT STRANGE.
YEAH, ALL RIGHT, POINT TAKEN.
BUT DO ME A FAVOR? LOOK INTO HER FOR ME.
YOU CAN DO THAT, RIGHT?
I'M LIMITED TO WHAT I CAN DO...
...I MEAN SHE'S FBI...
IT'S NOT LIKE I CAN GO POKING AROUND IN THE FRONT LOBBY MAKING IDLE CHITCHAT.
I'D HAVE TO CALL IN FAVORS.
HAVE I EVER ASKED YOU FOR ANYTHING?

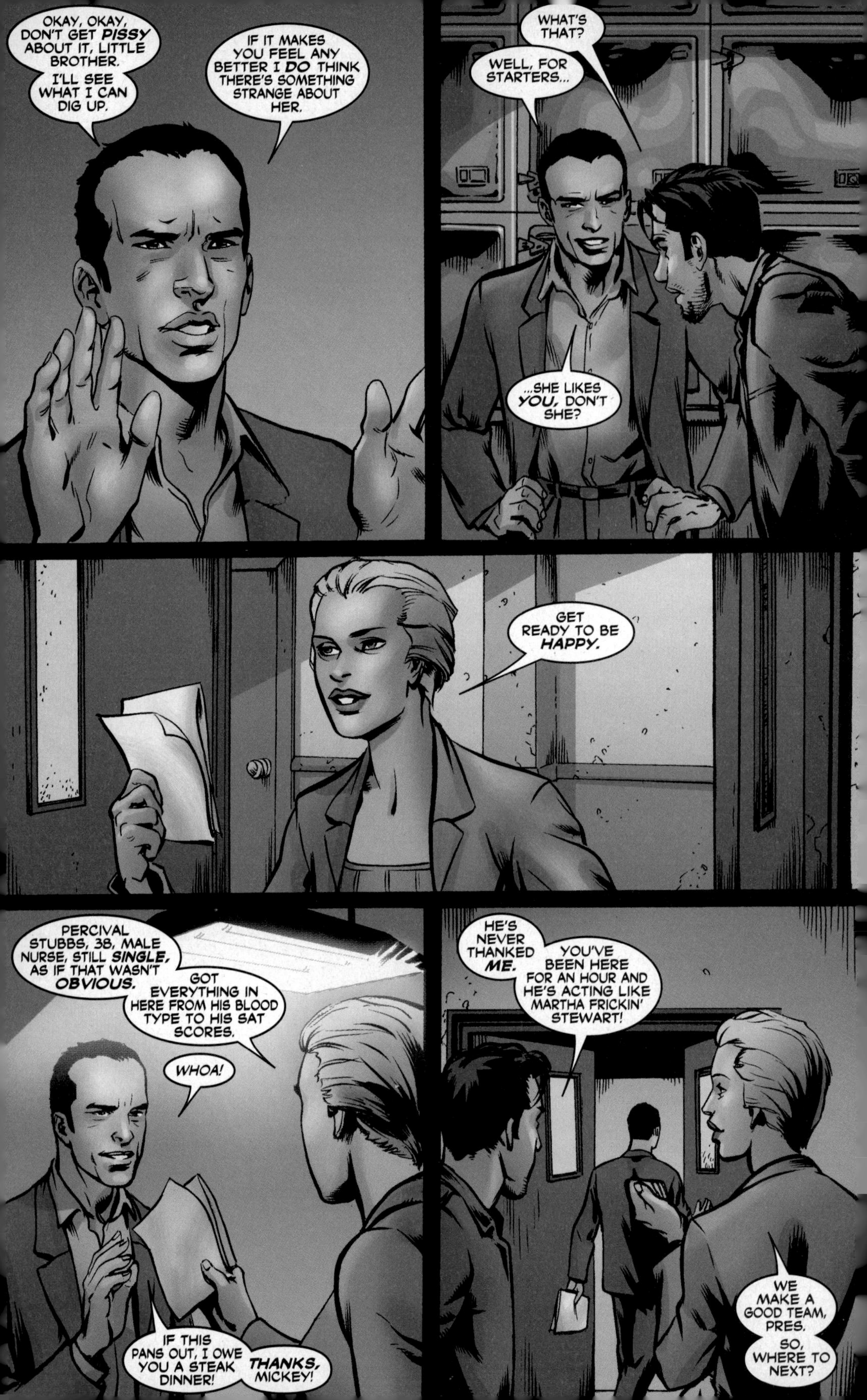
OKAY, OKAY, DON'T GET PISSY ABOUT IT, LITTLE BROTHER.
I'LL SEE WHAT I CAN DIG UP.
IF IT MAKES YOU FEEL ANY BETTER I DO THINK THERE'S SOMETHING STRANGE ABOUT HER.
WHAT'S THAT?
WELL, FOR STARTERS...
...SHE LIKES YOU, DON'T SHE?
GET READY TO BE HAPPY.
PERCIVAL STUBBS, 38, MALE NURSE, STILL SINGLE, AS IF THAT WASN'T OBVIOUS.
GOT EVERYTHING IN HERE FROM HIS BLOOD TYPE TO HIS SAT SCORES.
WHOA!
IF THIS PANS OUT, I OWE YOU A STEAK DINNER!
THANKS, MICKEY!
HE'S NEVER THANKED ME.
YOU'VE BEEN HERE FOR AN HOUR AND HE'S ACTING LIKE MARTHA FRICKIN' STEWART!
WE MAKE A GOOD TEAM, PRES.
SO, WHERE TO NEXT?

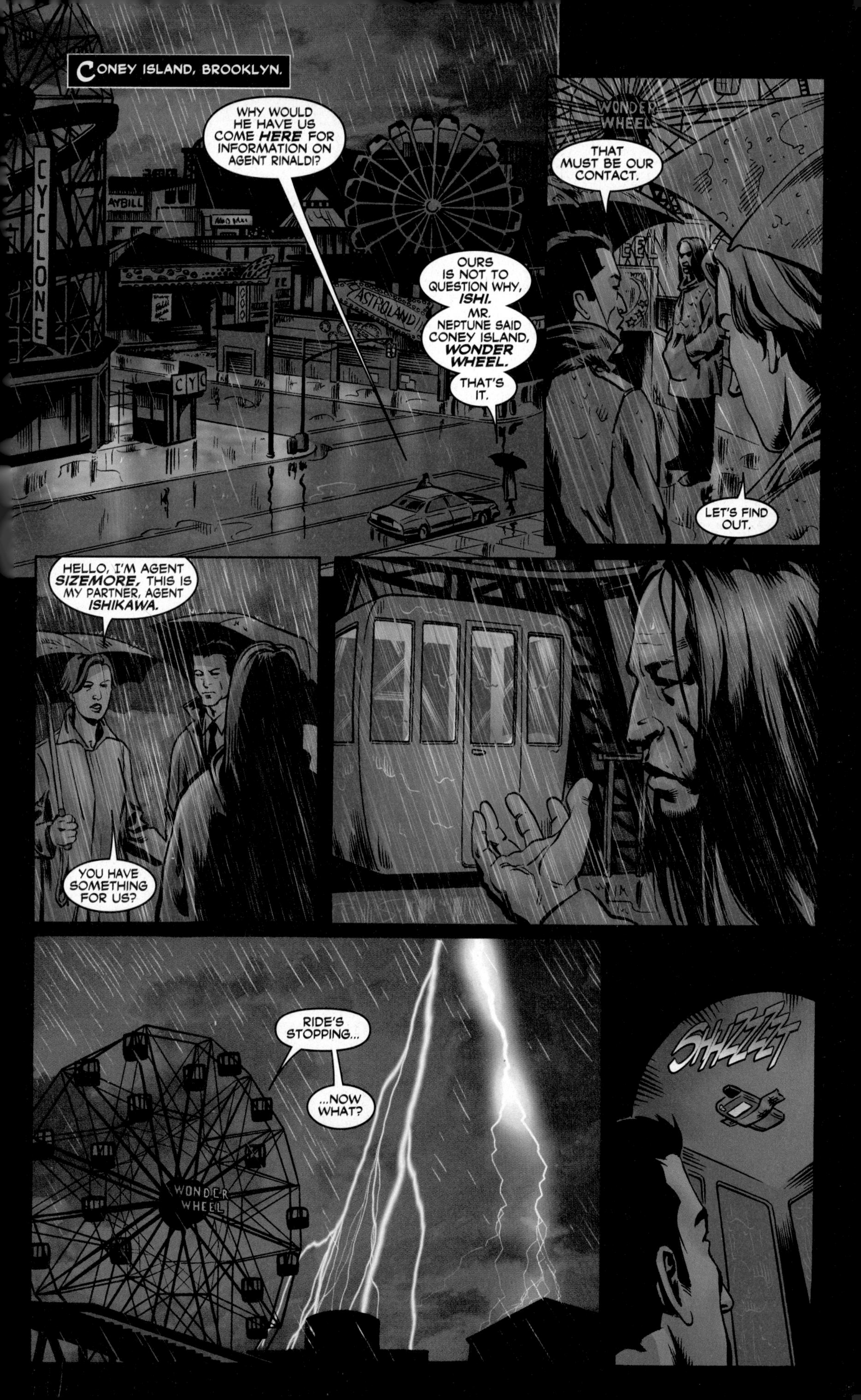
CONEY ISLAND, BROOKLYN.
CYCLONE
WHY WOULD HE HAVE US COME HERE FOR INFORMATION ON AGENT RINALDI?
ASTROLAND
OURS IS NOT TO QUESTION WHY, ISHI.
MR. NEPTUNE SAID CONEY ISLAND, WONDER WHEEL.
THAT'S IT.
WONDER WHEEL
THAT MUST BE OUR CONTACT.
LET'S FIND OUT.
HELLO, I'M AGENT SIZEMORE, THIS IS MY PARTNER, AGENT ISHIKAWA.
YOU HAVE SOMETHING FOR US?
RIDE'S STOPPING...
...NOW WHAT?
WONDER WHEEL
SHHZZZZT

LOOKS LIKE WE GOT OURSELVES A REAL TOAD CHOKER.

WHAT?

THE RAIN, SON.

I GUESS YOU AIN'T BEEN TO TEXAS.

WORD 'ROUND THE CAMPFIRE IS YOU'RE ON THE LOOKOUT FOR A FILLY THAT BROKE FROM THE STABLE.

YOU KNOW SOMETHING ABOUT MICKEY RINALDI?

HAVE A PEEK UNDER YOUR SEAT.

THERE ARE THREE KINDS OF PEOPLE:

THE ONES THAT LEARN BY READING, THE FEW WHICH LEARN BY OBSERVATION...

...AND THE REST OF THEM WHO HAVE TO TOUCH THE FIRE TO SEE FOR THEMSELVES IF IT'S REALLY HOT.

SOFT TARGETS:

JA'NELL MOORHEAD
ETHAN YORK
HARMONY PETERSON
GWEN MATSURA
PRESTON KILLS = MICKEY RINALDI
HAMZA AL-SHARIF RASHATI
JACK LAHANA
MILES TEHGO.

THE FOLLOWING IS A COMPRE- LIST OF OBJECTIVES WITH LOC MARKERS AND ELECTRONIC INFORM TO MAPPING LOREM IPSUM DOLO CONSECTETUER ADIPISCING NIBH EUISMO

I'M ASSUMING YOU'RE THE READING VARIETY.

IF NOT... YOU'LL SEE ME AGAIN.

RIDE'S MOVING.

OKAY, SO WHAT'S UP WITH THE FREAKY-ASS VILLAGE PEOPLE?

GHOST OPS.

DON'T ASK.

BETTER QUESTION IS HOW THE HELL DO WE GET OFF THIS THING?

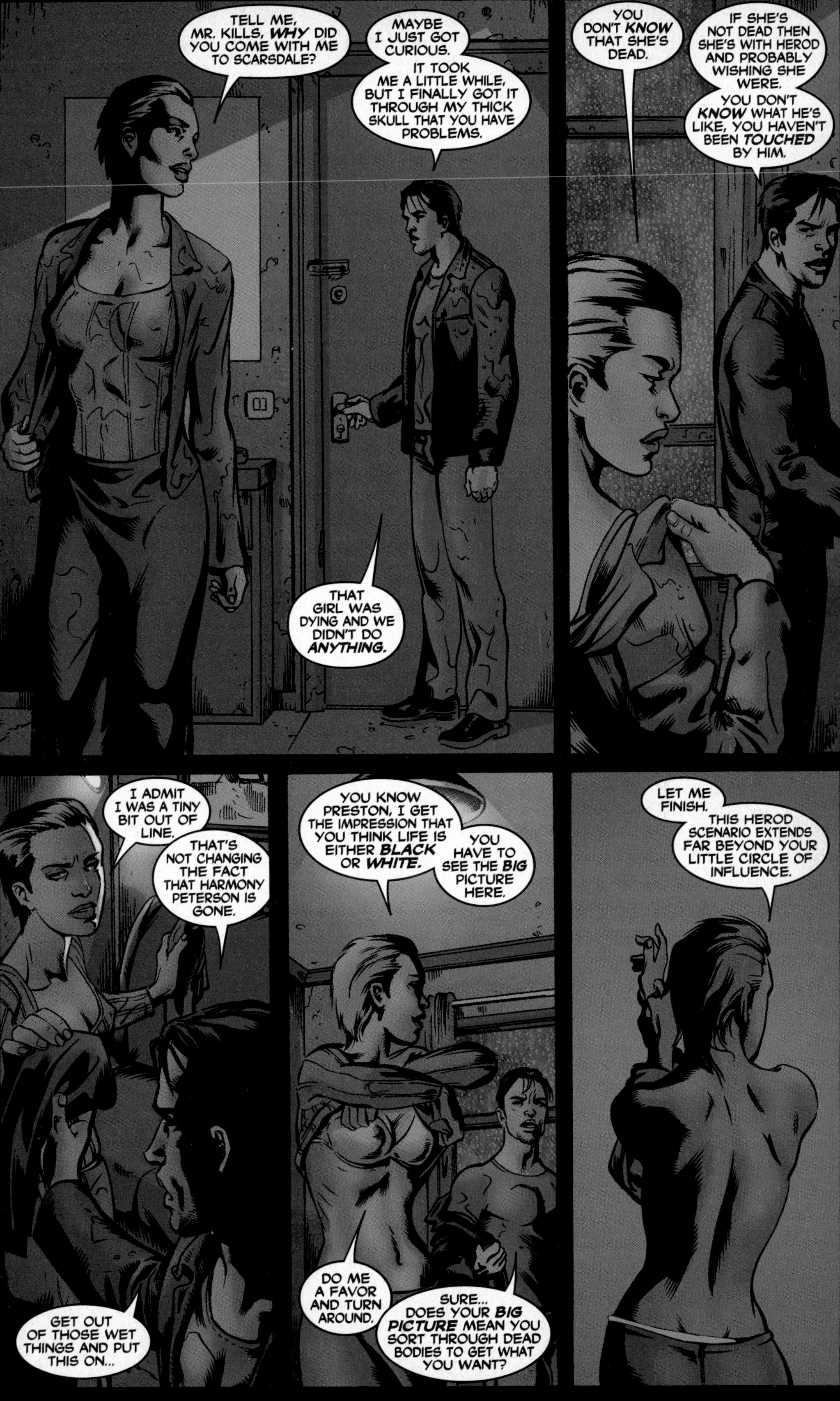
TELL ME, MR. KILLS, WHY DID YOU COME WITH ME TO SCARSDALE?
MAYBE I JUST GOT CURIOUS.
IT TOOK ME A LITTLE WHILE, BUT I FINALLY GOT IT THROUGH MY THICK SKULL THAT YOU HAVE PROBLEMS.
THAT GIRL WAS DYING AND WE DIDN'T DO ANYTHING.
YOU DON'T KNOW THAT SHE'S DEAD.
IF SHE'S NOT DEAD THEN SHE'S WITH HEROD AND PROBABLY WISHING SHE WERE.
YOU DON'T KNOW WHAT HE'S LIKE, YOU HAVEN'T BEEN TOUCHED BY HIM.
I ADMIT I WAS A TINY BIT OUT OF LINE.
THAT'S NOT CHANGING THE FACT THAT HARMONY PETERSON IS GONE.
GET OUT OF THOSE WET THINGS AND PUT THIS ON...
YOU KNOW PRESTON, I GET THE IMPRESSION THAT YOU THINK LIFE IS EITHER BLACK OR WHITE.
YOU HAVE TO SEE THE BIG PICTURE HERE.
DO ME A FAVOR AND TURN AROUND.
SURE... DOES YOUR BIG PICTURE MEAN YOU SORT THROUGH DEAD BODIES TO GET WHAT YOU WANT?
LET ME FINISH.
THIS HEROD SCENARIO EXTENDS FAR BEYOND YOUR LITTLE CIRCLE OF INFLUENCE.

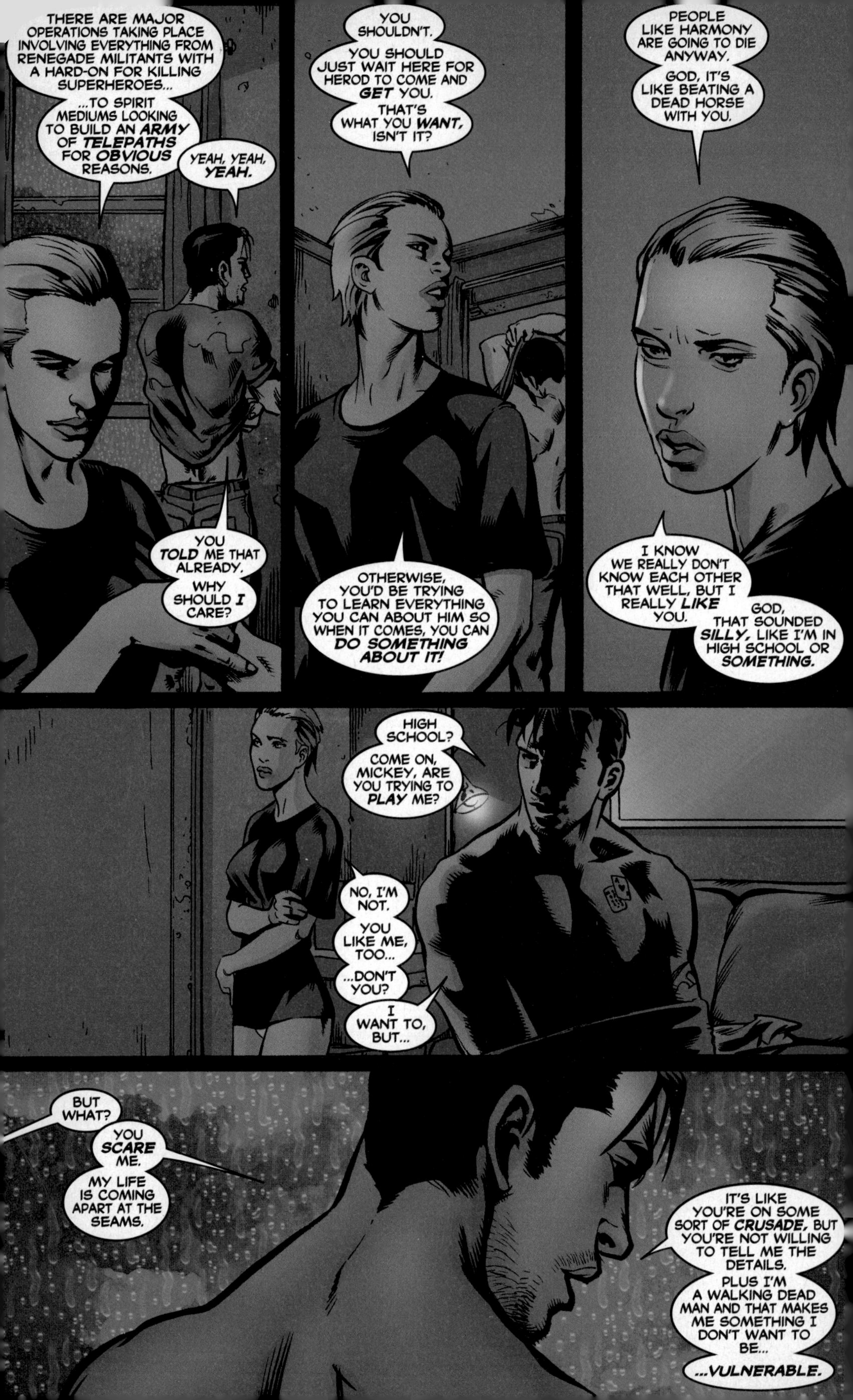
THERE ARE MAJOR OPERATIONS TAKING PLACE INVOLVING EVERYTHING FROM RENEGADE MILITANTS WITH A HARD-ON FOR KILLING SUPERHEROES...
...TO SPIRIT MEDIUMS LOOKING TO BUILD AN ARMY OF TELEPATHS FOR OBVIOUS REASONS.
YEAH, YEAH, YEAH.
YOU TOLD ME THAT ALREADY.
WHY SHOULD I CARE?
YOU SHOULDN'T.
YOU SHOULD JUST WAIT HERE FOR HEROD TO COME AND GET YOU.
THAT'S WHAT YOU WANT, ISN'T IT?
OTHERWISE, YOU'D BE TRYING TO LEARN EVERYTHING YOU CAN ABOUT HIM SO WHEN IT COMES, YOU CAN DO SOMETHING ABOUT IT!
PEOPLE LIKE HARMONY ARE GOING TO DIE ANYWAY.
GOD, IT'S LIKE BEATING A DEAD HORSE WITH YOU.
I KNOW WE REALLY DON'T KNOW EACH OTHER THAT WELL, BUT I REALLY LIKE YOU.
GOD, THAT SOUNDED SILLY, LIKE I'M IN HIGH SCHOOL OR SOMETHING.
HIGH SCHOOL?
COME ON, MICKEY, ARE YOU TRYING TO PLAY ME?
NO, I'M NOT.
YOU LIKE ME, TOO...
...DON'T YOU?
I WANT TO, BUT...
BUT WHAT?
YOU SCARE ME.
MY LIFE IS COMING APART AT THE SEAMS.
IT'S LIKE YOU'RE ON SOME SORT OF CRUSADE, BUT YOU'RE NOT WILLING TO TELL ME THE DETAILS.
PLUS I'M A WALKING DEAD MAN AND THAT MAKES ME SOMETHING I DON'T WANT TO BE...
...VULNERABLE.

WE'RE BOTH VULNERABLE, PRES...

...BUT THERE IS SOMETHING INSIDE *YOU*, A HEROIC SPIRIT AND I SEE THAT IT WANTS TO COME OUT.

YOU KEEP PUSHING IT DOWN, *HIDING* IT.

WHY?

HEROIC SPIRIT *KILLED* MY *PARENTS* AND IT'S THE SAME THING THAT MAKES MY BROTHER SUCH A *PRICK*.

I DON'T WANT TO BE A FRIGGIN' HERO.

IT'S NOT SOMETHING YOU CAN CHOOSE.

IT CHOOSES *YOU* AND I HAVE TO THINK THAT'S WHY HEROD GAVE YOU THIS POWER YOU HATE SO MUCH.

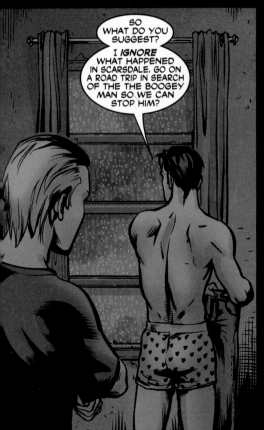

SO WHAT DO YOU SUGGEST?

I *IGNORE* WHAT HAPPENED IN SCARSDALE, GO ON A ROAD TRIP IN SEARCH OF THE THE BOOGEY MAN SO WE CAN STOP HIM?

ISN'T THAT WHAT HEROES *DO?* IF YOU'RE GOING TO DIE... YOU MIGHT AS WELL DIE *TRYING.*

NICE BOXERS, TOUGH GUY.

UGGGHHH... LONG STORY.

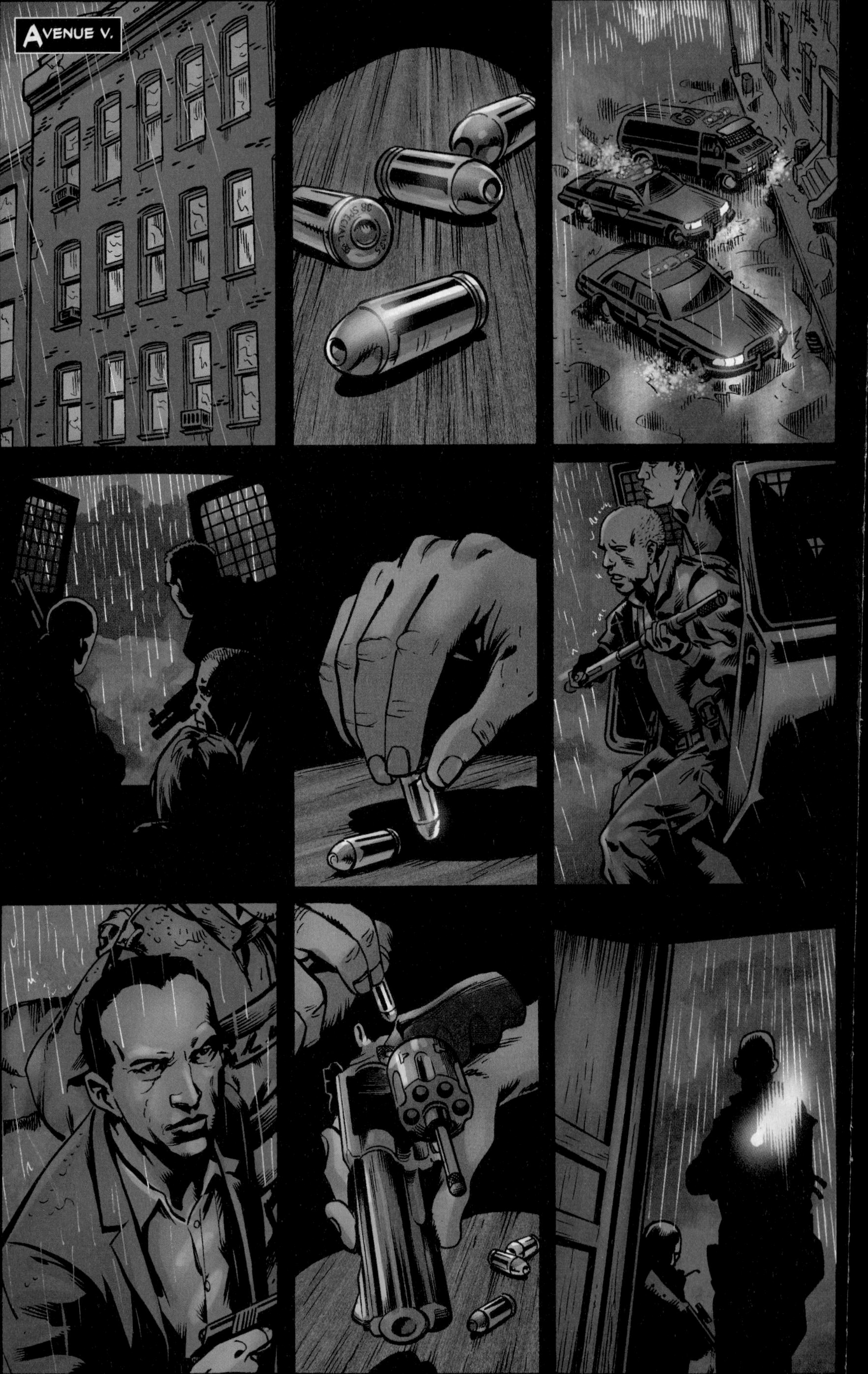
Avenue V.

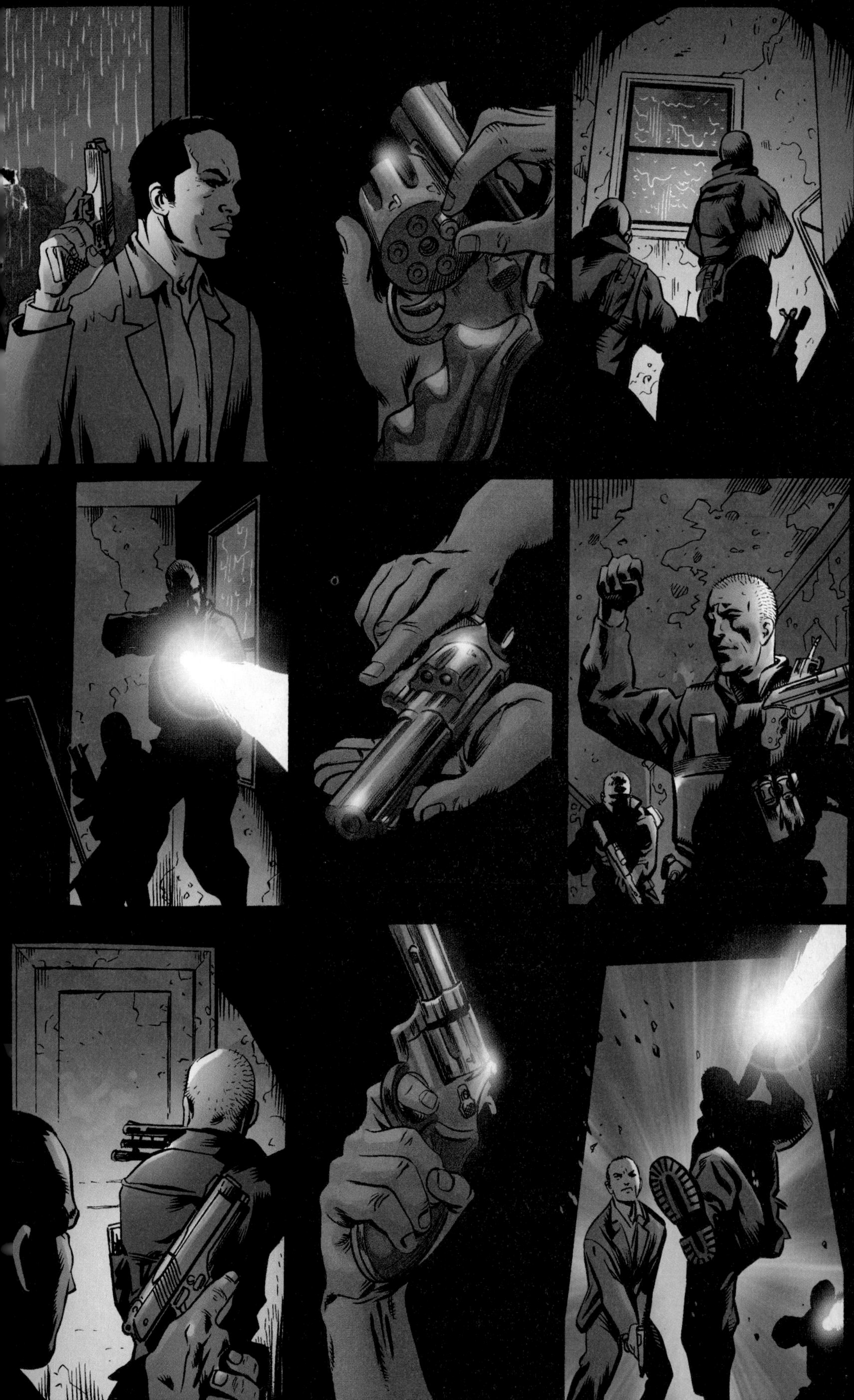

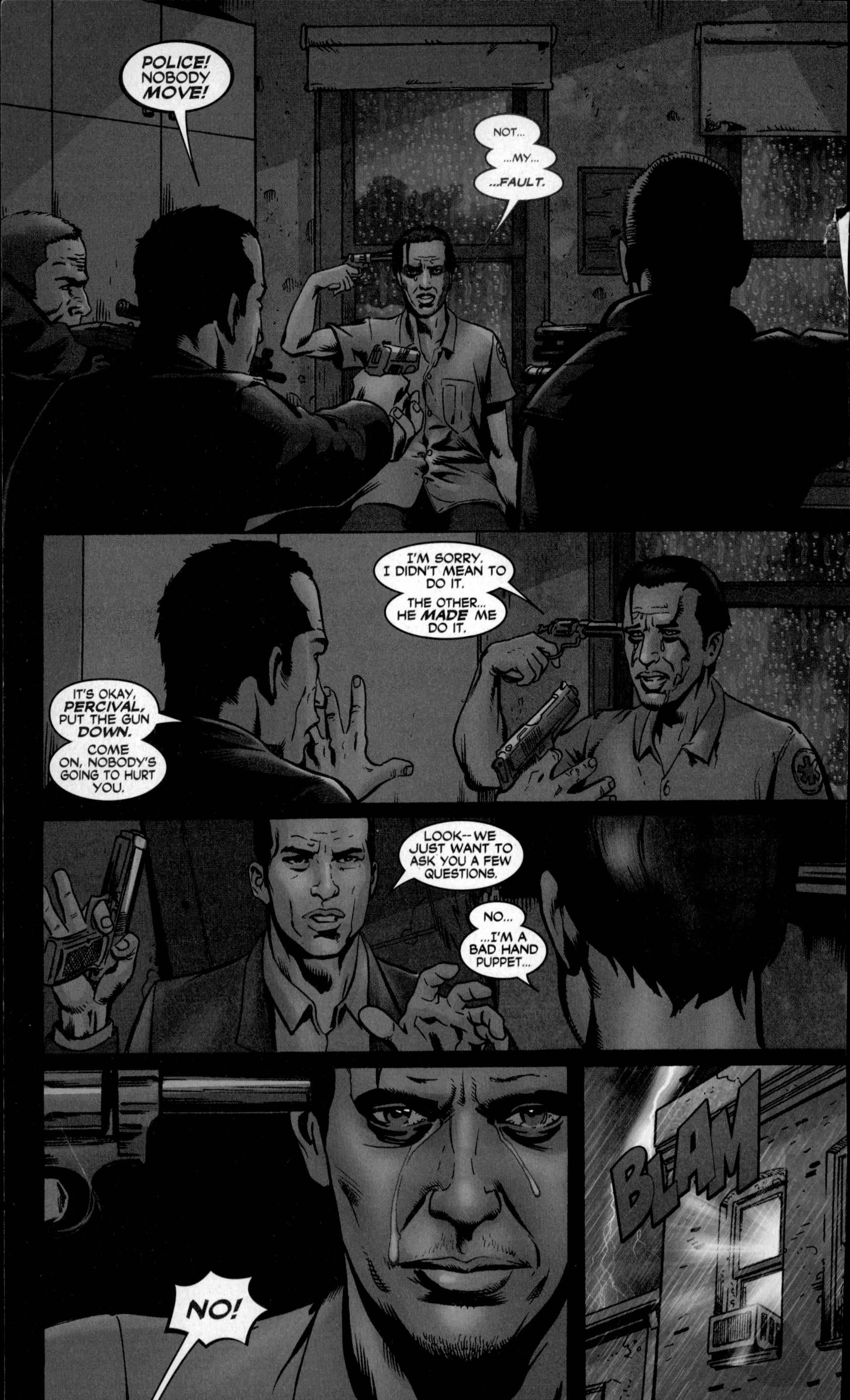

POLICE! NOBODY MOVE!
NOT...
...MY...
...FAULT.
I'M SORRY. I DIDN'T MEAN TO DO IT.
THE OTHER... HE MADE ME DO IT.
IT'S OKAY, PERCIVAL, PUT THE GUN DOWN.
COME ON, NOBODY'S GOING TO HURT YOU.
LOOK--WE JUST WANT TO ASK YOU A FEW QUESTIONS.
NO...
...I'M A BAD HAND PUPPET...
NO!
BLAM

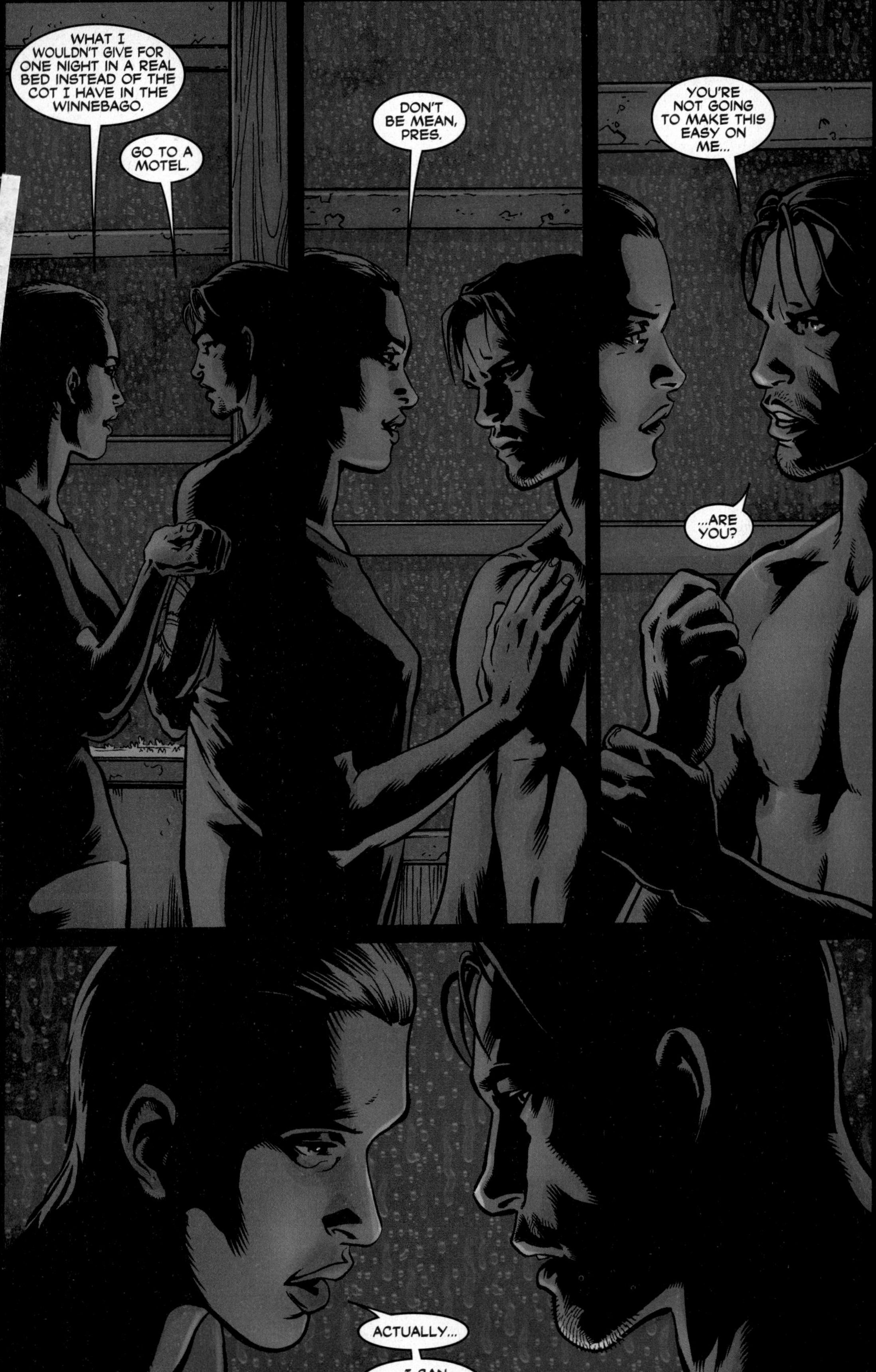
WHAT I WOULDN'T GIVE FOR ONE NIGHT IN A REAL BED INSTEAD OF THE COT I HAVE IN THE WINNEBAGO.
GO TO A MOTEL.
DON'T BE MEAN, PRES.
YOU'RE NOT GOING TO MAKE THIS EASY ON ME...
...ARE YOU?
ACTUALLY...
...I CAN MAKE IT *VERY* EASY.

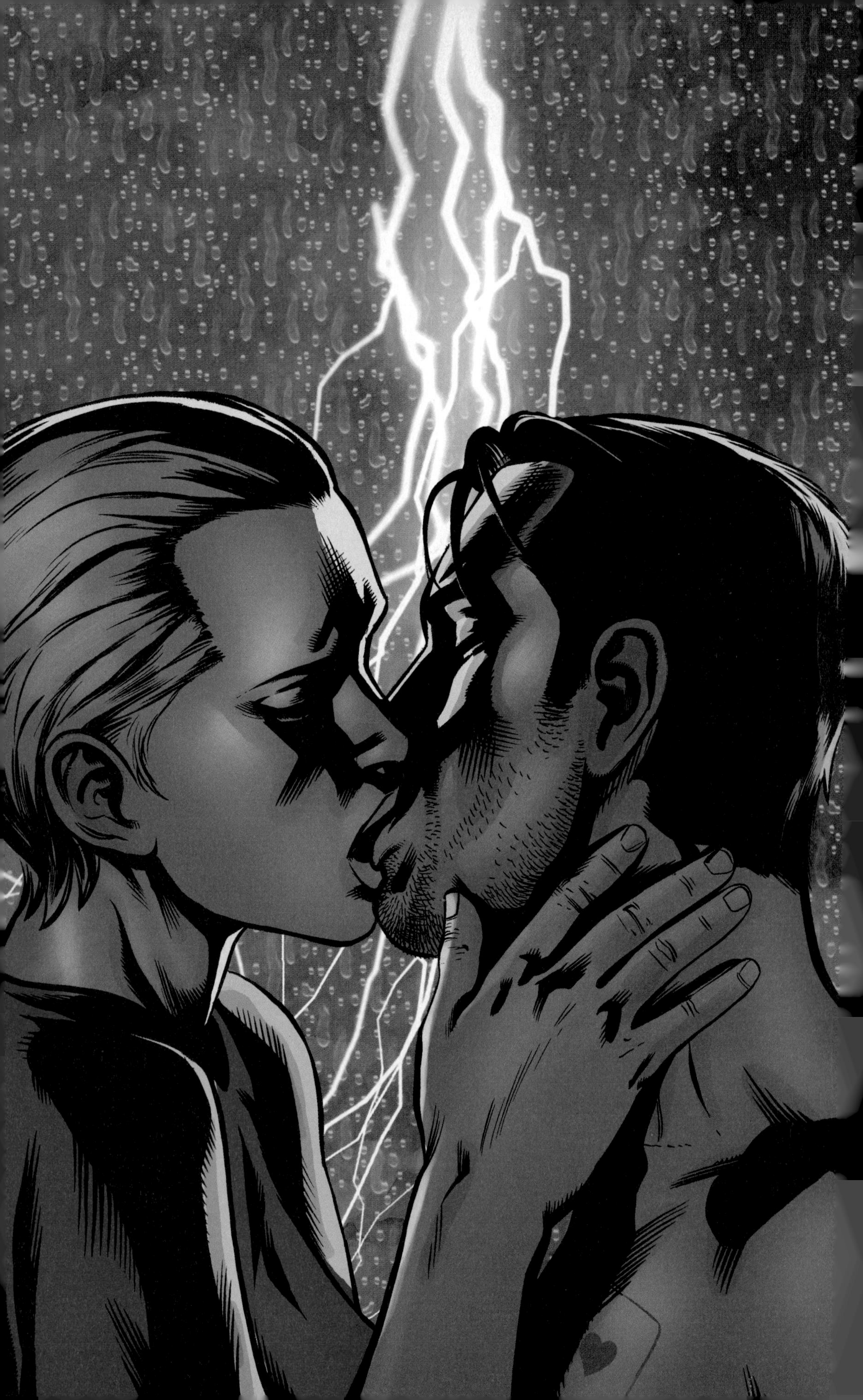

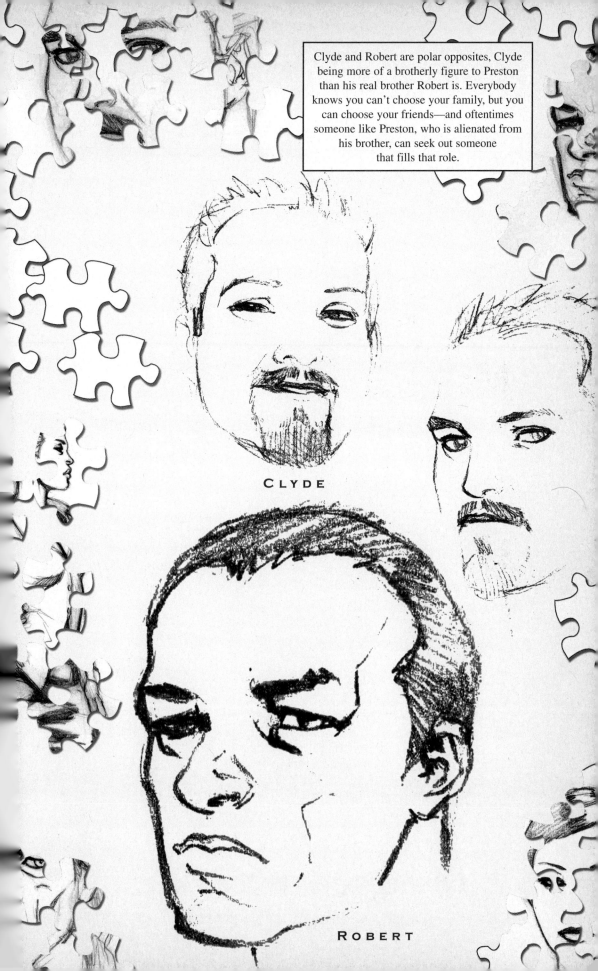

Clyde and Robert are polar opposites, Clyde being more of a brotherly figure to Preston than his real brother Robert is. Everybody knows you can't choose your family, but you can choose your friends—and oftentimes someone like Preston, who is alienated from his brother, can seek out someone that fills that role.

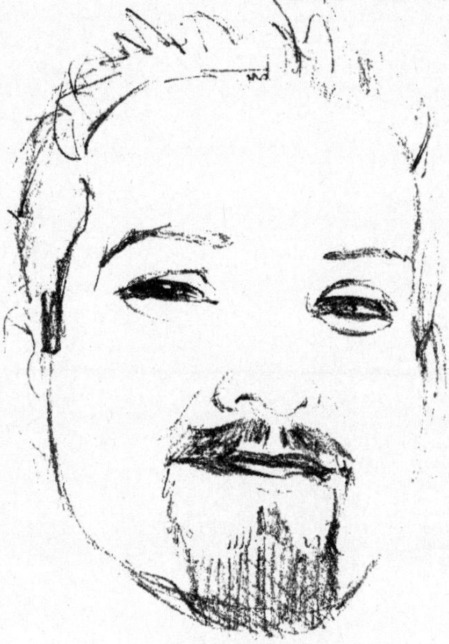

CLYDE

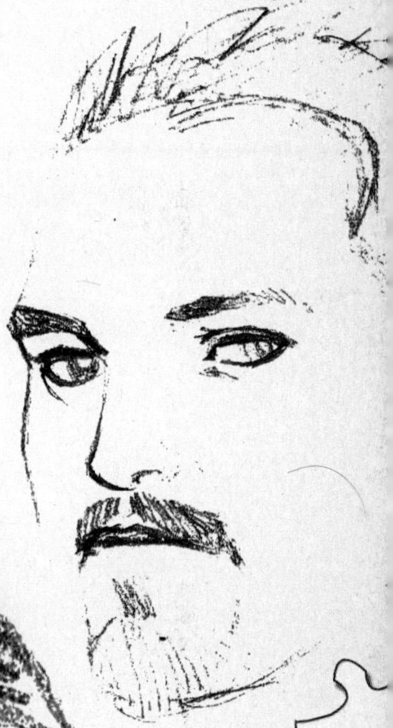

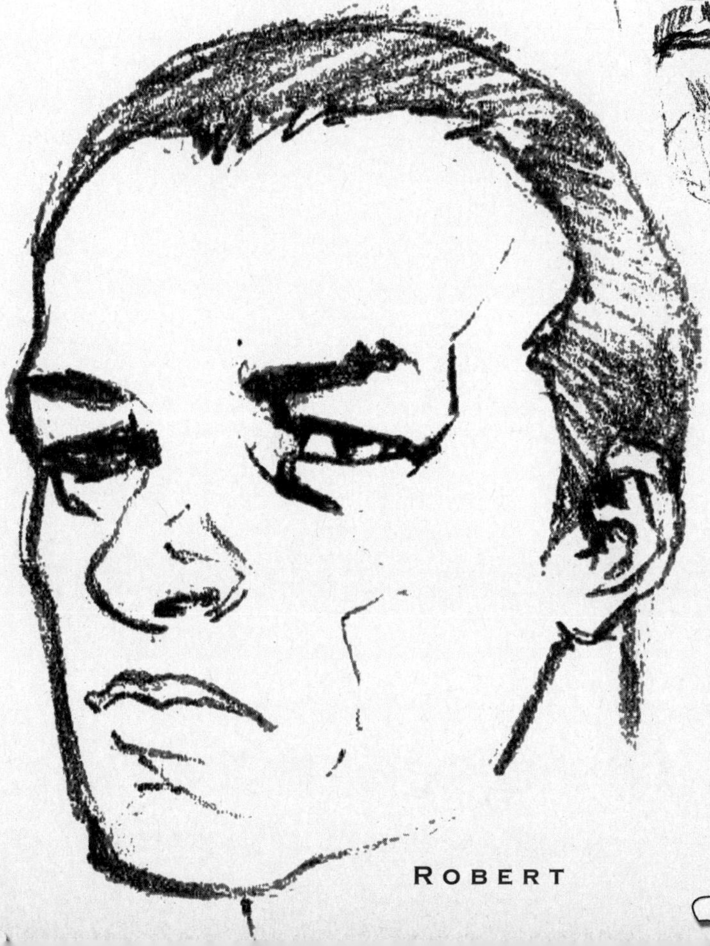

ROBERT

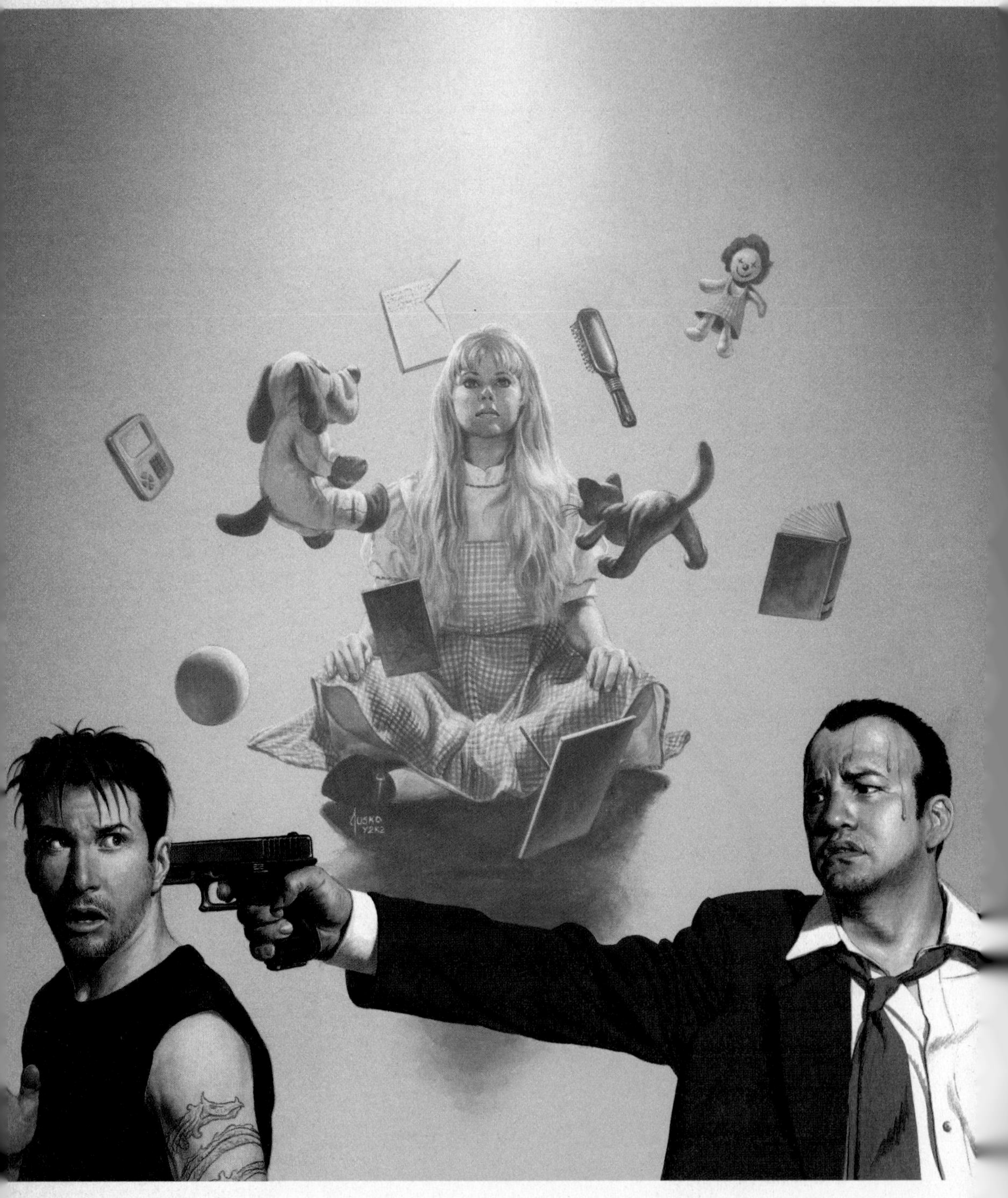

DISTANCE FROM ONE INTO THE OTHER

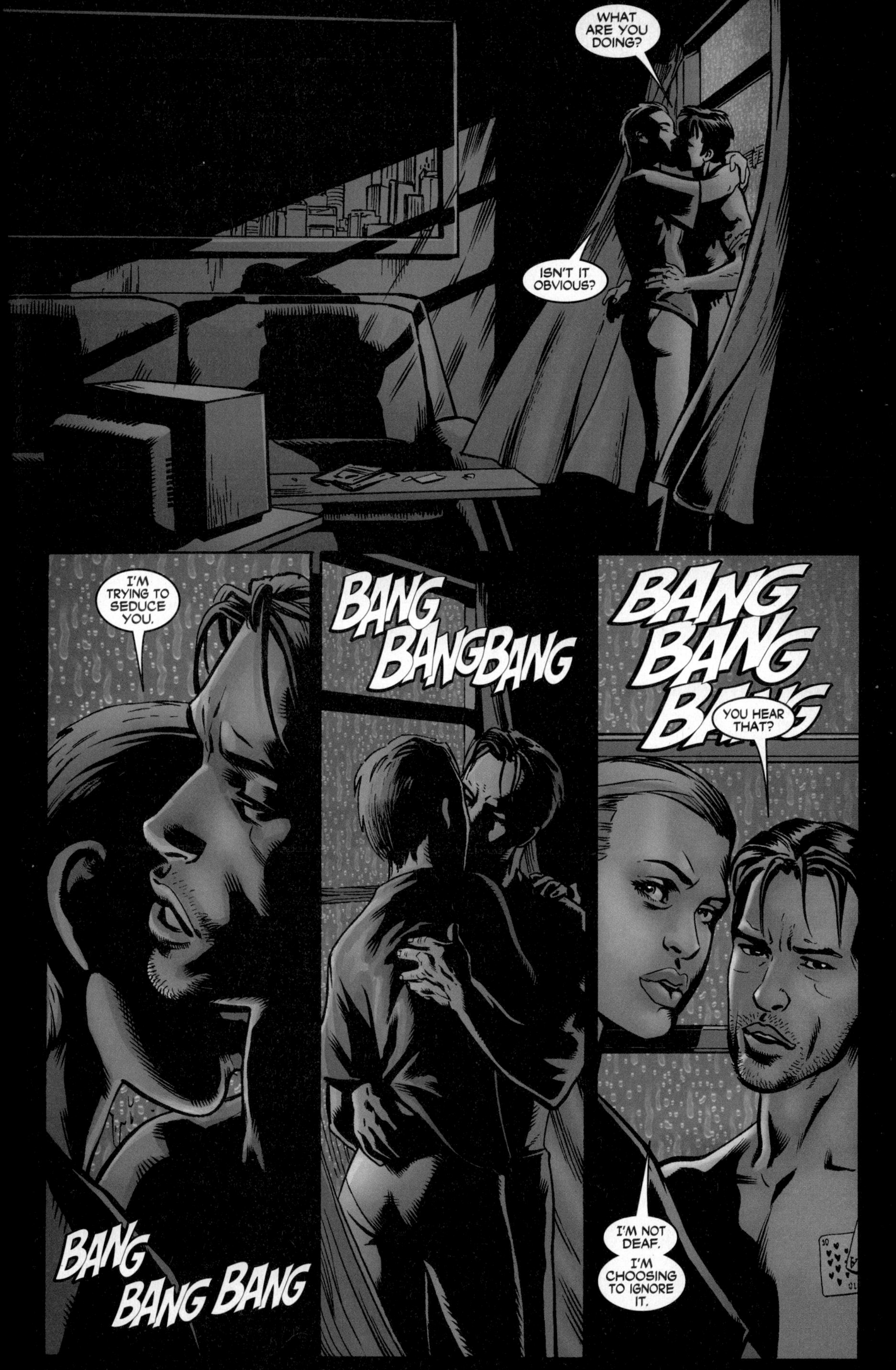
WHAT ARE YOU DOING?
ISN'T IT OBVIOUS?
I'M TRYING TO SEDUCE YOU.
BANG BANG BANG
BANG BANGBANG
BANG BANG BANG
YOU HEAR THAT?
I'M NOT DEAF. I'M CHOOSING TO IGNORE IT.

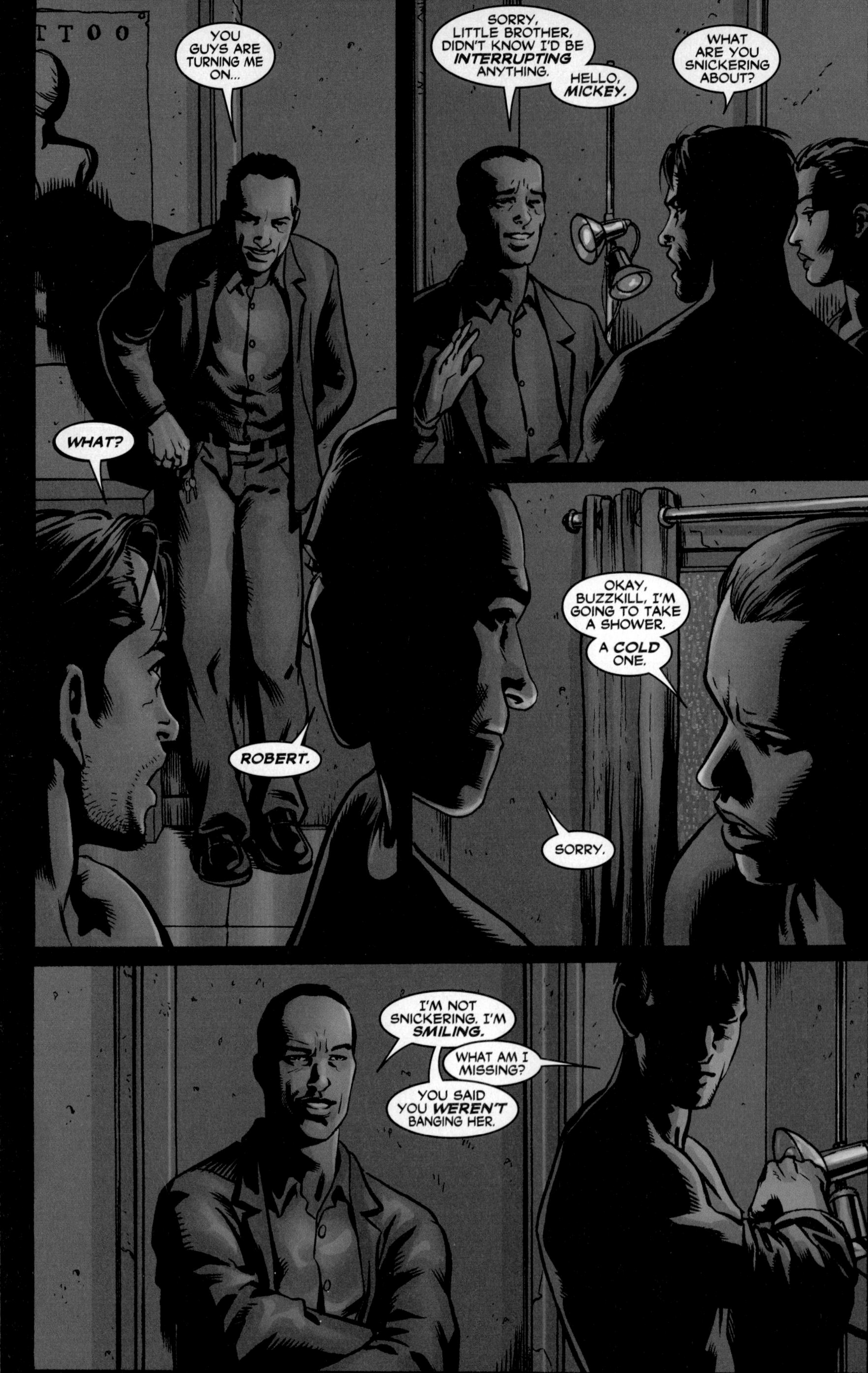
TTOO
YOU GUYS ARE TURNING ME ON...
SORRY, LITTLE BROTHER, DIDN'T KNOW I'D BE INTERRUPTING ANYTHING.
HELLO, MICKEY.
WHAT ARE YOU SNICKERING ABOUT?
WHAT?
ROBERT.
OKAY, BUZZKILL, I'M GOING TO TAKE A SHOWER.
A COLD ONE.
SORRY.
I'M NOT SNICKERING. I'M SMILING.
WHAT AM I MISSING?
YOU SAID YOU WEREN'T BANGING HER.

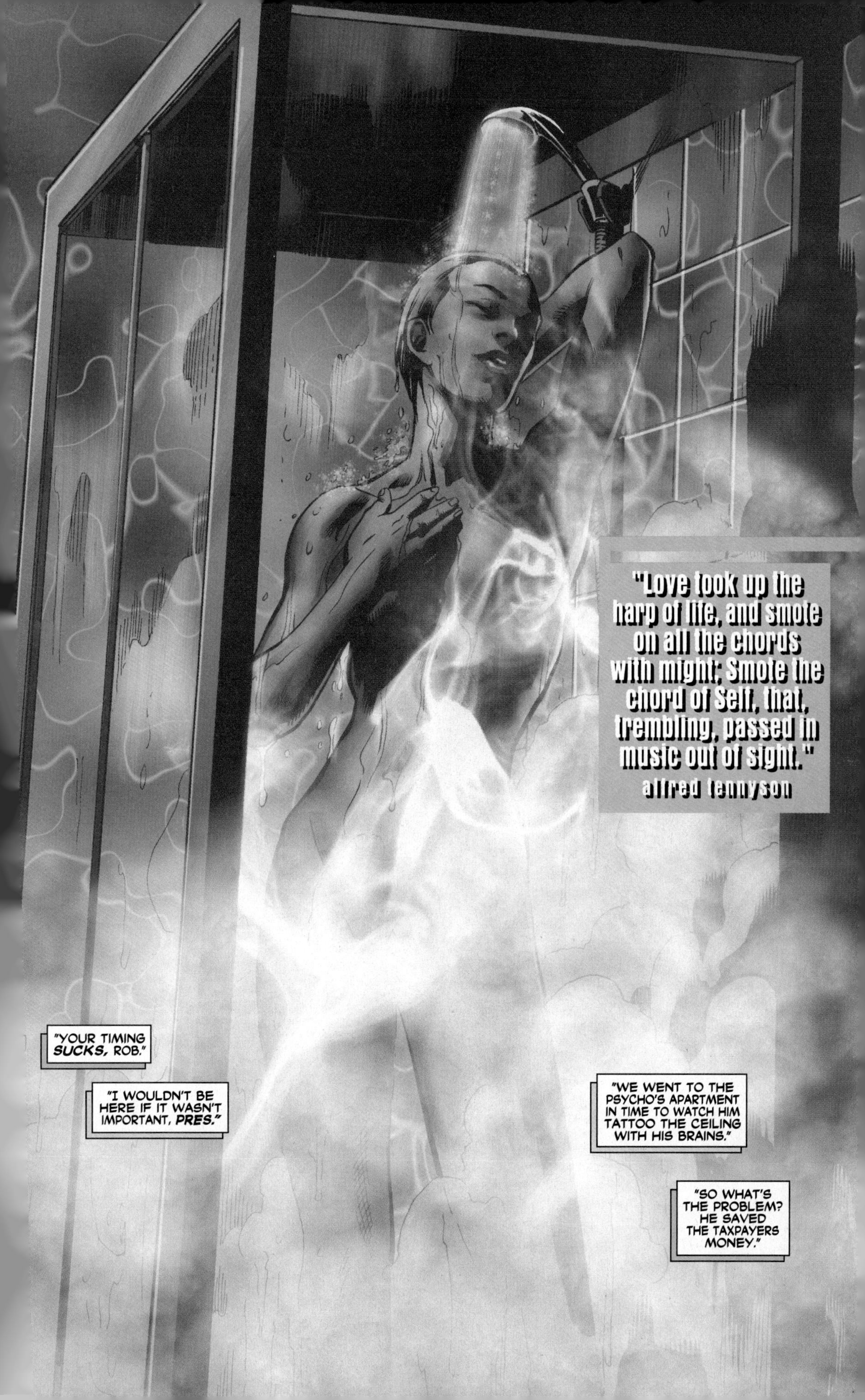
"Love took up the harp of life, and smote on all the chords with might; Smote the chord of Self, that, trembling, passed in music out of sight."
alfred tennyson
"YOUR TIMING SUCKS, ROB."
"I WOULDN'T BE HERE IF IT WASN'T IMPORTANT, PRES."
"WE WENT TO THE PSYCHO'S APARTMENT IN TIME TO WATCH HIM TATTOO THE CEILING WITH HIS BRAINS."
"SO WHAT'S THE PROBLEM? HE SAVED THE TAXPAYERS MONEY."

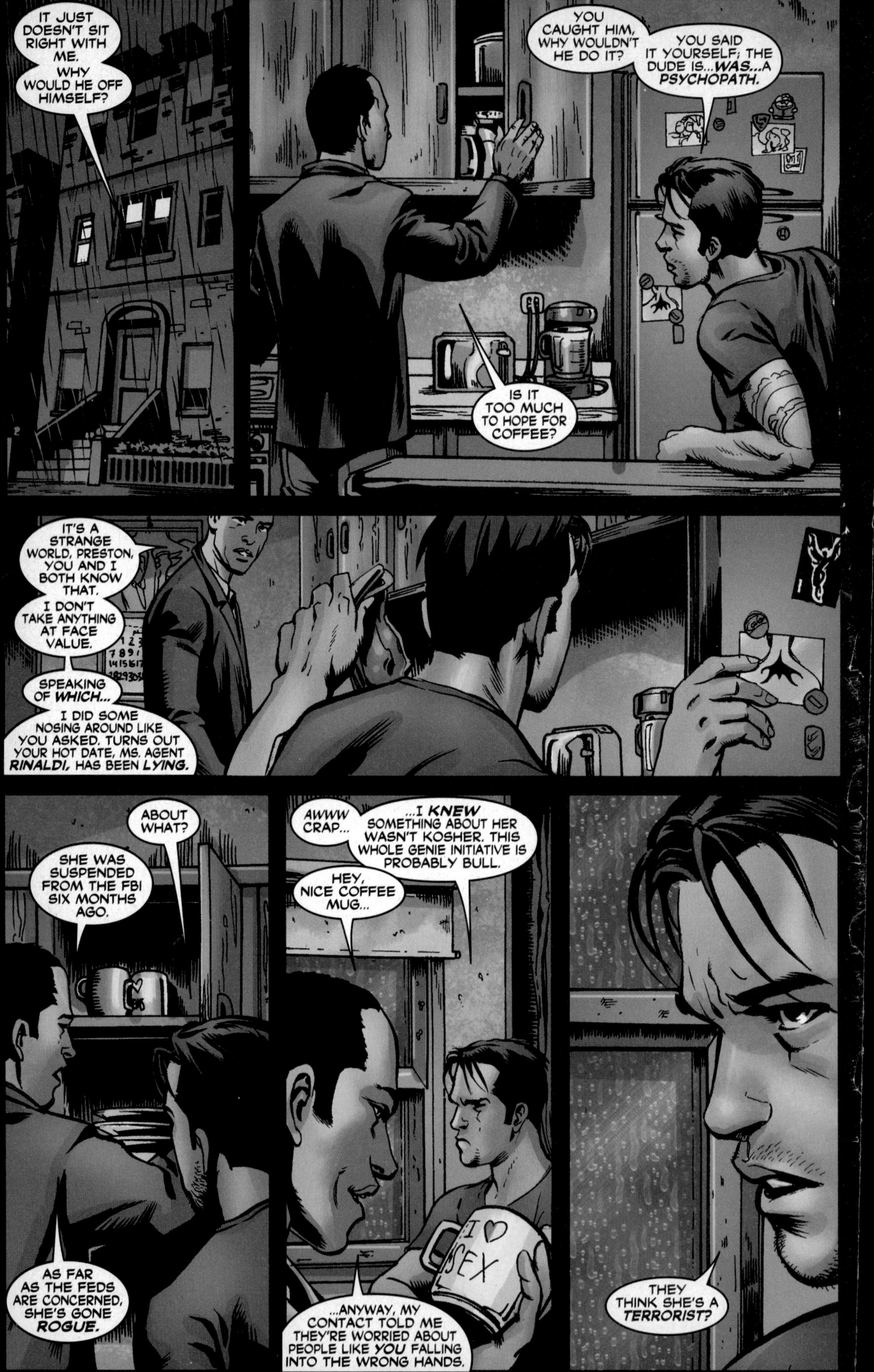

IT JUST DOESN'T SIT RIGHT WITH ME.
WHY WOULD HE OFF HIMSELF?
YOU CAUGHT HIM, WHY WOULDN'T HE DO IT?
YOU SAID IT YOURSELF; THE DUDE IS...WAS...A PSYCHOPATH.
IS IT TOO MUCH TO HOPE FOR COFFEE?
IT'S A STRANGE WORLD, PRESTON, YOU AND I BOTH KNOW THAT.
I DON'T TAKE ANYTHING AT FACE VALUE.
SPEAKING OF WHICH...
I DID SOME NOSING AROUND LIKE YOU ASKED. TURNS OUT YOUR HOT DATE, MS. AGENT RINALDI, HAS BEEN LYING.
ABOUT WHAT?
SHE WAS SUSPENDED FROM THE FBI SIX MONTHS AGO.
AS FAR AS THE FEDS ARE CONCERNED, SHE'S GONE ROGUE.
AWWW CRAP...
...I KNEW SOMETHING ABOUT HER WASN'T KOSHER. THIS WHOLE GENIE INITIATIVE IS PROBABLY BULL.
HEY, NICE COFFEE MUG...
I ♥ SEX
...ANYWAY, MY CONTACT TOLD ME THEY'RE WORRIED ABOUT PEOPLE LIKE YOU FALLING INTO THE WRONG HANDS.
THEY THINK SHE'S A TERRORIST?

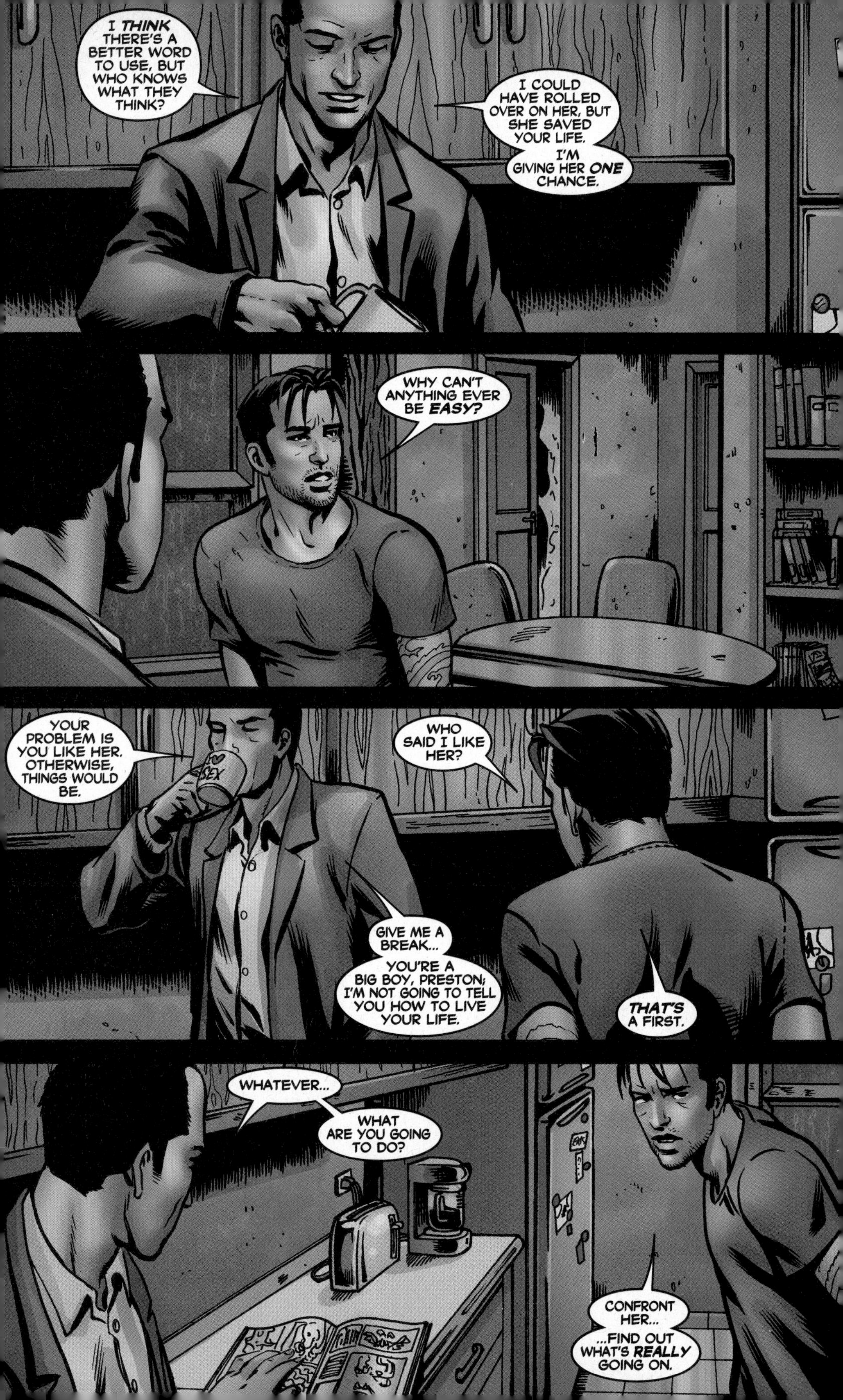
I THINK THERE'S A BETTER WORD TO USE, BUT WHO KNOWS WHAT THEY THINK?
I COULD HAVE ROLLED OVER ON HER, BUT SHE SAVED YOUR LIFE.
I'M GIVING HER ONE CHANCE.
WHY CAN'T ANYTHING EVER BE EASY?
YOUR PROBLEM IS YOU LIKE HER. OTHERWISE, THINGS WOULD BE.
WHO SAID I LIKE HER?
GIVE ME A BREAK...
YOU'RE A BIG BOY, PRESTON; I'M NOT GOING TO TELL YOU HOW TO LIVE YOUR LIFE.
THAT'S A FIRST.
WHATEVER...
WHAT ARE YOU GOING TO DO?
CONFRONT HER...
...FIND OUT WHAT'S REALLY GOING ON.

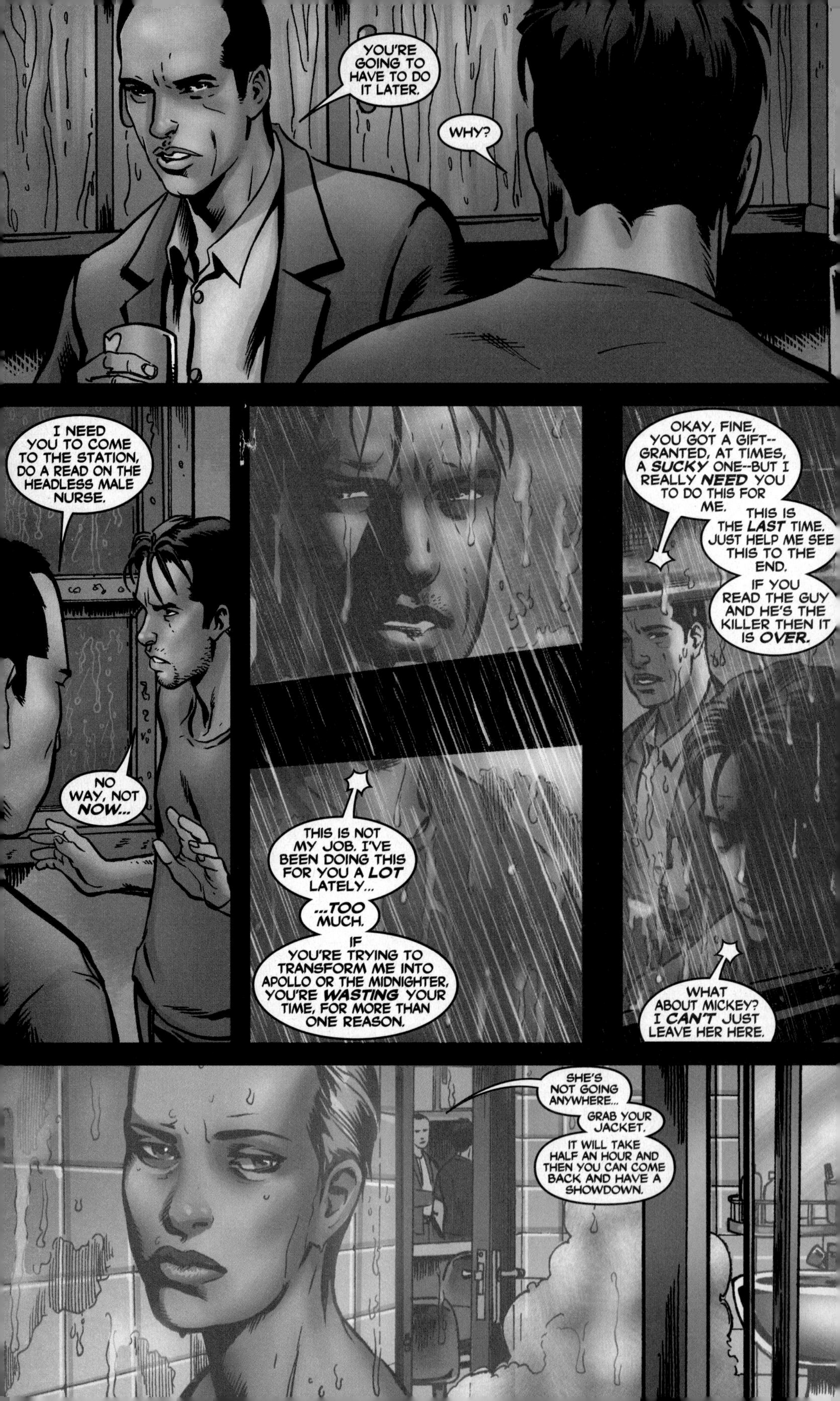
YOU'RE GOING TO HAVE TO DO IT LATER.
WHY?
I NEED YOU TO COME TO THE STATION, DO A READ ON THE HEADLESS MALE NURSE.
NO WAY, NOT NOW...
THIS IS NOT MY JOB. I'VE BEEN DOING THIS FOR YOU A LOT LATELY...
...TOO MUCH.
IF YOU'RE TRYING TO TRANSFORM ME INTO APOLLO OR THE MIDNIGHTER, YOU'RE WASTING YOUR TIME, FOR MORE THAN ONE REASON.
OKAY, FINE, YOU GOT A GIFT-- GRANTED, AT TIMES, A SUCKY ONE--BUT I REALLY NEED YOU TO DO THIS FOR ME.
THIS IS THE LAST TIME. JUST HELP ME SEE THIS TO THE END.
IF YOU READ THE GUY AND HE'S THE KILLER THEN IT IS OVER.
WHAT ABOUT MICKEY? I CAN'T JUST LEAVE HER HERE.
SHE'S NOT GOING ANYWHERE...
GRAB YOUR JACKET.
IT WILL TAKE HALF AN HOUR AND THEN YOU CAN COME BACK AND HAVE A SHOWDOWN.

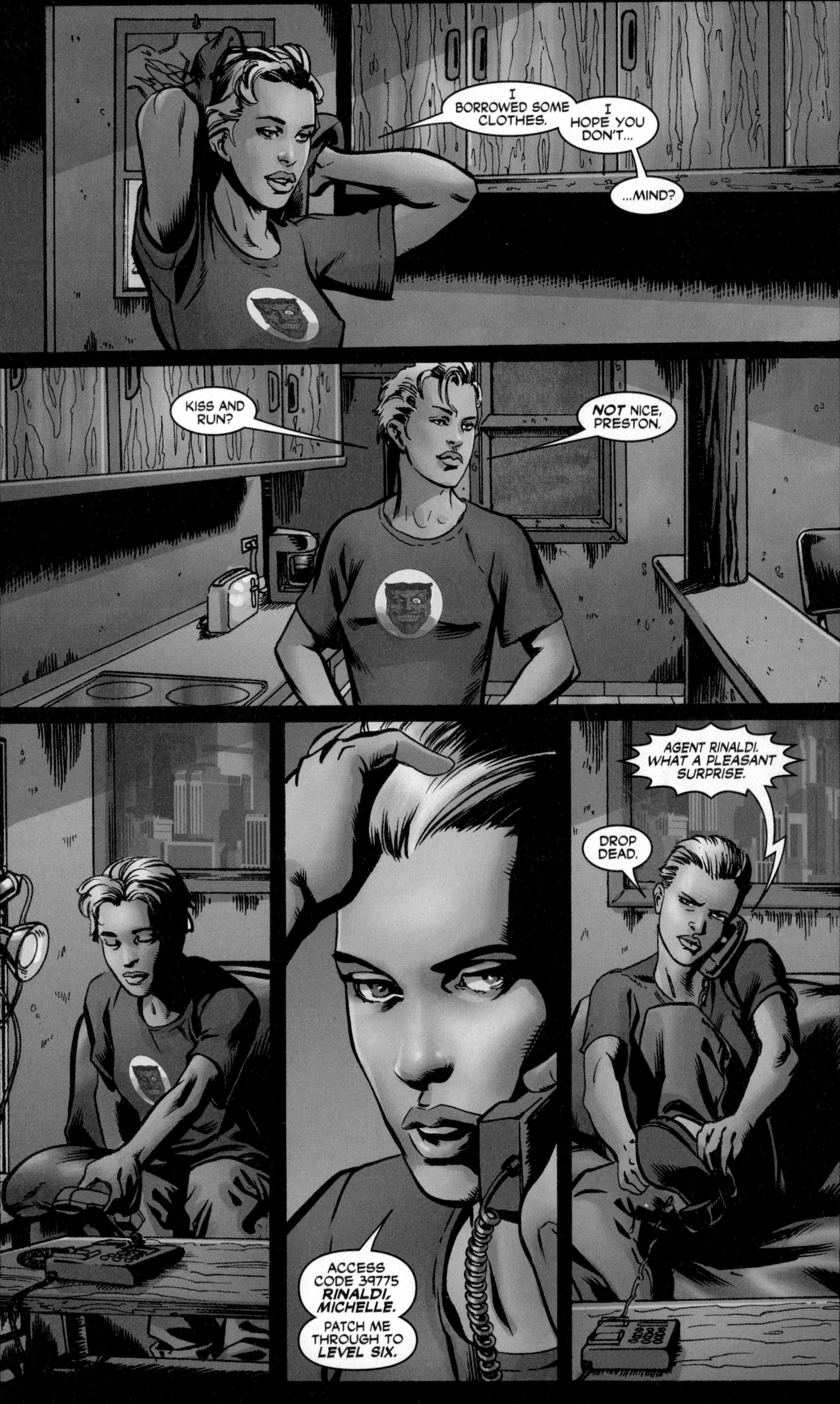
I BORROWED SOME CLOTHES.
I HOPE YOU DON'T...
...MIND?
KISS AND RUN?
NOT NICE, PRESTON.
ACCESS CODE 39775 RINALDI, MICHELLE.
PATCH ME THROUGH TO LEVEL SIX.
AGENT RINALDI. WHAT A PLEASANT SURPRISE.
DROP DEAD.

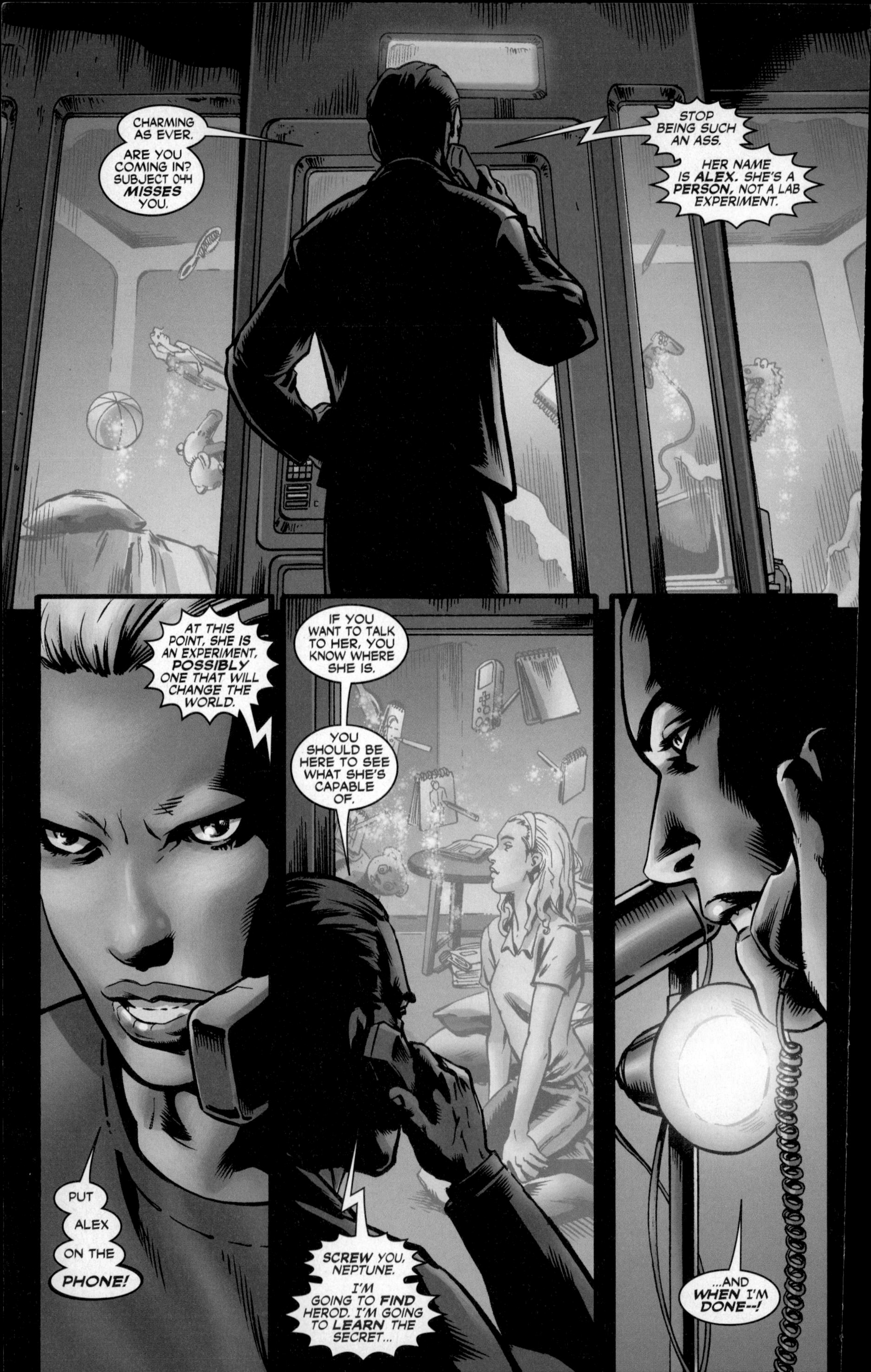

CHARMING AS EVER.
ARE YOU COMING IN? SUBJECT 044 **MISSES** YOU.
STOP BEING SUCH AN ASS.
HER NAME IS **ALEX.** SHE'S A **PERSON,** NOT A LAB EXPERIMENT.
AT THIS POINT, SHE IS AN EXPERIMENT, **POSSIBLY** ONE THAT WILL CHANGE THE WORLD.
PUT ALEX ON THE **PHONE!**
IF YOU WANT TO TALK TO HER, YOU KNOW WHERE SHE IS.
YOU SHOULD BE HERE TO SEE WHAT SHE'S CAPABLE OF.
SCREW *YOU, NEPTUNE.*
I'M GOING TO ***FIND*** *HEROD. I'M GOING TO* ***LEARN*** *THE SECRET...*
...AND **WHEN** I'M **DONE--!**

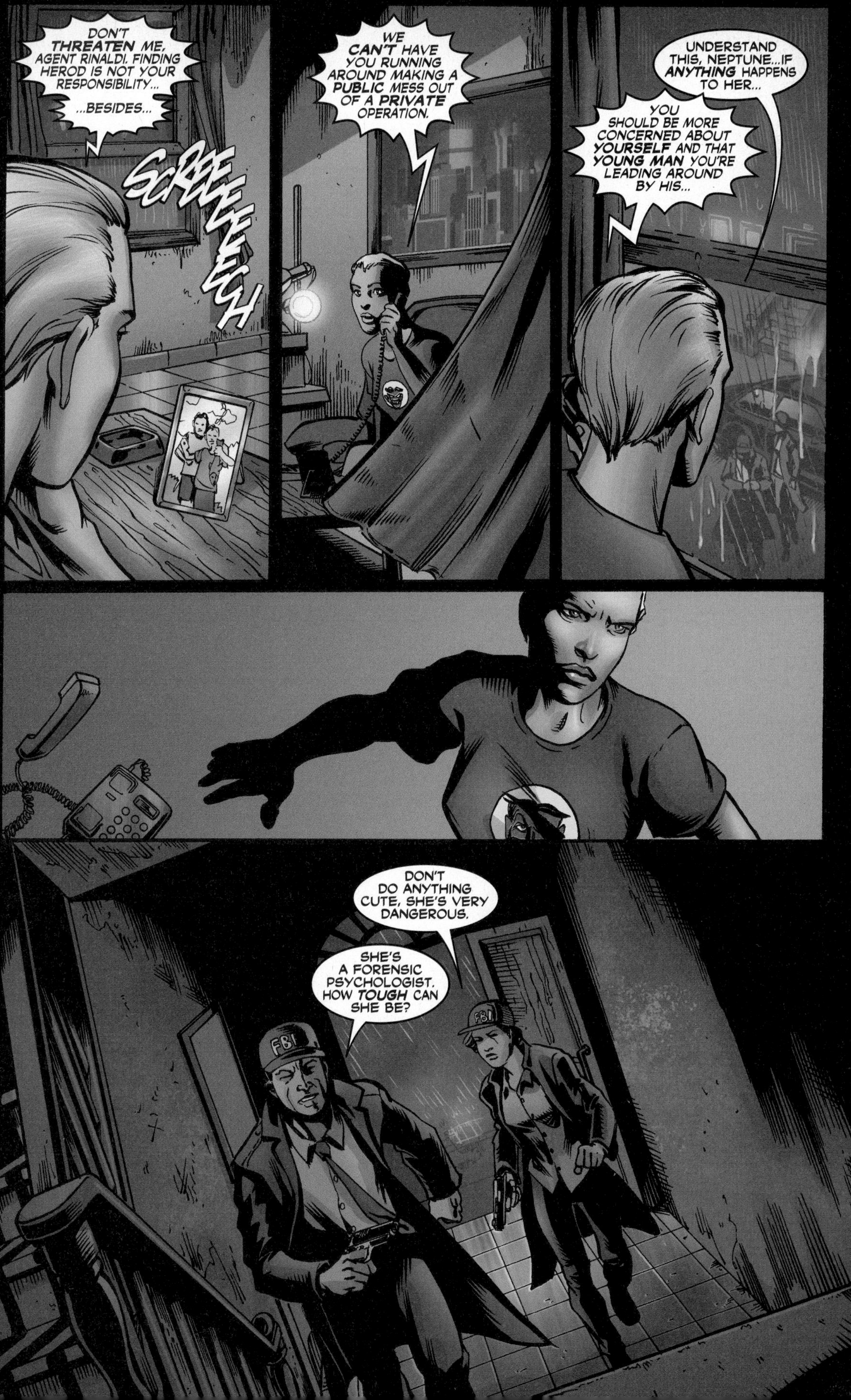

DON'T THREATEN ME, AGENT RINALDI. FINDING HEROD IS NOT YOUR RESPONSIBILITY...
...BESIDES...
SCREEEEECH
WE CAN'T HAVE YOU RUNNING AROUND MAKING A PUBLIC MESS OUT OF A PRIVATE OPERATION.
UNDERSTAND THIS, NEPTUNE...IF ANYTHING HAPPENS TO HER...
YOU SHOULD BE MORE CONCERNED ABOUT YOURSELF AND THAT YOUNG MAN YOU'RE LEADING AROUND BY HIS...
DON'T DO ANYTHING CUTE, SHE'S VERY DANGEROUS.
SHE'S A FORENSIC PSYCHOLOGIST. HOW TOUGH CAN SHE BE?
FBI
FBI

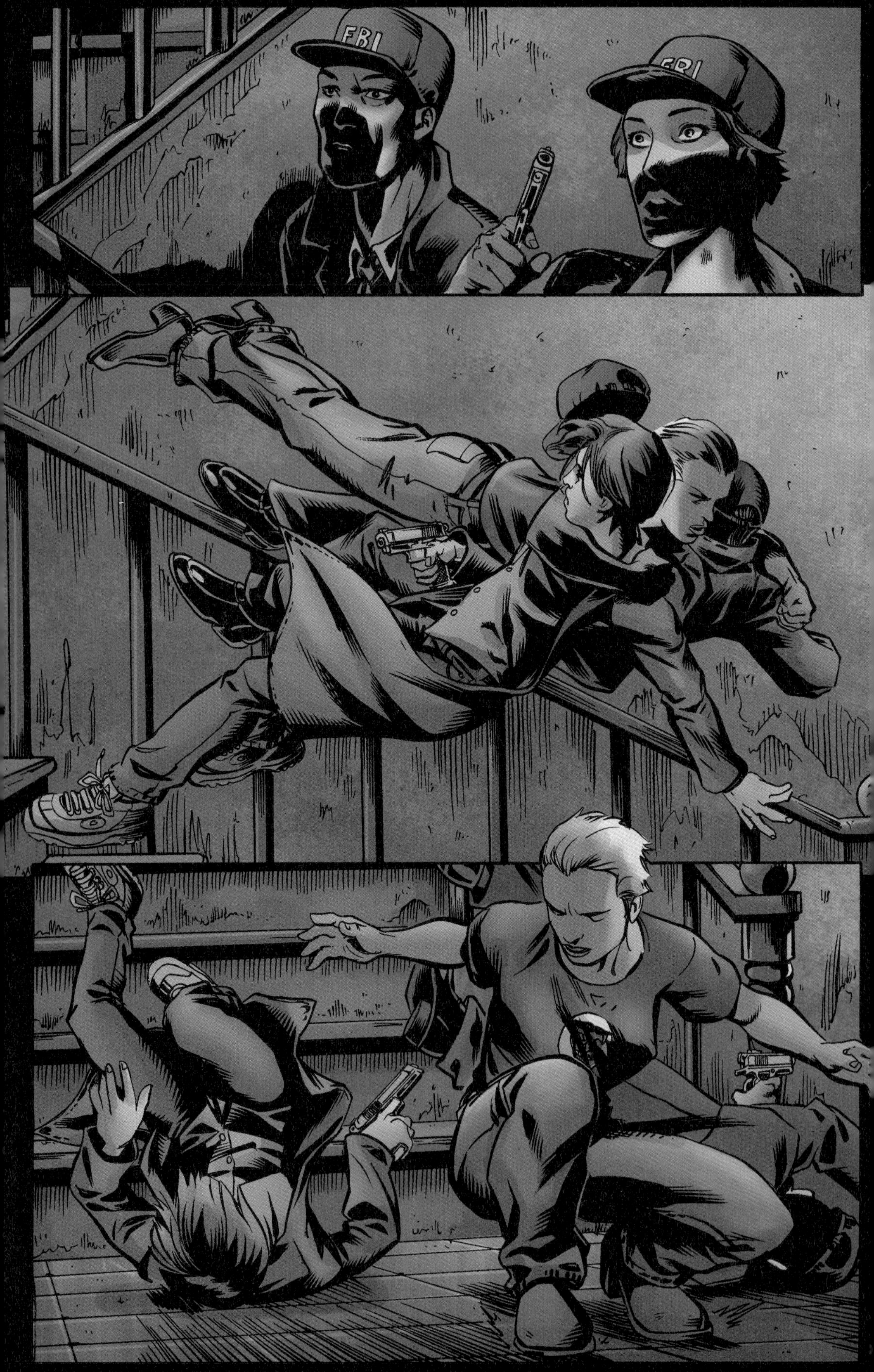
FBI
FBI

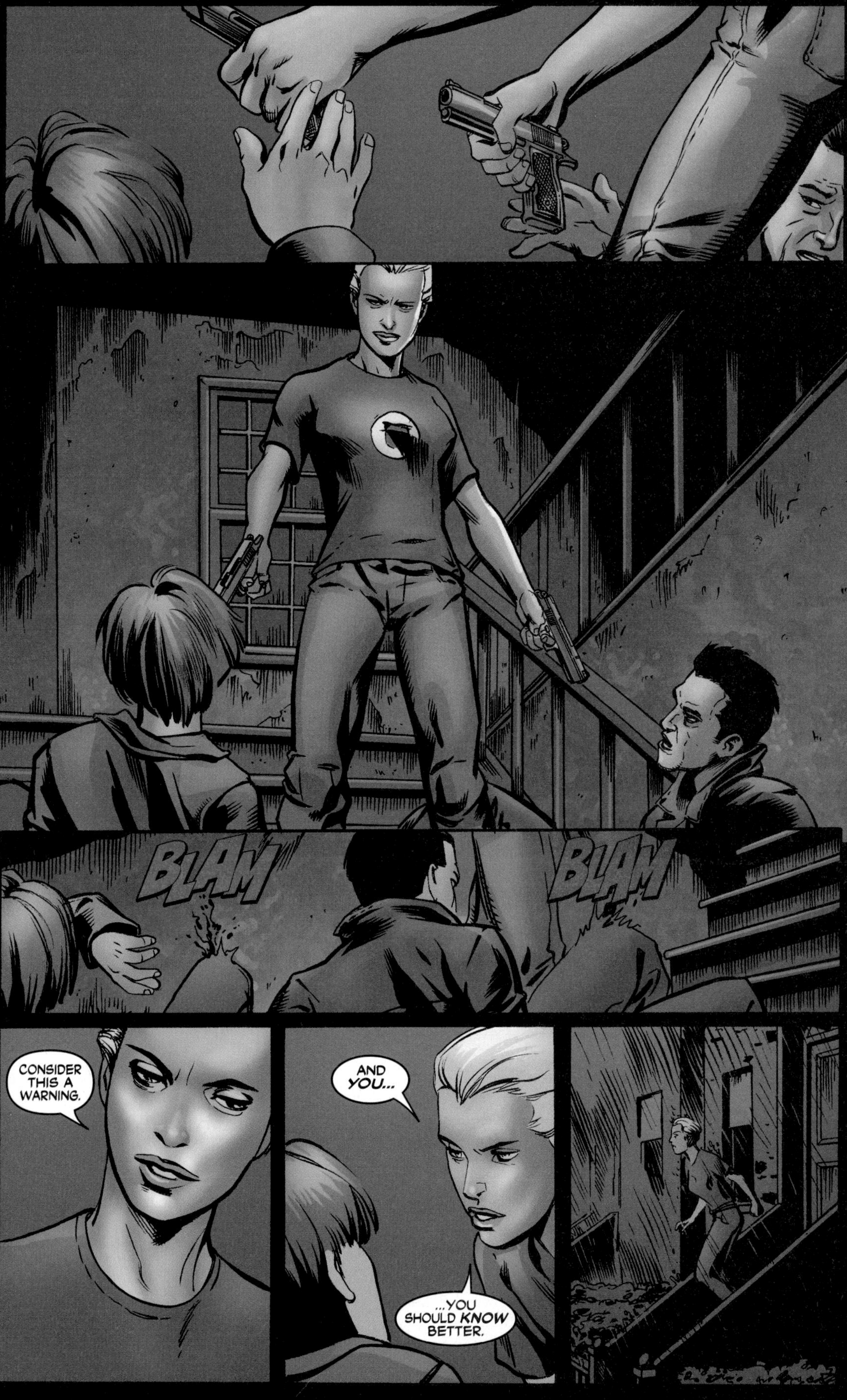
BLAM
BLAM
CONSIDER THIS A WARNING.
AND *YOU*...
...YOU SHOULD *KNOW* BETTER.

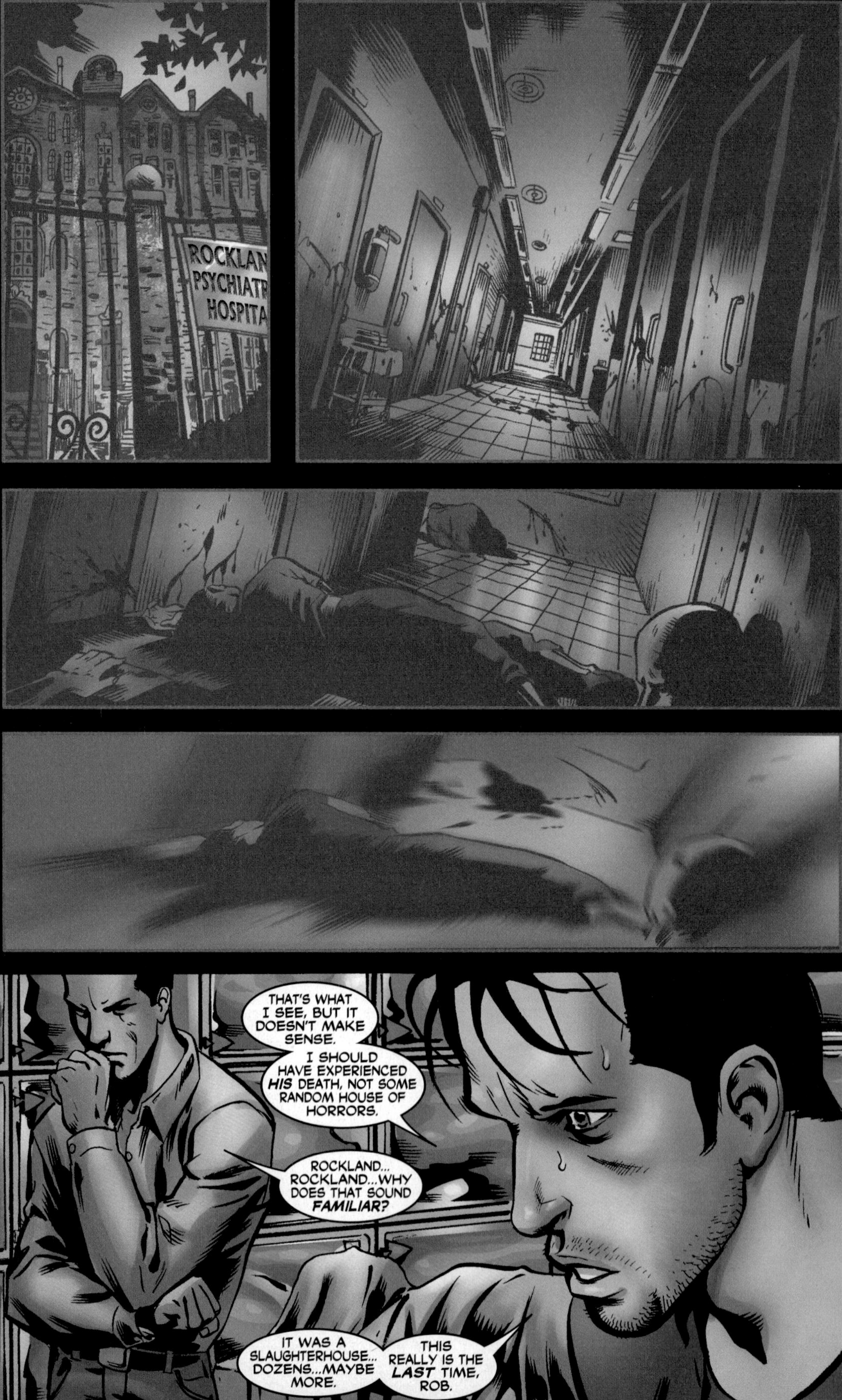

ROCKLAN
PSYCHIATR
HOSPITA
THAT'S WHAT I SEE, BUT IT DOESN'T MAKE SENSE.
I SHOULD HAVE EXPERIENCED *HIS* DEATH, NOT SOME RANDOM HOUSE OF HORRORS.
ROCKLAND... ROCKLAND...WHY DOES THAT SOUND *FAMILIAR?*
IT WAS A SLAUGHTERHOUSE... DOZENS...MAYBE MORE.
THIS REALLY IS THE *LAST* TIME, ROB.

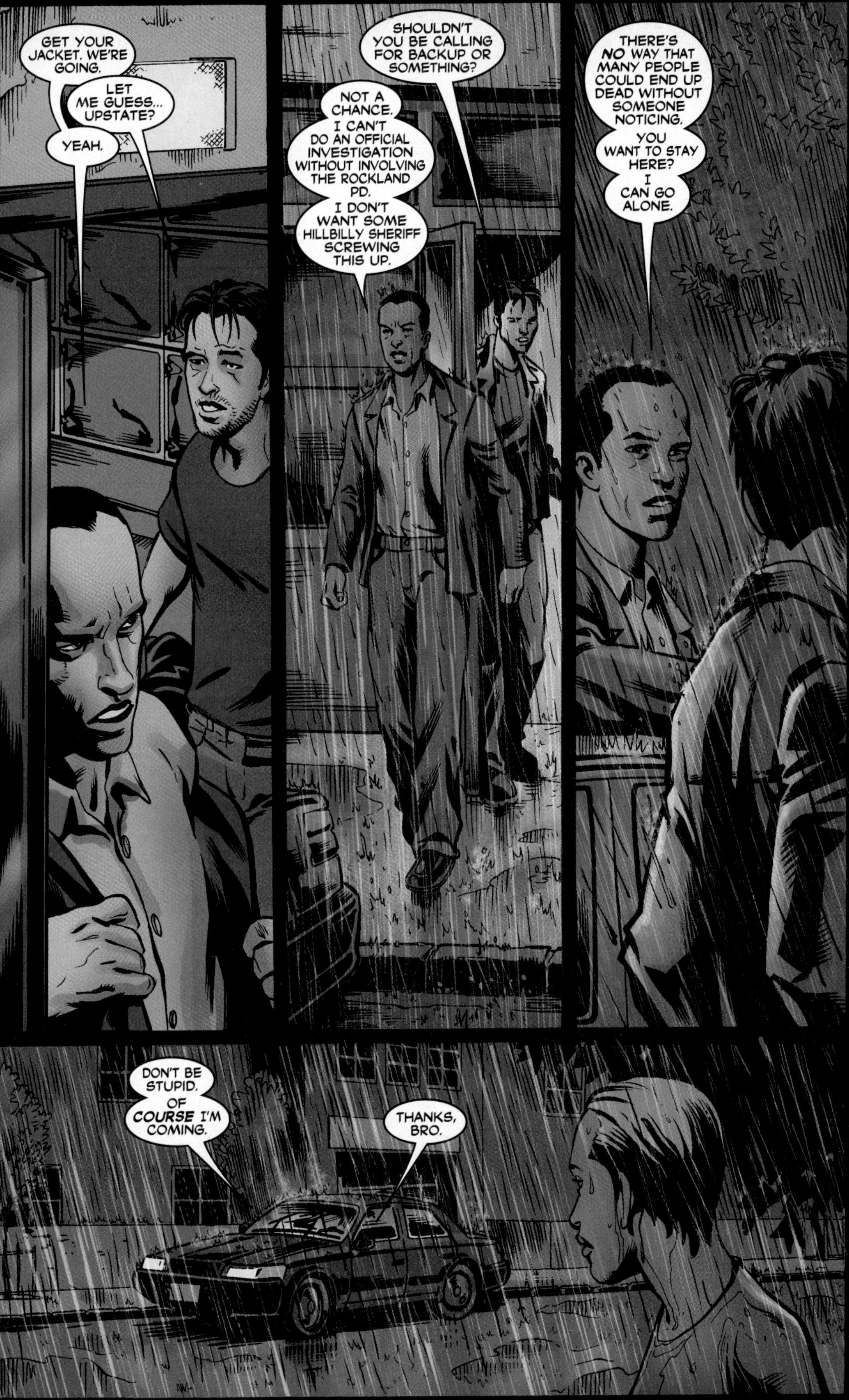
GET YOUR JACKET. WE'RE GOING.
LET ME GUESS... UPSTATE?
YEAH.
SHOULDN'T YOU BE CALLING FOR BACKUP OR SOMETHING?
NOT A CHANCE.
I CAN'T DO AN OFFICIAL INVESTIGATION WITHOUT INVOLVING THE ROCKLAND PD.
I DON'T WANT SOME HILLBILLY SHERIFF SCREWING THIS UP.
THERE'S NO WAY THAT MANY PEOPLE COULD END UP DEAD WITHOUT SOMEONE NOTICING.
YOU WANT TO STAY HERE?
I CAN GO ALONE.
DON'T BE STUPID.
OF COURSE I'M COMING.
THANKS, BRO.

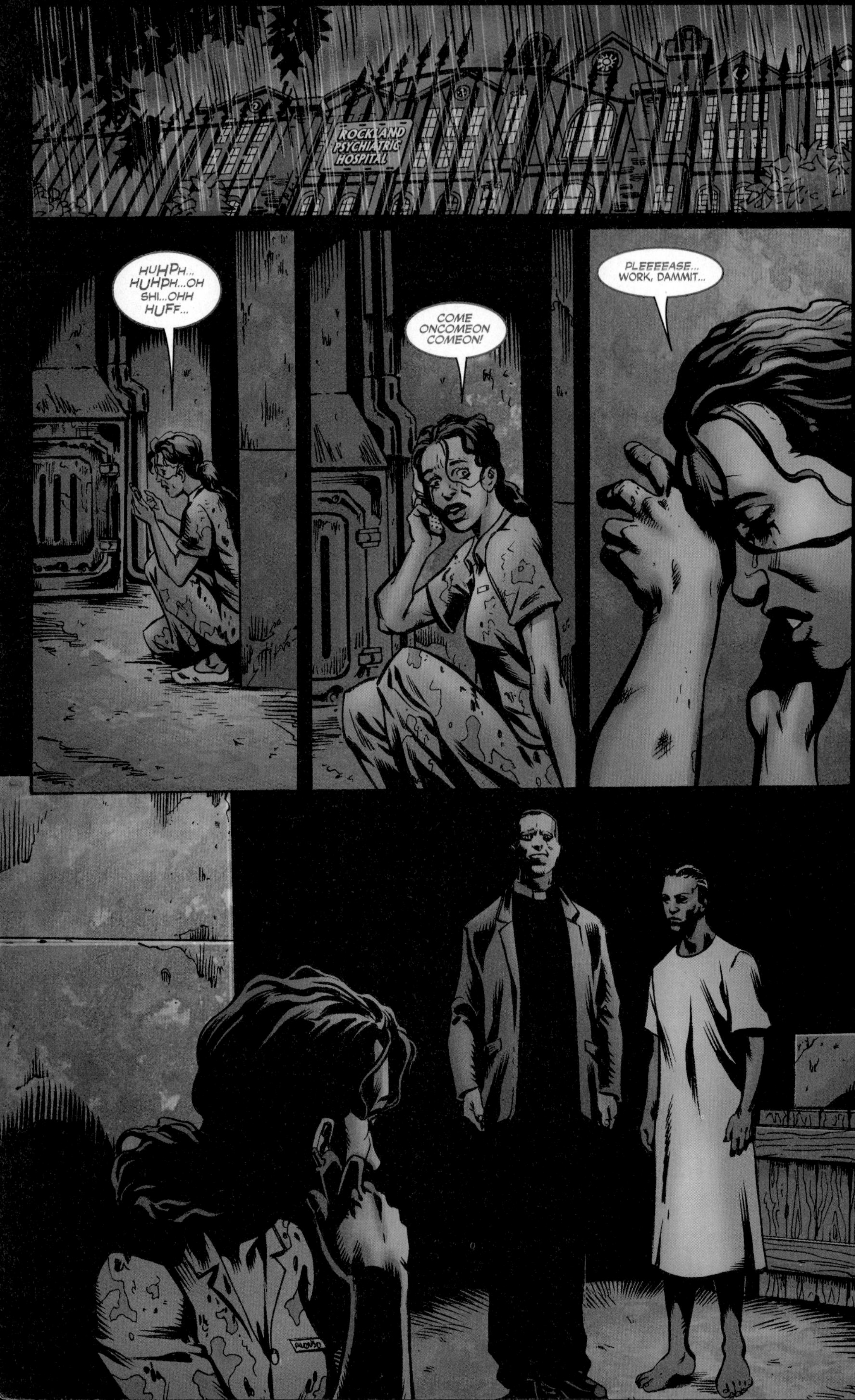
ROCKLAND PSYCHIATRIC HOSPITAL
HUHPH... HUHPH...OH SHI...OHH HUFF...
COME ONCOMEON COMEON!
PLEEEEASE... WORK, DAMMIT...

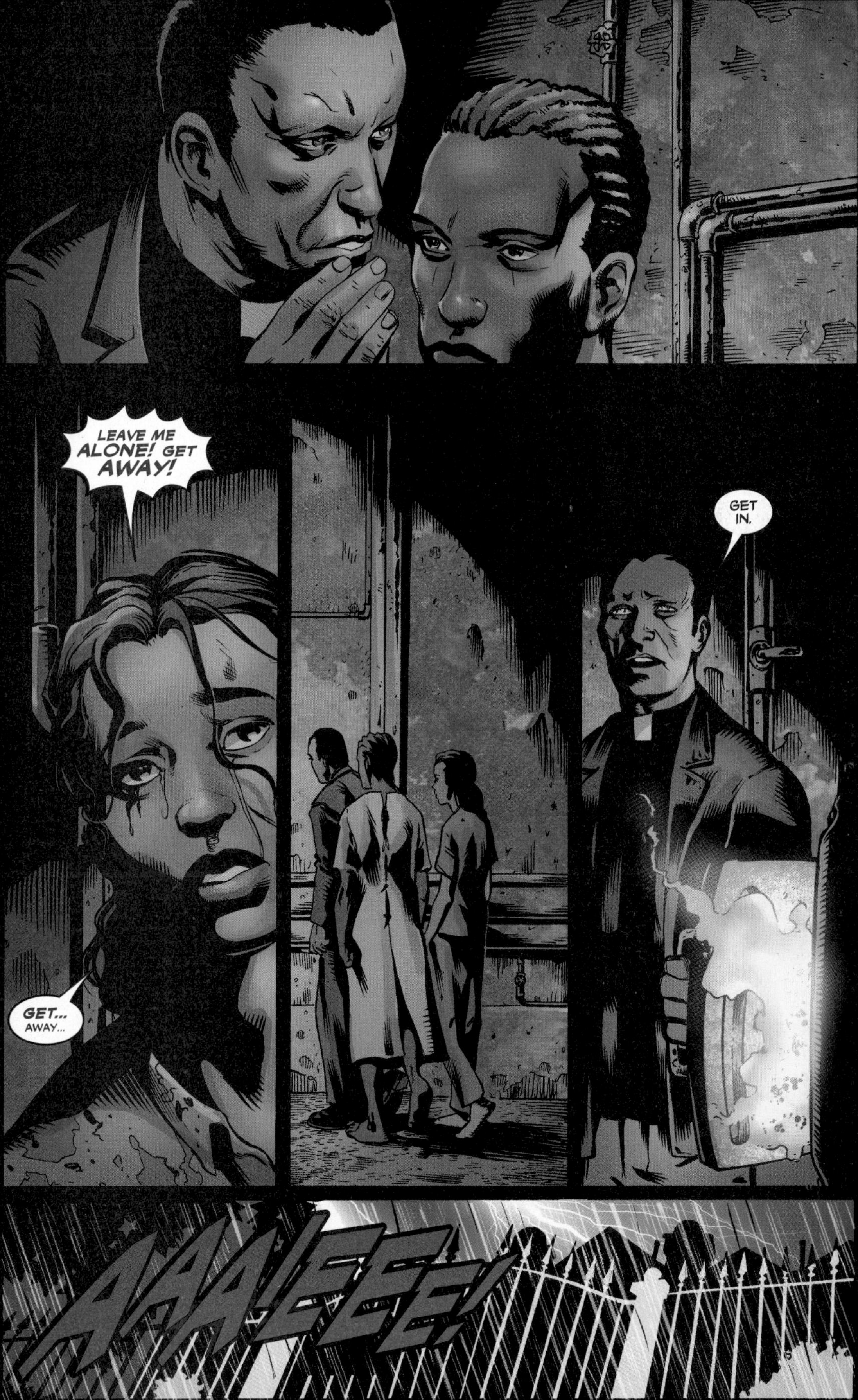
LEAVE ME ALONE! GET AWAY!
GET... AWAY...
GET IN.
AAAIEEE!

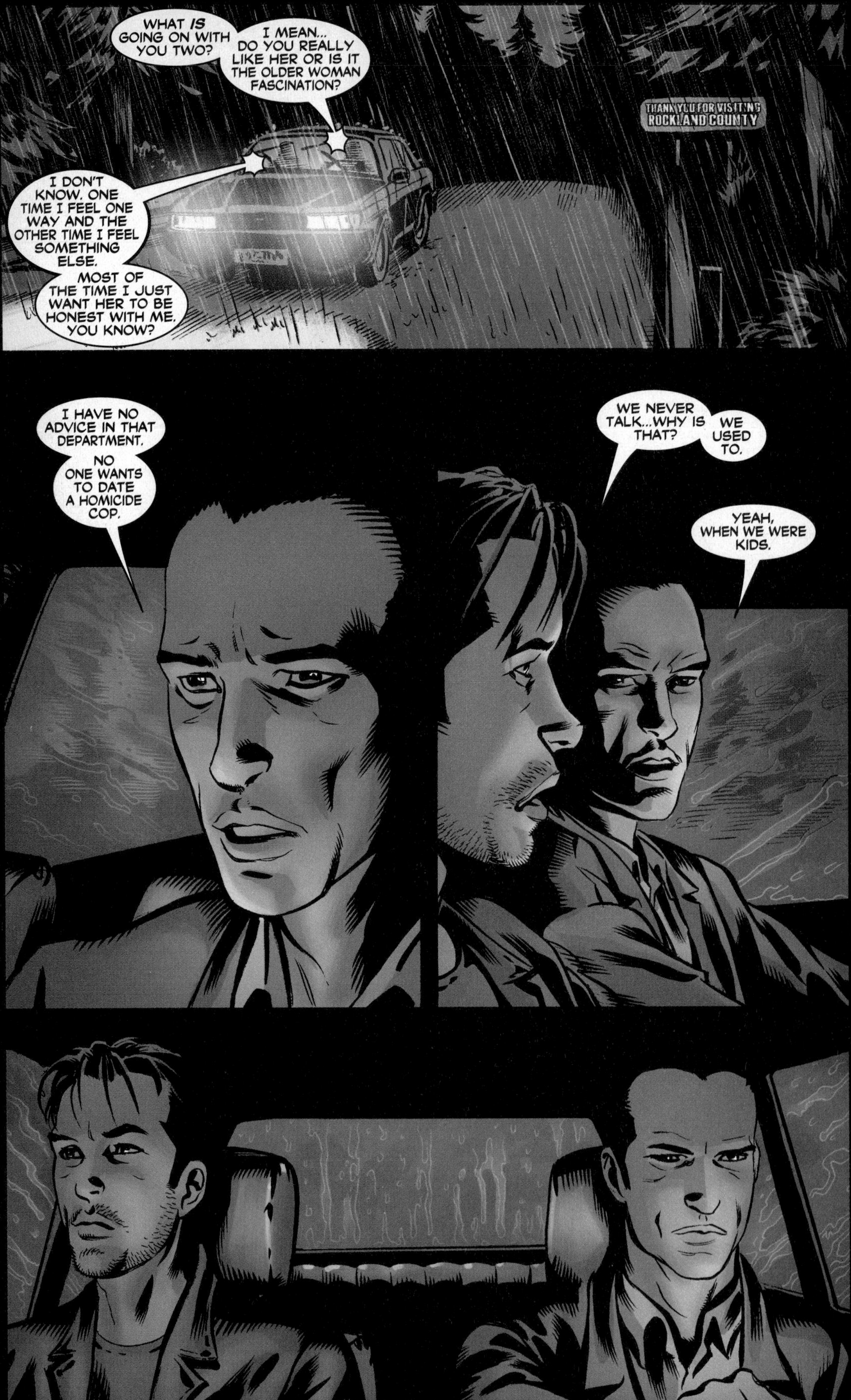
WHAT IS GOING ON WITH YOU TWO?
I MEAN... DO YOU REALLY LIKE HER OR IS IT THE OLDER WOMAN FASCINATION?
THANK YOU FOR VISITING ROCKLAND COUNTY
I DON'T KNOW. ONE TIME I FEEL ONE WAY AND THE OTHER TIME I FEEL SOMETHING ELSE.
MOST OF THE TIME I JUST WANT HER TO BE HONEST WITH ME. YOU KNOW?
I HAVE NO ADVICE IN THAT DEPARTMENT.
NO ONE WANTS TO DATE A HOMICIDE COP.
WE NEVER TALK...WHY IS THAT?
WE USED TO.
YEAH, WHEN WE WERE KIDS.

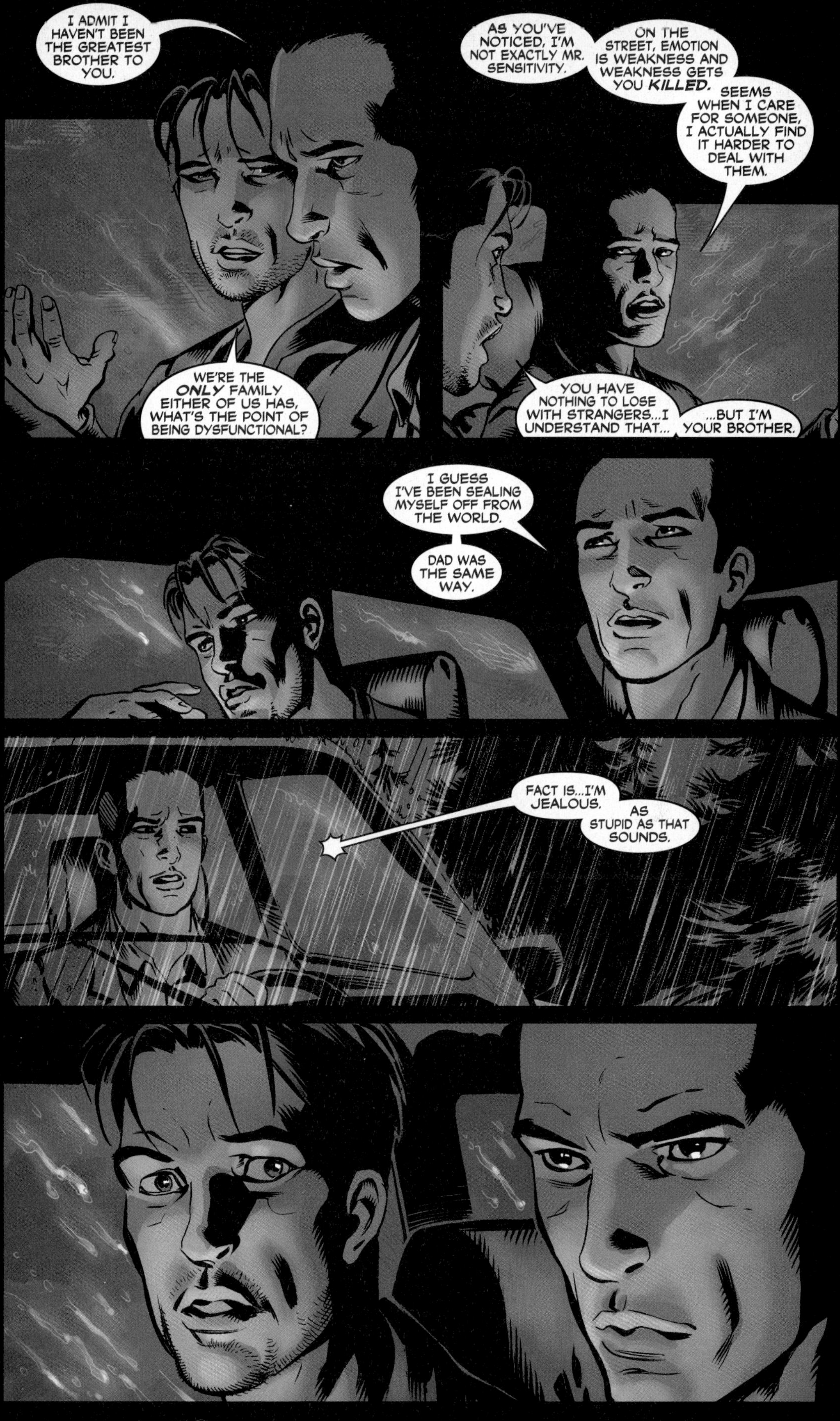
I ADMIT I HAVEN'T BEEN THE GREATEST BROTHER TO YOU.
WE'RE THE ONLY FAMILY EITHER OF US HAS, WHAT'S THE POINT OF BEING DYSFUNCTIONAL?
AS YOU'VE NOTICED, I'M NOT EXACTLY MR. SENSITIVITY.
ON THE STREET, EMOTION IS WEAKNESS AND WEAKNESS GETS YOU KILLED.
SEEMS WHEN I CARE FOR SOMEONE, I ACTUALLY FIND IT HARDER TO DEAL WITH THEM.
YOU HAVE NOTHING TO LOSE WITH STRANGERS...I UNDERSTAND THAT...
...BUT I'M YOUR BROTHER.
I GUESS I'VE BEEN SEALING MYSELF OFF FROM THE WORLD.
DAD WAS THE SAME WAY.
FACT IS...I'M JEALOUS.
AS STUPID AS THAT SOUNDS.

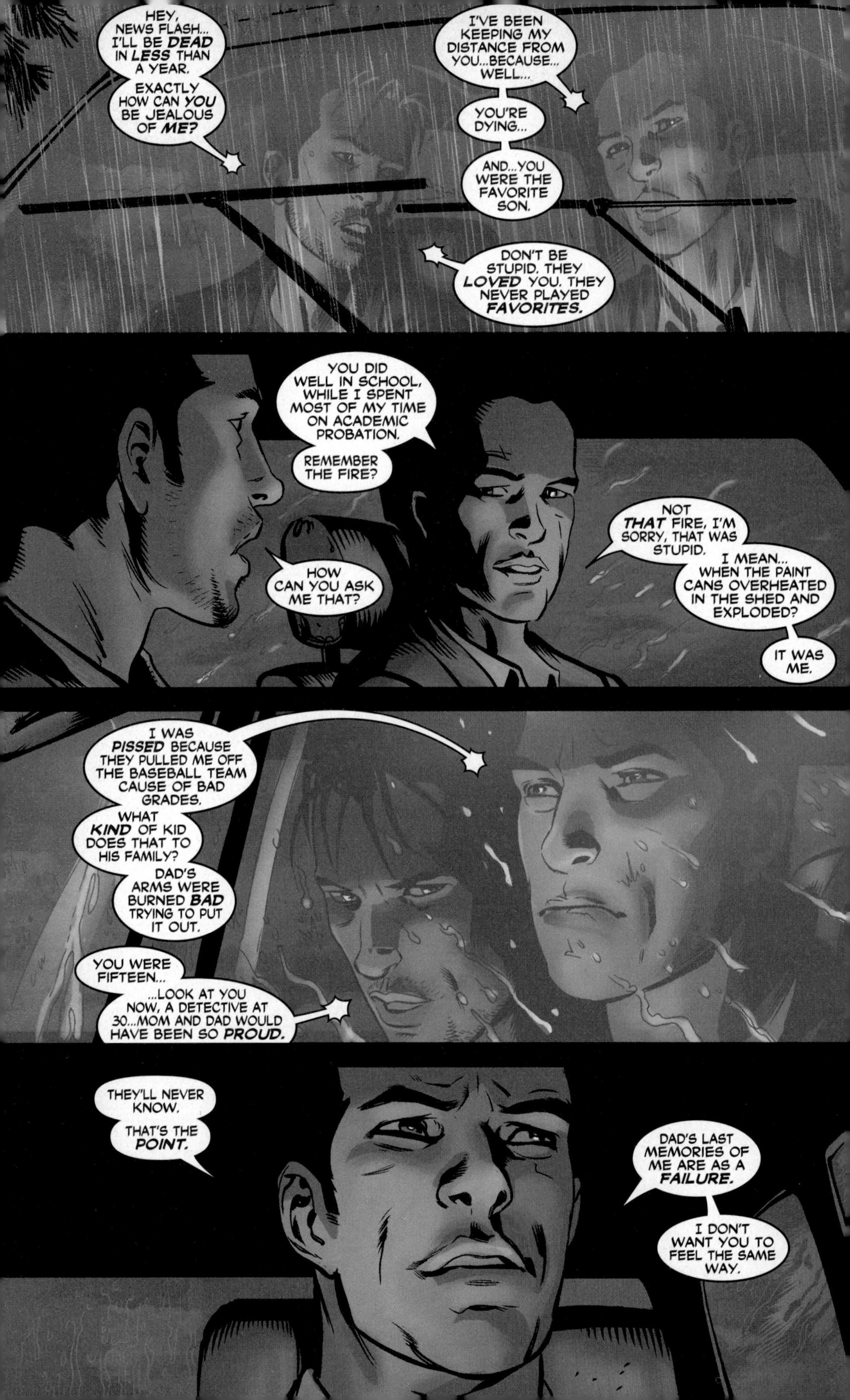
HEY, NEWS FLASH... I'LL BE DEAD IN LESS THAN A YEAR.
EXACTLY HOW CAN YOU BE JEALOUS OF ME?
I'VE BEEN KEEPING MY DISTANCE FROM YOU...BECAUSE... WELL...
YOU'RE DYING...
AND...YOU WERE THE FAVORITE SON.
DON'T BE STUPID. THEY LOVED YOU. THEY NEVER PLAYED FAVORITES.
YOU DID WELL IN SCHOOL, WHILE I SPENT MOST OF MY TIME ON ACADEMIC PROBATION.
REMEMBER THE FIRE?
HOW CAN YOU ASK ME THAT?
NOT THAT FIRE, I'M SORRY, THAT WAS STUPID.
I MEAN... WHEN THE PAINT CANS OVERHEATED IN THE SHED AND EXPLODED?
IT WAS ME.
I WAS PISSED BECAUSE THEY PULLED ME OFF THE BASEBALL TEAM CAUSE OF BAD GRADES.
WHAT KIND OF KID DOES THAT TO HIS FAMILY?
DAD'S ARMS WERE BURNED BAD TRYING TO PUT IT OUT.
YOU WERE FIFTEEN...
...LOOK AT YOU NOW, A DETECTIVE AT 30...MOM AND DAD WOULD HAVE BEEN SO PROUD.
THEY'LL NEVER KNOW.
THAT'S THE POINT.
DAD'S LAST MEMORIES OF ME ARE AS A FAILURE.
I DON'T WANT YOU TO FEEL THE SAME WAY.

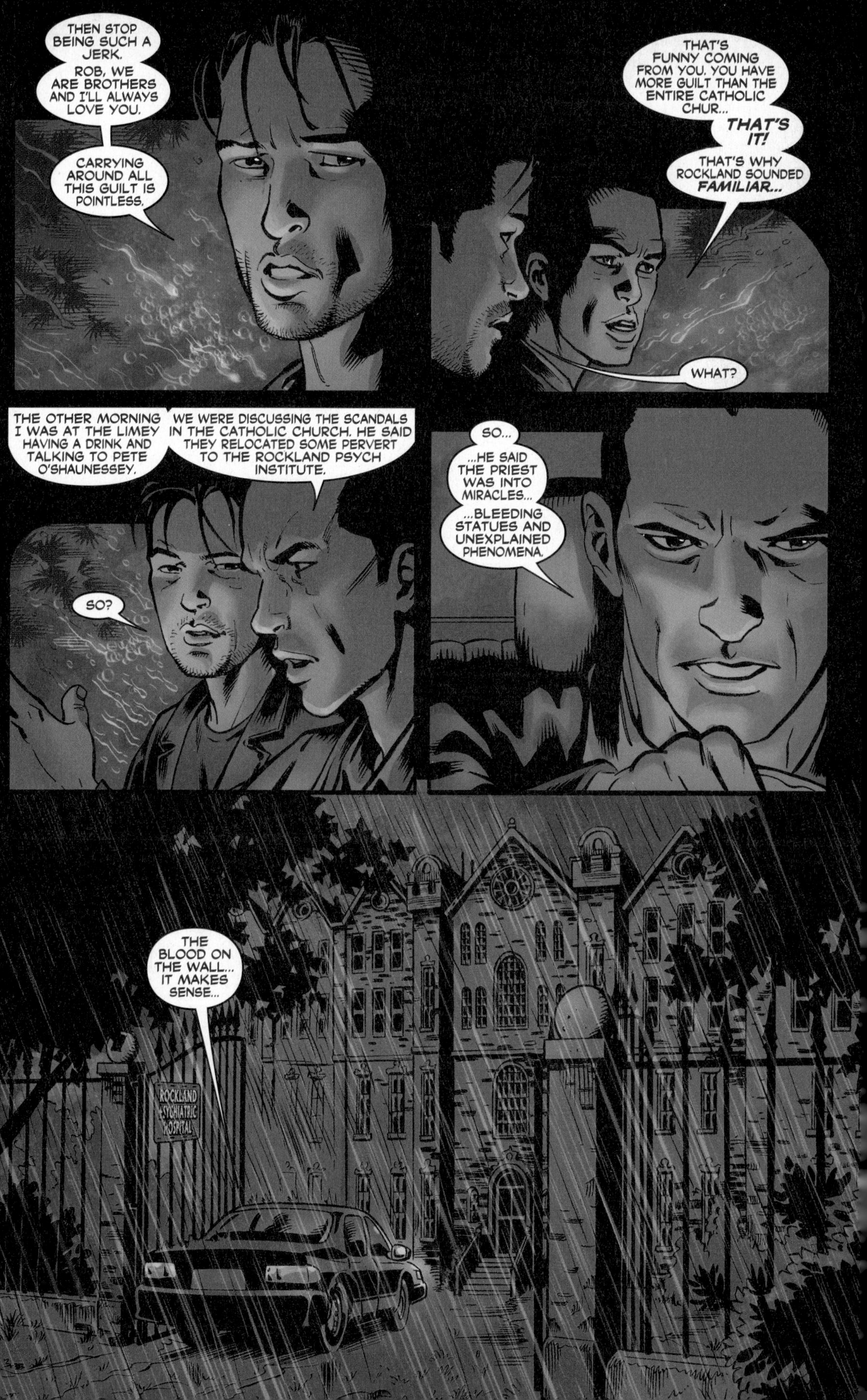
THEN STOP BEING SUCH A JERK.
ROB, WE ARE BROTHERS AND I'LL ALWAYS LOVE YOU.
CARRYING AROUND ALL THIS GUILT IS POINTLESS.
THAT'S FUNNY COMING FROM YOU. YOU HAVE MORE GUILT THAN THE ENTIRE CATHOLIC CHUR...
THAT'S IT!
THAT'S WHY ROCKLAND SOUNDED FAMILIAR...
WHAT?
THE OTHER MORNING I WAS AT THE LIMEY HAVING A DRINK AND TALKING TO PETE O'SHAUNESSEY.
WE WERE DISCUSSING THE SCANDALS IN THE CATHOLIC CHURCH. HE SAID THEY RELOCATED SOME PERVERT TO THE ROCKLAND PSYCH INSTITUTE.
SO?
SO...
...HE SAID THE PRIEST WAS INTO MIRACLES...
...BLEEDING STATUES AND UNEXPLAINED PHENOMENA.
THE BLOOD ON THE WALL... IT MAKES SENSE...
ROCKLAND PSYCHIATRIC HOSPITAL

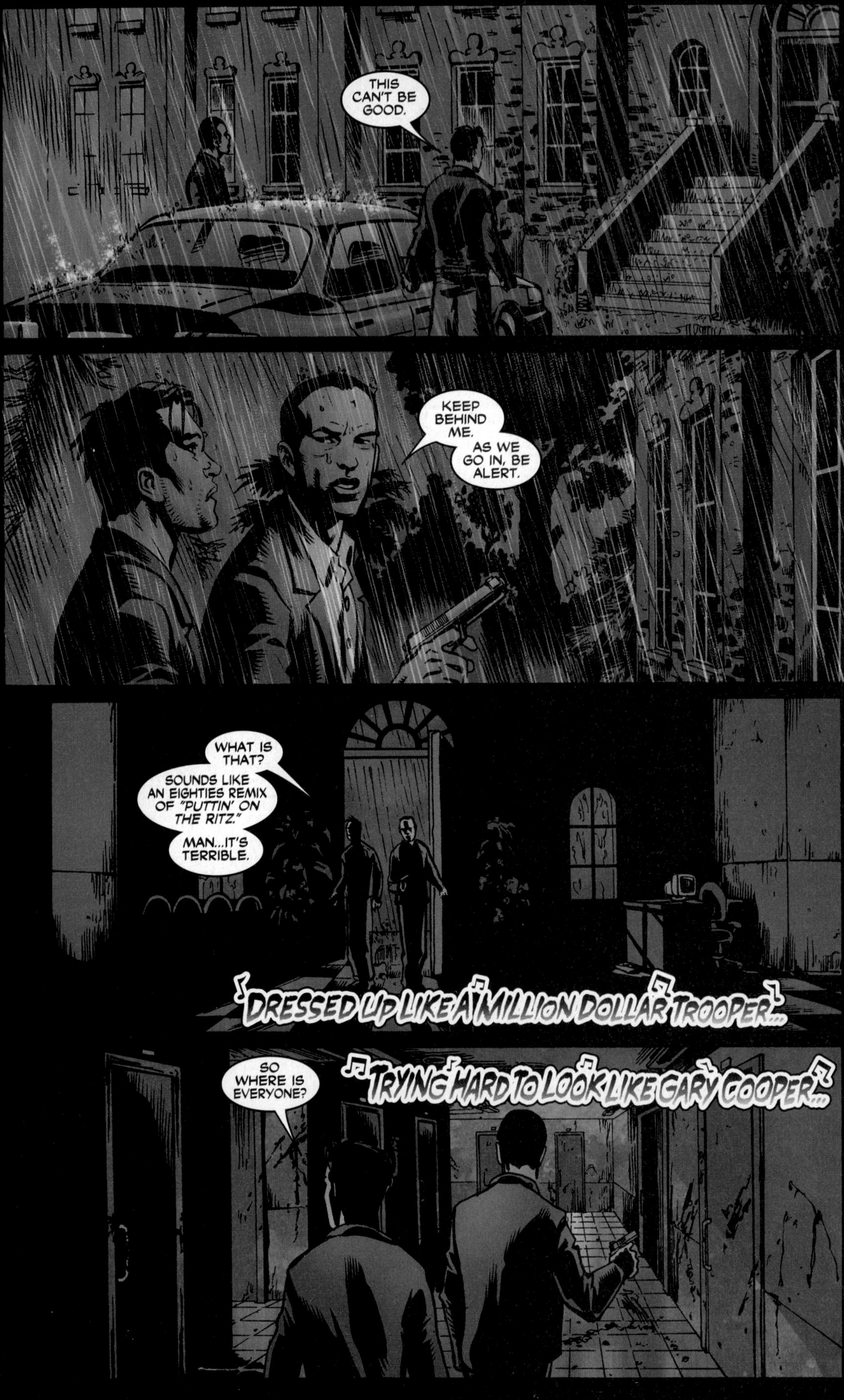
THIS CAN'T BE GOOD.
KEEP BEHIND ME.
AS WE GO IN, BE ALERT.
WHAT IS THAT?
SOUNDS LIKE AN EIGHTIES REMIX OF "PUTTIN' ON THE RITZ."
MAN...IT'S TERRIBLE.
DRESSED UP LIKE A MILLION DOLLAR TROOPER...
SO WHERE IS EVERYONE?
TRYING HARD TO LOOK LIKE GARY COOPER...

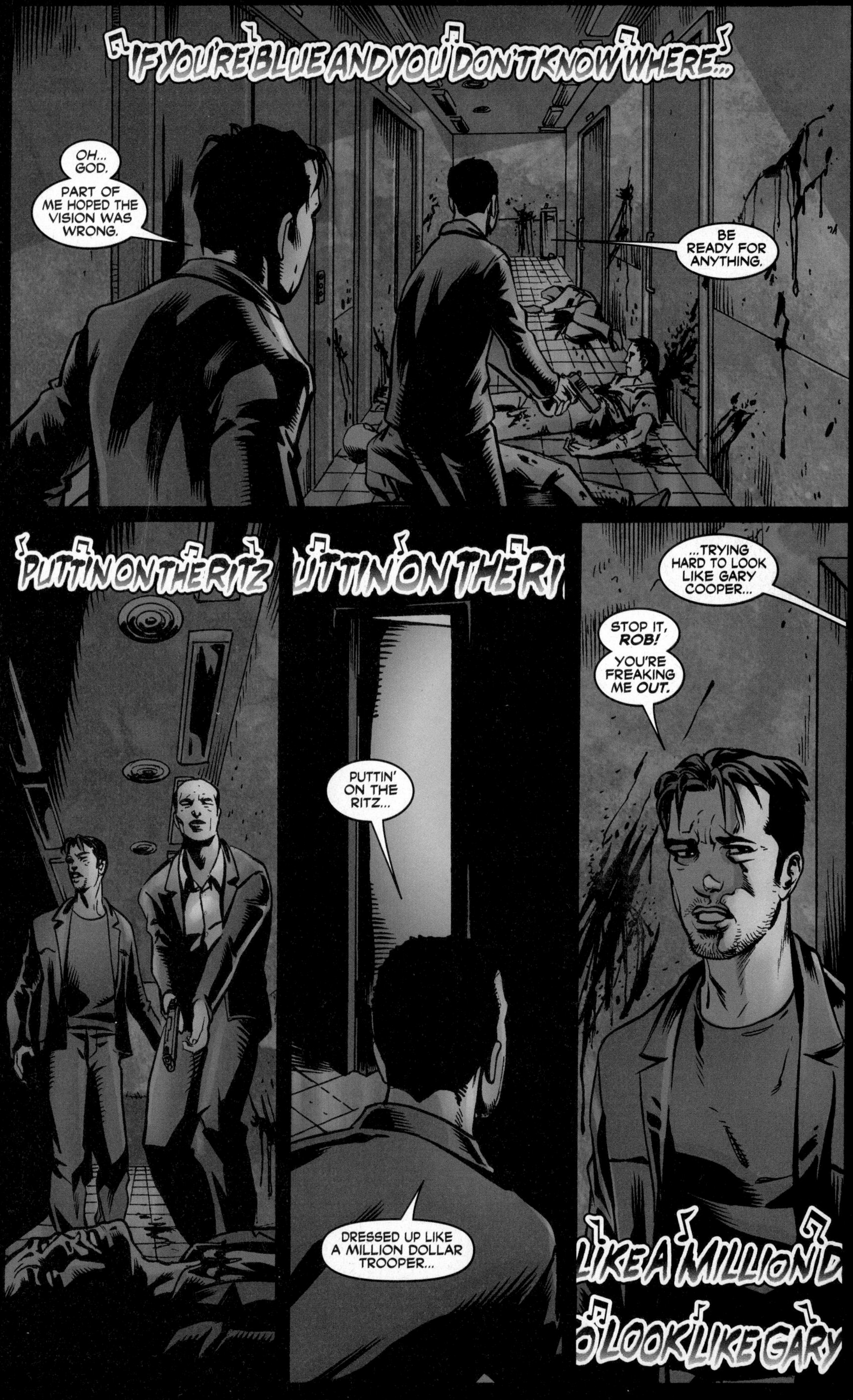
IF YOU'RE BLUE AND YOU DON'T KNOW WHERE...
OH... GOD.
PART OF ME HOPED THE VISION WAS WRONG.
BE READY FOR ANYTHING.
PUTTIN ON THE RITZ
UTTIN ON THE RI
PUTTIN' ON THE RITZ...
DRESSED UP LIKE A MILLION DOLLAR TROOPER...
...TRYING HARD TO LOOK LIKE GARY COOPER...
STOP IT, ROB! YOU'RE FREAKING ME OUT.
LIKE A MILLION D
O LOOK LIKE GARY

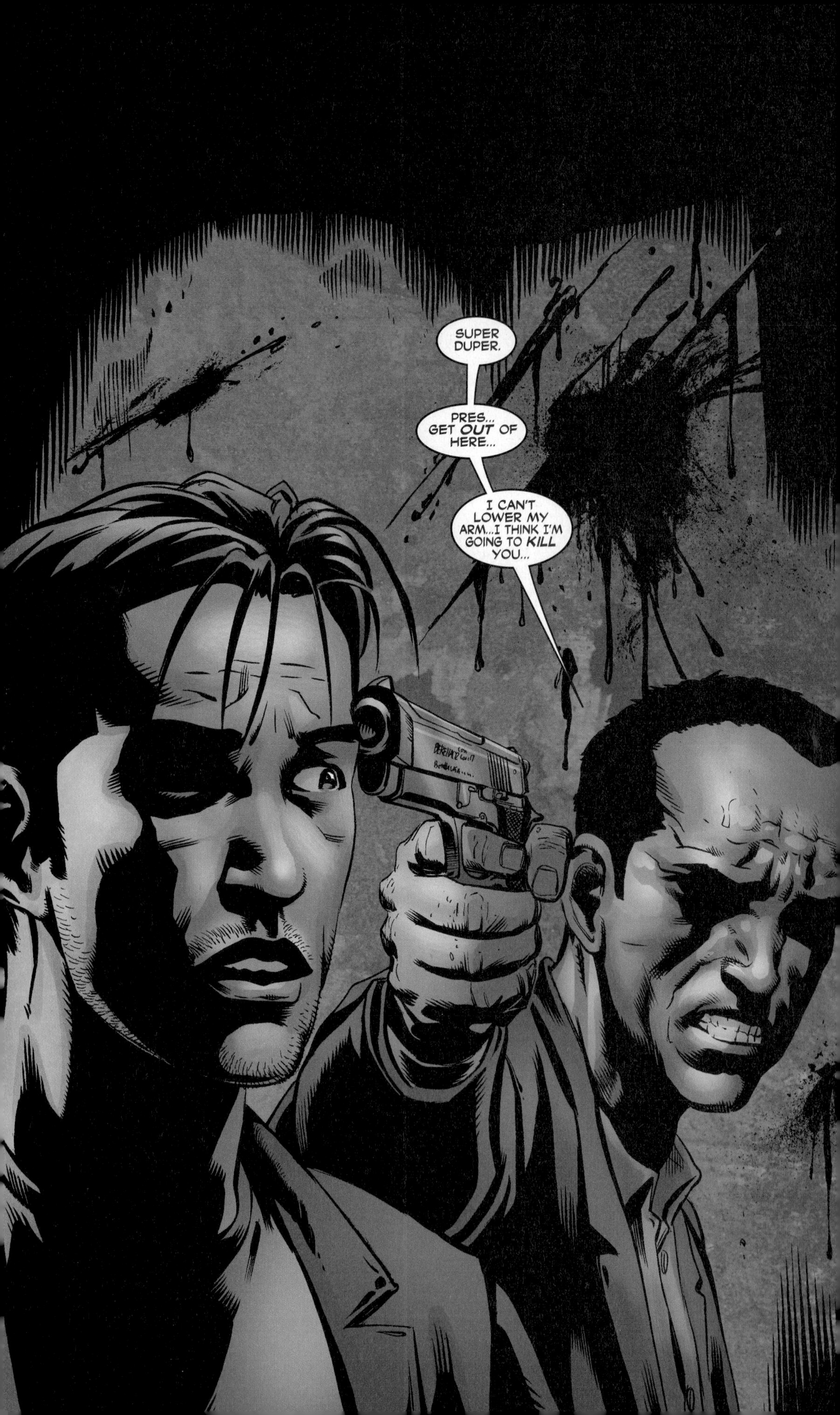
SUPER DUPER.
PRES... GET OUT OF HERE...
I CAN'T LOWER MY ARM...I THINK I'M GOING TO KILL YOU...

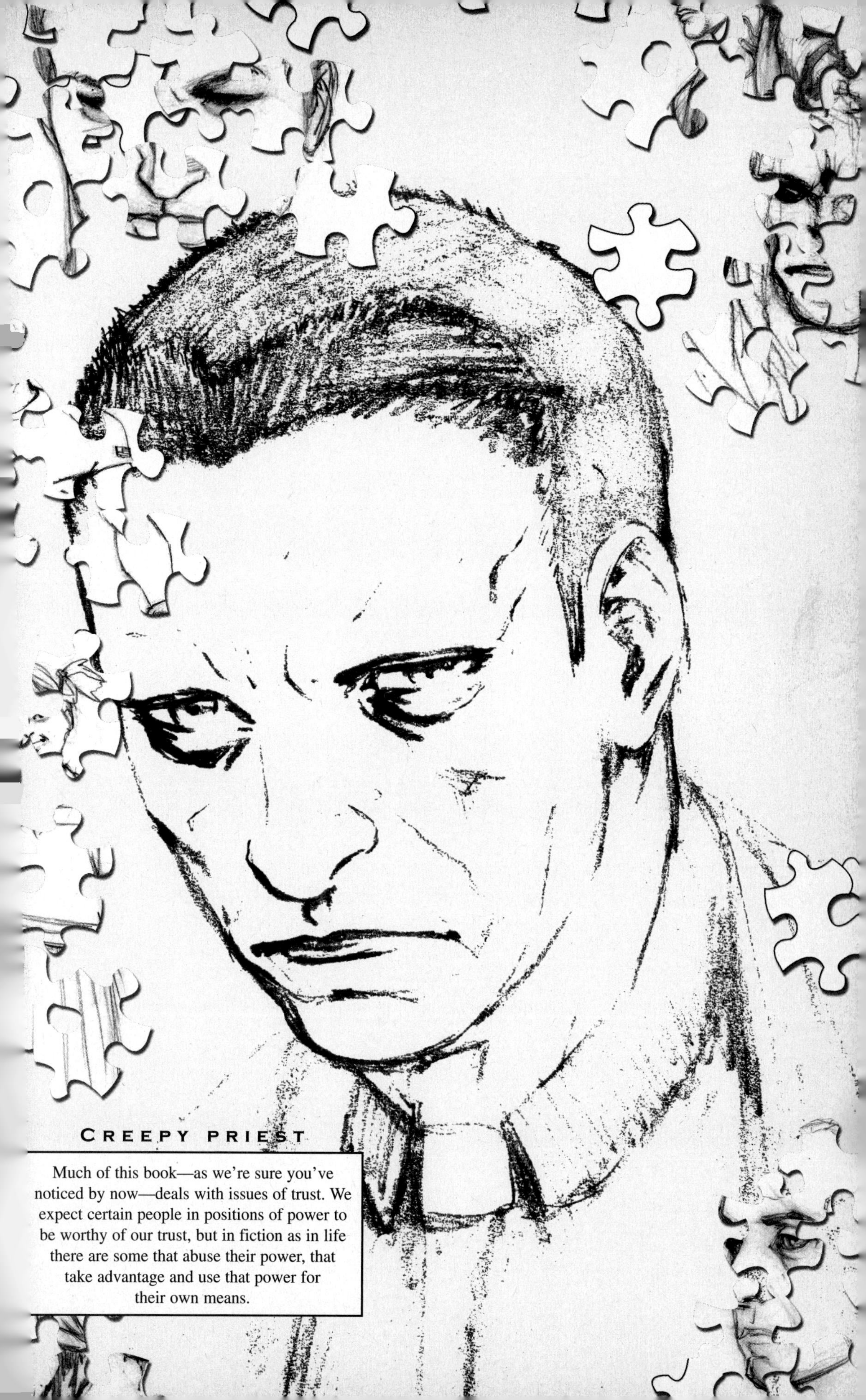

Creepy Priest

Much of this book—as we're sure you've noticed by now—deals with issues of trust. We expect certain people in positions of power to be worthy of our trust, but in fiction as in life there are some that abuse their power, that take advantage and use that power for their own means.

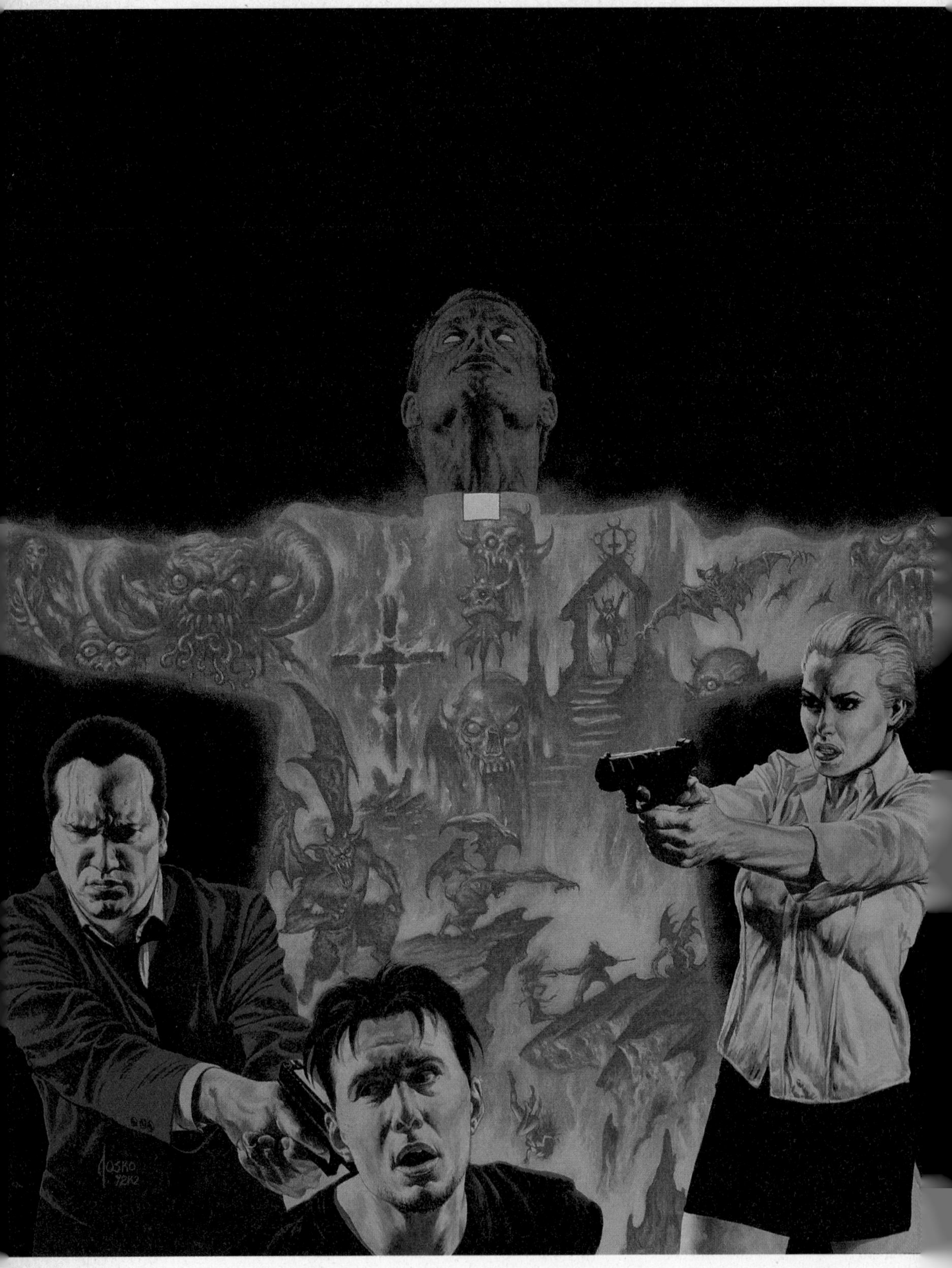

End of Night

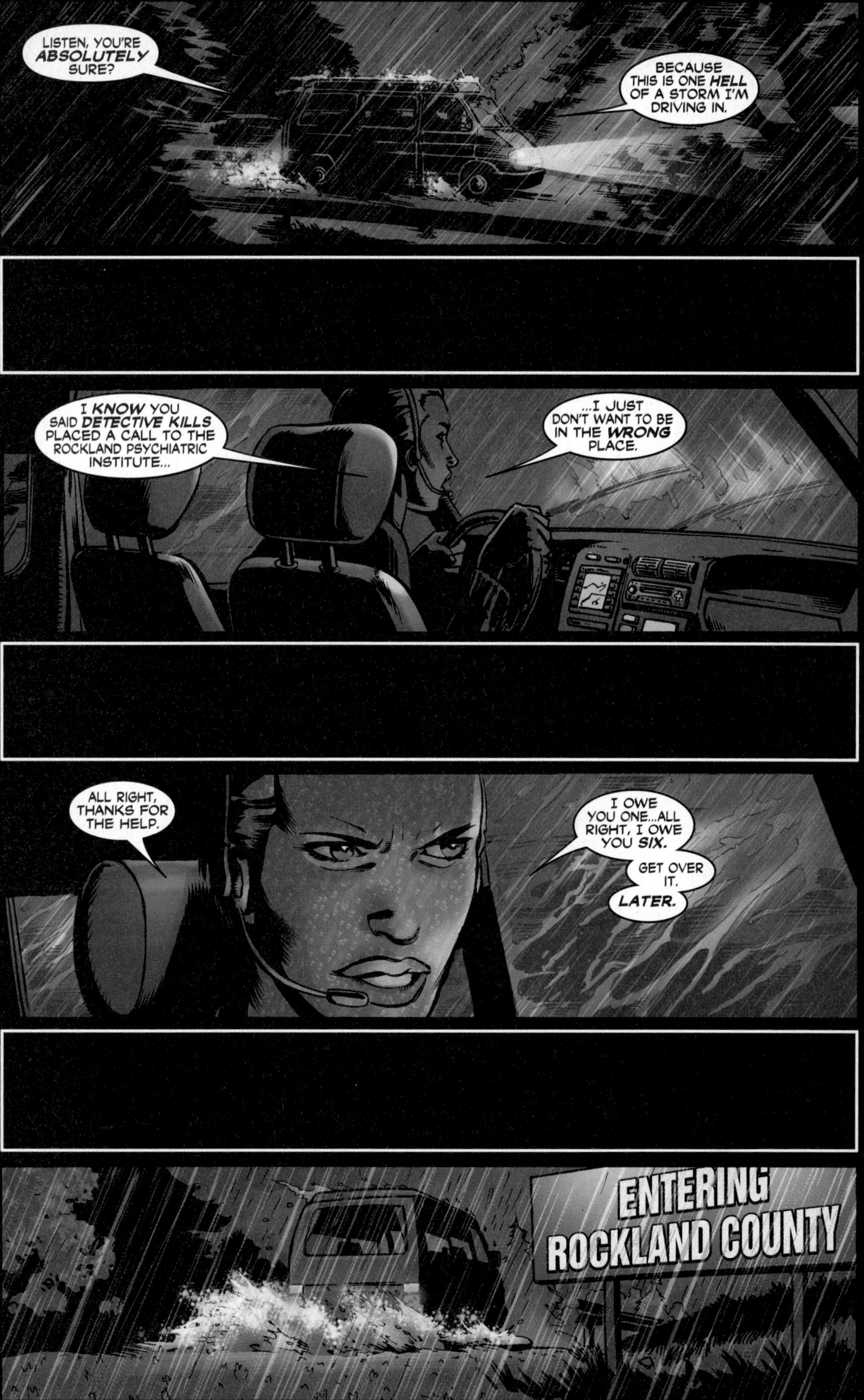
LISTEN, YOU'RE ABSOLUTELY SURE?
BECAUSE THIS IS ONE HELL OF A STORM I'M DRIVING IN.
I KNOW YOU SAID DETECTIVE KILLS PLACED A CALL TO THE ROCKLAND PSYCHIATRIC INSTITUTE...
...I JUST DON'T WANT TO BE IN THE WRONG PLACE.
ALL RIGHT, THANKS FOR THE HELP.
I OWE YOU ONE...ALL RIGHT, I OWE YOU SIX.
GET OVER IT.
LATER.
ENTERING ROCKLAND COUNTY

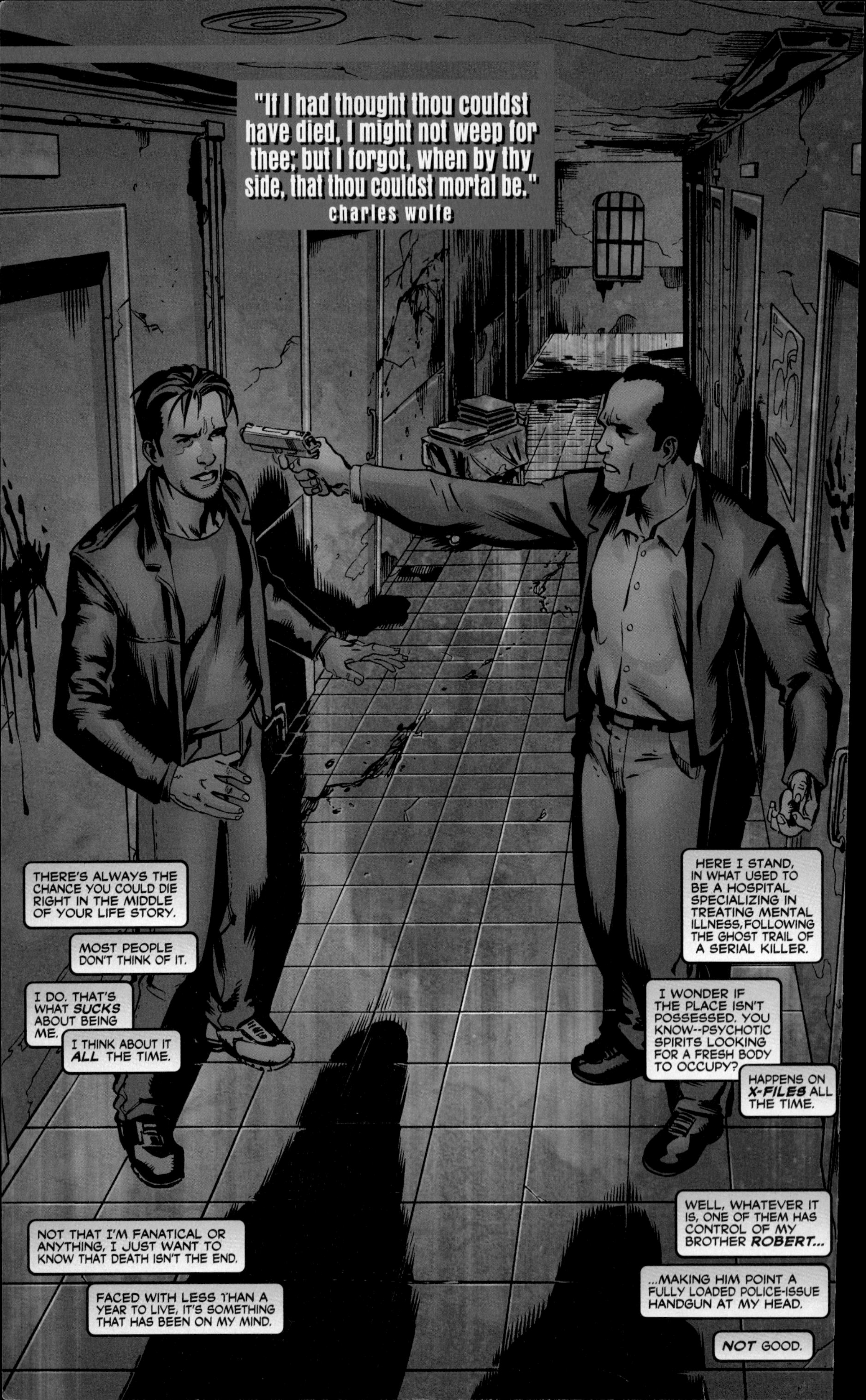
"If I had thought thou couldst have died, I might not weep for thee; but I forgot, when by thy side, that thou couldst mortal be."
charles wolfe
THERE'S ALWAYS THE CHANCE YOU COULD DIE RIGHT IN THE MIDDLE OF YOUR LIFE STORY.
MOST PEOPLE DON'T THINK OF IT.
I DO. THAT'S WHAT SUCKS ABOUT BEING ME.
I THINK ABOUT IT ALL THE TIME.
NOT THAT I'M FANATICAL OR ANYTHING, I JUST WANT TO KNOW THAT DEATH ISN'T THE END.
FACED WITH LESS THAN A YEAR TO LIVE, IT'S SOMETHING THAT HAS BEEN ON MY MIND.
HERE I STAND, IN WHAT USED TO BE A HOSPITAL SPECIALIZING IN TREATING MENTAL ILLNESS, FOLLOWING THE GHOST TRAIL OF A SERIAL KILLER.
I WONDER IF THE PLACE ISN'T POSSESSED. YOU KNOW--PSYCHOTIC SPIRITS LOOKING FOR A FRESH BODY TO OCCUPY?
HAPPENS ON X-FILES ALL THE TIME.
WELL, WHATEVER IT IS, ONE OF THEM HAS CONTROL OF MY BROTHER ROBERT...
...MAKING HIM POINT A FULLY LOADED POLICE-ISSUE HANDGUN AT MY HEAD.
NOT GOOD.

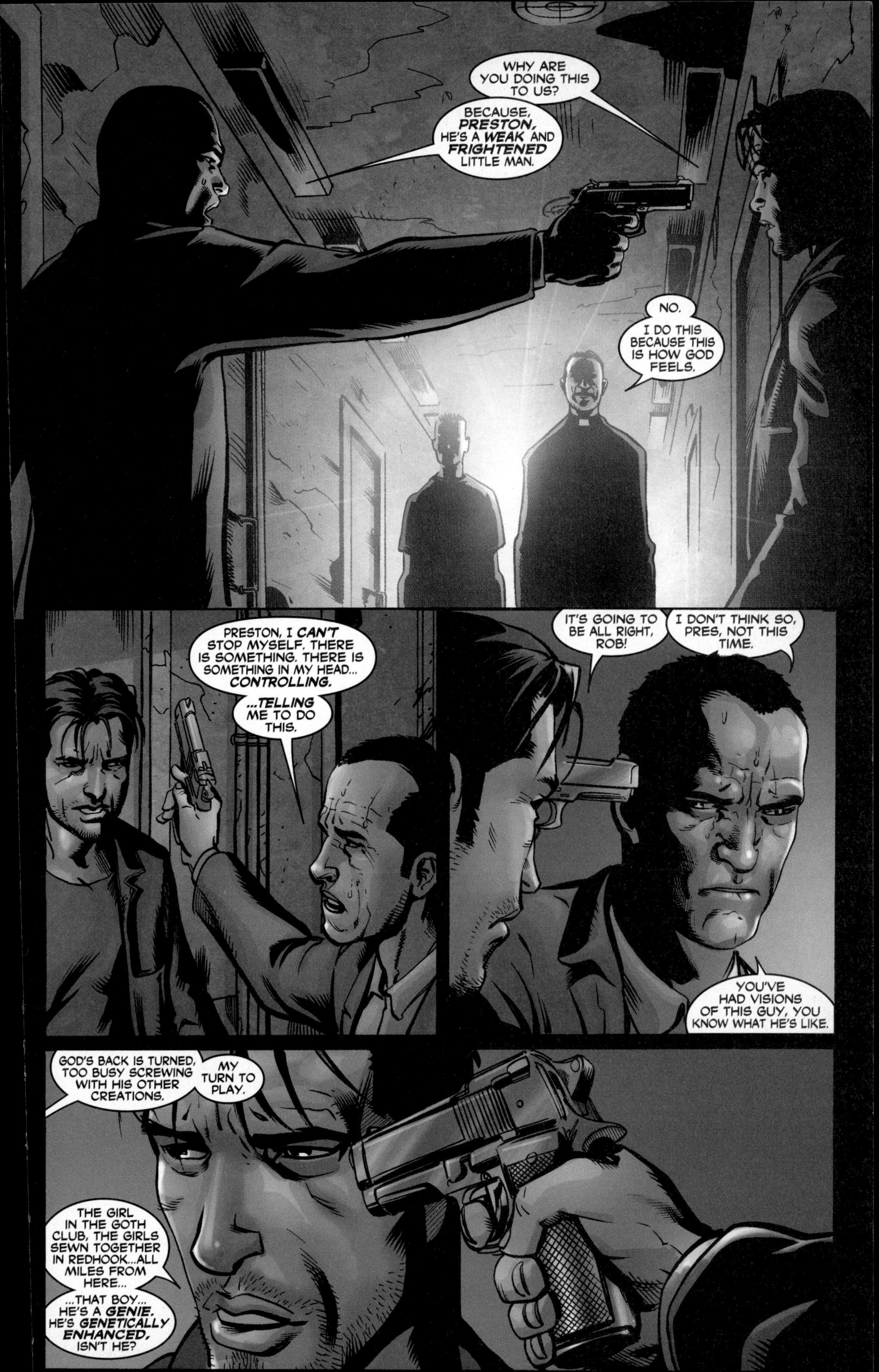
WHY ARE YOU DOING THIS TO US?
BECAUSE, PRESTON, HE'S A WEAK AND FRIGHTENED LITTLE MAN.
NO. I DO THIS BECAUSE THIS IS HOW GOD FEELS.
PRESTON, I CAN'T STOP MYSELF. THERE IS SOMETHING. THERE IS SOMETHING IN MY HEAD... CONTROLLING.
...TELLING ME TO DO THIS.
IT'S GOING TO BE ALL RIGHT, ROB!
I DON'T THINK SO, PRES, NOT THIS TIME.
YOU'VE HAD VISIONS OF THIS GUY, YOU KNOW WHAT HE'S LIKE.
GOD'S BACK IS TURNED, TOO BUSY SCREWING WITH HIS OTHER CREATIONS.
MY TURN TO PLAY.
THE GIRL IN THE GOTH CLUB, THE GIRLS SEWN TOGETHER IN REDHOOK...ALL MILES FROM HERE...
...THAT BOY... HE'S A GENIE. HE'S GENETICALLY ENHANCED, ISN'T HE?

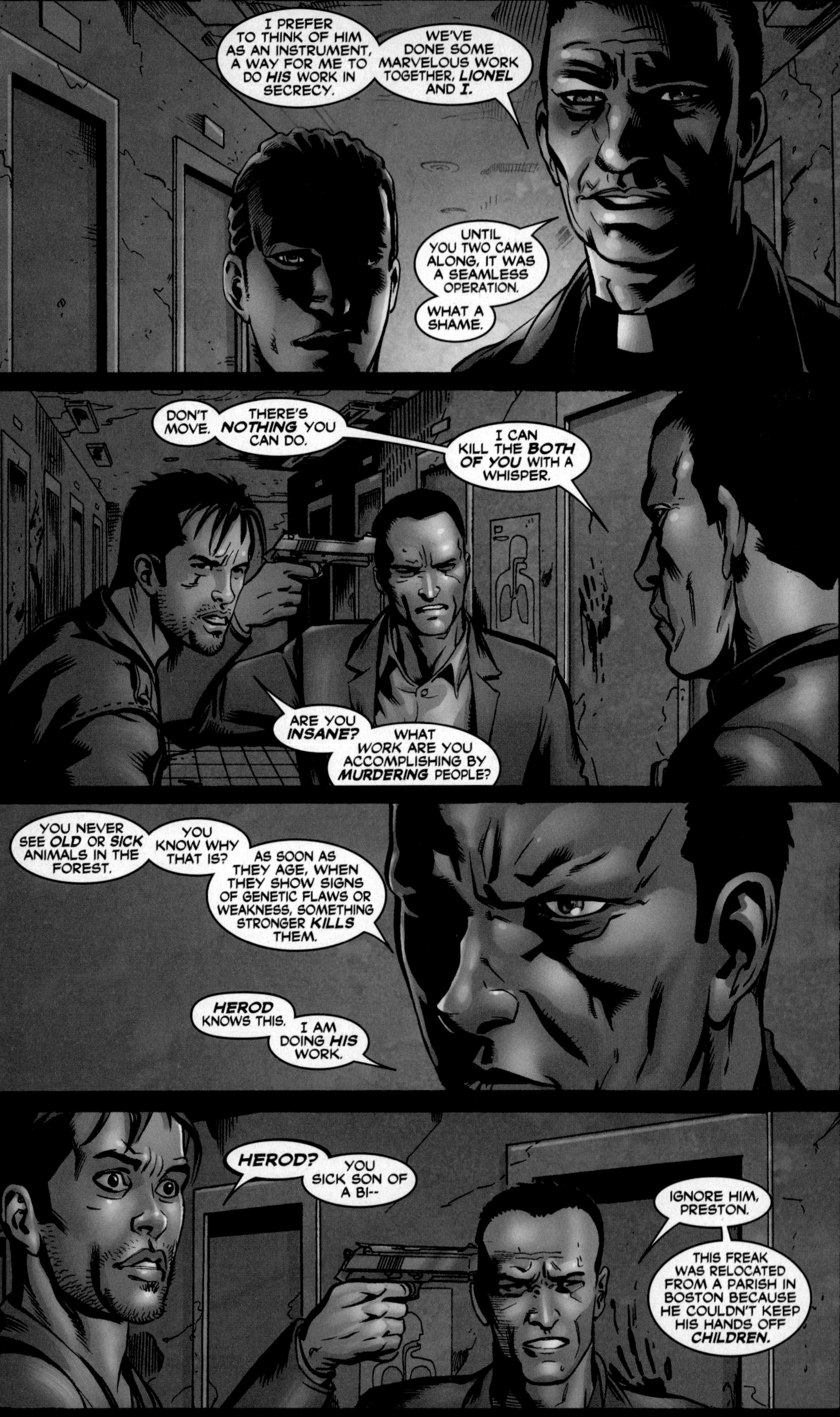
I PREFER TO THINK OF HIM AS AN INSTRUMENT, A WAY FOR ME TO DO HIS WORK IN SECRECY.
WE'VE DONE SOME MARVELOUS WORK TOGETHER, LIONEL AND I.
UNTIL YOU TWO CAME ALONG, IT WAS A SEAMLESS OPERATION.
WHAT A SHAME.
DON'T MOVE.
THERE'S NOTHING YOU CAN DO.
I CAN KILL THE BOTH OF YOU WITH A WHISPER.
ARE YOU INSANE?
WHAT WORK ARE YOU ACCOMPLISHING BY MURDERING PEOPLE?
YOU NEVER SEE OLD OR SICK ANIMALS IN THE FOREST.
YOU KNOW WHY THAT IS?
AS SOON AS THEY AGE, WHEN THEY SHOW SIGNS OF GENETIC FLAWS OR WEAKNESS, SOMETHING STRONGER KILLS THEM.
HEROD KNOWS THIS.
I AM DOING HIS WORK.
HEROD?
YOU SICK SON OF A BI--
IGNORE HIM, PRESTON.
THIS FREAK WAS RELOCATED FROM A PARISH IN BOSTON BECAUSE HE COULDN'T KEEP HIS HANDS OFF CHILDREN.

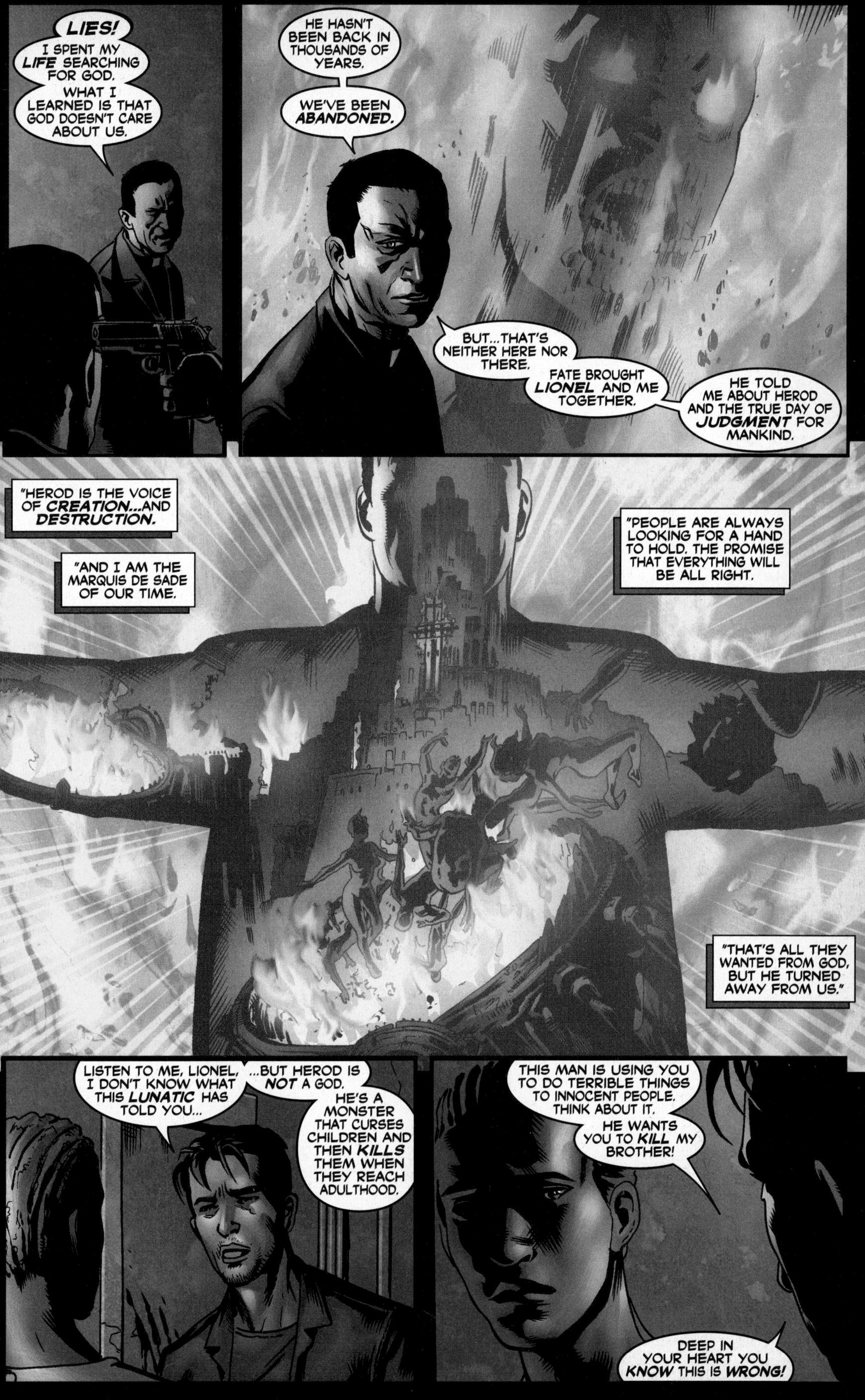
LIES!
I SPENT MY LIFE SEARCHING FOR GOD.
WHAT I LEARNED IS THAT GOD DOESN'T CARE ABOUT US.
HE HASN'T BEEN BACK IN THOUSANDS OF YEARS.
WE'VE BEEN ABANDONED.
BUT...THAT'S NEITHER HERE NOR THERE.
FATE BROUGHT LIONEL AND ME TOGETHER.
HE TOLD ME ABOUT HEROD AND THE TRUE DAY OF JUDGMENT FOR MANKIND.
"HEROD IS THE VOICE OF CREATION...AND DESTRUCTION.
"AND I AM THE MARQUIS DE SADE OF OUR TIME.
"PEOPLE ARE ALWAYS LOOKING FOR A HAND TO HOLD. THE PROMISE THAT EVERYTHING WILL BE ALL RIGHT.
"THAT'S ALL THEY WANTED FROM GOD, BUT HE TURNED AWAY FROM US."
LISTEN TO ME, LIONEL, I DON'T KNOW WHAT THIS LUNATIC HAS TOLD YOU...
...BUT HEROD IS NOT A GOD.
HE'S A MONSTER THAT CURSES CHILDREN AND THEN KILLS THEM WHEN THEY REACH ADULTHOOD.
THIS MAN IS USING YOU TO DO TERRIBLE THINGS TO INNOCENT PEOPLE. THINK ABOUT IT.
HE WANTS YOU TO KILL MY BROTHER!
DEEP IN YOUR HEART YOU KNOW THIS IS WRONG!

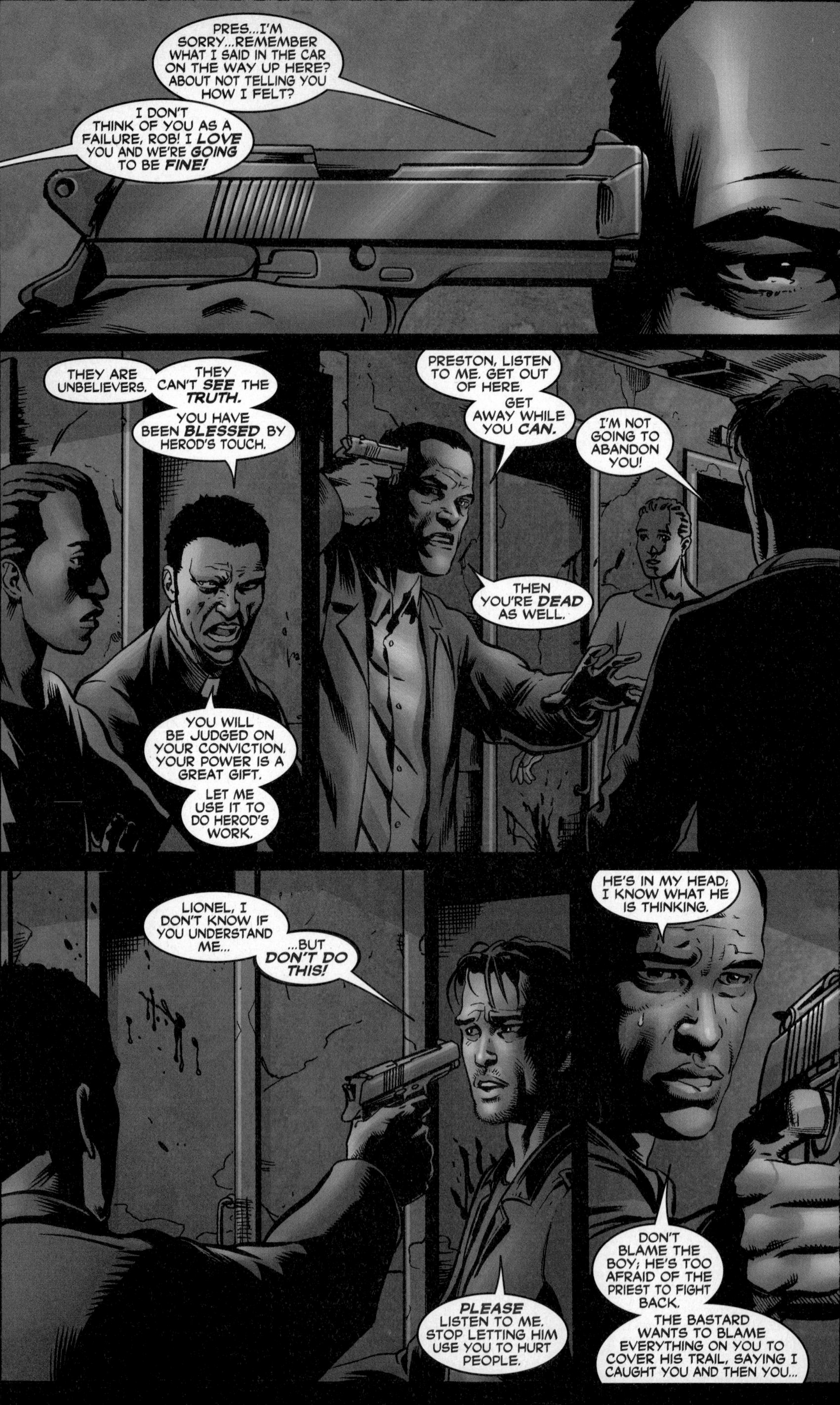
PRES...I'M SORRY...REMEMBER WHAT I SAID IN THE CAR ON THE WAY UP HERE? ABOUT NOT TELLING YOU HOW I FELT?
I DON'T THINK OF YOU AS A FAILURE, ROB! I *LOVE* YOU AND WE'RE *GOING* TO BE *FINE!*
THEY ARE UNBELIEVERS.
THEY CAN'T *SEE* THE *TRUTH.*
YOU HAVE BEEN *BLESSED* BY HEROD'S TOUCH.
YOU WILL BE JUDGED ON YOUR CONVICTION. YOUR POWER IS A GREAT GIFT.
LET ME USE IT TO DO HEROD'S WORK.
PRESTON, LISTEN TO ME. GET OUT OF HERE.
GET AWAY WHILE YOU *CAN.*
I'M NOT GOING TO ABANDON YOU!
THEN YOU'RE *DEAD* AS WELL.
LIONEL, I DON'T KNOW IF YOU UNDERSTAND ME...
...BUT *DON'T DO THIS!*
PLEASE LISTEN TO ME. STOP LETTING HIM USE YOU TO HURT PEOPLE.
HE'S IN MY HEAD; I KNOW WHAT HE IS THINKING.
DON'T BLAME THE BOY; HE'S TOO AFRAID OF THE PRIEST TO FIGHT BACK.
THE BASTARD WANTS TO BLAME EVERYTHING ON YOU TO COVER HIS TRAIL, SAYING I CAUGHT YOU AND THEN YOU...

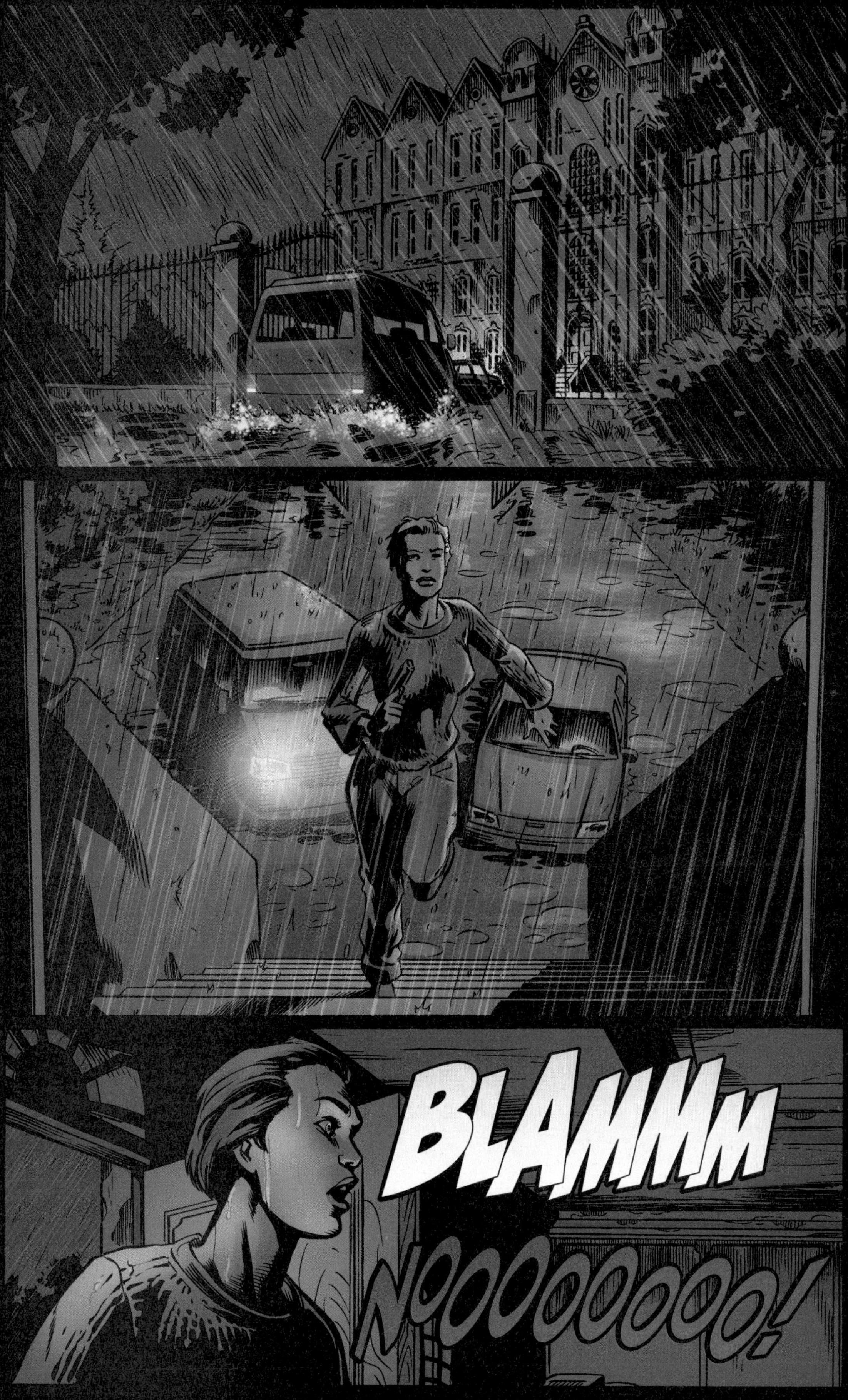
BLAMMM
NOOOOOOOO!

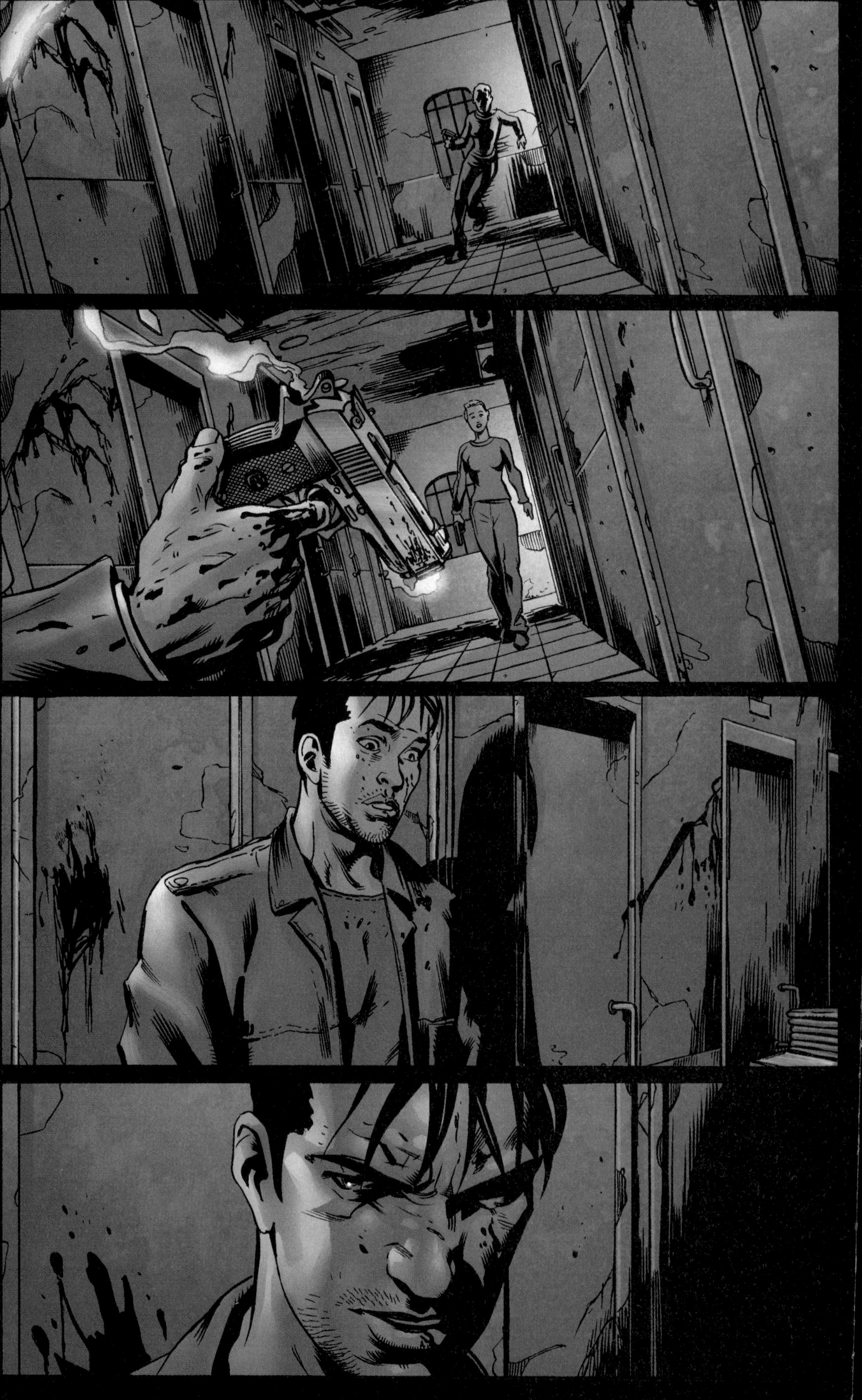

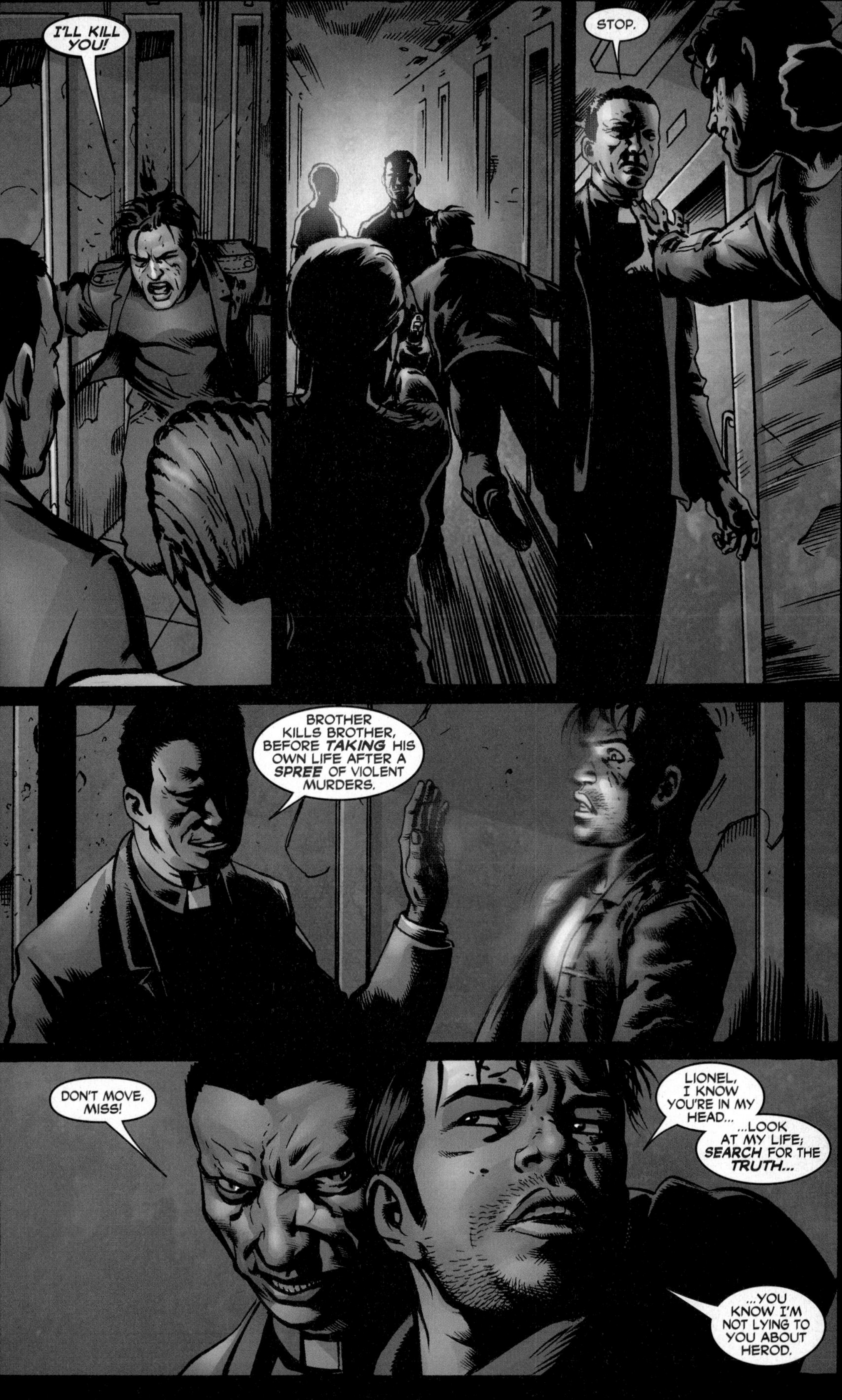
I'LL KILL YOU!
STOP.
BROTHER KILLS BROTHER, BEFORE TAKING HIS OWN LIFE AFTER A SPREE OF VIOLENT MURDERS.
DON'T MOVE, MISS!
LIONEL, I KNOW YOU'RE IN MY HEAD... ...LOOK AT MY LIFE; SEARCH FOR THE TRUTH...
...YOU KNOW I'M NOT LYING TO YOU ABOUT HEROD.

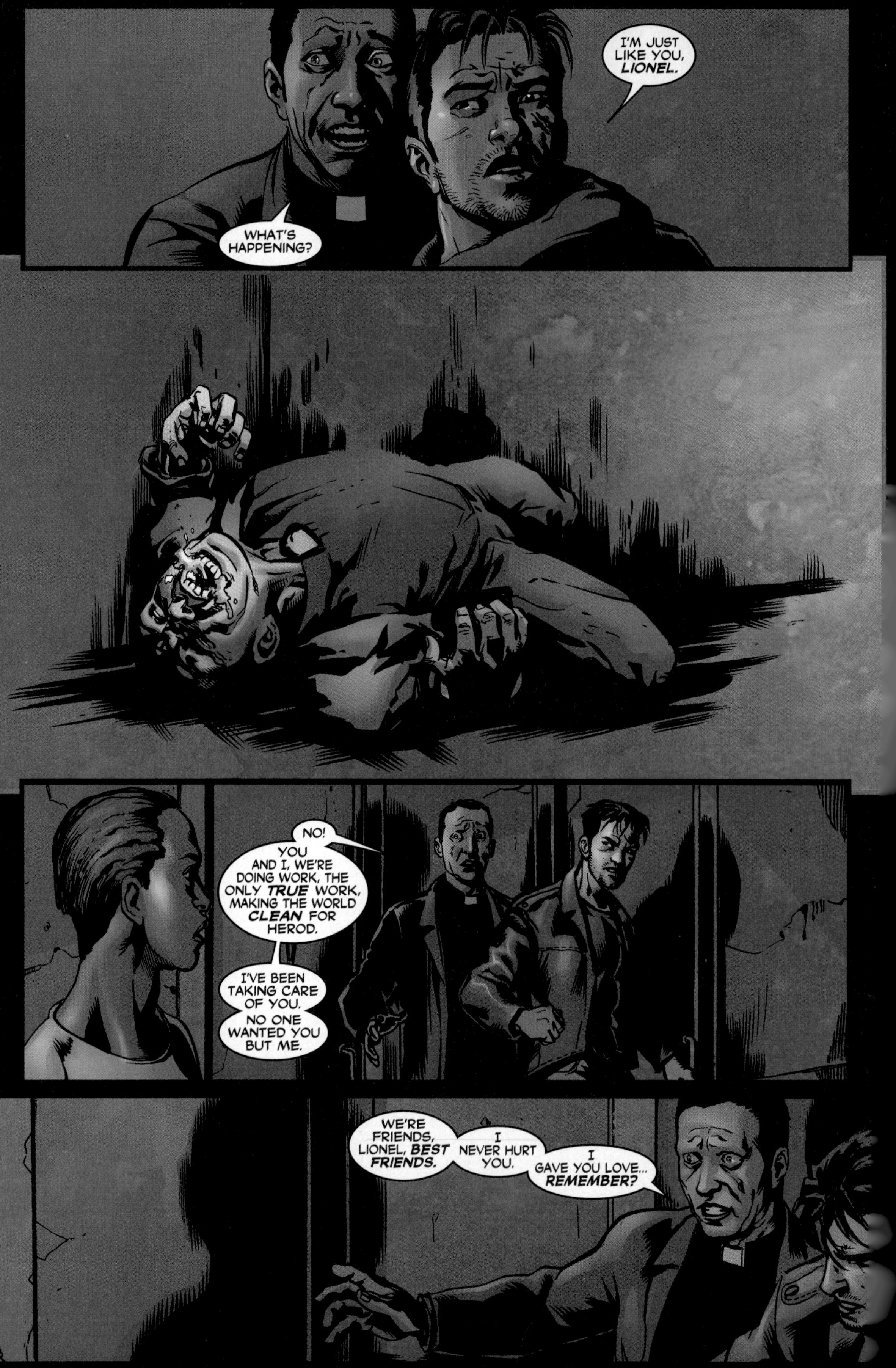
I'M JUST LIKE YOU, LIONEL.
WHAT'S HAPPENING?
NO!
YOU AND I, WE'RE DOING WORK, THE ONLY TRUE WORK, MAKING THE WORLD CLEAN FOR HEROD.
I'VE BEEN TAKING CARE OF YOU.
NO ONE WANTED YOU BUT ME.
WE'RE FRIENDS, LIONEL, BEST FRIENDS.
I NEVER HURT YOU.
I GAVE YOU LOVE... REMEMBER?

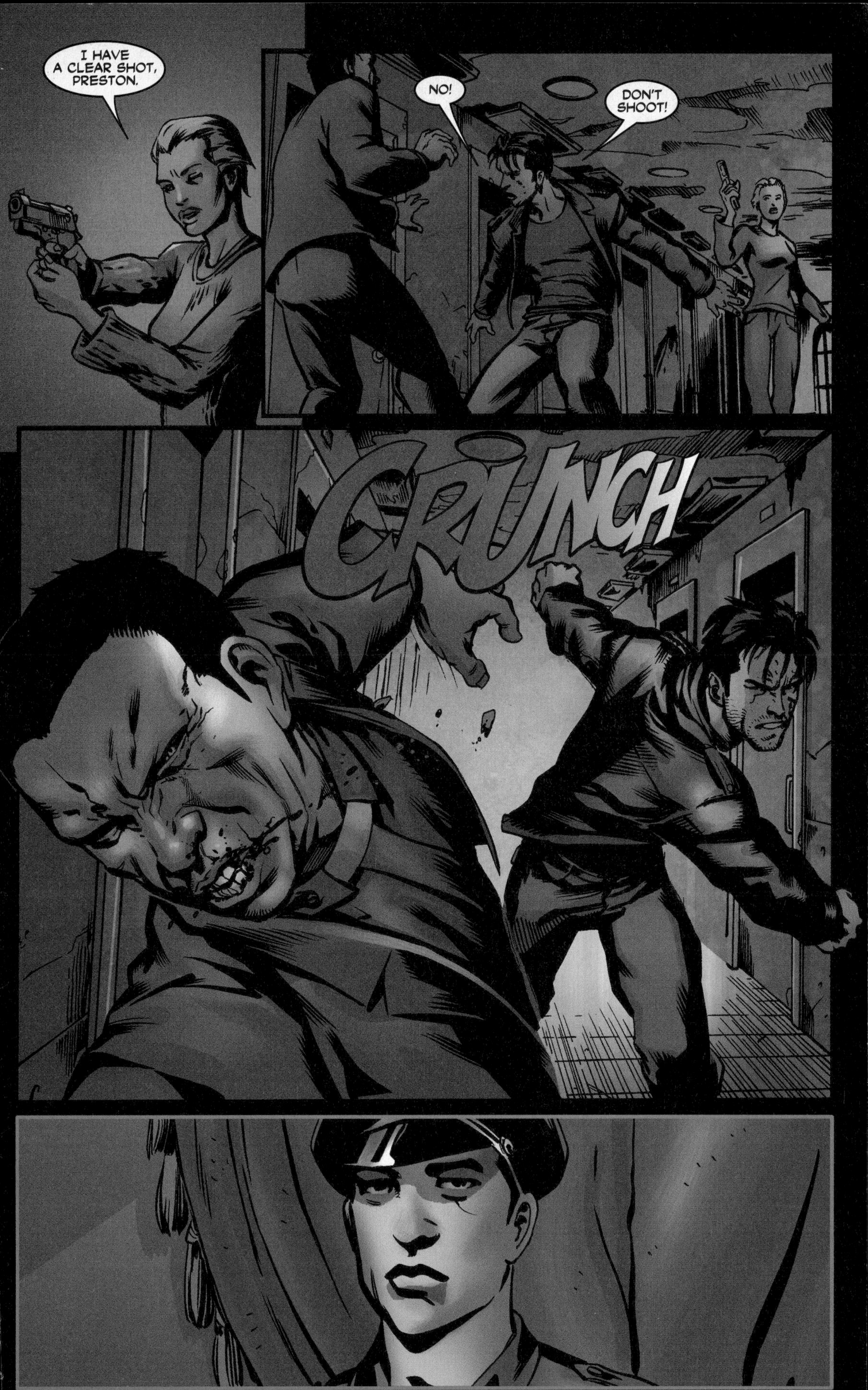
I HAVE A CLEAR SHOT, PRESTON.
NO!
DON'T SHOOT!
CRUNCH

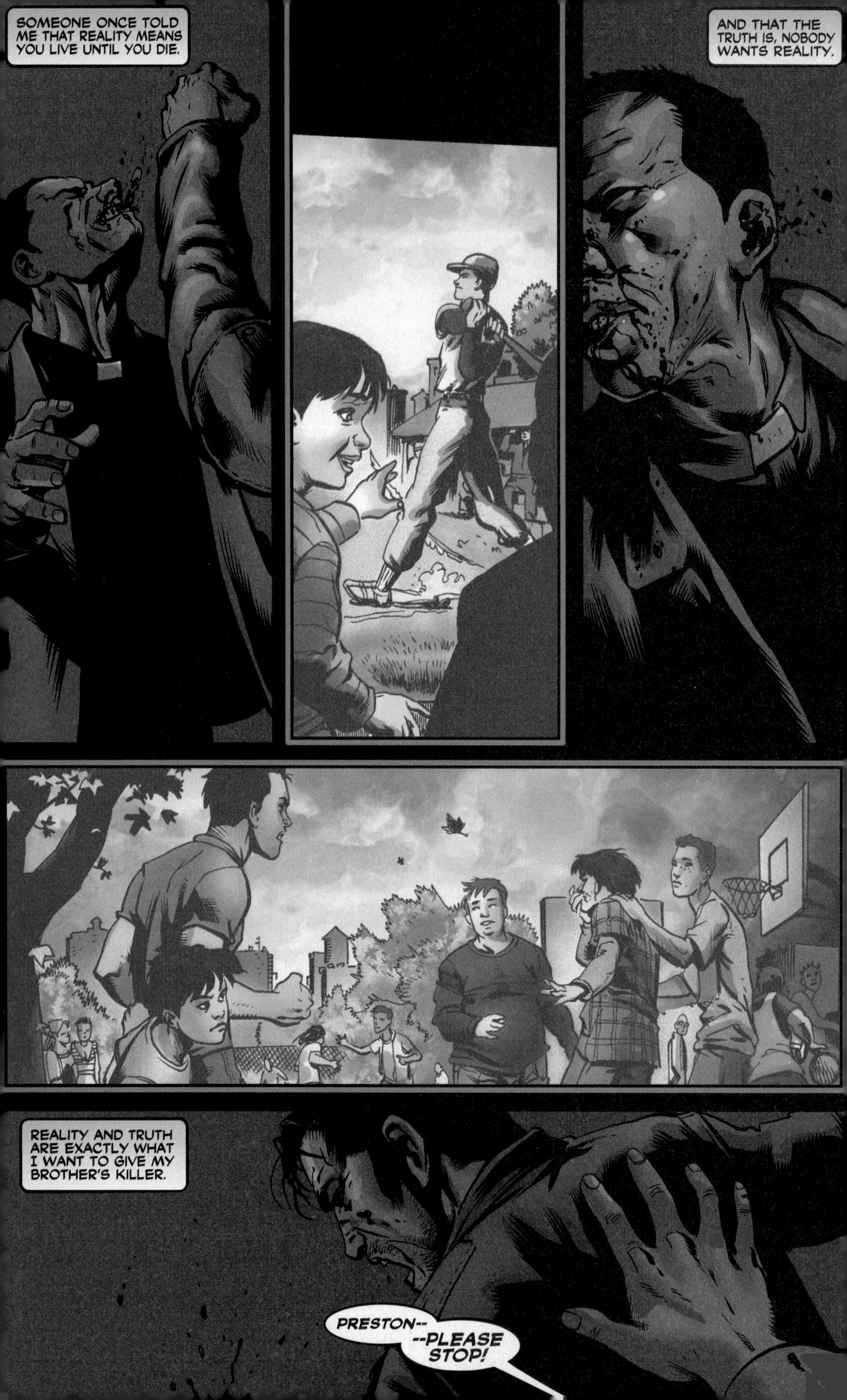
SOMEONE ONCE TOLD ME THAT REALITY MEANS YOU LIVE UNTIL YOU DIE.
AND THAT THE TRUTH IS, NOBODY WANTS REALITY.
REALITY AND TRUTH ARE EXACTLY WHAT I WANT TO GIVE MY BROTHER'S KILLER.
PRESTON--
--PLEASE STOP!

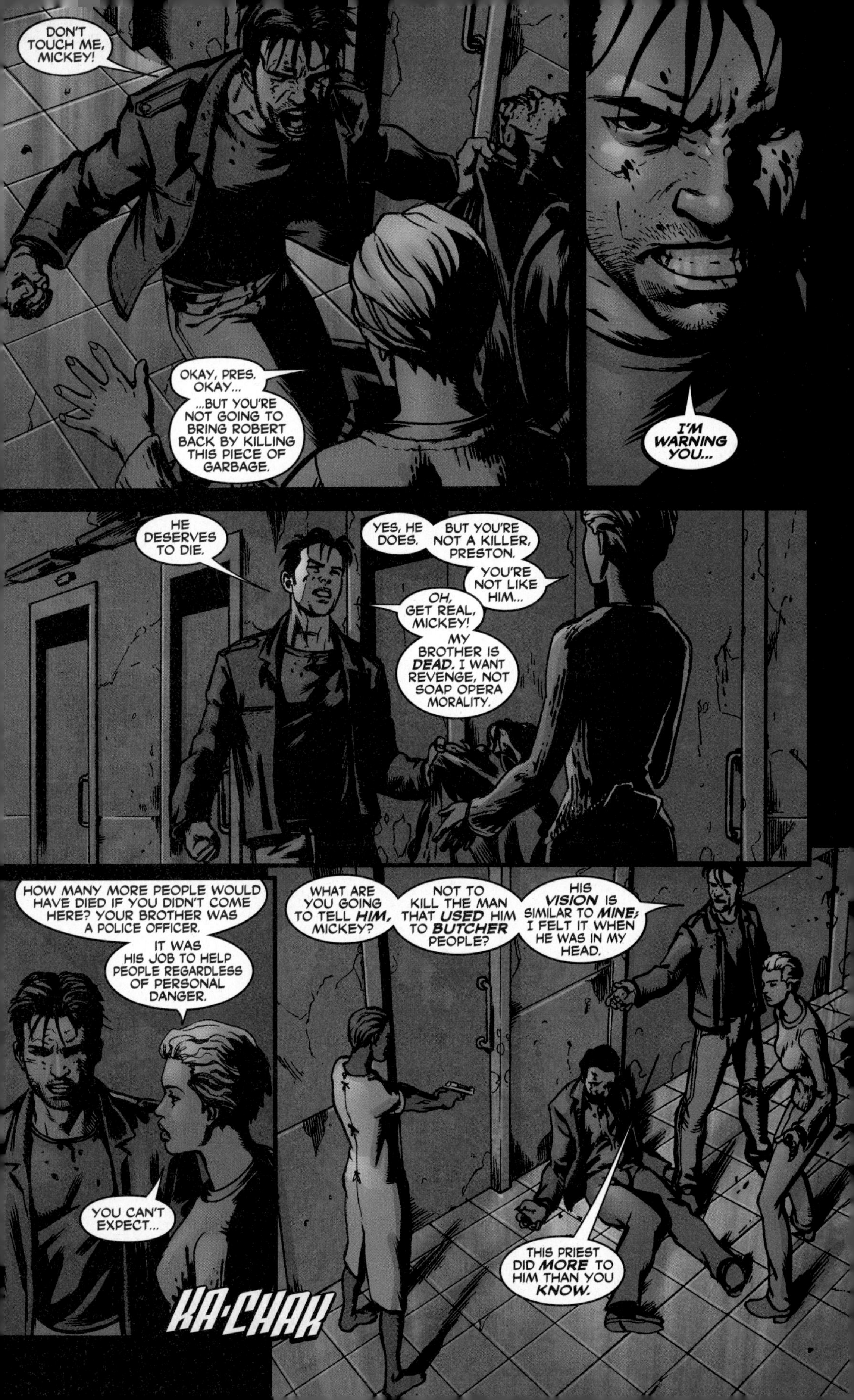
DON'T TOUCH ME, MICKEY!
OKAY, PRES. OKAY...
...BUT YOU'RE NOT GOING TO BRING ROBERT BACK BY KILLING THIS PIECE OF GARBAGE.
I'M WARNING YOU...
HE DESERVES TO DIE.
YES, HE DOES.
BUT YOU'RE NOT A KILLER, PRESTON.
YOU'RE NOT LIKE HIM...
OH, GET REAL, MICKEY!
MY BROTHER IS DEAD. I WANT REVENGE, NOT SOAP OPERA MORALITY.
HOW MANY MORE PEOPLE WOULD HAVE DIED IF YOU DIDN'T COME HERE? YOUR BROTHER WAS A POLICE OFFICER.
IT WAS HIS JOB TO HELP PEOPLE REGARDLESS OF PERSONAL DANGER.
YOU CAN'T EXPECT...
KA-CHAK
WHAT ARE YOU GOING TO TELL HIM, MICKEY?
NOT TO KILL THE MAN THAT USED HIM TO BUTCHER PEOPLE?
HIS VISION IS SIMILAR TO MINE; I FELT IT WHEN HE WAS IN MY HEAD.
THIS PRIEST DID MORE TO HIM THAN YOU KNOW.

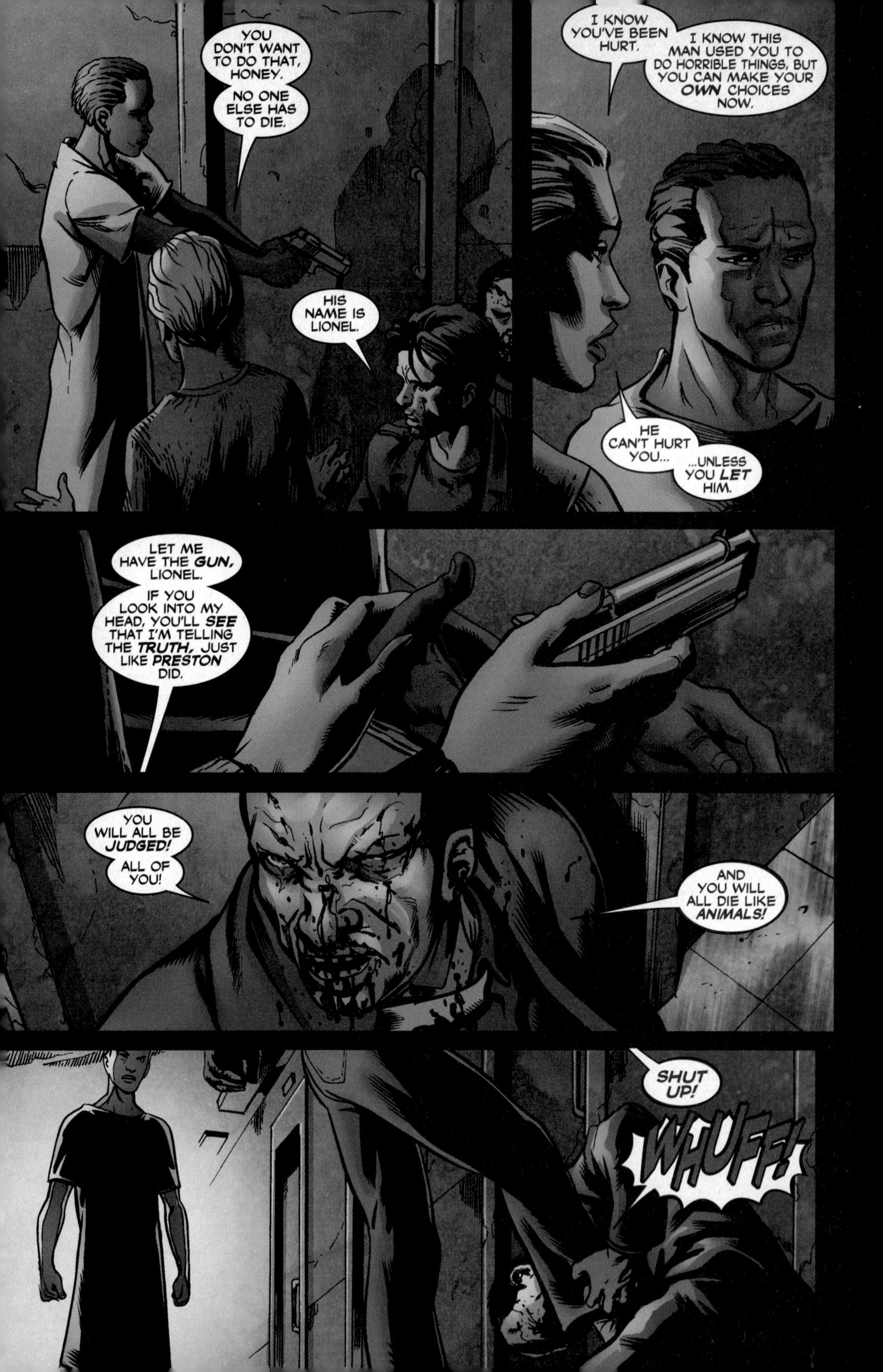
YOU DON'T WANT TO DO THAT, HONEY.
NO ONE ELSE HAS TO DIE.
HIS NAME IS LIONEL.
I KNOW YOU'VE BEEN HURT.
I KNOW THIS MAN USED YOU TO DO HORRIBLE THINGS, BUT YOU CAN MAKE YOUR OWN CHOICES NOW.
HE CAN'T HURT YOU...
...UNLESS YOU LET HIM.
LET ME HAVE THE GUN, LIONEL.
IF YOU LOOK INTO MY HEAD, YOU'LL SEE THAT I'M TELLING THE TRUTH, JUST LIKE PRESTON DID.
YOU WILL ALL BE JUDGED!
ALL OF YOU!
AND YOU WILL ALL DIE LIKE ANIMALS!
SHUT UP!
WHUFF!

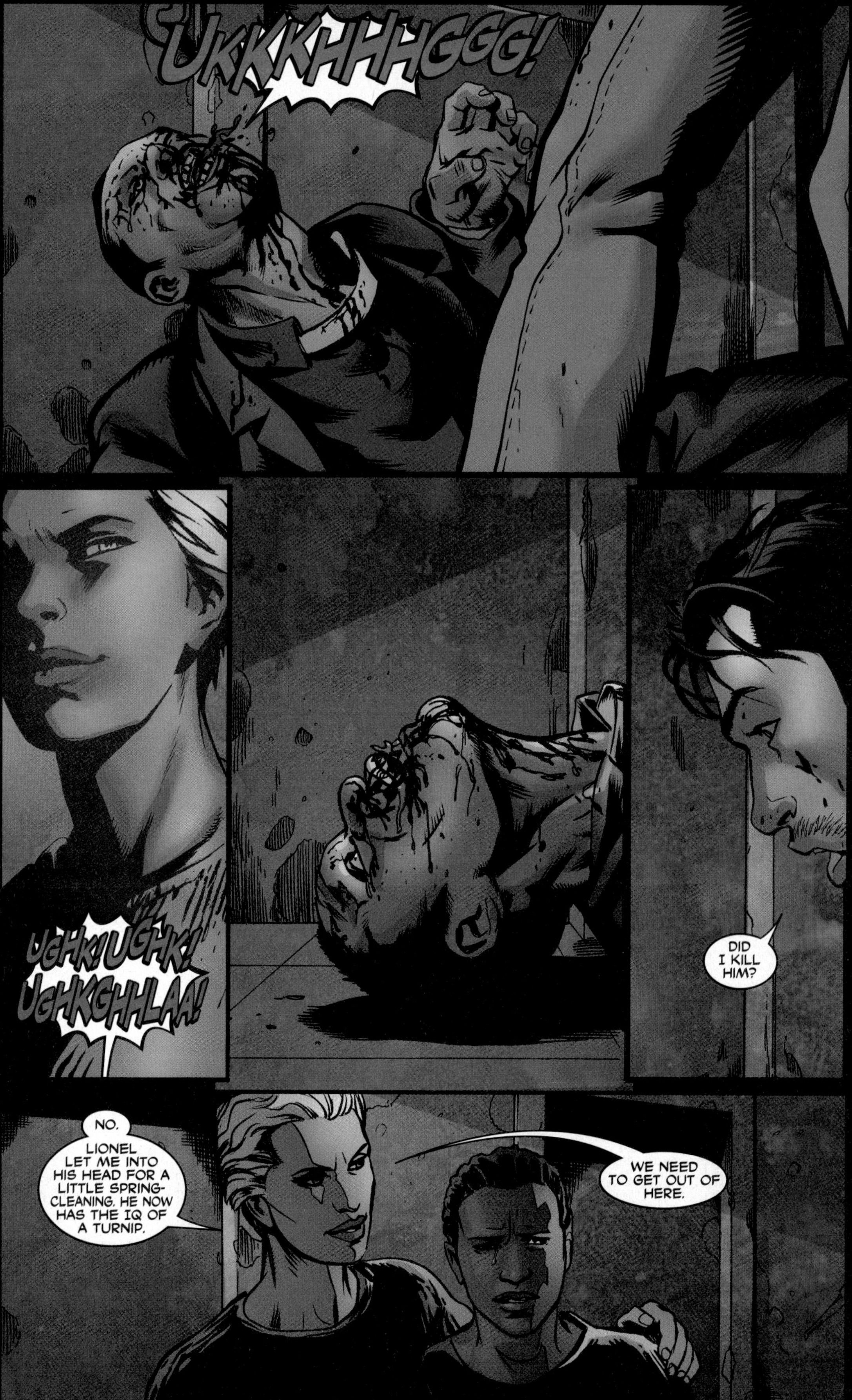

UKKKHHHGGG!
UGHK! UGHK! UGHKGHHLAA!
DID I KILL HIM?
NO. LIONEL LET ME INTO HIS HEAD FOR A LITTLE SPRING-CLEANING. HE NOW HAS THE IQ OF A TURNIP.
WE NEED TO GET OUT OF HERE.

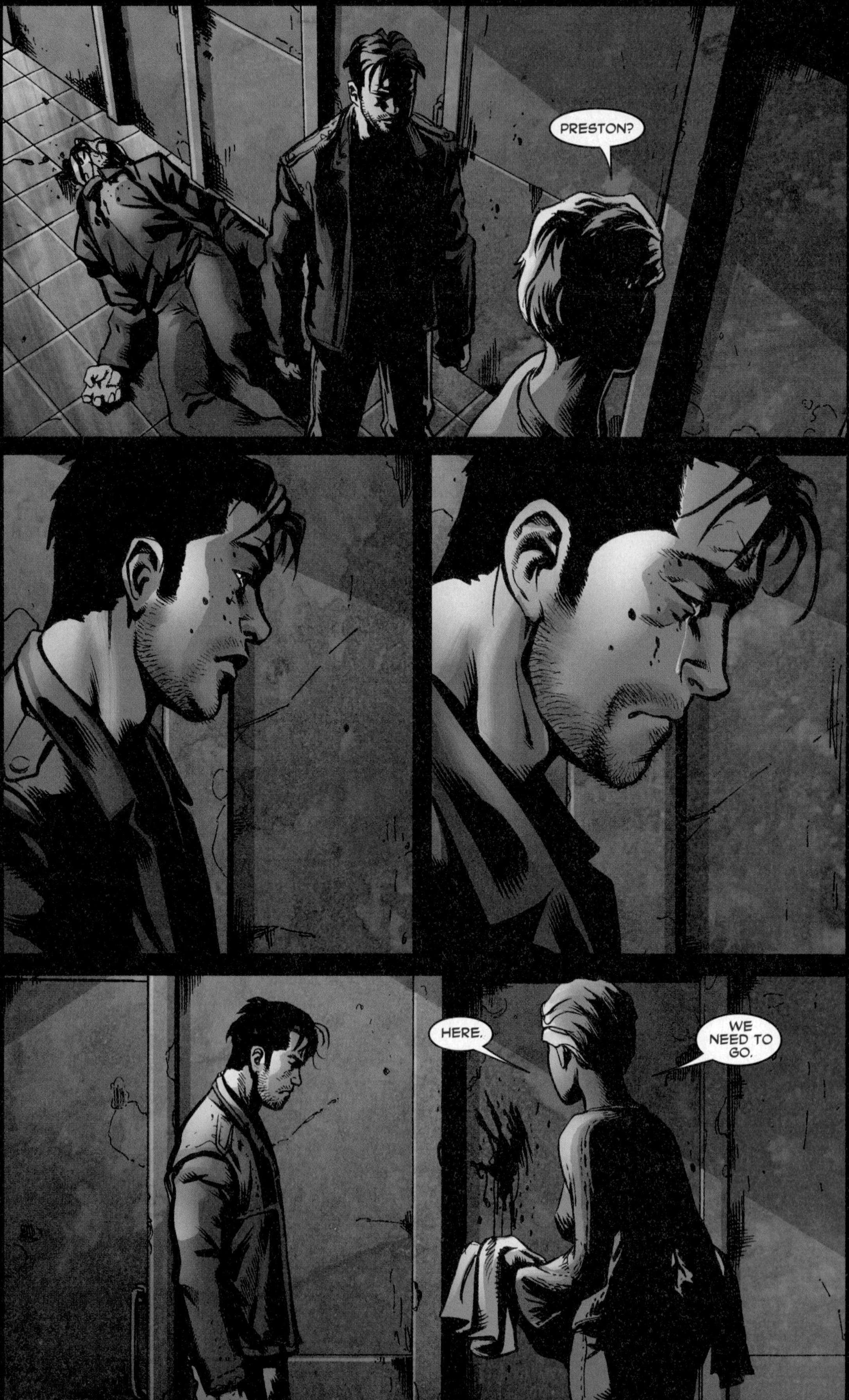
PRESTON?
HERE.
WE NEED TO GO.

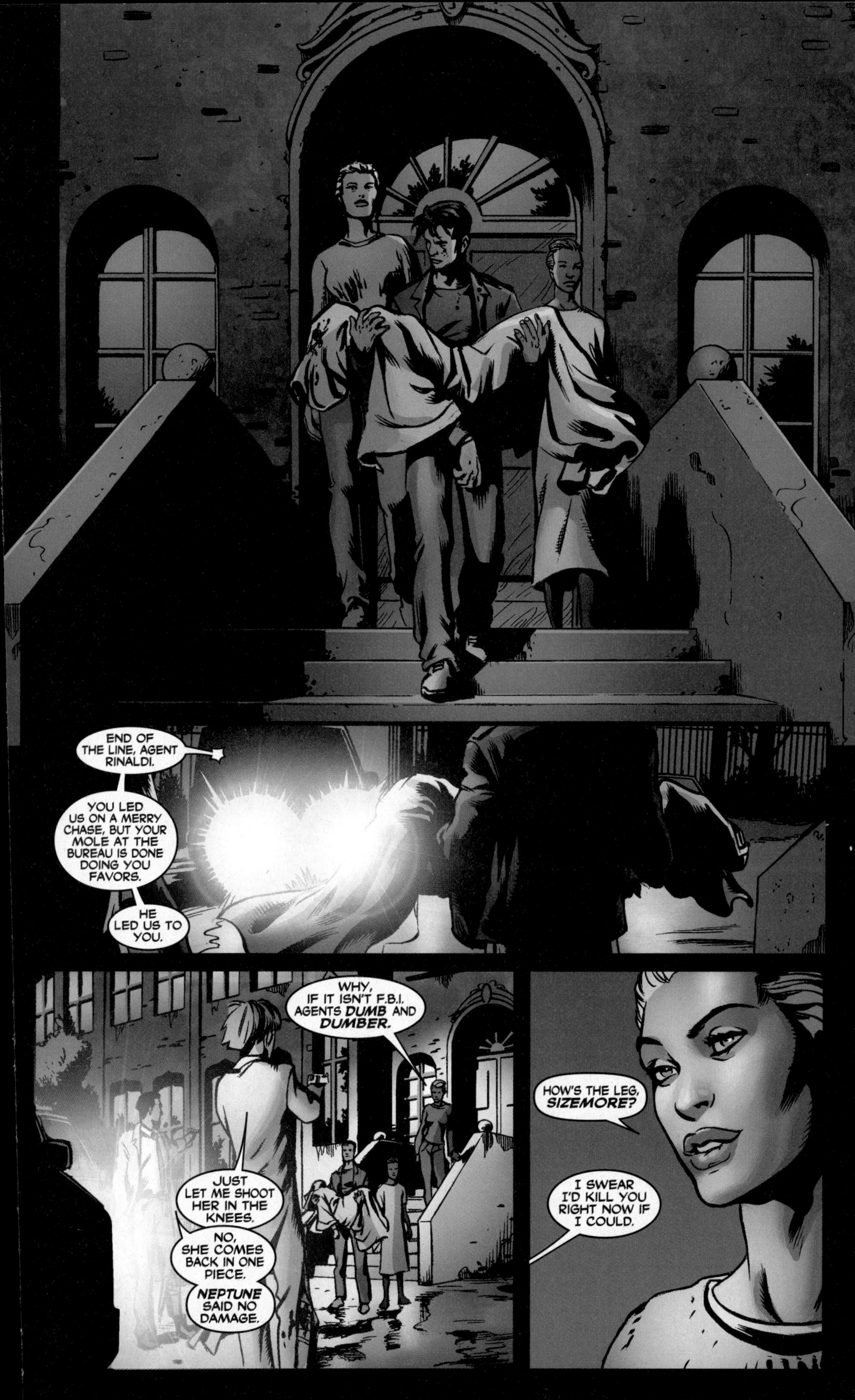
END OF THE LINE, AGENT RINALDI.
YOU LED US ON A MERRY CHASE, BUT YOUR MOLE AT THE BUREAU IS DONE DOING YOU FAVORS.
HE LED US TO YOU.
WHY, IF IT ISN'T F.B.I. AGENTS DUMB AND DUMBER.
JUST LET ME SHOOT HER IN THE KNEES.
NO, SHE COMES BACK IN ONE PIECE.
NEPTUNE SAID NO DAMAGE.
HOW'S THE LEG, SIZEMORE?
I SWEAR I'D KILL YOU RIGHT NOW IF I COULD.

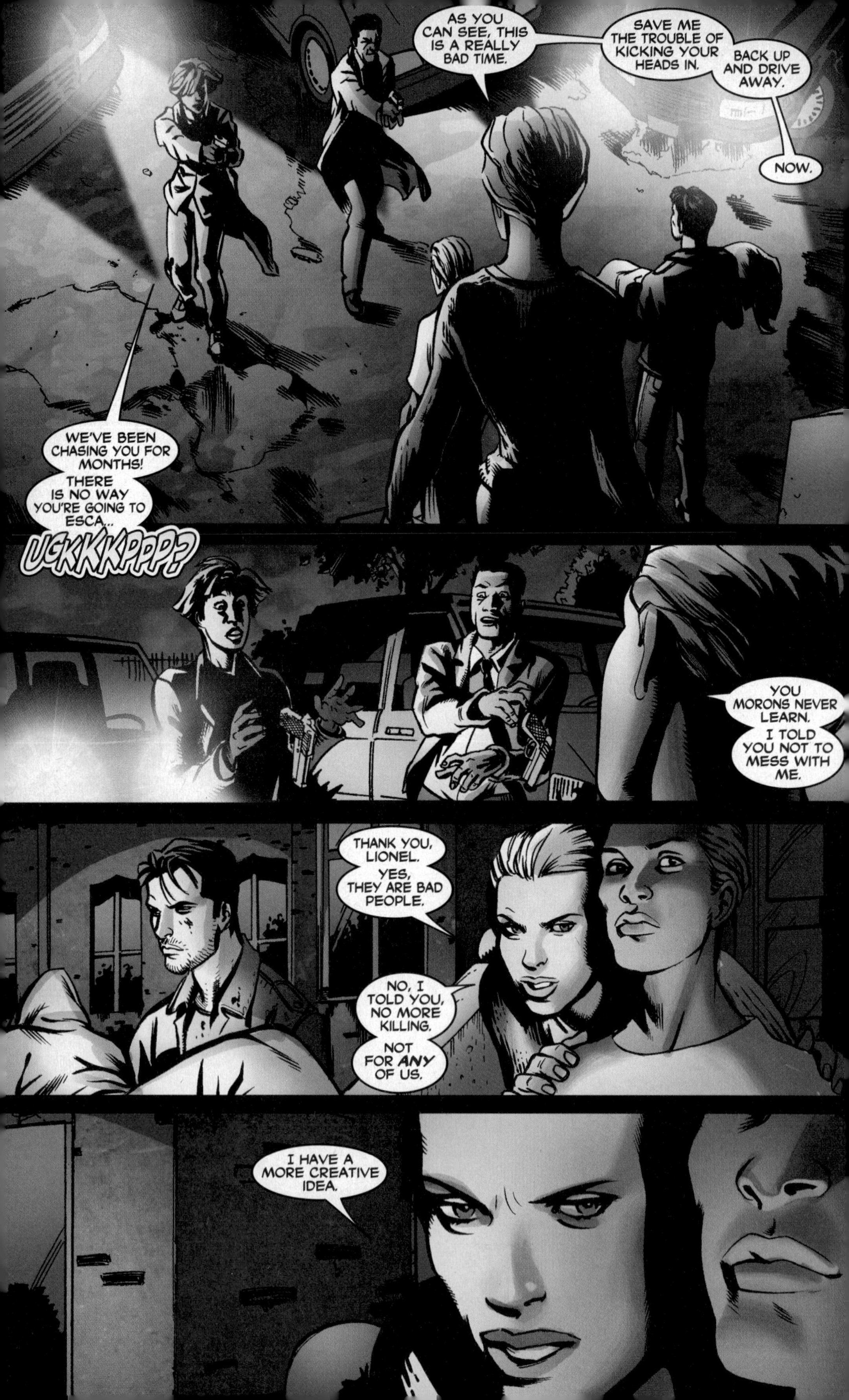
AS YOU CAN SEE, THIS IS A REALLY BAD TIME.
SAVE ME THE TROUBLE OF KICKING YOUR HEADS IN.
BACK UP AND DRIVE AWAY.
NOW.
WE'VE BEEN CHASING YOU FOR MONTHS!
THERE IS NO WAY YOU'RE GOING TO ESCA...
UGKKKPPP?
YOU MORONS NEVER LEARN.
I TOLD YOU NOT TO MESS WITH ME.
THANK YOU, LIONEL.
YES, THEY ARE BAD PEOPLE.
NO, I TOLD YOU, NO MORE KILLING.
NOT FOR ANY OF US.
I HAVE A MORE CREATIVE IDEA.

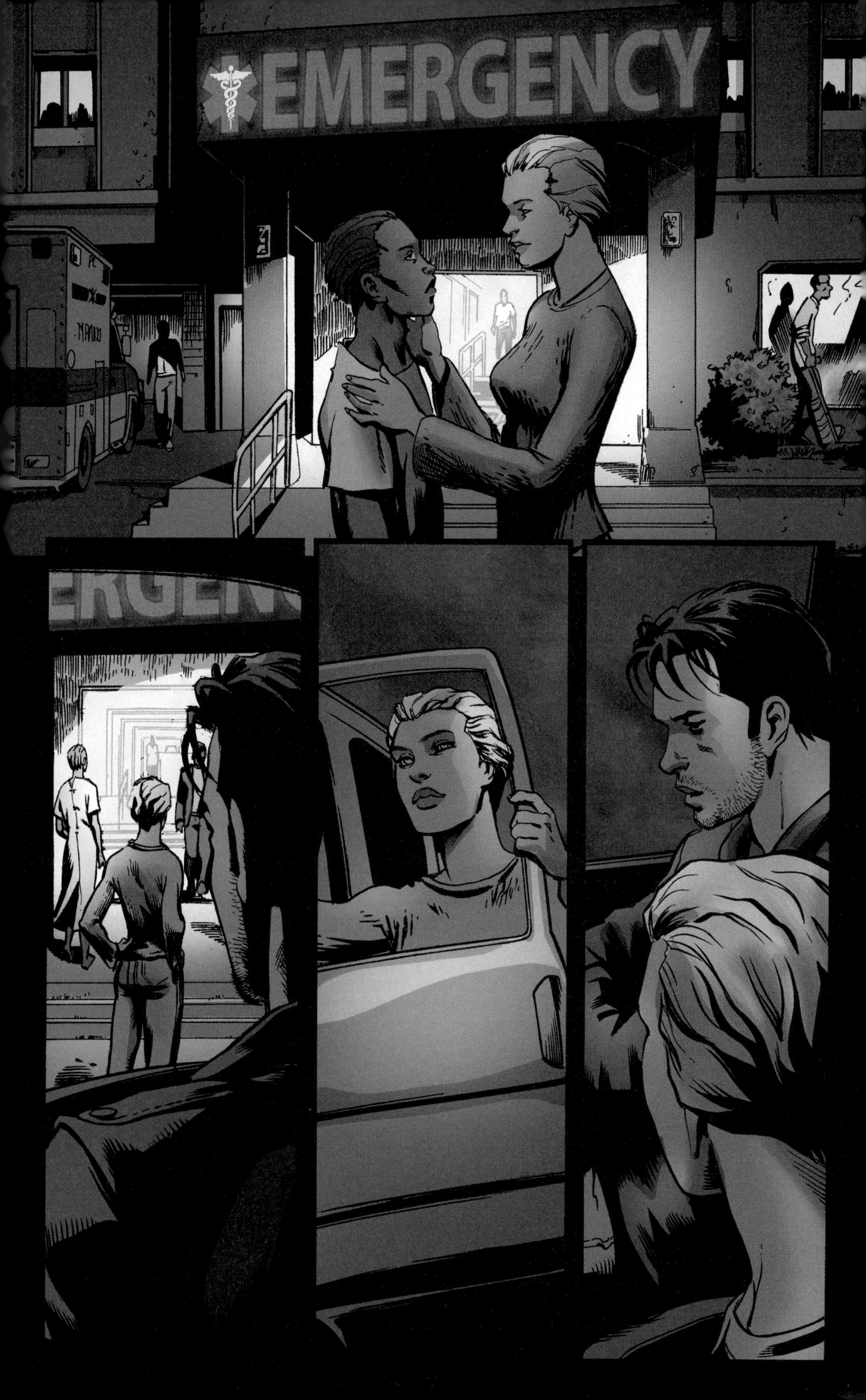
EMERGENCY

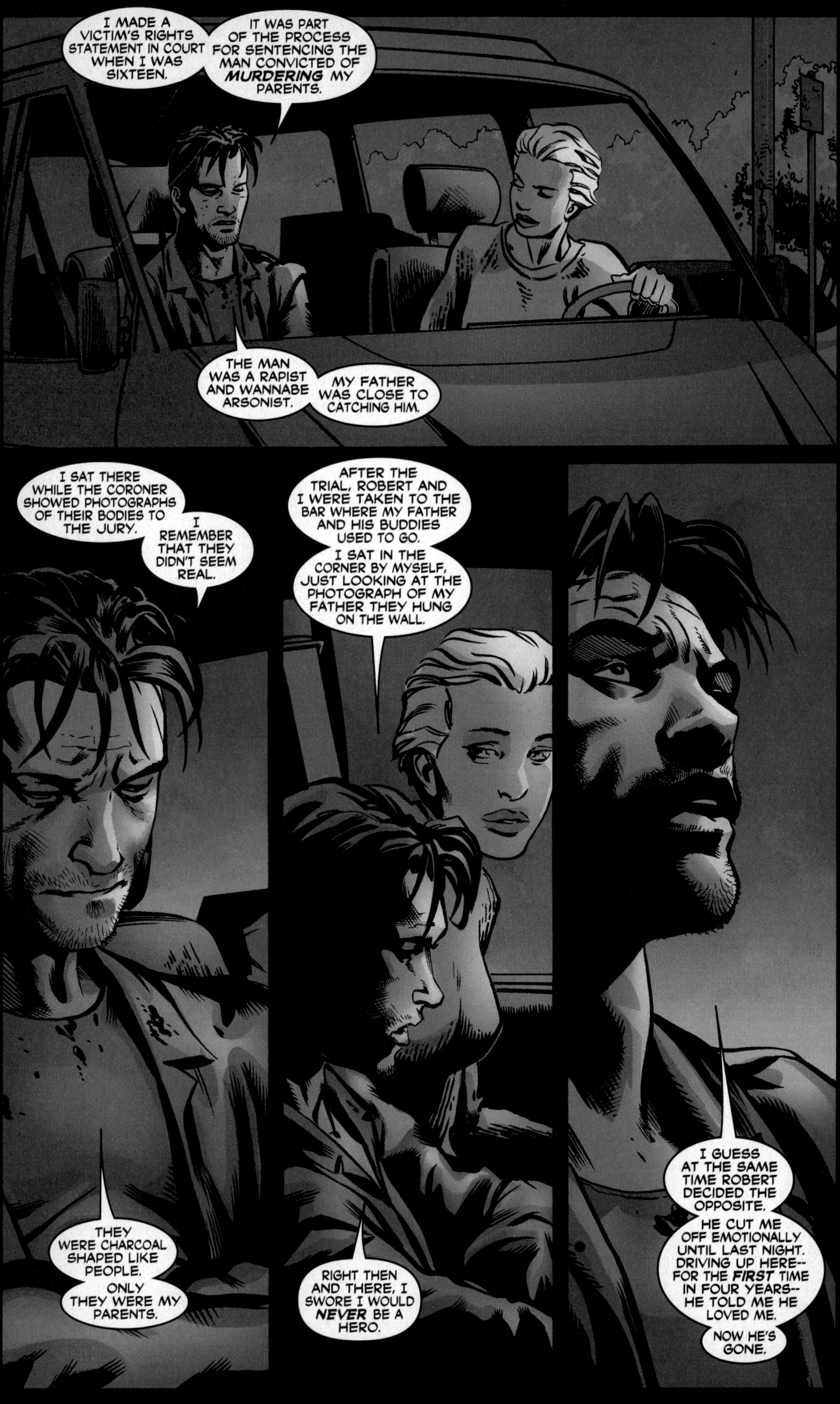
I MADE A VICTIM'S RIGHTS STATEMENT IN COURT WHEN I WAS SIXTEEN.
IT WAS PART OF THE PROCESS FOR SENTENCING THE MAN CONVICTED OF MURDERING MY PARENTS.
THE MAN WAS A RAPIST AND WANNABE ARSONIST.
MY FATHER WAS CLOSE TO CATCHING HIM.
I SAT THERE WHILE THE CORONER SHOWED PHOTOGRAPHS OF THEIR BODIES TO THE JURY.
I REMEMBER THAT THEY DIDN'T SEEM REAL.
THEY WERE CHARCOAL SHAPED LIKE PEOPLE.
ONLY THEY WERE MY PARENTS.
AFTER THE TRIAL, ROBERT AND I WERE TAKEN TO THE BAR WHERE MY FATHER AND HIS BUDDIES USED TO GO.
I SAT IN THE CORNER BY MYSELF, JUST LOOKING AT THE PHOTOGRAPH OF MY FATHER THEY HUNG ON THE WALL.
RIGHT THEN AND THERE, I SWORE I WOULD NEVER BE A HERO.
I GUESS AT THE SAME TIME ROBERT DECIDED THE OPPOSITE.
HE CUT ME OFF EMOTIONALLY UNTIL LAST NIGHT. DRIVING UP HERE-- FOR THE FIRST TIME IN FOUR YEARS-- HE TOLD ME HE LOVED ME.
NOW HE'S GONE.

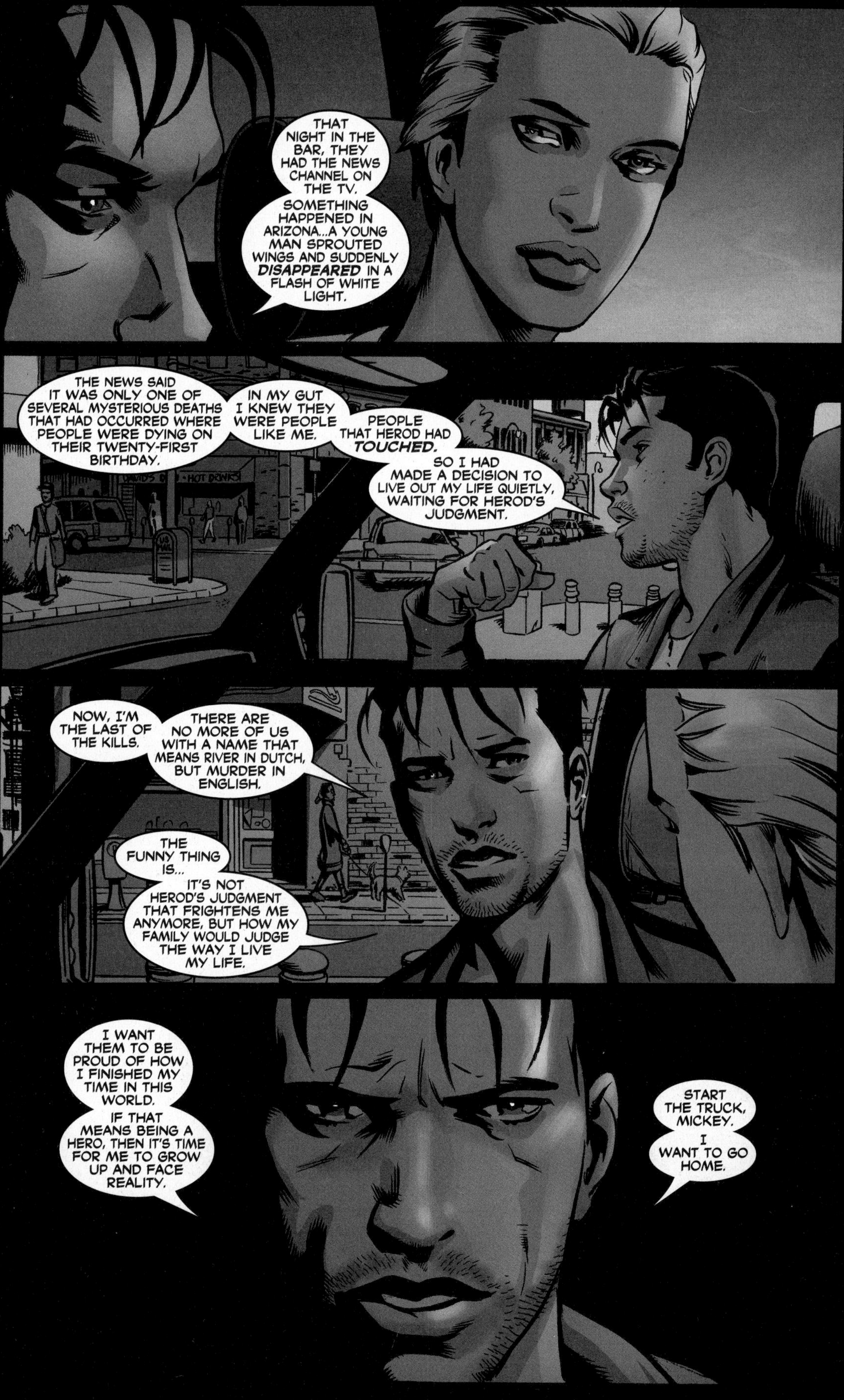
THAT NIGHT IN THE BAR, THEY HAD THE NEWS CHANNEL ON THE TV.
SOMETHING HAPPENED IN ARIZONA...A YOUNG MAN SPROUTED WINGS AND SUDDENLY DISAPPEARED IN A FLASH OF WHITE LIGHT.
THE NEWS SAID IT WAS ONLY ONE OF SEVERAL MYSTERIOUS DEATHS THAT HAD OCCURRED WHERE PEOPLE WERE DYING ON THEIR TWENTY-FIRST BIRTHDAY.
IN MY GUT I KNEW THEY WERE PEOPLE LIKE ME.
PEOPLE THAT HEROD HAD TOUCHED.
SO I HAD MADE A DECISION TO LIVE OUT MY LIFE QUIETLY, WAITING FOR HEROD'S JUDGMENT.
HOT DRINKS
NOW, I'M THE LAST OF THE KILLS.
THERE ARE NO MORE OF US WITH A NAME THAT MEANS RIVER IN DUTCH, BUT MURDER IN ENGLISH.
THE FUNNY THING IS...
IT'S NOT HEROD'S JUDGMENT THAT FRIGHTENS ME ANYMORE, BUT HOW MY FAMILY WOULD JUDGE THE WAY I LIVE MY LIFE.
I WANT THEM TO BE PROUD OF HOW I FINISHED MY TIME IN THIS WORLD.
IF THAT MEANS BEING A HERO, THEN IT'S TIME FOR ME TO GROW UP AND FACE REALITY.
START THE TRUCK, MICKEY.
I WANT TO GO HOME.

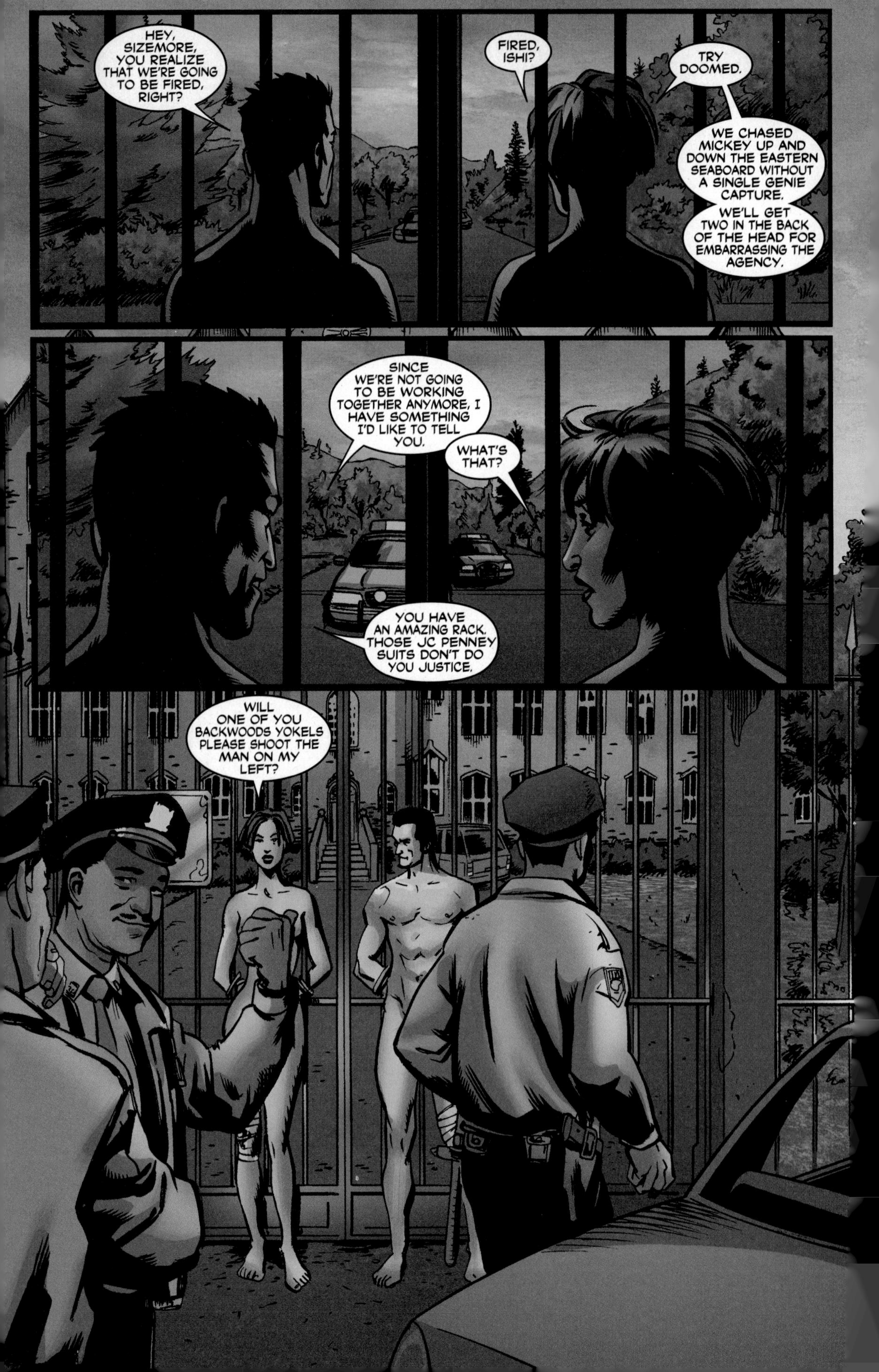
HEY, SIZEMORE, YOU REALIZE THAT WE'RE GOING TO BE FIRED, RIGHT?
FIRED, ISHI?
TRY DOOMED.
WE CHASED MICKEY UP AND DOWN THE EASTERN SEABOARD WITHOUT A SINGLE GENIE CAPTURE.
WE'LL GET TWO IN THE BACK OF THE HEAD FOR EMBARRASSING THE AGENCY.
SINCE WE'RE NOT GOING TO BE WORKING TOGETHER ANYMORE, I HAVE SOMETHING I'D LIKE TO TELL YOU.
WHAT'S THAT?
YOU HAVE AN AMAZING RACK. THOSE JC PENNEY SUITS DON'T DO YOU JUSTICE.
WILL ONE OF YOU BACKWOODS YOKELS PLEASE SHOOT THE MAN ON MY LEFT?

When Jimmy and I introduced you to Preston, you saw him attending a meeting for people suffering from brain cancer. You saw a young man struggling for a means of coping with the idea that he has only a year to live. I have always had a profound and irrational fear of death, but there is a difference between being afraid to die and having a date marked on the calendar.

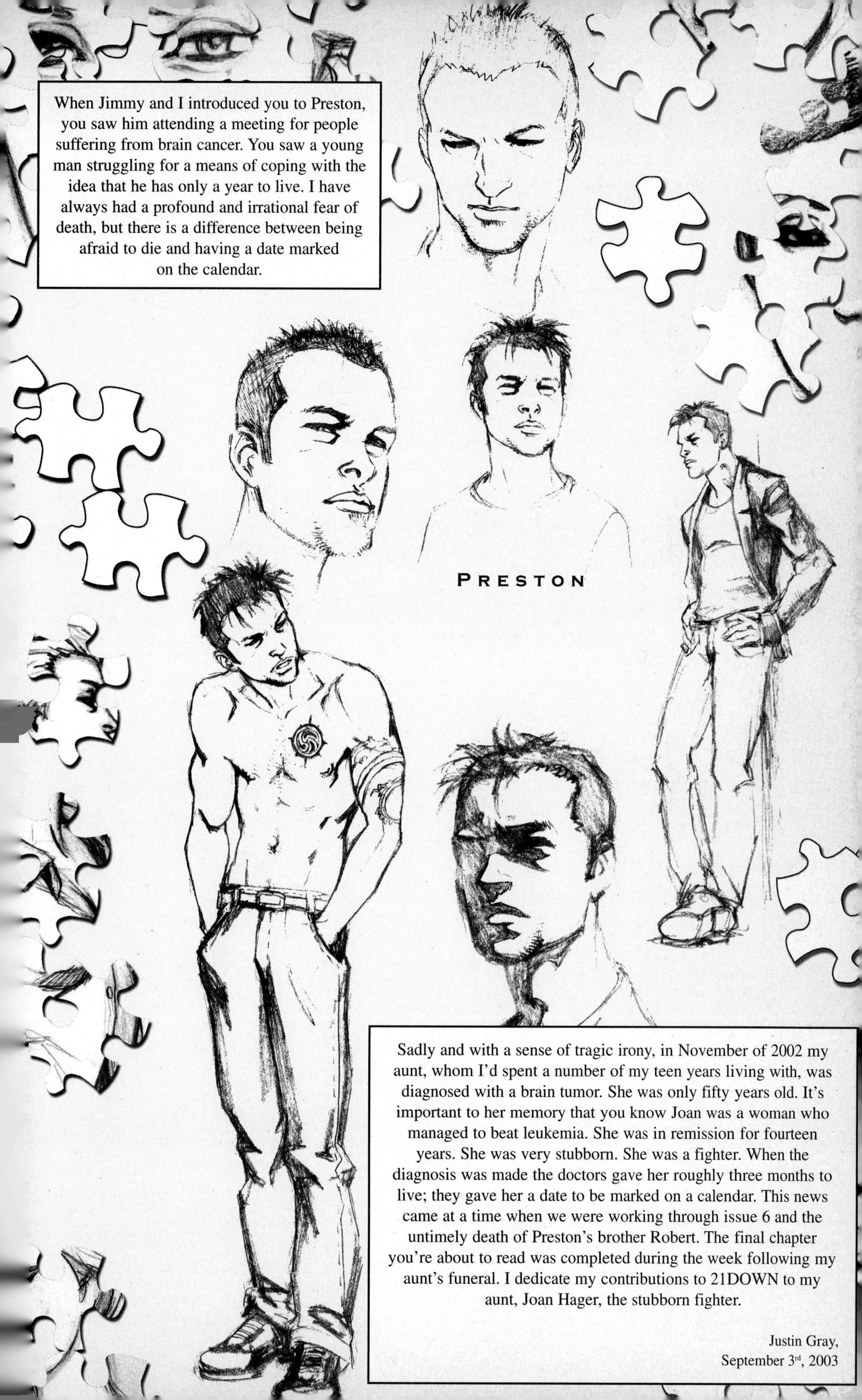
PRESTON

Sadly and with a sense of tragic irony, in November of 2002 my aunt, whom I'd spent a number of my teen years living with, was diagnosed with a brain tumor. She was only fifty years old. It's important to her memory that you know Joan was a woman who managed to beat leukemia. She was in remission for fourteen years. She was very stubborn. She was a fighter. When the diagnosis was made the doctors gave her roughly three months to live; they gave her a date to be marked on a calendar. This news came at a time when we were working through issue 6 and the untimely death of Preston's brother Robert. The final chapter you're about to read was completed during the week following my aunt's funeral. I dedicate my contributions to 21DOWN to my aunt, Joan Hager, the stubborn fighter.

Justin Gray,
September 3rd, 2003

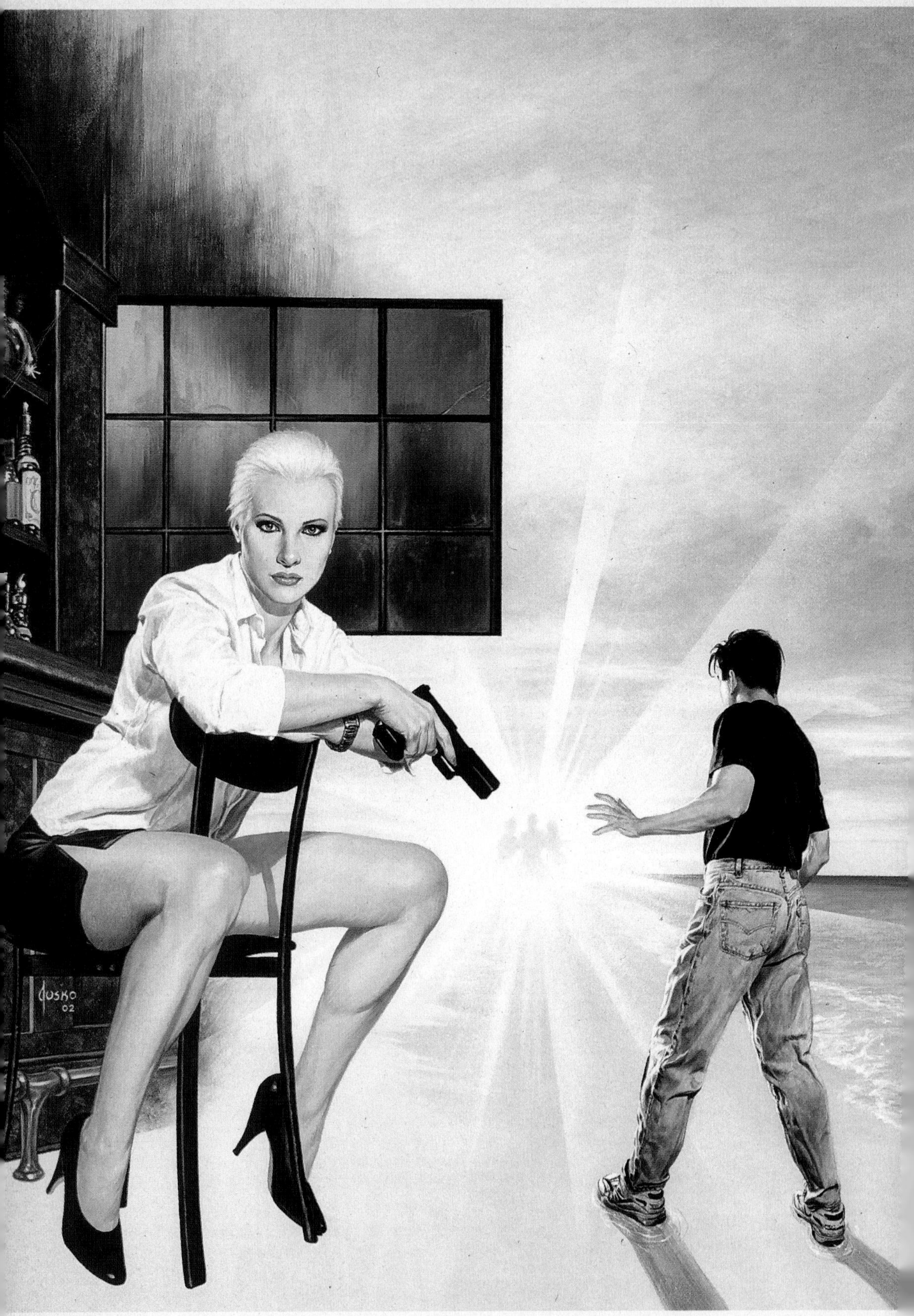

TRANSITIONS

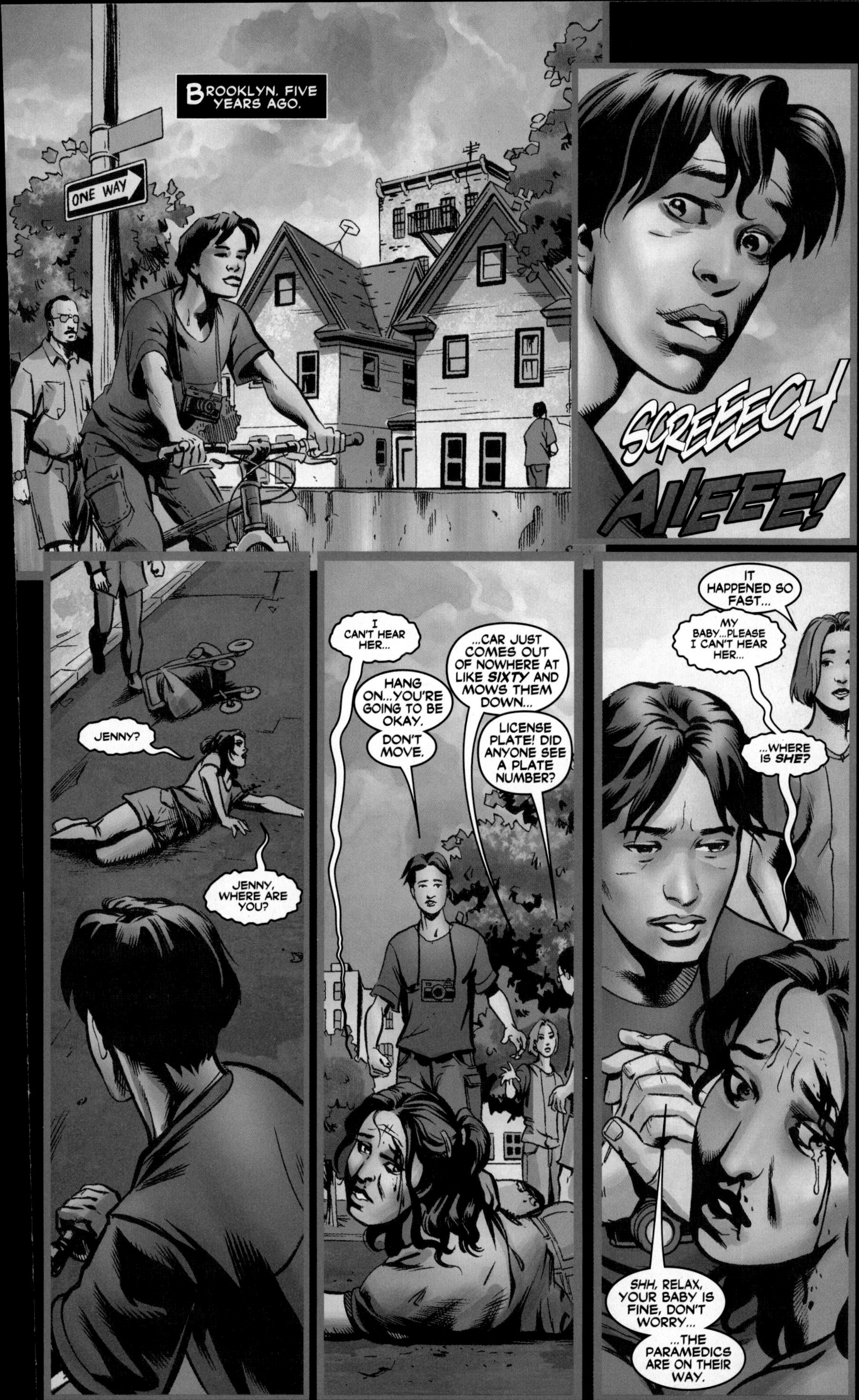
BROOKLYN, FIVE YEARS AGO.
ONE WAY
SCREEEECH
AIIEEE!
JENNY?
JENNY, WHERE ARE YOU?
I CAN'T HEAR HER...
HANG ON...YOU'RE GOING TO BE OKAY.
DON'T MOVE.
...CAR JUST COMES OUT OF NOWHERE AT LIKE *SIXTY* AND MOWS THEM DOWN...
LICENSE PLATE! DID ANYONE SEE A PLATE NUMBER?
IT HAPPENED SO FAST...
MY BABY...PLEASE I CAN'T HEAR HER...
...WHERE IS *SHE?*
SHH, RELAX, YOUR BABY IS FINE, DON'T WORRY...
...THE PARAMEDICS ARE ON THEIR WAY.

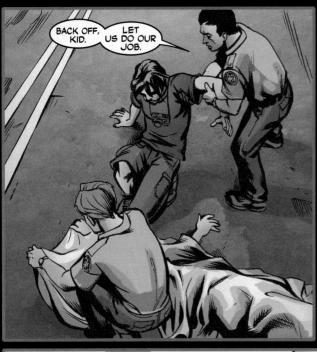

BACK OFF, KID. LET US DO OUR JOB.

PRESTON! MY GOD, WHAT ARE YOU DOING HERE?

ROB! I... THIS THING HAPPENED TO ME...I SAW--

--I HAD A VISION. I SAW THE CAR THAT HIT HER...

WHAT? YOU SAW THE ACCIDENT? DID YOU GET A LOOK AT THE DRIVER?

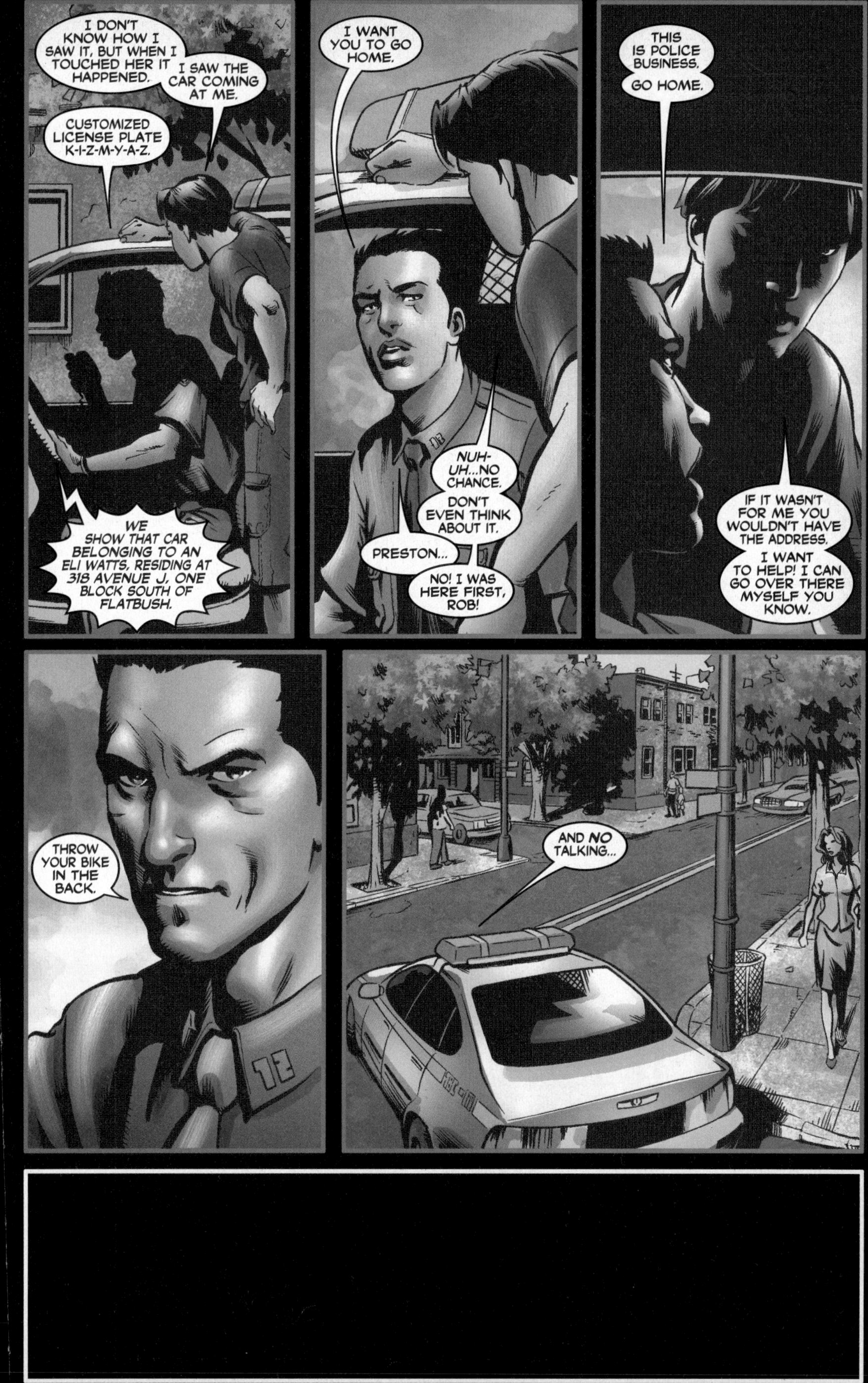

I DON'T KNOW HOW I SAW IT, BUT WHEN I TOUCHED HER IT HAPPENED.
I SAW THE CAR COMING AT ME.
CUSTOMIZED LICENSE PLATE K-I-Z-M-Y-A-Z.
WE SHOW THAT CAR BELONGING TO AN ELI WATTS, RESIDING AT 318 AVENUE J, ONE BLOCK SOUTH OF FLATBUSH.
I WANT YOU TO GO HOME.
NUH-UH...NO CHANCE.
DON'T EVEN THINK ABOUT IT.
PRESTON...
NO! I WAS HERE FIRST, ROB!
THIS IS POLICE BUSINESS.
GO HOME.
IF IT WASN'T FOR ME YOU WOULDN'T HAVE THE ADDRESS.
I WANT TO HELP! I CAN GO OVER THERE MYSELF YOU KNOW.
THROW YOUR BIKE IN THE BACK.
AND NO TALKING...

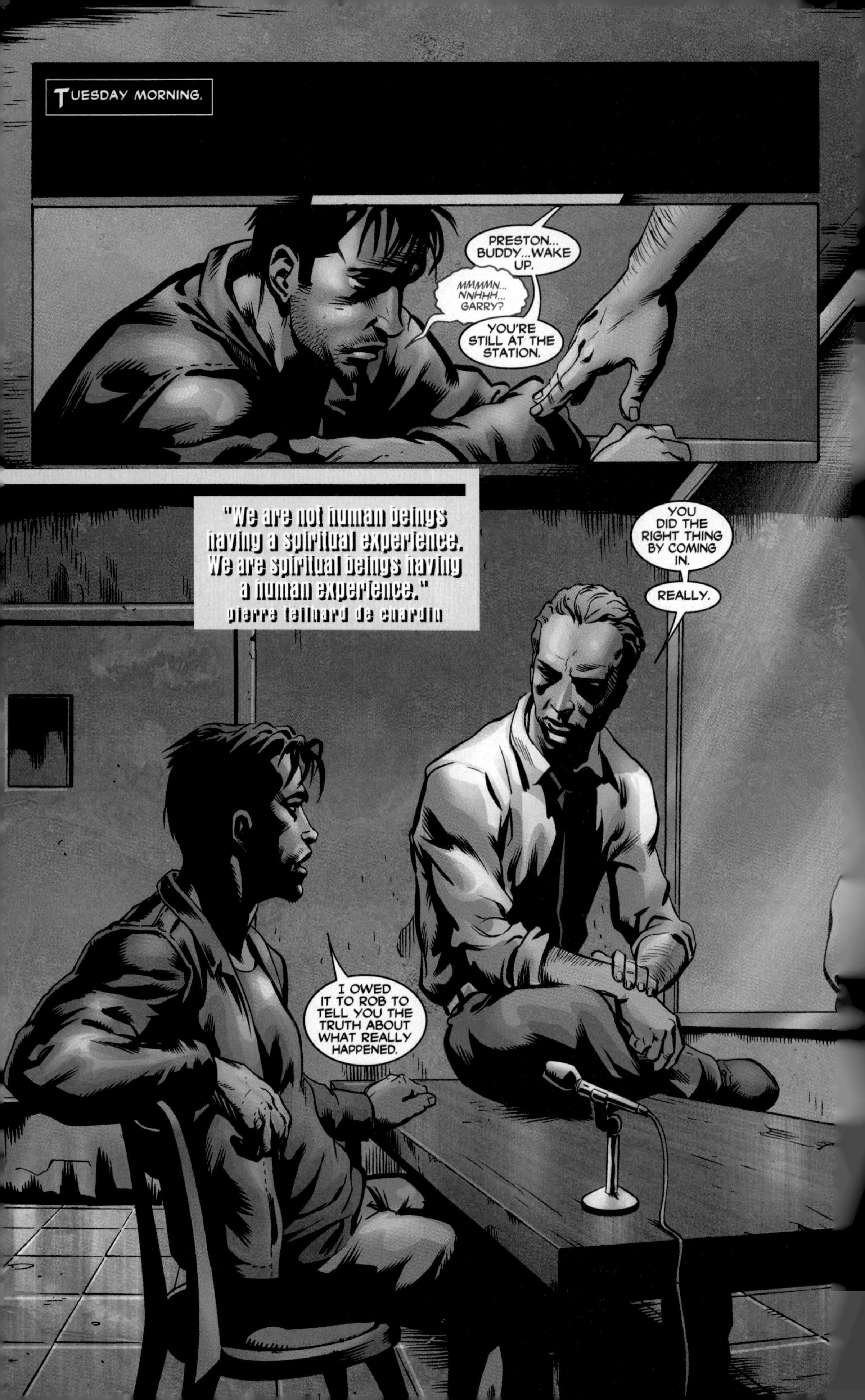
TUESDAY MORNING.
PRESTON... BUDDY...WAKE UP.
MMMMN... NNHHH... GARRY?
YOU'RE STILL AT THE STATION.
"We are not human beings having a spiritual experience. We are spiritual beings having a human experience."
pierre teilhard de chardin
YOU DID THE RIGHT THING BY COMING IN.
REALLY.
I OWED IT TO ROB TO TELL YOU THE TRUTH ABOUT WHAT REALLY HAPPENED.

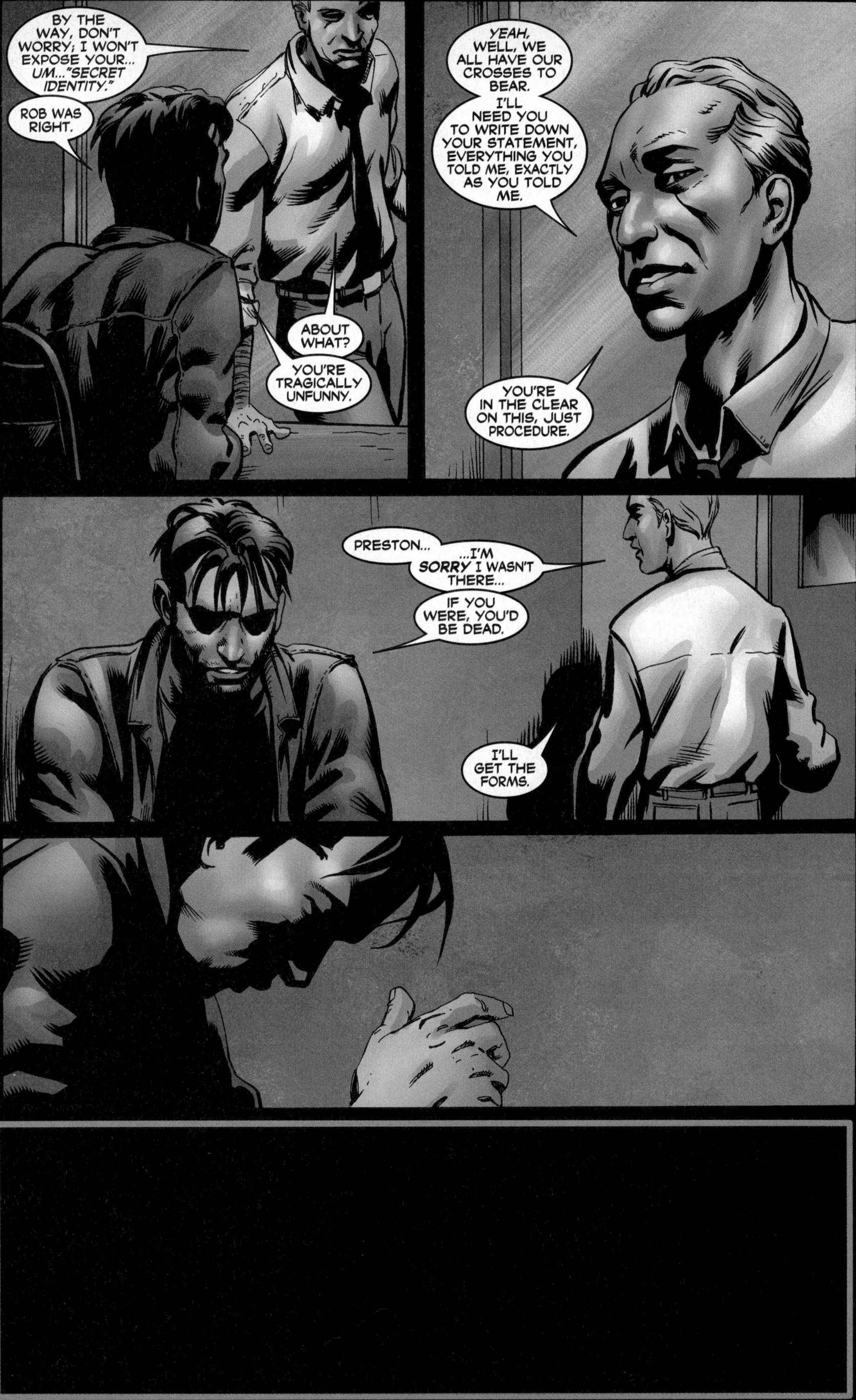
BY THE WAY, DON'T WORRY; I WON'T EXPOSE YOUR... UM..."SECRET IDENTITY."
ROB WAS RIGHT.
ABOUT WHAT?
YOU'RE TRAGICALLY UNFUNNY.
YEAH, WELL, WE ALL HAVE OUR CROSSES TO BEAR.
I'LL NEED YOU TO WRITE DOWN YOUR STATEMENT, EVERYTHING YOU TOLD ME, EXACTLY AS YOU TOLD ME.
YOU'RE IN THE CLEAR ON THIS, JUST PROCEDURE.
PRESTON...
...I'M SORRY I WASN'T THERE...
IF YOU WERE, YOU'D BE DEAD.
I'LL GET THE FORMS.

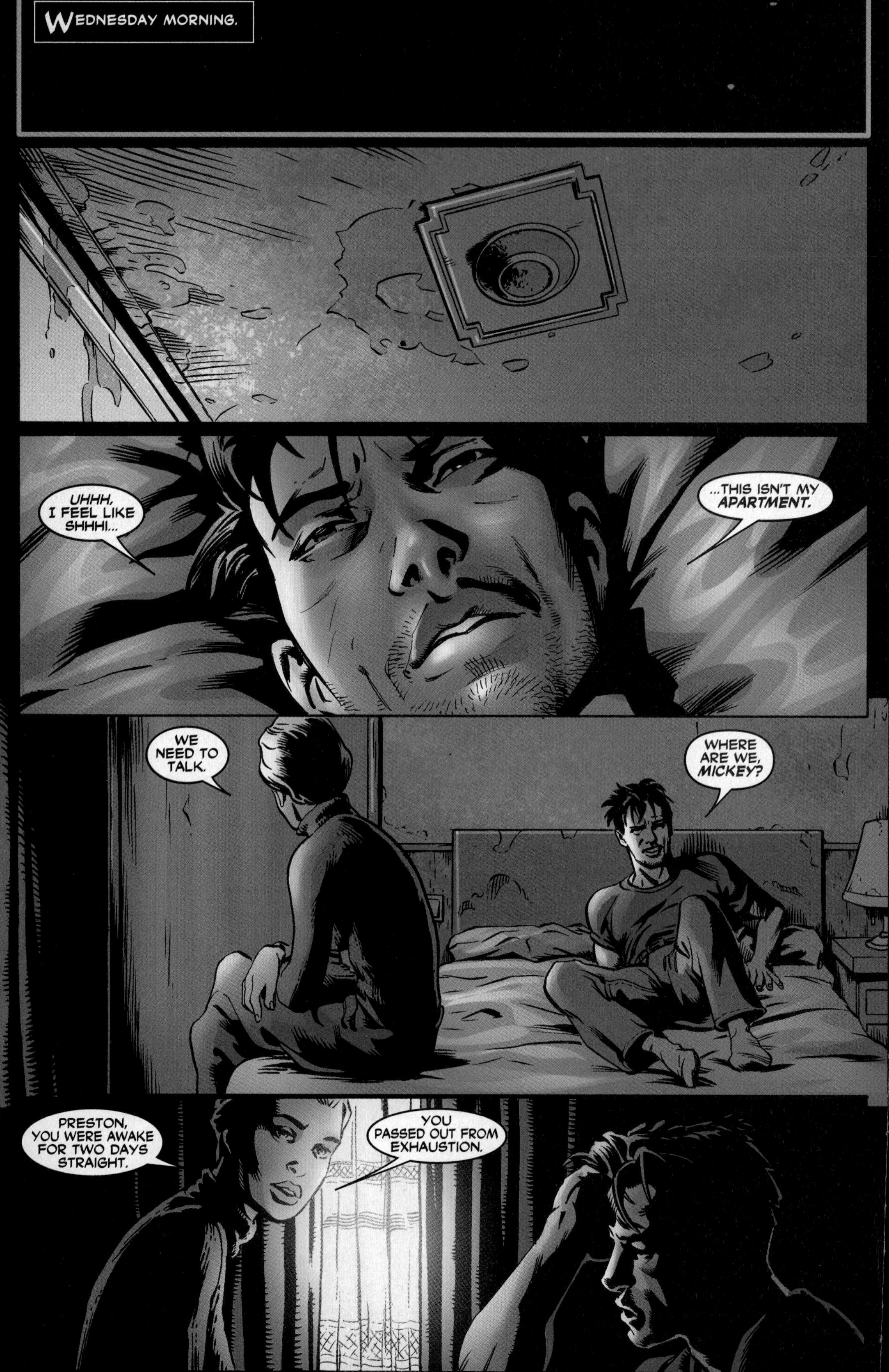
WEDNESDAY MORNING.
UHHH, I FEEL LIKE SHHHI...
...THIS ISN'T MY APARTMENT.
WE NEED TO TALK.
WHERE ARE WE, MICKEY?
PRESTON, YOU WERE AWAKE FOR TWO DAYS STRAIGHT.
YOU PASSED OUT FROM EXHAUSTION.

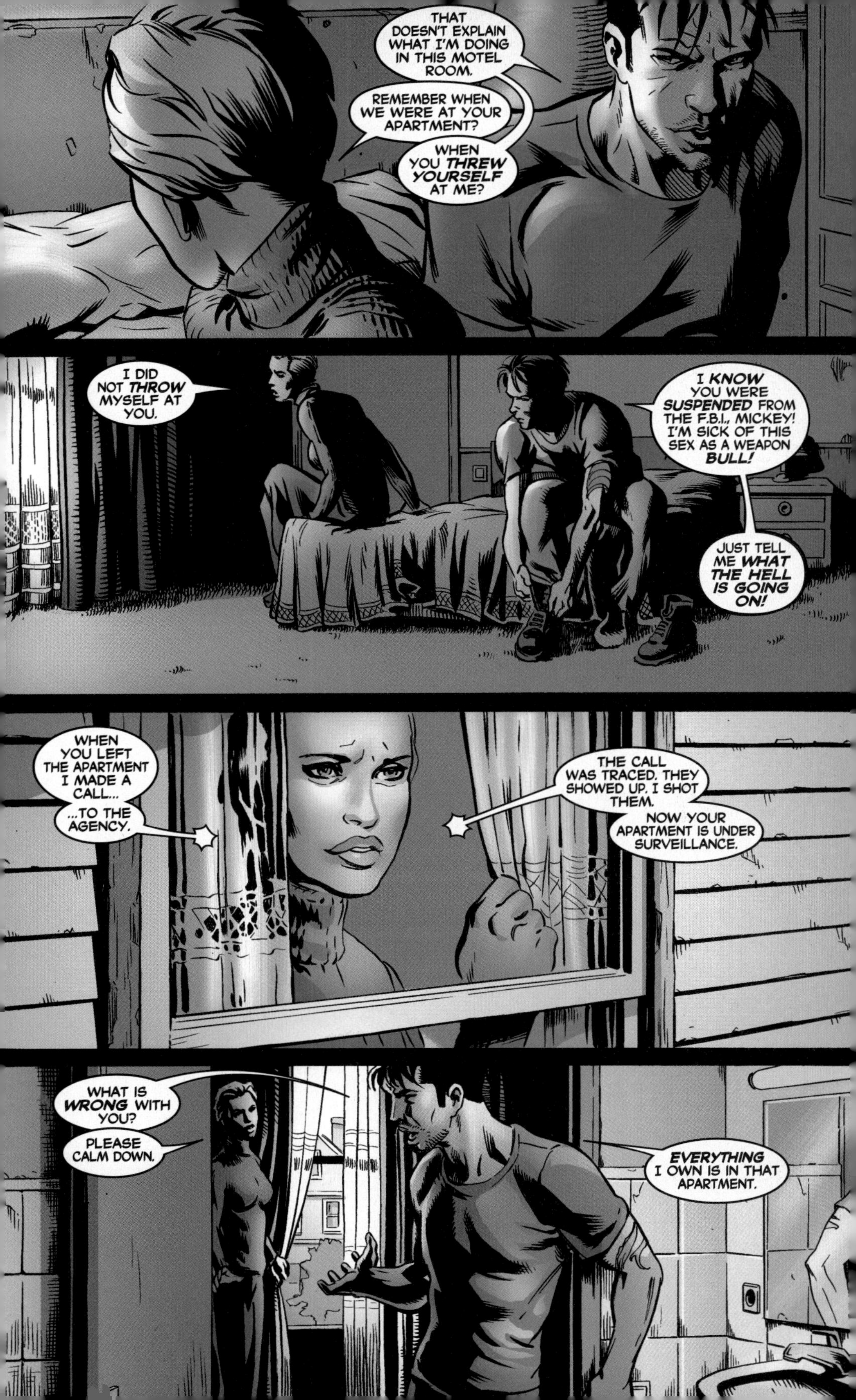
THAT DOESN'T EXPLAIN WHAT I'M DOING IN THIS MOTEL ROOM.
REMEMBER WHEN WE WERE AT YOUR APARTMENT?
WHEN YOU THREW YOURSELF AT ME?
I DID NOT THROW MYSELF AT YOU.
I KNOW YOU WERE SUSPENDED FROM THE F.B.I., MICKEY! I'M SICK OF THIS SEX AS A WEAPON BULL!
JUST TELL ME WHAT THE HELL IS GOING ON!
WHEN YOU LEFT THE APARTMENT I MADE A CALL...
...TO THE AGENCY.
THE CALL WAS TRACED. THEY SHOWED UP. I SHOT THEM.
NOW YOUR APARTMENT IS UNDER SURVEILLANCE.
WHAT IS WRONG WITH YOU?
PLEASE CALM DOWN.
EVERYTHING I OWN IS IN THAT APARTMENT.

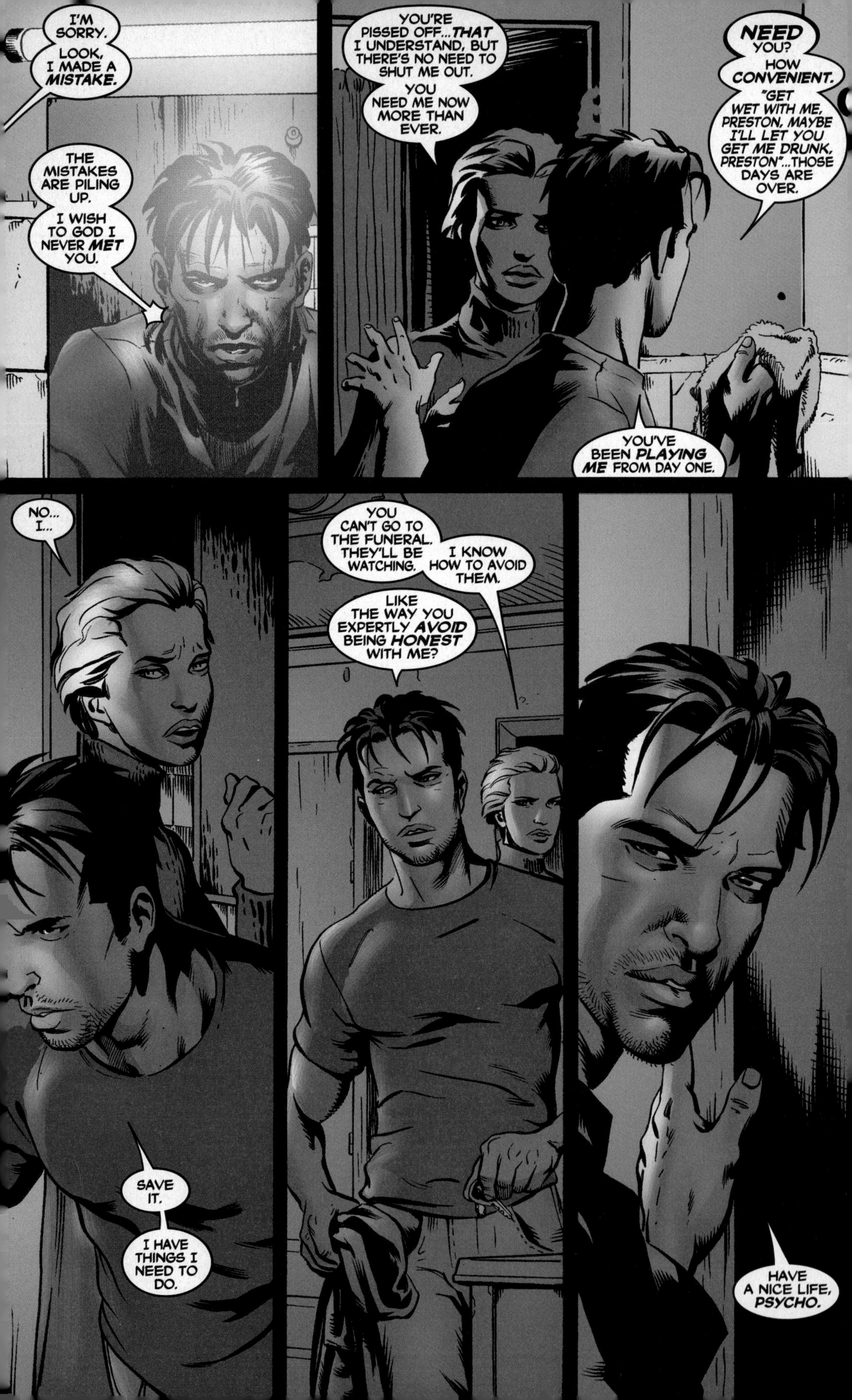
I'M SORRY.
LOOK, I MADE A MISTAKE.
THE MISTAKES ARE PILING UP.
I WISH TO GOD I NEVER MET YOU.
YOU'RE PISSED OFF...THAT I UNDERSTAND, BUT THERE'S NO NEED TO SHUT ME OUT.
YOU NEED ME NOW MORE THAN EVER.
NEED YOU?
HOW CONVENIENT.
"GET WET WITH ME, PRESTON, MAYBE I'LL LET YOU GET ME DRUNK, PRESTON"...THOSE DAYS ARE OVER.
YOU'VE BEEN PLAYING ME FROM DAY ONE.
NO... I...
SAVE IT.
I HAVE THINGS I NEED TO DO.
YOU CAN'T GO TO THE FUNERAL. THEY'LL BE WATCHING.
I KNOW HOW TO AVOID THEM.
LIKE THE WAY YOU EXPERTLY AVOID BEING HONEST WITH ME?
HAVE A NICE LIFE, PSYCHO.

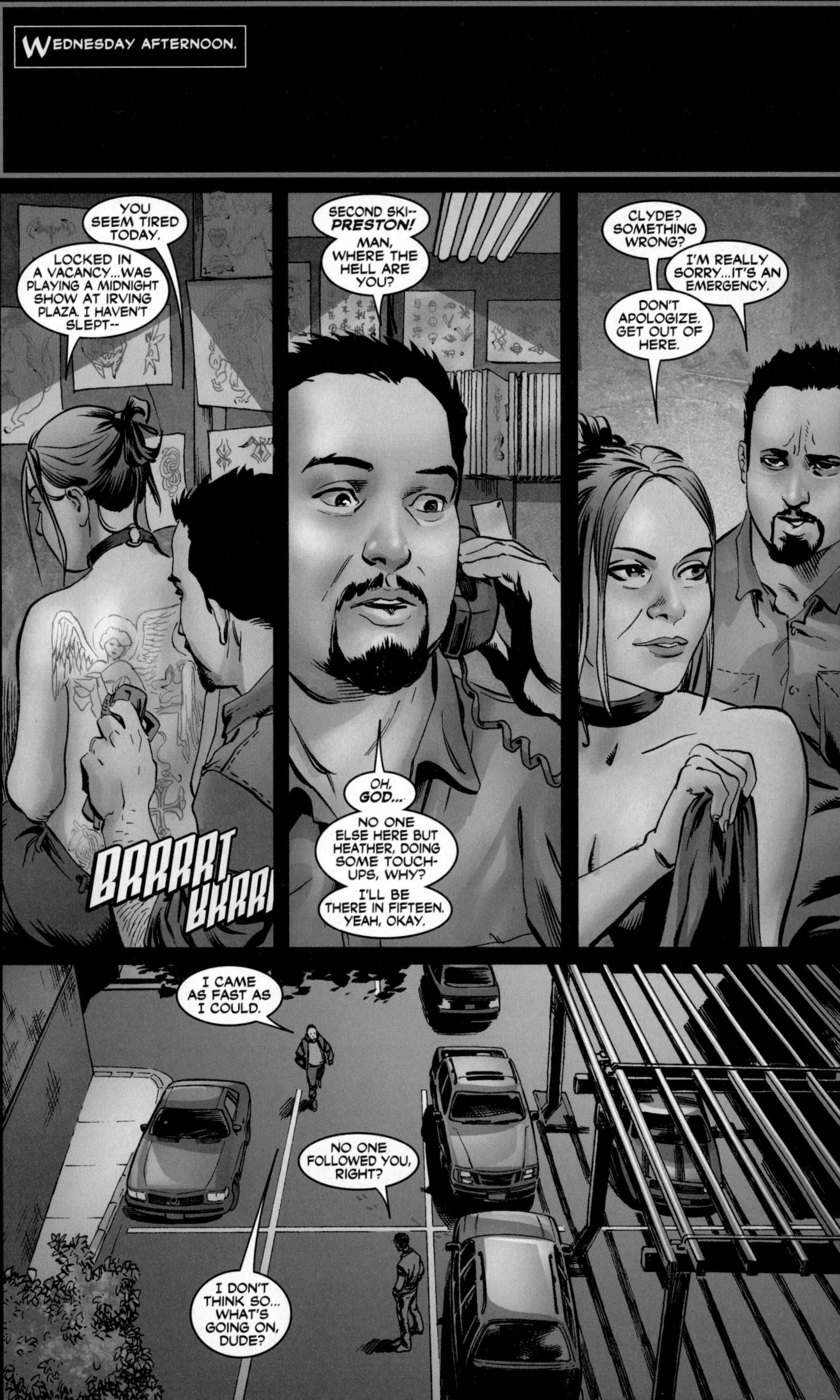

WEDNESDAY AFTERNOON.
YOU SEEM TIRED TODAY.
LOCKED IN A VACANCY...WAS PLAYING A MIDNIGHT SHOW AT IRVING PLAZA. I HAVEN'T SLEPT--
BRRRRT
SECOND SKI-- *PRESTON!* MAN, WHERE THE HELL ARE YOU?
OH, *GOD...*
NO ONE ELSE HERE BUT HEATHER, DOING SOME TOUCH-UPS, WHY?
I'LL BE THERE IN FIFTEEN. YEAH, OKAY.
CLYDE? SOMETHING WRONG?
I'M REALLY SORRY...IT'S AN EMERGENCY.
DON'T APOLOGIZE. GET OUT OF HERE.
I CAME AS FAST AS I COULD.
NO ONE FOLLOWED YOU, RIGHT?
I DON'T THINK SO... WHAT'S GOING ON, DUDE?

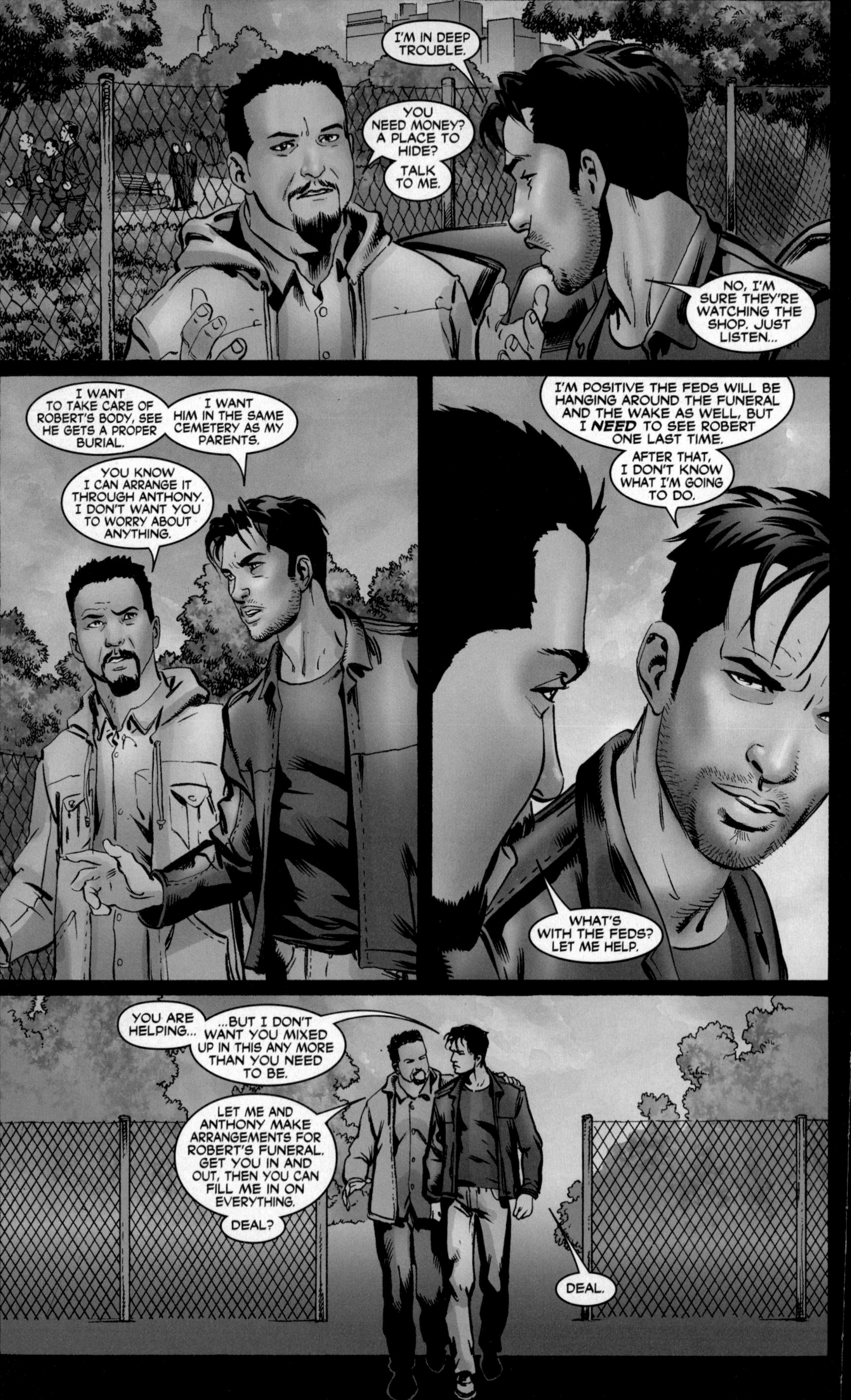
I'M IN DEEP TROUBLE.
YOU NEED MONEY? A PLACE TO HIDE?
TALK TO ME.
NO, I'M SURE THEY'RE WATCHING THE SHOP. JUST LISTEN...
I WANT TO TAKE CARE OF ROBERT'S BODY, SEE HE GETS A PROPER BURIAL.
I WANT HIM IN THE SAME CEMETERY AS MY PARENTS.
YOU KNOW I CAN ARRANGE IT THROUGH ANTHONY. I DON'T WANT YOU TO WORRY ABOUT ANYTHING.
I'M POSITIVE THE FEDS WILL BE HANGING AROUND THE FUNERAL AND THE WAKE AS WELL, BUT I NEED TO SEE ROBERT ONE LAST TIME.
AFTER THAT, I DON'T KNOW WHAT I'M GOING TO DO.
WHAT'S WITH THE FEDS? LET ME HELP.
YOU ARE HELPING...
...BUT I DON'T WANT YOU MIXED UP IN THIS ANY MORE THAN YOU NEED TO BE.
LET ME AND ANTHONY MAKE ARRANGEMENTS FOR ROBERT'S FUNERAL. GET YOU IN AND OUT, THEN YOU CAN FILL ME IN ON EVERYTHING.
DEAL?
DEAL.

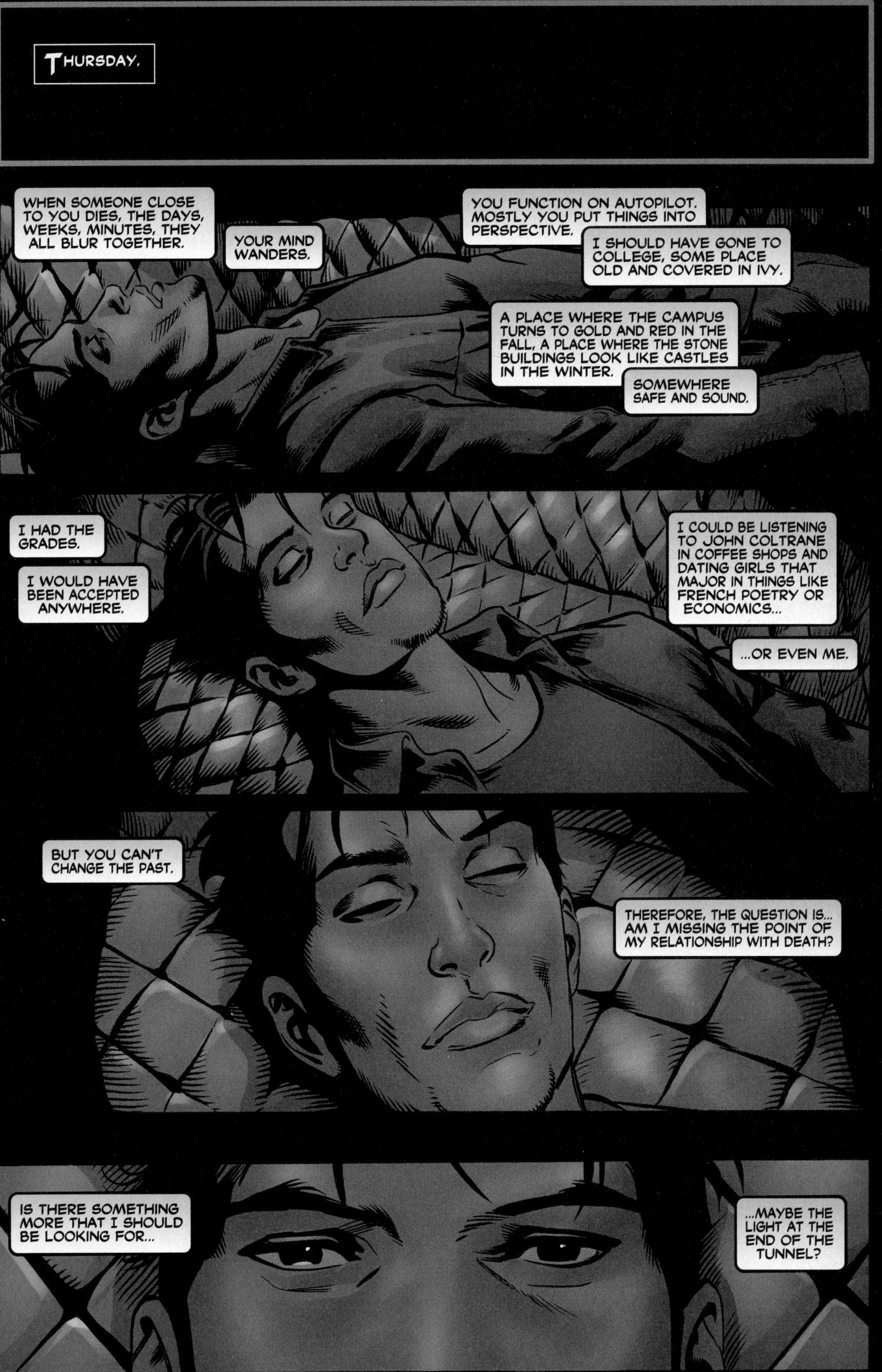
THURSDAY.
WHEN SOMEONE CLOSE TO YOU DIES, THE DAYS, WEEKS, MINUTES, THEY ALL BLUR TOGETHER.
YOUR MIND WANDERS.
YOU FUNCTION ON AUTOPILOT. MOSTLY YOU PUT THINGS INTO PERSPECTIVE.
I SHOULD HAVE GONE TO COLLEGE, SOME PLACE OLD AND COVERED IN IVY.
A PLACE WHERE THE CAMPUS TURNS TO GOLD AND RED IN THE FALL, A PLACE WHERE THE STONE BUILDINGS LOOK LIKE CASTLES IN THE WINTER.
SOMEWHERE SAFE AND SOUND.
I HAD THE GRADES.
I WOULD HAVE BEEN ACCEPTED ANYWHERE.
I COULD BE LISTENING TO JOHN COLTRANE IN COFFEE SHOPS AND DATING GIRLS THAT MAJOR IN THINGS LIKE FRENCH POETRY OR ECONOMICS...
...OR EVEN ME.
BUT YOU CAN'T CHANGE THE PAST.
THEREFORE, THE QUESTION IS... AM I MISSING THE POINT OF MY RELATIONSHIP WITH DEATH?
IS THERE SOMETHING MORE THAT I SHOULD BE LOOKING FOR...
...MAYBE THE LIGHT AT THE END OF THE TUNNEL?

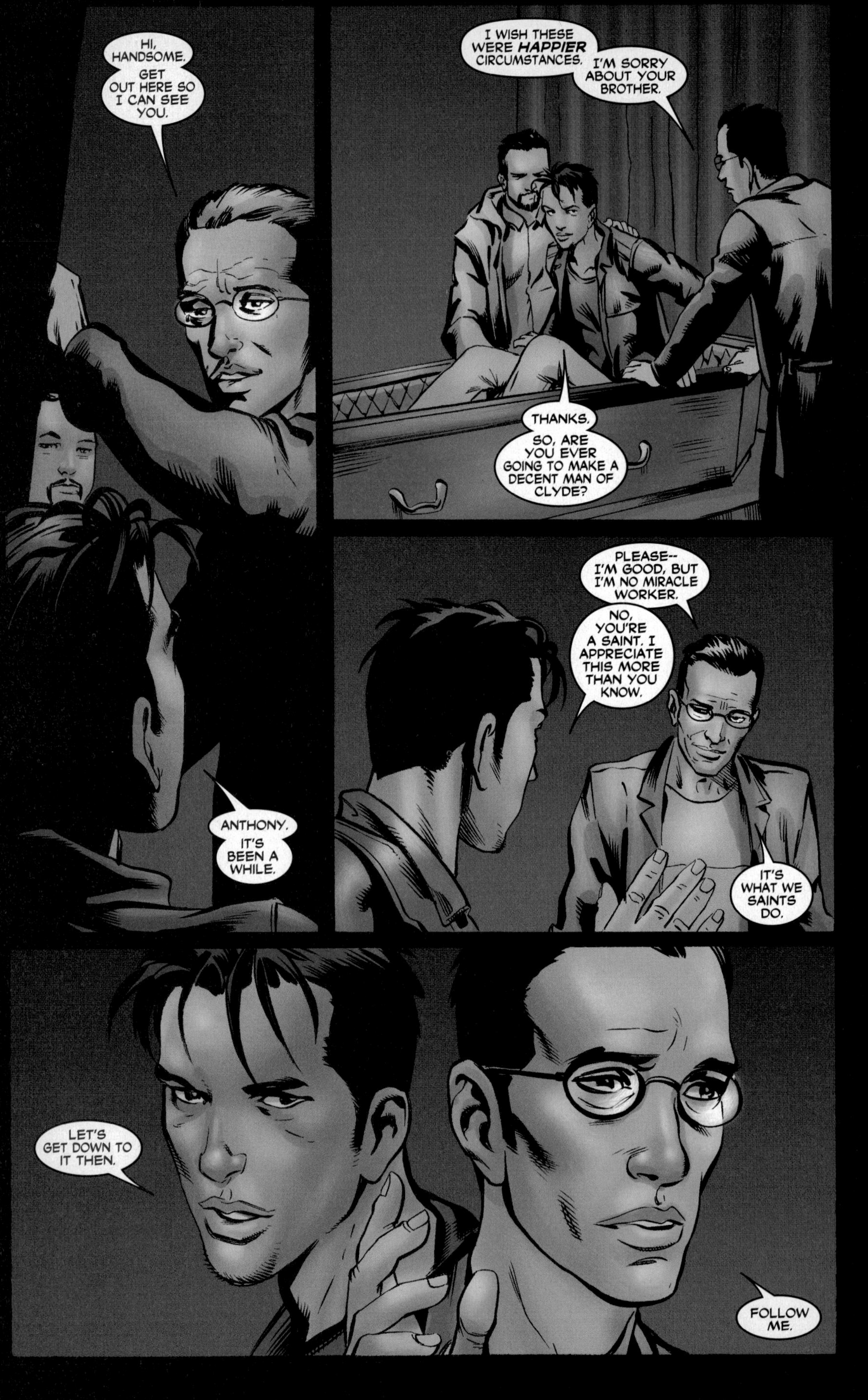
HI, HANDSOME. GET OUT HERE SO I CAN SEE YOU.
ANTHONY. IT'S BEEN A WHILE.
I WISH THESE WERE *HAPPIER* CIRCUMSTANCES.
I'M SORRY ABOUT YOUR BROTHER.
THANKS. SO, ARE YOU EVER GOING TO MAKE A DECENT MAN OF CLYDE?
PLEASE-- I'M GOOD, BUT I'M NO MIRACLE WORKER.
NO, YOU'RE A SAINT. I APPRECIATE THIS MORE THAN YOU KNOW.
IT'S WHAT WE SAINTS DO.
LET'S GET DOWN TO IT THEN.
FOLLOW ME.

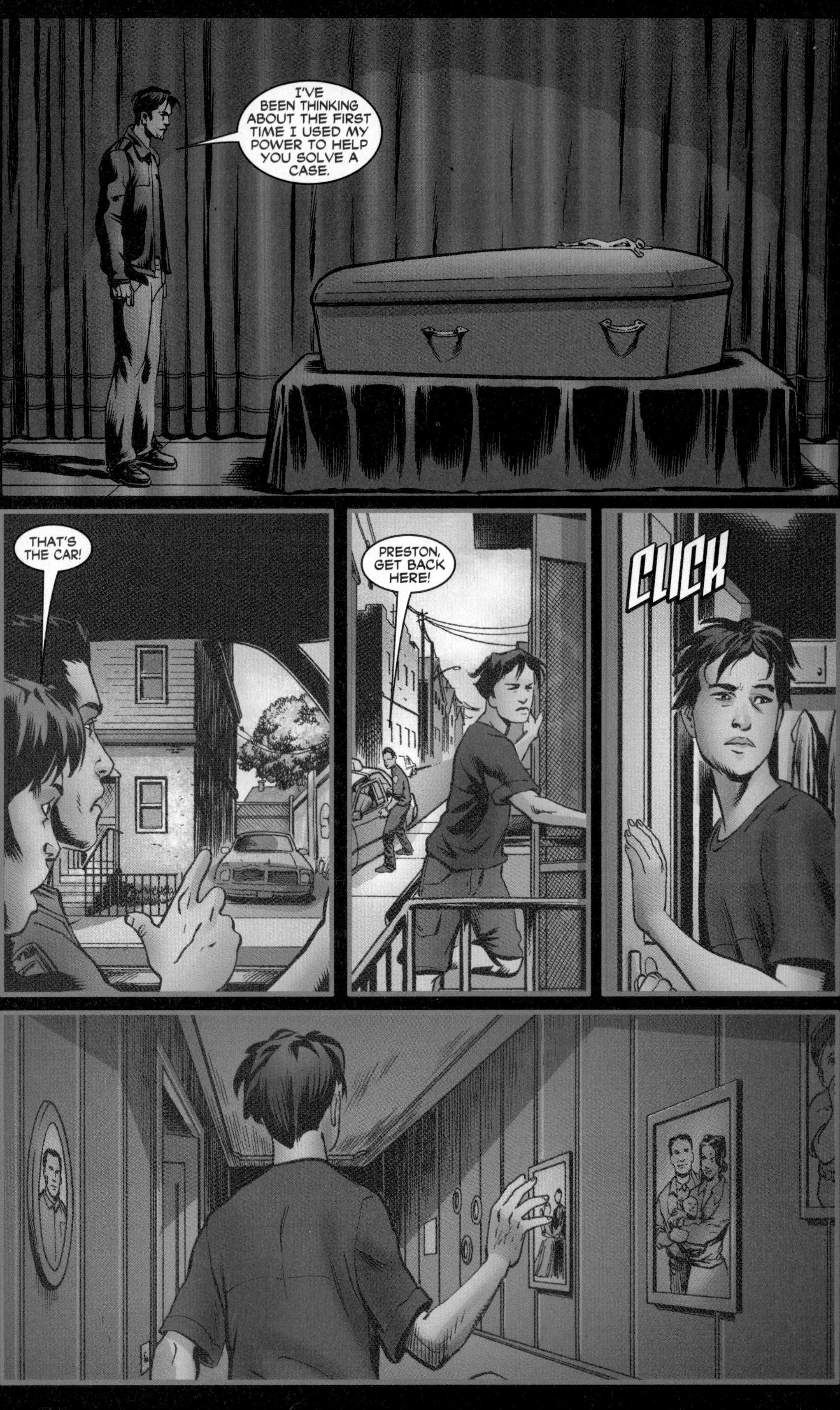
I'VE BEEN THINKING ABOUT THE FIRST TIME I USED MY POWER TO HELP YOU SOLVE A CASE.
THAT'S THE CAR!
PRESTON, GET BACK HERE!
CLICK

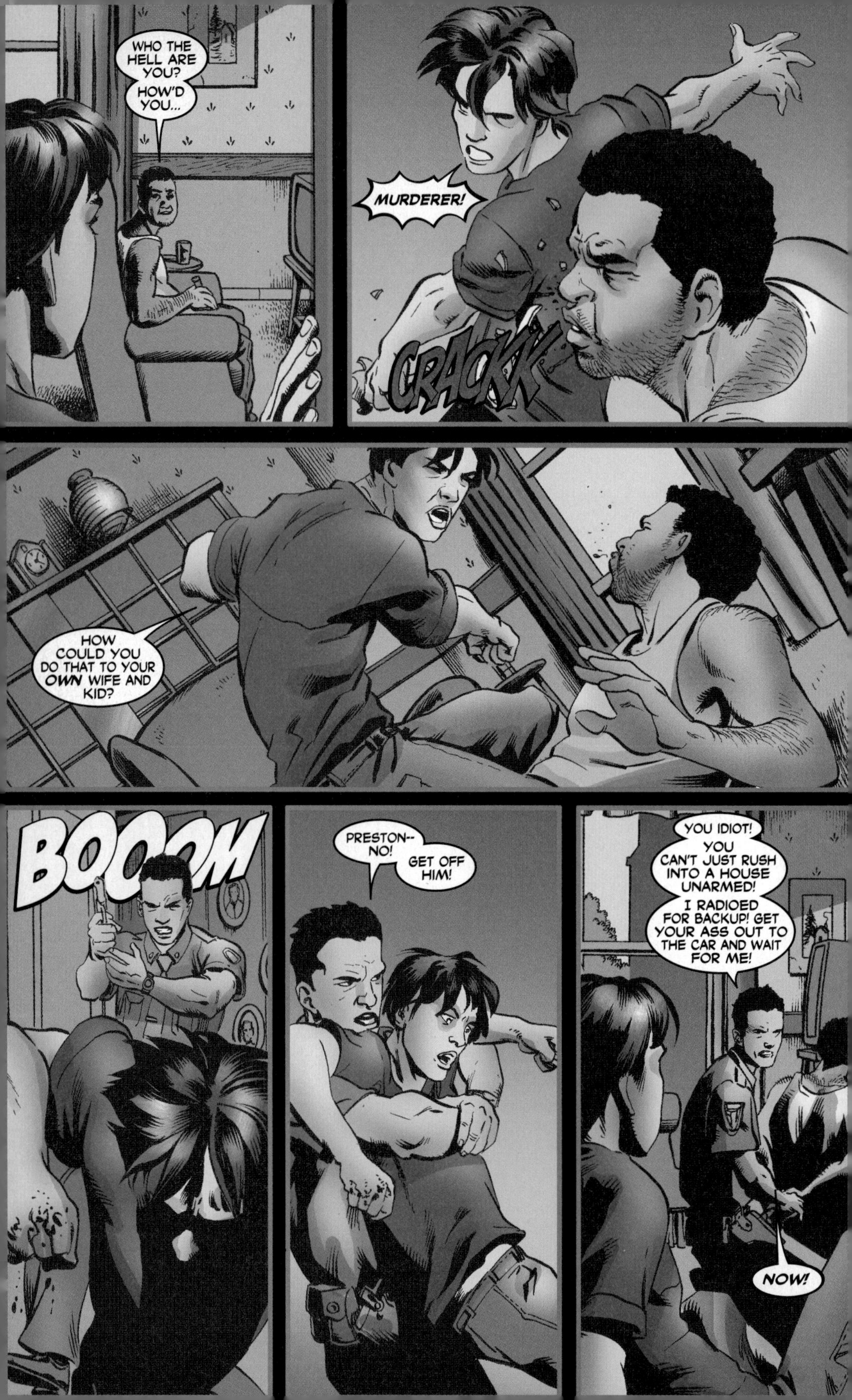
WHO THE HELL ARE YOU?
HOW'D YOU...
MURDERER!
CRACKK
HOW COULD YOU DO THAT TO YOUR *OWN* WIFE AND KID?
BOOOM
PRESTON-- NO!
GET OFF HIM!
YOU IDIOT!
YOU CAN'T JUST RUSH INTO A HOUSE UNARMED!
I RADIOED FOR BACKUP! GET YOUR ASS OUT TO THE CAR AND WAIT FOR ME!
NOW!

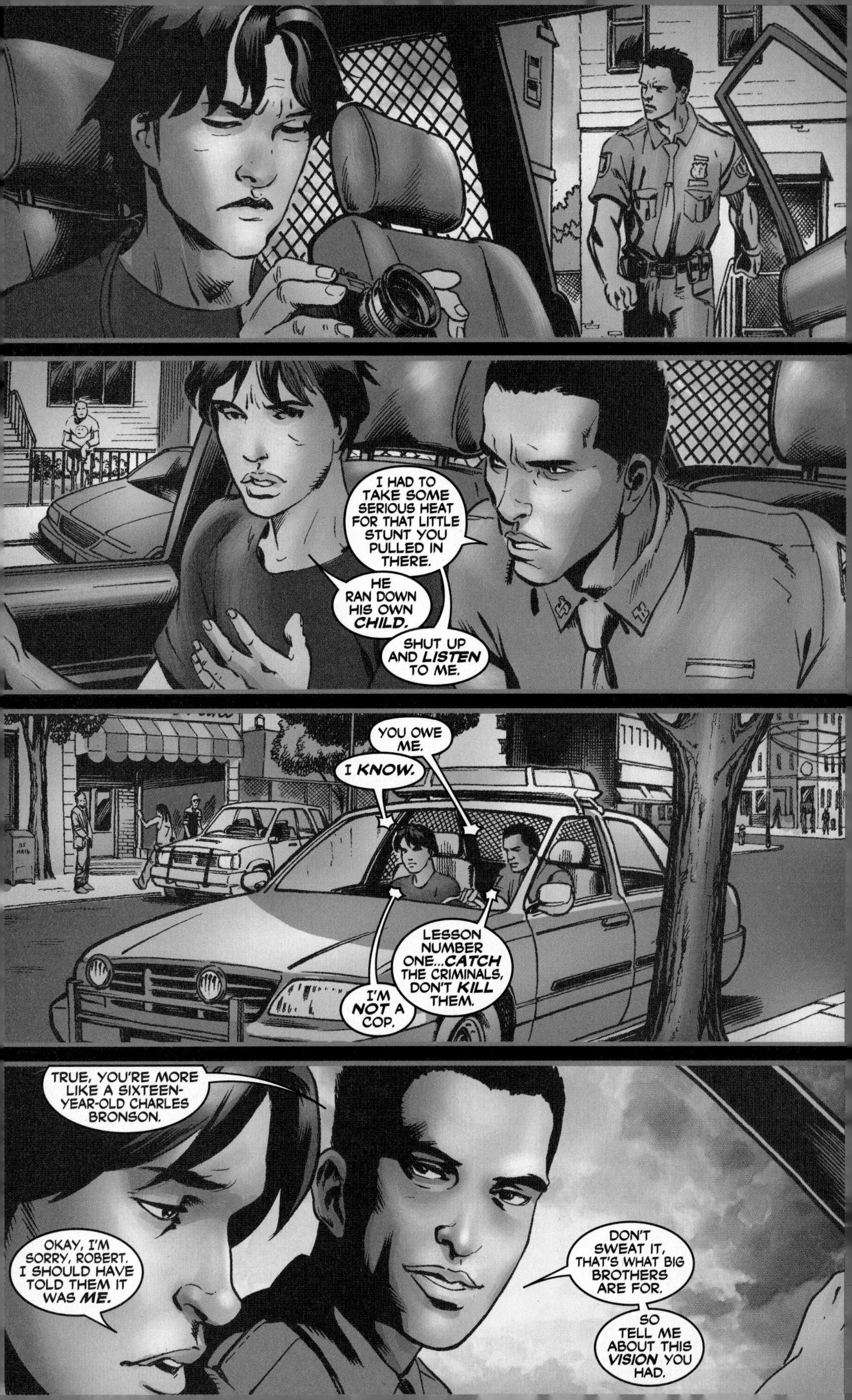
I HAD TO TAKE SOME SERIOUS HEAT FOR THAT LITTLE STUNT YOU PULLED IN THERE.
HE RAN DOWN HIS OWN CHILD.
SHUT UP AND LISTEN TO ME.
YOU OWE ME.
I KNOW.
LESSON NUMBER ONE...CATCH THE CRIMINALS, DON'T KILL THEM.
I'M NOT A COP.
TRUE, YOU'RE MORE LIKE A SIXTEEN-YEAR-OLD CHARLES BRONSON.
OKAY, I'M SORRY, ROBERT. I SHOULD HAVE TOLD THEM IT WAS ME.
DON'T SWEAT IT, THAT'S WHAT BIG BROTHERS ARE FOR.
SO TELL ME ABOUT THIS VISION YOU HAD.

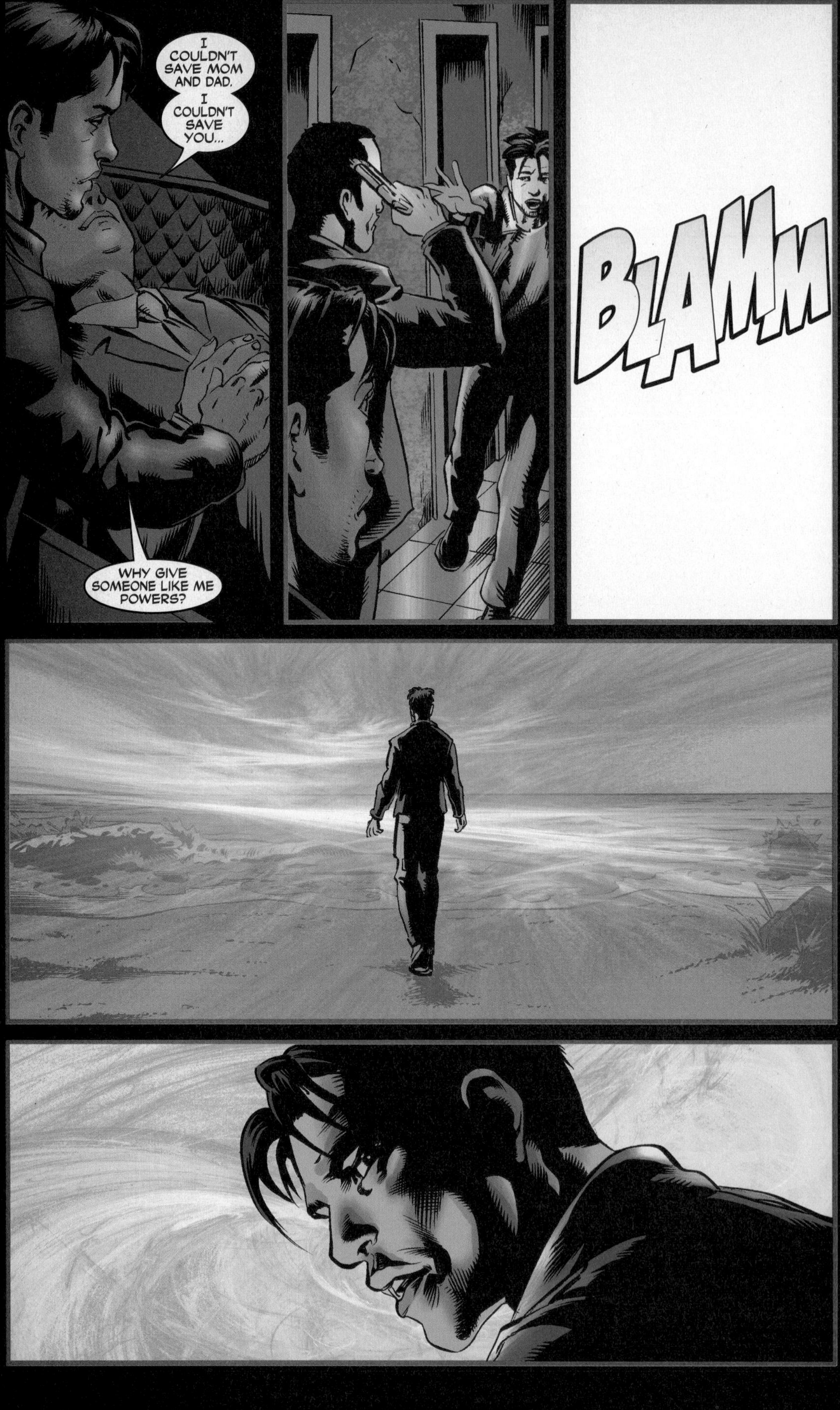
I COULDN'T SAVE MOM AND DAD.
I COULDN'T SAVE YOU...
WHY GIVE SOMEONE LIKE ME POWERS?
BLAMM

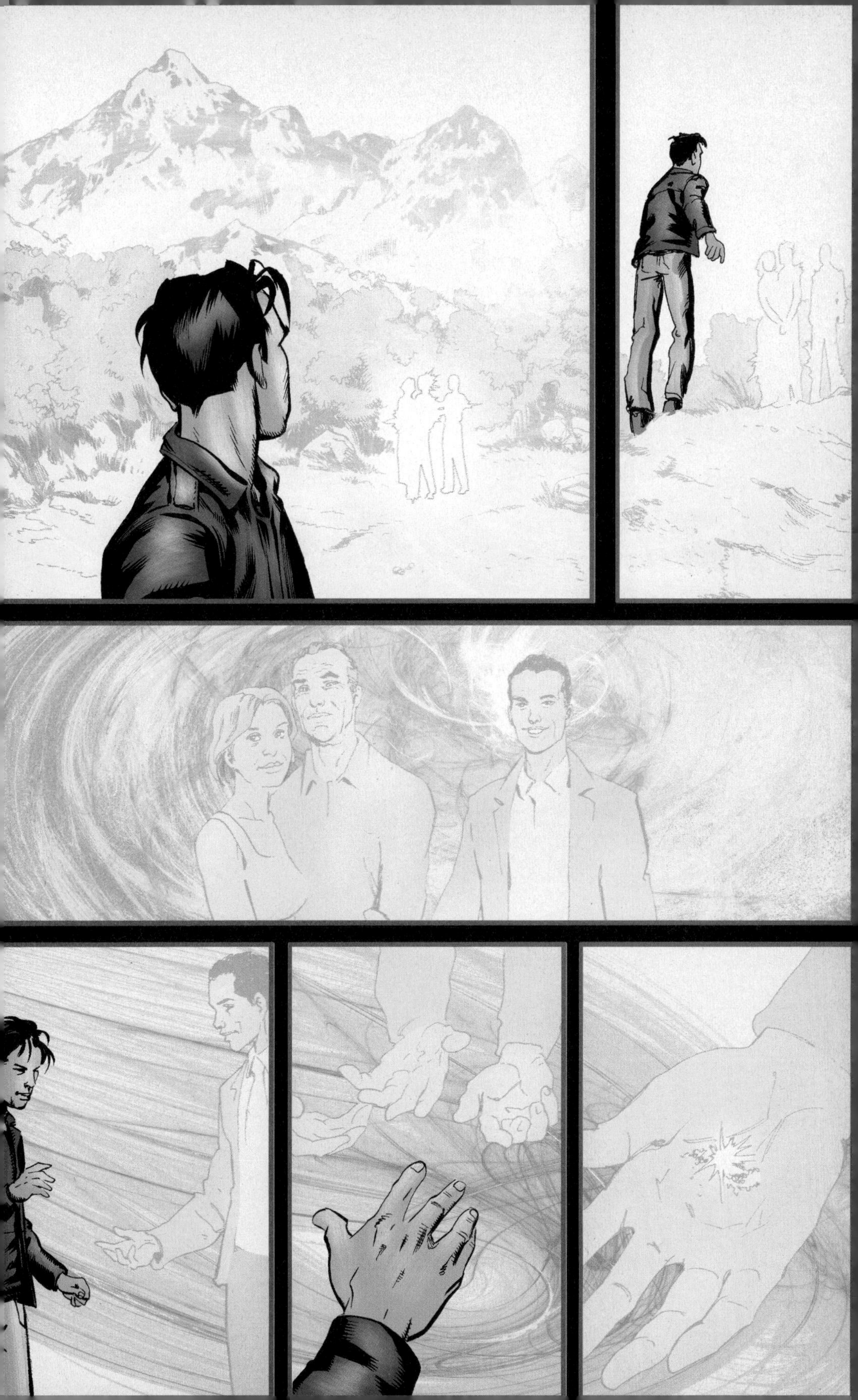

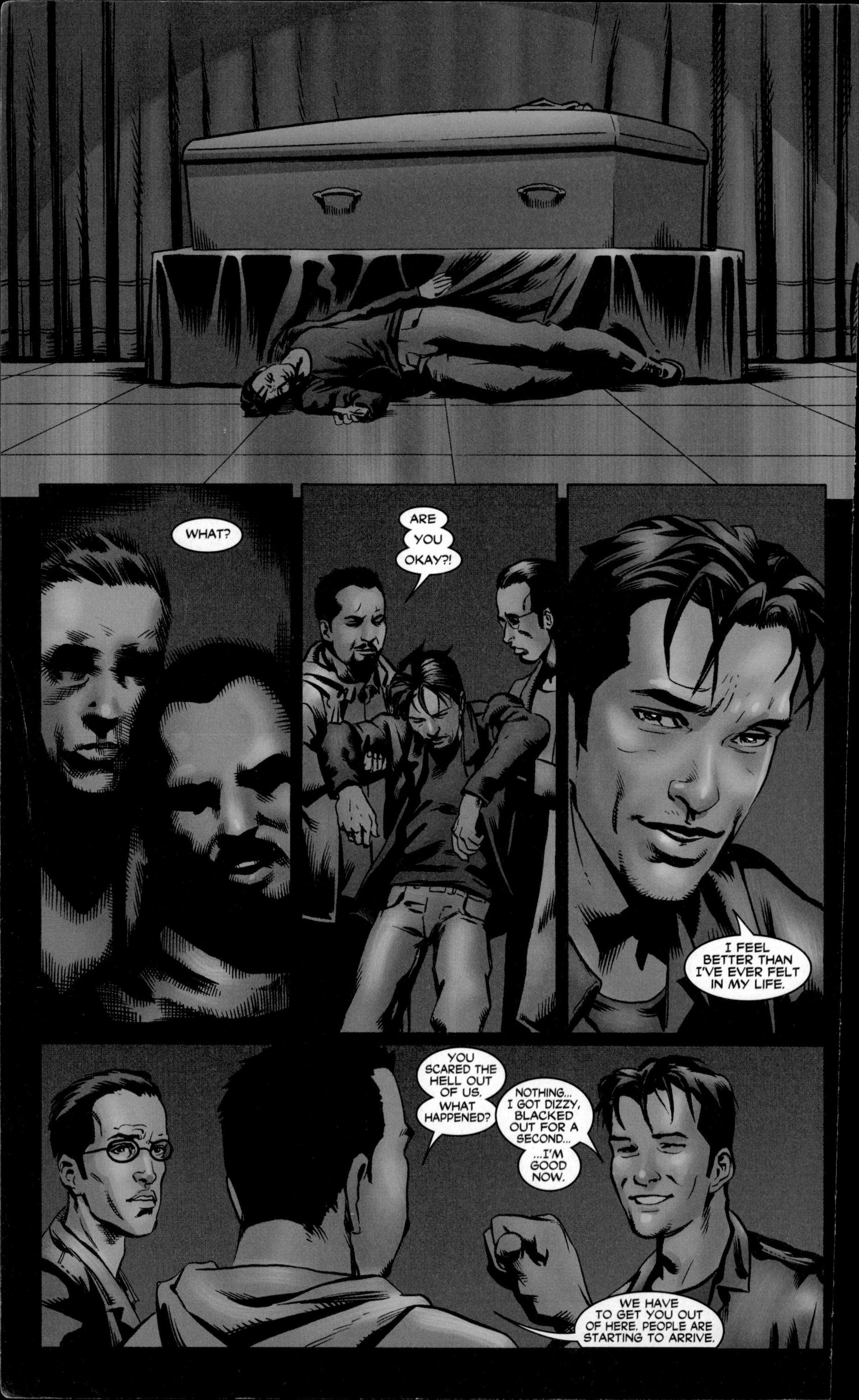
WHAT?
ARE YOU OKAY?!
I FEEL BETTER THAN I'VE EVER FELT IN MY LIFE.
YOU SCARED THE HELL OUT OF US. WHAT HAPPENED?
NOTHING... I GOT DIZZY, BLACKED OUT FOR A SECOND...
...I'M GOOD NOW.
WE HAVE TO GET YOU OUT OF HERE. PEOPLE ARE STARTING TO ARRIVE.

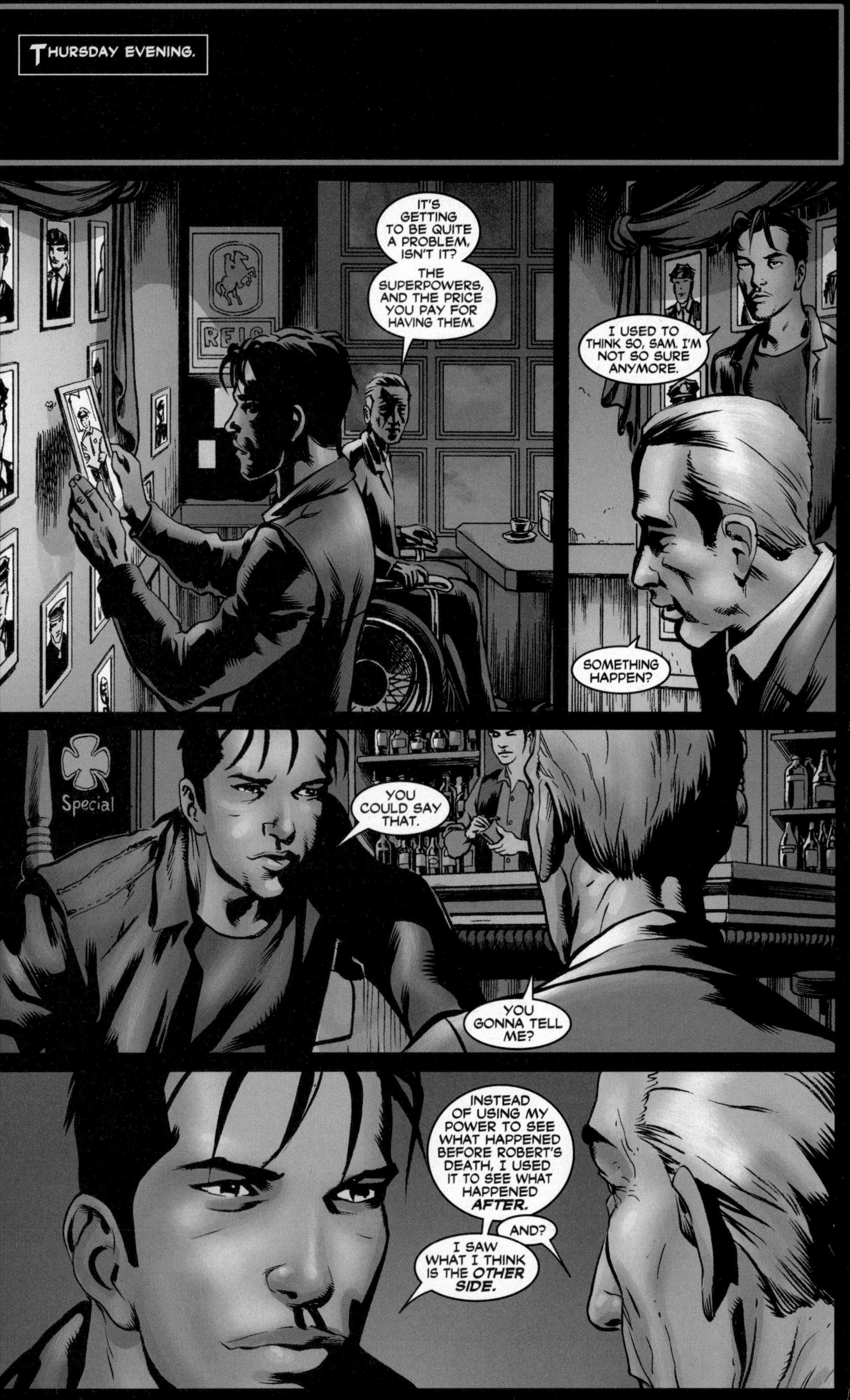
THURSDAY EVENING.
IT'S GETTING TO BE QUITE A PROBLEM, ISN'T IT?
THE SUPERPOWERS, AND THE PRICE YOU PAY FOR HAVING THEM.
I USED TO THINK SO, SAM. I'M NOT SO SURE ANYMORE.
SOMETHING HAPPEN?
Special
YOU COULD SAY THAT.
YOU GONNA TELL ME?
INSTEAD OF USING MY POWER TO SEE WHAT HAPPENED BEFORE ROBERT'S DEATH, I USED IT TO SEE WHAT HAPPENED AFTER.
AND?
I SAW WHAT I THINK IS THE OTHER SIDE.

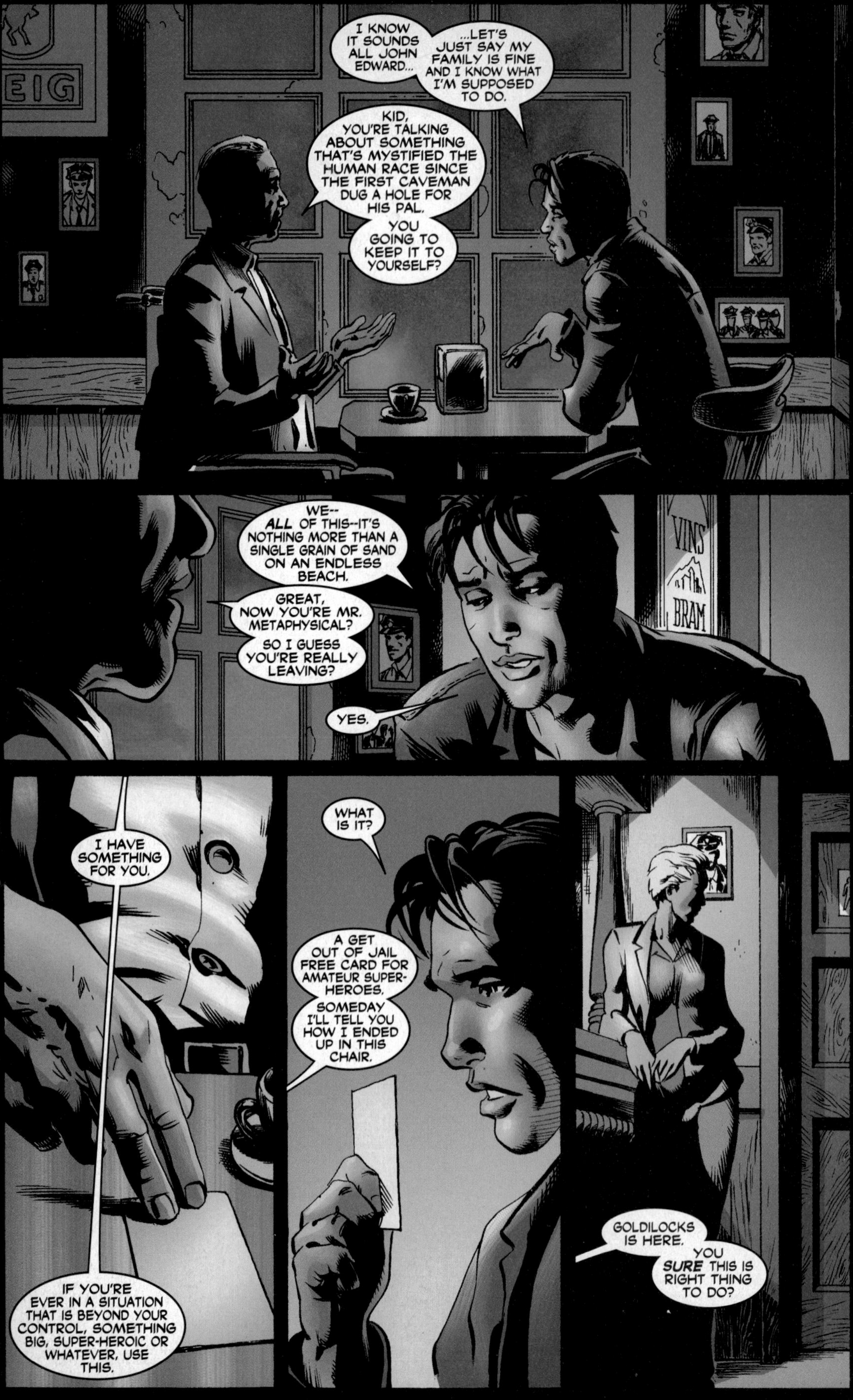
EIG
I KNOW IT SOUNDS ALL JOHN EDWARD...
...LET'S JUST SAY MY FAMILY IS FINE AND I KNOW WHAT I'M SUPPOSED TO DO.
KID, YOU'RE TALKING ABOUT SOMETHING THAT'S MYSTIFIED THE HUMAN RACE SINCE THE FIRST CAVEMAN DUG A HOLE FOR HIS PAL.
YOU GOING TO KEEP IT TO YOURSELF?
WE-- ALL OF THIS--IT'S NOTHING MORE THAN A SINGLE GRAIN OF SAND ON AN ENDLESS BEACH.
GREAT, NOW YOU'RE MR. METAPHYSICAL?
SO I GUESS YOU'RE REALLY LEAVING?
YES.
VINS
BRAM
I HAVE SOMETHING FOR YOU.
IF YOU'RE EVER IN A SITUATION THAT IS BEYOND YOUR CONTROL, SOMETHING BIG, SUPER-HEROIC OR WHATEVER, USE THIS.
WHAT IS IT?
A GET OUT OF JAIL FREE CARD FOR AMATEUR SUPER-HEROES.
SOMEDAY I'LL TELL YOU HOW I ENDED UP IN THIS CHAIR.
GOLDILOCKS IS HERE.
YOU SURE THIS IS RIGHT THING TO DO?